Music, Sound, and Architecture in Islam

Music, Sound, and Architecture in Islam

Edited by
Michael Frishkopf
and Federico Spinetti

Foreword by
Ali S. Asani

The University of Texas Press *Austin*

Printed in the United States of America
First edition, 2018

This research was supported by the Social Sciences and Humanities Research Council of Canada.

Social Sciences and Humanities Research Council of Canada
Conseil de recherches en sciences humaines du Canada

Canada

Requests for permission to reproduce material from this work should be sent to:
Permissions
University of Texas Press
P.O. Box 7819
Austin, TX 78713-7819
http://utpress.utexas.edu/index.php/rp-form

♾ The paper used in this book meets the minimum requirements of ANSI/NISO Z39.48-1992 (R1997) (Permanence of Paper).

Library of Congress Cataloging-in-Publication Data
Names: Frishkopf, Michael Aaron, editor. | Spinetti, Federico, editor.
Title: Music, sound, and architecture in Islam / edited by Michael Frishkopf and Federico Spinetti.
Description: First edition. | Austin : University of Texas Press, 2018. | Includes bibliographical references and index.
Identifiers: LCCN 2017036820| ISBN 978-1-4773-1245-2 (cloth : alk. paper) | ISBN 978-1-4773-1246-9 (pbk. : alk. paper) | ISBN 978-1-4773-1247-6 (library e-book) | ISBN 978-1-4773-1248-3 (nonlibrary e-book)
Subjects: LCSH: Music and architecture—Islamic countries. | Art and architecture—Islamic countries. | Music—Social aspects—Islamic countries. | Music—Islamic countries—History and criticism. | Architecture—Islamic countries—History and criticism.
Classification: LCC ML3849 .M9393 2018 | DDC 700.917/67—dc23
LC record available at https://lccn.loc.gov/2017036820
doi:10.7560/312452

CONTENTS

Image and sound files to accompany this volume are available at **https://archnet.org**

ILLUSTRATIONS

FIGURES

PLATES (following page 108)

CHARTS

TABLES

Foreword

ALI S. ASANI

It is a great privilege and honor for me to write a foreword to this volume—an innovative exploration of the relationship between the aural/sonic arts and the visual/spatial arts in Muslim societies. Comprising contributions from scholars working in an array of disciplines, the collection examines how the sonic arts, such as music, shape and are shaped by the physical spaces in which they are performed. In so doing, it provides us with new perspectives on the dynamic relationship between various forms of art in cultural, sociopolitical, and religious spaces. More important, the volume's essays demonstrate how a multisensory approach—one that combines sound with built structure, music with architecture, time with space—can lead to a deeper and more nuanced understanding of Muslim cultures.

Professor Mohammed Arkoun, the influential Arab intellectual, often called for audacious, free, and productive thinking about Islam and indeed Islamicate civilizations. He writes that our understandings of Islam as a religious phenomenon are woefully inadequate since we do not pay sufficient attention to a crucial element: "silent Islam." He defines "silent Islam" as "the Islam of true believers who attach more importance to the religious relationship with the absolute of God than to the vehement demonstrations of political movements."[1] Instead of focusing on this aspect, Professor Arkoun argues, scholarly discussions about Islam are monopolized by sociopolitical ideologies, such as Islamic revivalism. These, he claims, are in reality secular movements "disguised by religious discourse, rites, and collected behaviors."[2] Given Professor Arkoun's definition of "silent Islam," we may posit that these ideologies and their discourses of power, orthodoxy, and hegemony underlie a "loud Islam" whose voice has been greatly amplified in political, social, and cultural spaces, including the media.

The arts are particularly well suited to provide us access to "silent Islam." Historically, the vast majority of Muslims have experienced and understood their faith principally through the aural, visual, and literary arts, and they continue to do so today. Traditionally, the arts have provided important vehicles through which religious ideas and teachings are transmitted and given expression; indeed, for many Muslims, the arts aptly evoke the complexity, beauty, and aesthetic power of their faith. The arts thus constitute not only a form of religious experience but also a type of knowledge that is emotive. Most Muslims do not derive knowledge of Islam simply from a close reading of scriptures and works of theology. Instead, their knowledge is inextricably enmeshed in the experience with and production of various arts. In this regard, the arts have played a pivotal role in shaping the development of the Islamic tradition. Ultimately, Islam experienced and understood in a multisensory way through the arts is not "silent" at all. On the contrary, it is a "strong" voice, many centuries old, still confident and beautiful.

Let us take, for example, the Qurʾan, which is connected in significant ways with various arts in Muslim societies. While we commonly conceive of it as a book, its verses were actually transmitted by the Prophet Muhammad to his followers not in writing but orally, as a performance—a fact reflected in its name, "The Recitation." Early Muslim accounts provide vivid depictions of the experiential aspect of the revelation of the Qurʾan to Muhammad. If we look in particular at accounts of the first revelation, the Prophet heard these words: "Recite in the Name of Your Lord!" He then found that it was as if they had been "written on his heart." The Qurʾan's form and style shows great sensitivity to the poetic sensibility of Arab culture, one that prized the beauty of oral expression. Not surprisingly, Muhammad's opponents accused him of being a poet, inspired by jinn, to which he responded by asserting that he was a prophet receiving revelation from the one God.

Even though the oral revelations the Prophet received were codified as a written text after his death under the auspices of a state-initiated project, the Qurʾan continued to be manifest as sacred sound that should be personally experienced by each individual. Its emotionally transforming and inimitable aesthetic qualities came to be seen as proof of its divine origin. For the believer, the sound of a Qurʾan recitation is immediately a personal, intellectual encounter with meaning as well as an aesthetic encounter with the transcendent.

The aural/oral and written forms of the Qur'an have complemented each other in this way from the very beginning and continue to do so today. In fact, the medium through which most Muslims today interact with this holiest scripture of Islam is still sound, with the written text serving as an *aide de memoire*. Although some Muslims devote themselves to the art of *tajwid*—the rigorous study of the correct articulation and elongation of Arabic phonemes—many more encounter Qur'anic recitation more organically, whether in the home, in the mosque, or through recordings played in markets, on buses, and in hospitals throughout many Muslim-majority countries. Indeed, the Qur'an is at the center of an Islamic soundscape that permeates the arts of poetry, music, and dance.

Engagement with the Qur'anic revelation, of course, is not only aural experience. Calligraphic representations of its verses grace the covers of greeting cards, appear on bumper stickers, and adorn the walls of many Muslim homes. Indeed, the arts in Islam extend beyond its central text. They appear also in architecture, pottery, film, and literature; in short, Muslims may encounter religious meaning in almost all spheres of their lives through diverse forms of art appealing to multiple senses.

Although the arts provide us significant insight into the multisensory nature of Muslim devotional life, it is uncommon to find them being incorporated into the study and teaching of Islam as a religious tradition. As Professor Arkoun has pointed out, this is the result of a strong bias toward constructing Islam as a sociopolitical ideology, neglecting the Islam of faith experienced by millions of Muslims around the world every day. Frequently, artistic expressions of faith and their experiential dimensions are either dismissed or considered peripheral to the study of Islamic religion. "The arts are icing on the cake," one scholar explained to me, while another remarked, "If I taught Islam through the arts at my university, it would not be tolerated—I would be laughed out of the classroom."

Notwithstanding such biases, for many years I have sought to foster literacy about Islam and Muslim societies through a multisensory approach incorporating the arts.[3] Instead of following the conventional orientalist narrative of Islam as a religion of empire associated with various dynasties, my approach is premised on the notion that religion as a cultural phenomenon is intricately embedded in and constantly being shaped and reshaped by various interrelated contexts—political, social, economic, literary, and artistic. We therefore need multiple lenses through which to understand its multivalent social and cultural influences.[4] Employing the arts as the primary lens to study Islam and Muslim cultures allows students not only to appreciate their seminal role in the tradition but also to situate them within historical and sociopolitical contexts. For example, it enables students to question widely prevalent conceptualizations of Qurʾan as scripture based on assumptions of Christian theology and Old Testament scholarship in particular. I also employ a broad range of artistic expressions to discuss notions of the sacred, authority, theology, and mysticism, as well as issues affecting contemporary Muslim societies, such as colonialism and its aftermath, reform and revival movements, and globalization. Through such discussions, the students learn that the arts often play a subversive role in societies and become powerful means of expressing dissent by critiquing constructions of orthodoxy and power. Since I encourage students to respond to the course material through creative assignments that engage them in making art, they come to realize that the arts, as they are both experienced and practiced, are "irreplaceable instruments of knowledge."[5]

In embracing this arts-based pedagogic approach, I have been inspired by the work of my own teacher, the late Professor Annemarie Schimmel, who introduced me to the potential of the arts as lenses for understanding Muslim societies. During her distinguished career, she was widely recognized and honored by universities, governments, and civic organizations for promoting better understanding of Islam and Muslim cultures. Professor Schimmel's scholarship and teaching about Islam straddled and explored the intricate and complex relationships among many distinct fields (including history of religion, phenomenology, theology and mysticism, numerology, languages and literatures, and Islamic art history). Since she was fluent in several languages—including Arabic, Persian, Turkish, Urdu, and Sindhi—and had lived and traveled extensively in different Muslim-majority countries, she developed an intimate familiarity with different aspects of Muslim cultures. A strong advocate of the power of the arts to educate and transform, she endorsed the perspective of the German philosopher Johann Herder (d. 1803), who wrote, "From poetry we learn about eras and nations in much greater depth than through the deceitful and miserable ways of political and military war-histories."[6] During a speech she delivered at a March 1996 ceremony where she was awarded the 1995 Peace Prize of the German Book Trade (Friedenspreis des Deutschen Buchhandels) for her achievements in generating understanding between East and West, Professor Schimmel cited the importance of poetry in her own development as a scholar:

> I have discovered Istanbul corner by corner through the verses which Turkish poets had sung for five centuries about this wonderful city; I have learnt to love the culture of Pakistan through the songs that resound in all of its provinces, and when one of my Harvard students had the misfortune to be among the American hostages in Tehran, he experienced a great change in his jailers' attitude when he recited Persian poetry; here, suddenly, a common idiom emerged and helped to bridge deep ideological differences.[7]

She published more than a hundred books in English and German, many of which were translations and commentaries on Arabic, Persian, Turkish, Urdu, and Sindhi poetry. Here she followed the model of her hero, the Romantic poet and orientalist Friedrich Rückert, for whom world poetry offered a means of global reconciliation and peace. Like Rückert, she also wrote her own poetry, in German as well as in English, often in an orientalized style inspired by Rumi, the poet-philosopher Sir Muhammad Iqbal, and many of the Sufi folk poets of South Asia. Professor Schimmel was firmly convinced of the potential of not only poetry but also other forms of art, particularly calligraphy, as pedagogic bridges to approach the study of Islam and Muslim societies.

While Professor Schimmel's engagement with the arts focused on the appreciation of their religious and literary dimensions, the strength of this volume is that it significantly expands the discussion to the sociocultural dimensions by drawing on various disciplines such as sociology, history, art history, ethnomusicology, and anthropology. This multidisciplinary approach focused on the arts is a particularly important contribution, for it projects the fostering of literacy into a broader civilizational framework, recognizing the pluralistic dimensions of Muslim civilizations and their multiple identities. It plays a key role in dismantling unidimensional discourses about Muslim societies—discourses often steeped in the polarizing and dehumanizing language of civilizational superiority, nationalism, and patriotism, premised on the notion of the Muslim as "the other."

NOTES

1 Arkoun 2003, 19.
2 Ibid., 38.
3 Asani 2011.
4 For more on the cultural studies approach briefly outlined here, see Moore 2007.
5 Task Force on the Arts 2008, 1.
6 As quoted in Schimmel 2007, 296.
7 Schimmel 1996.

Acknowledgments

The editors gratefully acknowledge support from Canada's Social Sciences and Humanities Research Council (Standard Research Grant 410-2011-0838) for research and publication, as well as a publication subvention grant from the University of Alberta, jointly funded by the Office of the VP of Research and the Faculty of Arts. Our gratitude also to the editorial board and staff at the University of Texas Press for their very collegial and supportive work on this volume. We sincerely thank the Aga Khan Documentation Center at MIT for hosting audiovisual content on their website, archnet.org. We are most grateful to our authors, to the organizations who provided illustrations reproduced in this volume, and to our families for their patience and help. Finally, we would like to thank the many people around the globe—too numerous to mention individually—who supported the research published herein.

INTRODUCTION

Music, Sound, and Architecture in Islam

MICHAEL FRISHKOPF AND FEDERICO SPINETTI

This innovative, interdisciplinary collection explores the multiple relations of music, sound, and architecture as socially lived and experienced in Muslim cultures, both in the contemporary world and historically. It aims to open a pioneering and productive forum for academic fields and domains of intellectual reflection that have rarely been in dialogue, showing the possibilities offered by such an exchange for a greater understanding of both musical/aural experiences and built environments. The collection brings together a unique array of scholars, contributing perspectives from ethnomusicology, anthropology, art history, architecture, history of architecture, religious studies, and Islamic studies.

The book centers on Islamic contexts. We regard Islam as a broad historical, religious, and sociopolitical milieu of considerable complexity and diversity. Rather than a preconfigured category or "value system" determining the interpretive grid of our analyses, Islam is here explored from the ground up as we scrutinize the specificity of a wide range of socio-cultural, historical, and geographical settings. At the same time, the present collection of essays reflects a keen interest in shared historical linkages and heritages, as well as coherent sociocultural traits across the Muslim world. These commonalities are of great significance for a multiauthored exploration of the music-architecture nexus by enabling meaningful connections to be drawn. In particular, the volume explores and lays specific emphasis on the centrality of sound production in built environments in Muslim religious and cultural expression, as exemplified by the intimate relationship between prominent

Muslim sonic performances, such as the recitation of the Qur'an or devotional songs, and core Muslim architectural spaces, ranging from mosques and Sufi shrines to historic aristocratic villas, gardens, or traditional gymnasia. In the process, we approach Islam as an ideal site for theoretical investigations of the general relationship between sound and architecture and, in parallel, propose this relationship as an innovative and particularly significant angle from which to explore Muslim cultures.

We live in and through architecture, and we live in and through sound, usually simultaneously. What is more, architecture is not only an eminently spatial and visual configuration but also a temporal, auditory, and social one: we access and inhabit architectural spaces in time, and we experience and evaluate architectural structures through hearing, listening, and aural communication within them. Conversely, music and sound utterances are not only eminently temporal and auditory phenomena but also spatial and visual ones: they guide our orientation and positioning; they demarcate social spaces; they are performed according to specific spatial and visual arrangements among participants in sonic events; they may evoke visual narratives or be experienced visually as gesture and bodily movement. Music and architecture thus emerge as interlinked temporal-spatial phenomena, affording coordinates for intersubjective meaning creation, as well as behavioral and performative interaction.

The volume considers sonic performances broadly conceived as "aesthetically meaningful"—ranging from poetry recitation to art, folk, popular, and ritual musics, as well as religious sonic utterances not usually labeled "music" from an Islamic perspective—in relation to built environments broadly conceived as encompassing monumental, vernacular, ephemeral, and landscape architectures, interior design, decoration and furniture, urban planning, and geography. Here, the study of architecture moves beyond the analysis of physical structures to consider the social interactions, historical narratives, and cultural meanings that architecture defines, demarcates, or enables.

In exploring the sociocultural dimensions of the sound-space nexus, this volume is concerned both to elaborate theory and to ground it in specific ethnographic and historical evidence. We bring together research projects concentrating on selected regions and musical/sonic traditions of the Islamic world, highlighting the diverse area expertise of our contributors and offering a variety of ethnographic and historical perspectives while securing thematic consistency through the study of related cultural settings. In this way, the book aims at offering a significant contribution to scholarly discourse across anthropology, ethnomusicology, Islamic studies, art history, and architecture. In particular, it sets out to provide ethnomusicology with a groundbreaking, in-depth study of the relationship between music and the built environment, while offering the field of architecture a unique perspective on music that goes beyond the usual concerns with architectural acoustics or formal homomorphisms between visual and auditory domains.

The book fills a gap in both scholarly architectural and music studies. In addressing the relationship between music and place, ethnomusicological scholarship has interpreted "place" primarily as a dimension of cultural and territorial belonging,[1] often without considering music as a social and symbolic practice operating in concrete, material environments. On the other hand, scholarship devoting attention to music and architecture has predominantly focused on architectural acoustics,[2] or on symbolic and structural analogies viewed from the perspectives of music criticism, music composition, or architectural design,[3] without full consideration of the sociocultural aspects of the relationship between music performance and the architectural frames in which it takes place.

Building on and moving past this literature, we propose a mediation between emerging new directions in both architectural and music studies. On the one hand, we recapture anthropological antecedents in the cultural study of architecture[4] and further look with particular interest at architectural theory that both problematizes the traditional understanding of architecture as an essentially visual art and explores the multisensory dimensions of built environments,[5] including aural perception.[6] On the other hand, we detect in various contemporary streams of music scholarship a fruitful growing interest, beyond music per se, in auditory cultures and soundscapes at large and in aurality and hearing as forms of intersubjective action in, and knowledge of, the world,[7] with a few noteworthy contributions including a consideration of architectural spaces, landscapes, and urban geography.[8] By bringing these various theoretical streams and disciplinary approaches together, we intend to illuminate making music and living in buildings as profoundly interconnected social activities and the relationship between them as directly affecting the ways in which both humanly organized sounds and humanly organized spaces are experienced and interpreted.

Our theoretical frameworks are eclectic, drawing on a variety of perspectives and disciplines, and geared toward the exploration of broad classes of research problems. Three recurrent research themes, however, trace their way across chapters, disciplines, and areas.

The first theme involves the relationship between cultural meanings encoded aurally in musical (and, more generally, sonic) performances, on the one hand, and, on the other, cultural meanings encoded visually and spatially in architecture (and, more generally, the built environment), especially the ways in which meanings of sonic performance color architectural meaning and vice versa.[9] Here, moving from the contribution of studies highlighting the multiple sociocultural and ideological dimensions of the arts and architecture in the Middle East,[10] we look at theoretical paradigms from music semiotics[11] and from the semiotics of architecture[12] as a means to explore how these ostensibly distinct processes of signification come to be combined in architecturally framed performance events and to examine their intersections in terms of correspondences and complementarities, as well as dissonances and tensions. Drawing from performance theory and phenomenology,[13] especially as applied to ritual and performance,[14] we view musical meanings as situational and their relationship to architectural meanings as dependent on processes of embodiment, symbolization, and ritualization, as well as of negotiation and interpretation on the part of performers and participants.

The second pervasive theme comprises the implications of music performance practices for the ways in which architectural space is constructed, perceived, and experienced socially and pragmatically, as well as the bearings of architecturally framed space on the socio-communicative interactions of participants in sonic events. Here, architecture is viewed as an eminently social space that affords possibilities, poses constraints, and provides frames for specific social transactions. Germane to our discussion of the ways in which specific architectural spaces define possibilities for interaction within participatory musical performances are perspectives from nonverbal communication theory,[15] proxemics,[16] and symbolic interaction theory,[17] as well as studies directly concerned with architecture.[18] Social network theory provides another general paradigm for thinking about how communicative networks are established in performance under architectural constraints.[19]

The third theme concerns the politics of socio-architectural landscapes and their implications for musical life, situating the sound-architecture nexus in broader historical, sociopolitical, and economic contexts across the

Muslim world. Here, besides drawing on broadly critical social theory,[20] we look at the sociology of architecture,[21] as well as recent scholarly explorations of the politics of Islamic auditory cultures,[22] to situate musical life within the distribution of architectural complexes, the related social articulation of built environments, and the economic and political dimensions of urban and human geographies.

Working within—and beyond—this framework, the authors represented in this volume investigate how architecture as a material and social phenomenon shapes the social processes and meanings of sound and music, and—conversely—the ways in which sonic performances condition architecture's form and social meaning, tracing new pathways toward the study of the interconnections between humanly organized sound and humanly organized space. Some chapters, particularly those grounded in historiographic inquiry, examine visual representations of music or (sung) poetry in the figurative arts, often together with an inspection of their represented architectural settings. Here, songs featuring poetic representations of built environments and landscapes may complement in reverse these intertextual references. While a few chapters detect structural correspondences between spatial and sonic phenomena—for example, through the mirroring of geometric notions and poetic prosody, or the aurality inherent in the formal composition of manuscript pages—many of the authors highlight, across locales and epochs, the multiple intersections of sound and architecture at the level of semiosis (whether iconic, indexical, or symbolic/metaphorical). A rich array of culturally and socially significant referents are here implicated, ranging from social status and gender, to political and identity struggles, to modernist and nationalist ideologies, to religious and ethical discourses linked to Islamic philosophy, Sufism, or other localized belief systems. Other chapters focus on the music-architecture nexus on an experiential and pragmatic level, considering the performative interaction of spatial configurations and sonic utterances in a variety of contexts. Contributions from art history here converge with anthropologically informed studies in underscoring the multisensory and performative dimensions of built environments as an essential complement to the study of "solid" architectural frameworks.

While this book does not attempt to be encyclopedic in either disciplinary or global coverage, it is nonetheless topically and methodologically wide-ranging and aims to provide a multifaceted representation of the sound–

built environment nexus in the Islamic world. It is organized in six sections covering broad geo-cultural areas and highlighting interdisciplinary cross-pathways.

In part one, "Transregional," the historian of Islamic art and architecture D. Fairchild Ruggles's "Listening to Islamic Gardens and Landscapes" investigates the multisensory ecology of domesticated, designed natural environments from a variety of epochs across the Islamic world. Setting her discussion as a broader critique of the traditional visualist bias in the fields of art and architectural history, Ruggles calls for renewed attention to other senses, alongside sight, as constitutive of the human experience of built environments, thus advocating a full recognition that "the study of architecture has always required a study of space, which always exceeds visual perception and invites consideration of the *body* in space." The author focuses on historic Islamic gardens and highlights the importance of an examination of aural, olfactory, and tactile sensations, in addition to visually apprehended architectural forms, in understanding and reconstructing their sensorial and experiential dimensions. Turning specifically to aurality, she sets out to trace historical evidence of sound events in Islamic gardens.

Part two, "The Ottoman Empire and Turkey," begins with the art and architecture historian Nina Ergin, who argues for the importance of sound in understanding the social meaning of sixteenth-century Istanbul mosque architecture. In her chapter, "A Sound Status among the Ottoman Elite: Architectural Patrons of Sixteenth-Century Istanbul Mosques and Their Recitation Programs," mosque architectural forms—eminent spatial and visual markers in Istanbul's urban landscape—and Qur'anic recitation programs—distinctive aural phenomena animating the soundscape of those mosques—emerge as equally significant statements of social status for Ottoman architectural patrons. In a society as highly regulated along social ranks as was the Ottoman, decorum dictated that an architectural patron be wary of supporting buildings that, because of site, size, construction materials, or structural and decorative features, exceeded the patron's position on the social ladder. Ergin illustrates how, in this economy of status, the employment of Qur'an reciters "constituted a significant element of Ottoman mosque architecture, as much as domes, minarets, decorative tiles, and calligraphic inscriptions." By inspecting the endowment charters and the recitation programs of fourteen mosques, built in Istanbul by the sixteenth-century imperial master architect Mimar Sinan, Ergin shows how sonic parameters allowed a certain flexibility in the patrons' display of status, often consolidating, but to a certain extent also deflecting, the hierarchy of prestige encoded by architectural forms.

In his chapter "A Concert Platform: A Space for a Style in Turkish Music," the ethnomusicologist John Morgan O'Connell traces the impact of architectural space on musical style, delineating how both are implicated in complex, often contradictory, discourses of tradition, modernity, and Westernization that have bedeviled many newly formed nation-states throughout the twentieth century. O'Connell explores the emergence of large concert halls in nineteenth- and early twentieth-century Turkey as platforms for concert performance, venues not only for importing musical styles such as opera but also for presenting and transforming local styles. In particular, his chapter traces the career of musician Münir Nurettin Selçuk (1899–1981) alongside the socio-architectural history of Istanbul's Fransız Tiyatrosu ("French Theater"), founded in the mid-nineteenth century. O'Connell cogently demonstrates the impact of changing architectural spaces on *alaturka* (Turkish classical music, traditionally performed in more intimate venues) by examining the strategies by which Selçuk selected from and adapted to a series of Western-style concert halls, marked by different architectural features and built for different musical purposes, positioning musical and architectural styles within the broader discourses of an emerging Turkish modernity.

The ethnomusicologist Irene Markoff's chapter, entitled "Articulating Otherness in the Construction of Alevi-Bektaşi Rituals and Ritual Space in a Transnational Perspective," focuses on the portability of Alevi rituals and the mobility of ritual specialists and sacred objects (including musical instruments), all supporting a tenacious, fluid, and flexible Alevi identity largely independent of fixed structures. Alevis have historically feared persecution and perforce have practiced their faith clandestinely. They have learned to sanctify available space through adaptive, evanescent performance: highly affective sacred sound—language and music—and movement rather than through more durable, physical architecture or printed texts. In this way, minority and diasporic Alevi communities, whether residing in Turkey, Bulgaria, or Canada, can be locally empowered and globally connected, despite political oppression, rapidly shifting sociocultural climates, or migration. Markoff illuminates the resilience of Alevi-Bektaşi ritual through such spatial reconfigurations, as tied to a developing transnational network. Poetics of ritual is thus linked to politics of space, constructed through sacred movement, sung poetry, and the *bağlama* lute, known as the "stringed Qur'an" and deeply symbolic of the community and its beliefs.

In part three, "The Arab World," the ethnomusicologist Michael Frishkopf, in "Venerating Cairo's Saints through Monument and Ritual: Islamic Reform and the Rise of the Architext," contrasts architectural and sonic ritual veneration of saints in Islam. The saints, or *awliyāʾ*, are venerated architecturally through construction and maintenance of a shrine, while ritual veneration takes place through shrine visitation and a musical liturgy (*ḥaḍra*). Frishkopf asks: What is the relation between these two forms of veneration, and under what conditions does the balance shift from one to the other? During most of Egyptian history, they coexisted harmoniously, but more recently they have begun to conflict, the former ascendant, the latter in decline. Taking the Cairo shrine of Sidi ʿAli Zayn al-ʿAbidin as a case study, the author interprets the current decline of its *ḥaḍra* as representing a general shift from (1) dynamic, performative Islamic traditions, carried by people, transmitted orally, and adapting locally to forge a ramified, affective religious culture and localized social solidarities, toward (2) a more static, uniform, religious culture, carried by durable objects such as texts and architecture, which does not adapt but remains fixed, standardized, and standardizing and thus open to transnational connections, detaching from local culture toward a common, globalized Islam. The author calls this textual-architectural formation the "architext," arguing that its increasing dominance reflects a quest for political unification and empowerment of the global *umma* in order to confront power imbalances of the postcolonial world.

Also in part three, the anthropologist Jonathan H. Shannon's chapter, "Nightingales and Sweet Basil: The Cultural Geography of Aleppine Song," offers a phenomenological contribution to sound, architecture, and nostalgia, one that is particularly poignant in the wake of Aleppo's wholesale destruction since 2011. The author demonstrates the interrelation of soundscapes and the built environment, showing how music can induce a sense of longing for lost sonic and architectural spaces while fostering a critical engagement with the forces of modernity shaping the present. In this way, music helps pave the way for modernity by maintaining connections to sounds and places of the past. The author explores Aleppo's three zones (old city, new city, and peri-urban area), attending to the ways soundscape and built environment converge to reflect and shape cultural meaning, social life, and the distribution of power. Next, he reflects on sensory meanings of the old city and delineates how soundscape (including both musical and non-musical phenomena) and built environment authenticate each other in the auditory and visual domains, along with other sensory modalities. Finally, he discusses the *qudūd ḥalabiyya*, a traditional genre of Aleppine song, as a "sonic marker of authenticity," drawing out what he calls the "cultural geography of song" to illustrate how the *qudūd* evoke nostalgia for a disappearing sonic-spatial world, an object of contemporary longing as a hallmark of modernity.

Finally, in "Aural Geometry: Poetry, Music, and Architecture in the Arabic Tradition," the architecture historian and Islamic studies scholar Samer Akkach examines the intersection of geometric, prosodic, and musical notions in medieval Islamic theorization. Through a focus on the prosodic system codified by the eighth-century linguist al-Khalil bin Ahmad al-Farahidi, the author inspects the Islamic tradition of visual representation of prosodic cycles in circular diagrams and the ensuing translation of auditory patterns into geometrical ones. Drawing on a wider Islamic scholarly tradition, he highlights how this geometrical understanding of classical Arabic poetry is foundational for the closely related theorization and representation of musical rhythmic cycles. Akkach further interrogates this poetic-musical-geometric nexus in relation to the spatial structures of Islamic architecture. Here, lexical and conceptual analogies between musico-poetic and architectural domains testify to a semantic field imbued with metaphorical resonances between (sung) poetry and architecture. But, whereas a "geometrical and mathematical imagination . . . lay at the heart of classical Arabic poetry and music," we have very little evidence of corresponding equivalences between prosody and architecture for any level beyond the metaphorical, such as the formal or structural. Rather, the author argues, it is in philosophical discourse that music and architecture most directly converge, mediated by a common interpretive frame provided by the Platonic notions of harmony and beauty as recaptured and elaborated in medieval Islamic Neoplatonic thought.

Part four, "Andalusia and Europe," opens with the Islamic art historian Cynthia Robinson's "Tents of Silk and Trees of Light in the Lands of Najd: The Aural and the Visual at a *Mawlid* Celebration in the Alhambra," offering a study of the festivities for the commemoration of Prophet Mohammad's birthday (*mawlid*) in 1362 CE at the Alhambra palace, in Granada. Through a close reading of the fourteenth-century Andalusian scholar Lisan al-Din Ibn al-Khatib's account of the proceedings of the celebration, Robinson reconstructs the complex resonances between poetic symbolism and style, architectural design, and sonic performance playing into the experience of the event's participants. Robinson inspects the elaborate lighting devices adorning the open patio that was part of the carefully designed celebration setting and discusses the centrality of sonic performances in the ritual proceedings. Here, alongside Qur'anic recitation and *dhikr* chants, a prominent role was assigned to sung odes (*qaṣīdas*) composed for the occasion. Robinson's analysis of the intertextual ties between lighting-architectural mise-en-scène and musico-poetic performance, mediated by a shared universe of religious and mystical associations centered on the Prophet Muhammad, points to the actual sensory—visual and aural—experience of attendees at the *mawlid*, an experience that, by virtue of its manifold meaningful evocations, spurred them to ecstatic responses in what emerges as one specific, and at the same time emblematic, mystical séance in fourteenth-century Arab Andalusia.

Next, in her chapter entitled "Aristocratic Residences and the *Majlis* in Umayyad Córdoba," the Islamic art historian Glaire D. Anderson investigates the social and material dimensions of elite residences of tenth-century Umayyad Andalusia, particularly those of Córdoba's royal citadel and the villa of al-Rummaniyya. Grounding her discussion in historical sources as well as in the analysis of architectural frameworks and decorations, she uncovers the experiential and sensorial combination of visual, spatial, and auditory elements at the *majlis*, a term that in medieval Andalusia designated aristocratic musical gatherings as well as the reception halls that hosted them. The author argues that a consideration of music performance is key both to elucidating the historical function of reception spaces, their furnishings, and their decorations and, more generally, to "an enhanced understanding of how architecture and landscape worked in concert with material culture and social behavior in the context of the *majlis* in Umayyad Córdoba." Anderson considers the diverse social composition of *majlis* gatherings in terms of gender and legal status, noting the prominence of female slave musicians and singers performing for an audience of male guests. This gender distribution is significant for the interpretation of certain structural features of reception hall architecture. Drawing from Ibn Khaldun, Anderson further highlights the visual impact of bodily gestures of music performance as integral to the aesthetic appreciation of *majlis* participants. More generally, she delineates a multilayered sensory experience at the Córdoban *majlis* that binds together architectural frameworks and forms, including decorative motifs and textiles, landscape and garden sights, and auditory as well as visual musico-poetic signs.

Closing this part is the anthropologist Paul A. Silverstein's chapter, "Sounds of Love and Hate: Sufi Rap, Ghetto Patrimony, and the Concrete Politics of the French Urban Periphery." Here, the author shows how the built environment of gritty lower-class French suburbs, the *banlieues*—housing ethnically and religiously diverse communities, and expressly designed to repress cultural, social, and religious differences deemed incompatible with French state secularism—shapes subjectivities that are both expressed and reinforced in musical soundscapes that "re-spatialize" the *banlieue*, constructing aesthetic and social value out of the *banlieue*'s dilapidated forms. Yet the relation between built environment and soundscape is anything but deterministic; indeed, there is a reciprocal and dialogical relation between them, producing contrastive musical styles. One such style is hardcore "gangsta" hip-hop, expressing a "hypermasculine 'ghetto patrimony'" of streetwise street life, full of hatred, despair, and sharp political critique, stemming from institutionalized oppressions of class, gender, and race, but with little relation to religious identities. Contrasting to this hardcore style is an emerging Islamic music, especially Sufi hip-hop, offering spiritual love, hope, solace, and peace, in deliberate contrast to the violent, irreligious "gangsta" ethos. Sufi music—more transnational (via connections provided by global Sufi orders), more acceptable to authority (because it is anti-extremist), but still rooted in the particularities of Muslim life in the *banlieue*—delivers a completely different vision, even though gangsta and Sufi rappers emerge from the same built environment.

Part five, "Central and South Asia," begins with "Ideal Form and Meaning in Sufi Shrines of Pakistan: A Return to the Spirit," by the architect Kamil Khan Mumtaz. Adopting a Sufi Islamic position centered on Divine Reality, the author elucidates how both music and architecture in Islam express a common spiritual core, with particular reference to examples drawn from architectural and musical practices associated with Sufi tomb-shrines in Pakistan. The author highlights the centrality of the performing and plastic arts in Sufi ritual and devotional practice. For the Sufi, the highest form of worship is *iḥsān,* a word whose root form evokes the term meaning "beauty" (*ḥusn*). To create beauty is thus an act of both worship and invocation. But beauty is reflected rather than created; its degree depends on the extent to which a work exhibits Divine principles. While the possible range of sensible manifestations of these Divine principles is infinite, their source is essentially one. For this reason, traditional Muslim artists—whether musicians or architects—copy preexisting models; truly original creation of beauty is impossible, because God is always the source. Rather, the traditional arts support a spiritual quest for perfection, as a mirror reflecting Divine qualities and a ground for contemplating them. Congruence between music and architecture, as with other traditional Islamic arts, stems from deeper unifying principles and a common spiritual source. For Mumtaz, therefore, interarts relationships are essentially "vertical" and spiritual, not "horizontal" and sensory.

The following chapter, "The Social and Sacred Microcosm of the *Kiiz Üi*: Space and Sound in Rituals for the Dead among the Kazakhs of Mongolia," by the ethnomusicologist Saida Daukeyeva, presents an ethnographic study of funeral and commemorative lamentations (*joqtau*) among Muslim Kazakh seminomadic pastoralists in contemporary western Mongolia. Performed by female relatives of the deceased according to musically and poetically consistent formulas, lamentations are part of elaborate ritual proceedings taking place in the ephemeral vernacular architecture of the transportable yurt (*kiiz üi*). The author investigates the consonances between built environment and sonic performances of mourning, tracking their "dual spiritual-social significance" for ritual participants. Ethnographic evidence suggests that both the yurt's material configuration and these lamentations are replete with highly significant religious and cosmological meanings that relate directly to Kazakh beliefs about death, which display an integration of Islamic and indigenous shamanic elements. Daukeyeva further illustrates how codified spatial dispositions within the yurt, including the arrangement of objects and proxemic relations among participants, as well as the unfolding of social transactions among ritual participants by means of intoned lamentations and opportune movements in space, are of paramount importance in enacting social relations and responsibilities, including hierarchies along the lines of gender, seniority, and status. In her discussion, Daukeyeva thus addresses both the symbolic and the behavioral-performative interaction of spatial/visual and sonic/aural elements in ritual proceedings, highlighting how their interpenetration is instrumental in sustaining cosmological, religious, and societal notions in the Mongolian Kazakh community.

"Listening to Pictures in Iran," the title of the chapter by the Islamic art and architecture historian Anthony Welch that opens part six, "Iran," indicates his implicit premise: that the history of figurative visual art—as found in paintings, illuminated manuscripts, on the surfaces of functional objects such as bowls, or as inscribed on buildings—is not silent; rather, it evokes sound symbolically, through portrayals of musicians, instruments, and performance practices. In addition, such visual music is doubly located in relation to the built environment: the artwork itself is spatially located within a real built environment, and the artwork portrays musical practices and built environments together.

Through fanciful, stylized musical imagery—sometimes illuminating manuscripts that likewise speak of music and sometimes ornamenting architectural surfaces or objects placed within them—the scholar learns much, not only about musicians and musical practices, their social contexts, and their relation to the built environment, but also—through reading artistic style—about musical attitudes, meanings, and values in social, political, and religious arenas. From Welch's chapter, one begins to understand that "listening to pictures" may provide more cultural information than the musical sound itself, despite the ostensible silence of such visual arts, and is in any case crucial for unearthing musical meanings of a silent past. Figurative visual arts thus emerge as key for understanding architecturally emplaced soundscapes throughout history, with important implications for the broader political, social, and theological understanding of Islamic culture. For instance, his analysis clearly underscores the centrality of elaborate music, in conjunction with magnificent royal court architecture, for a Muslim monarch's prestige and reputation and for the construction of the broader aristocratic class. On the other hand, in some cases it also appears that silent visual music could displace sounded music, as when the latter is deemed to contravene Islamic law (for instance under the later reign of Shah Tahmasp). Through his detailed investigation of Persian relief sculptures and illuminated manuscripts, especially from the Timurid and Safavid periods, the author highlights the relation of music and the built environment and the significance of both throughout Persian history.

Finally, the ethnomusicologist Federico Spinetti's "Of Mirrors and Frames: Music, Sound, and Architecture at the Iranian *Zūrkhāneh*" offers an ethnographically based study of the complex relationship between sonic performance and auditory experience, athletic practice, and built environment in the traditional Iranian gymnasium known as *zūrkhāneh*. The author considers the ways in which the unique architectural and interior design features of *zūrkhāneh* gymnasia relate to both musical-poetic content and athletic exercises in a web of symbolic correspondences that articulate the tenets of the *zūrkhāneh* ethos. This referential mirroring of musical and architectural texts is key to the creation of meaning on the part of gymnasia affiliates. Moving beyond the symbolic dimension, Spinetti construes architecture as a frame for communicative and performative interaction. The author illustrates the spatial articulation of sound and movement, contending that architectural frames and the disposition of social actors within them are essential to the unfolding of performative interactions in the musico-athletic practice of the *zūrkhāneh*; conversely, he explores the sonic articulation of space, arguing that sonic events are central to the ways in which *zūrkhāneh* gymnasts interact meaningfully with the built environment. Through this symbolic-referential as well as pragmatic-performative exploration of how sound and material environment are experienced conjointly, the author proposes "a multisensory approach to both architecture and music, beyond the confines of putatively discrete auditory and visual or spatial domains."

NOTES

1 For a seminal study, see Stokes 1994a; see also Feld and Basso 1996 and, for similar perspectives from popular music studies, Whiteley et al. 2004.

2 See for example Beranek 1979 and 1992; Forsyth 1985; Thompson 2002; Howard and Moretti 2009; Kronenburg 2012.

3 See Waterhouse 1921; Kompridis 1993; Young et al. 1993; Martin 1994; Xenakis 2008; Grueneisen 2003. In this vein, see also more recent collaborative endeavors of music and architectural scholarship, such as Muecke and Zach 2007 and Ripley et al. 2007.

4 See Waterson 1990. See also Hirsch 1996, and Low and Lawrence-Zúñiga 2003.

5 See, for example, Pallasmaa 1996, and Holl et al. 2006. Relevant here are also contributions from the anthropology of the senses, especially Ingold 2000. See also Ingold and Lucas 2007.

6 Of particular significance for our volume is the concept of "aural architecture" as put forward and discussed in Blesser and Salter 2007. See also Sheridan and van Lengen 2003; Rasmussen 1962, 224–237.

7 See, among others, Schafer 1977; Feld 1996; Bull and Back 2003; Erlmann 2004b; Schulze 2008; Samuels et al. 2010; Pinch and Bijsterveld 2011; Sterne 2012.

8 See Cohen 1995 and 2012; Sterne 1997; Krims 2007; Born 2013; Prokopovych 2013; Bijsterveld 2013.

9 For a pioneering study see Ergin 2008.

10 See Ardalan and Bakhtiar 1973; El-Said and Parman 1976; Haider 1988; Tonna 1990; Lifchez 1992; Mortada 2003; Gharipour and Schick 2013. For a discussion specifically addressing music and visual arts in Islam, see Wright 2004.

11 See Turino 1999.

12 See Eco 1972 and 1980; Amor 2004.

13 See Schutz and Luckmann 1989.

14 See Turner 1977; Schechner and Turner 1985; Schechner 1988; Bell 1992; Small 1998.

15 See Birdwhistell 1970, and, in specific connection to architecture, Rapoport 1982.

16 See Hall 1966.

17 See Bateson 1972; Goffman 1974.

18 See Milligan 1998; Smith and Bugni 2002 and 2006; Nas and Brakus 2004.

19 See Scott 2000.

20 See Bourdieu 1977 and 1993; Habermas 1984 and 1987. See also, in relation to architecture and everyday spaces, Bourdieu 1979 and Lefebvre 1991.

21 See, for example, Ankerl 1981; Gieryn 2000 and 2002; Du Bois 2001.

22 See Hirschkind 2009.

PART ONE

Transregional

CHAPTER ONE

Listening to Islamic Gardens and Landscapes

D. FAIRCHILD RUGGLES

Like all gardens, those built in the Islamic world from the seventh century CE to the present, from the Alhambra in Spain to the Taj Mahal in India and modern gardens such as Azhar Park in Cairo, were and are fully sensory environments. Vision was the foremost of the senses attracted to the garden. Poetry and botanical texts tell us that the plants were diverse and the color palette was vibrant with brightly hued blooms. Arabic, Persian, and Turkish writers of the past admired the rich yellow of the lily and the deep red of the rose; when extolling the beauty of a landscape or a garden, they lavished so much praise on the contrast of white marble architecture against a backdrop of green that it became a poetic cliché. In those cases, it was not nature itself that was admired but the firm establishment of humankind in nature, taming it, making it productive and orderly, and giving it meaning. The relationship between Islamic society and nature is a sensory one in which the impact of nature—almost always in its domesticated garden form—was measured in human terms.

In addition to a visual component, sensory contact included smell. Islamic poetry is rich with references to fragrant plants, spices, and perfumes, and garden manuals list hundreds of plants that had pungent or sweet scents. Sensory contact also included the tactile experience of touching textured surfaces, of feeling the cool spray of water, of moving within the garden, and of shifts from hot sunlight to cool shade. Finally, the sensory perception of the garden occurred through its sounds, celebrated in poetry where a nightingale's song, the splashing of a fountain, or the murmuring of foliage riffled by a breeze can still be heard.

In trying to recapture the missing sensory experiences, one must work against the grain of traditional practices of art and architectural history, where the scholarship of the discipline has focused on vision to the exclusion of other senses. To explain why this is so, it helps to examine art history's roots. As a field first of aesthetic judgment and appreciation, and later of critical analytical study, art history began with painting and sculpture and addressed the challenge of decoding meaning from representations that are, by virtue of being representations, *not* the thing that they represent.[1] For art history to complete its task, the split between the thing and the representation that stands for it is a necessary precursor. Precisely how representation occurs in the visual field had been studied by Erwin Panofsky in the early twentieth century.[2] But the terms of engagement were dramatically changed when the visual field became not simply a spatial stage but a psychoanalytic field wherein subjectivity and objectivity were defined as positions. Lacanian psychoanalytic theory in the 1970s and 1980s explained subjectivity as emerging from the eternal, unbridgeable gap between self and otherness, imagined as reality (designated as the Real)—but a Real that is forever unknowable.[3] The photography historian John Tagg explained it thus: "In relation to Lacan's discussion of vision . . . it is clear that the Real is what cannot be encountered. It is what the eye must shield itself against and, indeed, it is in the recoil from this unwelcome, scorching encounter that the split occurs from which the subject emerges, separated from the world as object, but hanging on its loss, for which the elusive object of the look's desire will henceforth stand."[4]

These inquiries into representation, perspective, subjectivity, and the Real relied on a visual experience of the world, and it is not mere coincidence that some art history programs at that time—anxious to separate themselves from the older art historical practices of connoisseurship, formalism, and stylistic analysis—renamed themselves as departments of visual culture. The renaming announced the shift away from the object as the art history's primary focus of study to the study of vision itself, in which the object, the eye, the brain, and space were all studied as elements of both an expanded visual field and an expanded disciplinary field. In the shift, the sense of sight gained an even greater importance. Aural and other sensory experiences of the world had never been a particularly important part of art historical inquiry, except in those limited cases where the architectural historian considered the structural means by which resonance was enhanced in a church or mosque interior, or how prayer times were announced to the urban surround from belfries and minarets.

I recall a moment in a medieval studies conference twelve years ago when I asked an eminent elderly scholar to expand upon his explanation of a French cathedral's interior space in order to include its temperature, sounds, and aroma. In my own mind, I was recalling the awe and powerful sensations of entering a medieval cathedral: I remembered the interior as a vast, dark space that was perceived as much by echoes as by sight, and I remembered reaching out to the smooth, hard stone piers, the coolness of which I had already anticipated before actually touching them. However, at the conference, the request was dismissed out of hand as belonging to the realm of not art history but music. But why should we separate an echo (sound) from the material (architecture) that produces it? The study of architecture has always required a study of space, which always exceeds visual perception and invites consideration of the *body* in space. That human body is more than a pair of eyes. Fortunately, the perception of architectural history's limits is changing, as the essays in this volume, titled *Music, Sound, and Architecture in Islam*, demonstrate.

The power of the senses is that they stitch the interior world of the self to the exterior experience of the world. Vision simultaneously reaches out to and holds the exterior world at bay—seen as it is across that unbridgeable gap between the self and all else. It is that external world that becomes the object, the object being that thing that is *not* the self. In contrast, the other senses lack the ability to objectify. Indeed, sound is perceived by actual changes made to the human body as the surface of the skin or the ear's membrane responds to the pressure of sound waves. Similarly, the sense of smell is activated when odor molecules enter the nose and stimulate nerve cells. The catalyst may be "out there"; however, it does not remain out there very long and quickly becomes part of the subjective sensate self. Thus, while the jasmine plant releases the rich perfume that we inhale, our sensory appreciation of it is directed less at the emitting object than at the odor itself. Indeed, it is common when encountering a pleasant fragrance to close the eyes, blocking off the identification of the source so that the aroma can be savored not as an appreciable and external thing but as a bodily experience. To inhale a scent is not a scorching encounter with otherness but rather a brief adjustment in oneself.

My own work on Islamic gardens initially centered on visual experience.[5]

In part this was because the visual was all that endured. The olfactory, aural, and tactile aspects of being in a garden were ephemeral experiences that were not retrievable, except as repetitions in which the modern listener could only imagine the original impact of the musical concert. Subsequently, however, I began to realize that describing and analyzing the visual effects alone of a garden space is insufficient. I have come to see that the emphasis on vision is a projection of our own modern, highly scopophilic proclivities and to wonder if the casual dismissal of the other senses—particularly sound and smell—derives from our ability to control the sounds, odors, temperatures, and humidity of our surroundings. Because we have the ability to control the environment and suppress unpleasant sensory experiences, we can persuade ourselves that we are not subject to them. Thus protected from strong sensations in our own world, we do not attribute importance to the premodern experience of sensation. I am not claiming that the premodern world was more saturated with sensory stimuli than the modern world in which we live; rather, I am suggesting that modern art historians—such as the aforementioned historian of French cathedral architecture—have chosen to disregard such stimuli as unimportant.

In a fascinating essay, George Roeder analyzed the reasons for this dismissal, attributing it to the perceived rationality of the eye and to class prejudices, among other things.[6] He wrote that the senses were closely associated with the class division between those who labor with their bodies in the physical world and those who do not labor but write about the world from the sanitary distance of a desk. Such writers have not only avoided but have even disdained the effects of hard work, its filth and sweat, and they linked powerful sensory experiences with socially marginal status. The fact that historians themselves did not engage in physical labor has influenced, in Roeder's words, "how we regarded the historical role of sensory experience."[7] As an analytic practice, art history—a discipline that continues to have upper-class associations—has privileged the scopic.

Evidence of Sound

Garden history is the progeny of art history, and art historians studying gardens have often treated them as works of architecture, focusing on the planning, form, functioning, and symbolic meaning of gardens. But the transitory nature of a garden or landscape often demands a more amplified scope of analysis that addresses the passage of time and the performance aspects of gardens.[8] For one thing, the key formal elements (i.e., the plants) are ephemeral, in the sense of being short-lived but also materially in a state of constant change. Bulbs emerge, bloom, and then fade from view in a matter of weeks; trees that are lit with color when they blossom in the spring may become more subdued as the season progresses. I am once again (myopically, as it were) focusing on appearance; yet it is not only the colors of the tree that change but also the scent of those short-lived blooms and the sounds as birds trill from the branches in the morning and the fountains gurgle throughout the day. These were integral parts of the garden experience, but they are gone, leaving the historian with the challenge of how to assess a multisensory environment of which only coded representations and fragments of the material fabric survive.

What is the evidence for aurality in Islamic gardens? Because of the ephemerality of the gardens themselves (not to mention their sounds), most scholars asking about the sense of sound have resorted to visual and textual evidence. In Islamic art in general, the musicologist Owen Wright explains, there are two ways of finding the "sight of sound."[9] One is to study the representation of instruments and musical events in manuscripts, or what he calls musical iconography. The other is to seek parallels between music and visual art, for example, looking for echoes of musical meter and harmony in the geometry of architectural decoration, while at the same time examining how some elements of music are visualized in diagrams. In both the iconography and the parallels, he is looking specifically at *music* as a production that follows rules of design similar to those guiding art and architecture as well as poetry. However, in the following, I inquire into the presence of sound more generally, defined not exclusively as a composition made intentionally with instruments and voices but as an sonic entity (1) that can command full attention, as with a calculated production of musical performance, or (2) that can fulfill the role of backdrop, as in the sound of a constantly running fountain, or (3) that occurs incidentally and unpredictably, as with the cacophonous screech of a peacock. Employing the iconographic mode described by Wright, evidence for such sound in gardens can be found in pictorial representations, poetry and written descriptions, and architectural spaces.

From the seventh century CE to the present, from the Maghreb to Southeast Asia, Islamic gardens were much more than mere repositories for pavilions, plants, and trees. They were living environments animated by birds and animals, some of which flew in and out at whim, while others were specifically housed there. Many palaces had aviaries. For instance, the palace of Madinat al-Zahra', built outside of Córdoba in the tenth century CE, had fish ponds, a zoo, and an aviary with caged birds and animals that must have been heard on occasion throughout the palace grounds.[10] Some of the animals and birds were collected as exotic species (and to eat), but surely the birds were also enjoyed for their song. The city of al-Qata'i (in modern Cairo), built in the second half of the ninth century CE by Ibn Tulun, was a vast complex with gardens, a menagerie, and a hippodrome, to which his son added the Golden House and a nearby aviary.[11] Similarly, the seventeenth-century Topkapı Palace in Istanbul had an aviary formed of trees.[12] Poetry is full of evocative descriptions of birdsong, and of all the birds, nightingales and doves were enjoyed the most. For example, the ninth-century Andalusian poet Abu Marwan Ibn Razin wrote that the melodious cooing of doves is "better than the best of singers."[13]

Not sufficiently content with live birds and animals, wealthy patrons also had their artisans craft artificial versions that could be made to whistle or twitter when water, steam, or wind passed through interior pipes. In an Andalusian tenth-century palace outside of Córdoba, for example, there was a pool with tortoises wearing pearl necklaces. They were said to croak, but whether they were real tortoises or mechanical facsimiles is unclear from the description.[14] They could have been animals in the royal collection, or they may have been one of the many wondrous fountains and other machines—related to the Hellenistic and Byzantine automata—that were fabricated to create musical and other special effects.[15] Even the well-known lions fountain in the Alhambra's Court of the Lions in fourteenth-century Granada may have belonged to this category: a wondrous object that spewed water noisily and thus seemed alive (fig. 1.1a).

In early tenth-century Baghdad, on the occasion of a visit from the Byzantine ambassador to the Abbasid court, a splendid display was orchestrated with similar stagecraft. The entourage of visitors was led from one marvelous hall to another until they reached a courtyard in the New Palace. There they saw a large tree with eighteen gold and silver boughs on which artificial birds made from gold and silver chirped and sang. Proceeding onward to their audience with the caliph, they reached another hall where, on the caliph's

Figure 1.1. (a, *top*) The Court of the Lions, a fourteenth-century courtyard garden as it appeared in 2007, the Alhambra, Granada. (b, *bottom*) Patio de la Acequia, a fourteenth-century courtyard garden as it appeared in 2007, Palacio de Generalife, Granada. Photographs: D. F. Ruggles.

signal, a tree rose miraculously from the ground, while mechanical birds sang, and fountains gushed with rose water and musk.[16] In all of these descriptions, adding to the pleasure of hearing song from an ordinary bird was the delight of manufacturing that same sound and thus erasing the line between the natural and the ingeniously artificial.

Providing a sibilant aural backdrop to the chirps and growls of living fauna and automata, the garden's trees and fountains made a gentle and constant sound that was pleasing yet unobtrusive. One of the effects of such background sounds is that they mask other noises and can thus help to create a sense of privacy. On a hillside very near to the Alhambra, the Generalife Palace's Acequia Garden (Granada), an early fourteenth-century garden retreat named for its central water channel, had a pavilion at either end as well as a projecting mirador at the midpoint of the long covered gallery that ran along one side of the garden (fig. 1.1b).

Because walking along this gallery was the primary means of getting to the far pavilion, the experience of the garden was unavoidable. Visitors saw colors and foliage textures, set against the characteristically reddish clay soil typical of Granada. Perhaps they detected the light scent of whatever flowers were in bloom. Hieronymous Münzer, a German physician who went to Granada only two years after the surrender of the ruling Nasrid dynasty in 1492 CE, and Andrea Navagero, who traveled there as an ambassador from Venice in 1526, saw orange and lemon trees planted in the courtyards of the Alhambra. The sweet and slightly heavy scent of the flower and the much lighter scent of the fruit itself later in the season must have been a great delight, and surely the water made noise as it ran gently through the central channel.[17] Navagero related that there were also vigorous jets that shot upward. One can imagine both the physical sensation of the water spray as it cooled the skin and the sound of splashing as it fell back into the containing basin. The rows of jets that line the channel today may have been a later addition, but the singular jets observed in other courtyards indicate that the sound, at least, is authentic.[18] In addition, water rushes fast and generously into the courtyard from a source uphill, a sound loud enough to demand attention. It arrives with sufficient force to flow like a fast-moving stream. In a dry climate such as southern Spain, the sound of water comes as a relief.

Even where the gardens were less spectacular, we find evidence for multiple sensory dimensions. For example, the eleventh-century Persian traveler Nasir-i Khusraw saw rooftop gardens in Cairo where the trees were presumably grown in pots. The roof gardens were probably positioned thus to take advantage of breezes as well as to maximize real estate in the densely settled city. But their height required ingenious water-lifting devices, such as wheels. "There are places where the houses are fourteen stories tall and others seven. I heard from a reliable source that one person has on top of a seven-story house a garden where he raised a calf. He also has a water-wheel up there turned by this ox to lift water from a well down below. He has orange trees and also bananas and other fruit-bearing trees, flowers, and herbs planted on the roof."[19]

Waterwheels are never silent. They rotate for hours on end, and their creaking noise was sometimes regarded as detracting from the environment of the garden and sometimes adding to it. In al-Andalus the poet Lisan al-Din Ibn al-Khatib (1313–1374 CE) wrote of a waterwheel's "plaintive lovesong," and another, Abu Tammam Ghalib ibn Tammam al-Hayyam, praised the melody and chant of such wheels, likening them to the famous singer Ziryab who arrived in al-Andalus in 822.[20] Although the historical sounds themselves do not reverberate in the present, the accounts of birdsong, traces of fountains, and descriptions of waterwheels inform us not only that sound was present but that it was an intended part of the sensory design of gardens. Thus, in historic gardens today, when we hear the splashing of a fountain or the heavier rhythm of a waterwheel in motion, we are not hearing the actual sounds from the eleventh and fourteenth centuries, and yet we *are* hearing an authentic repetition of those sounds. The garden as a form is like a written musical composition; its "performance" today bears the same relation to its "performance" long ago as the performance of a medieval song today does to its performance in the era of its composition.

There is also evidence for staged musical events in garden settings. The playing of music is shown in manuscripts such as the romance of *Bayad wa Riyad*, a thirteenth-century illustrated Arabic manuscript from al-Andalus (fig. 1.2).[21] It is a tale of secret love between Bayad, a young merchant from Damascus, and Riyad, a slave girl, in which there are several illustrations of scenes set within walled gardens where singers played the *ʿūd* (lute). In the first, Riyad attends a get-together in a garden with other ladies attending to Riyad's mistress, the daughter of the *ḥajib* (prime minister). The narrative tells us that the garden was a lovely sight, with carpets, silken cushions, platters of food, and cups of wine. Painted scenes from the manuscript show the group sitting between high walls—an enclosed garden—under the shade

Figure 1.2. Bayad plays the ʿūd to the lady, in the *Bayad wa Riyad*. Biblioteca Apostolica Vaticana, Vatican City AR. 368; courtesy of Pictures From History/ Bridgeman Images.

of leafy trees. The mistress tells one of her slave girls to sing, whereupon the girl takes up the instrument and sings of forlorn love. When she finishes, the mistress cries, "By God, your song filled me with sadness—sing us another!" And one after another, the slave girls sing songs of unrequited love as the lute and another string instrument, the *ṭanbūr*, are passed among the singers, along with wine.

At this point Bayad arrives. He has already glimpsed Riyad in an orchard on the banks of the river and has engaged a go-between—who is present at the party and serves as the narrator of the events—and he and the go-between hatched a plan whereby he would attend the gathering to see if Riyad is as lovely and demure as he believes. When he arrives, he takes the lute himself and sings several love songs. When pressed by the mistress, he confesses that he has been smitten by one of her ladies whom he has seen only from a distance (thus attesting to her unbesmirched honor). The mistress asks others to sing, and eventually it becomes a back-and-forth of songs sung by Riyad and Bayad, in one of which Bayad composes and sings verses describing the garden's myrtle, lilies, golden narcissus, and white and red roses. The mistress is sympathetic to the lovers, perhaps as a result of having just heard twenty-five songs about romantic longing (according to the sequence in the manuscript). But she cannot give them to each other because, as she explains, Riyad is owned by the mistress's father, who wants the slave girl for himself. The group fears a scandal, and Bayad is quickly and secretly ushered from the garden.

The story continues with love letters and tearful sadness, and we do not know how it ends since the manuscript's final pages have been lost. But it is significant that the entire first scene (more than a third of the extant text) occurs in the garden and that the communication among the attendants at the garden party—and thus the communication to the reader as well—occurs in the form of songs. The scenes are illustrated as well as narrated. In addition to the first scene of lute playing, there are two similar scenes, one of Riyad singing and the other of the turbaned Bayad (seen in the painting reproduced here).

The *Bayad wa Riyad* is an unusual manuscript in that it is the only such fully illustrated manuscript to survive from Islamic Spain, but in its depictions of musical scenes in gardens, it is typical. Manuscripts, wall paintings, and scenes painted or carved in precious objects throughout the Islamic world show that gardens, whether enjoyed as places of leisure or organized ceremoniously on state occasions, were sonorous environments. Music was an expected entertainment not only in receptions held in gardens but also at court festivities, military parades, and the hunt.[22] Thus, the *Bayad wa Riyad* manuscript painting provides more than an image of a popular musical instrument: it shows the courtly garden context in which music was played and hints at its effect—winning the heart of the musician's beloved.

Music is shown at large scale in palace murals. An entire program of such scenes is represented in the Chihil Situn pavilion (finished in 1647 CE) in the Safavid palace complex of Isfahan. The Chihil Situn stood within a large walled garden with trees, garden beds, water channels, and large rectangular pools, and the pavilion opens up to its verdant environment via its broad *tālār* (wooden columned) porch and immense arched *īwāns* (large niches) (fig. 1.3a). On the walls in the interior of the hall are four large murals showing state receptions and historical battles, as well as several smaller ones showing festive scenes and some later paintings of figural types.[23] There is delightful consonance in the fact that the Chihil Situn is a real pavilion surrounded by a real garden, adorned with pictures that show a garden pavilion peopled by the shah, courtiers, visitors, and entertainers, the very people who would have constituted the viewing and listening audience on festive occasions.

On the south end of the western wall, there is a painting (made soon after 1647 CE) that depicts the feast given a hundred years earlier by Shah Tahmasp in honor of the visit of the Mughal emperor Humayun to Tabriz (fig. 1.3b). Humayun had sought the protection of the Safavids during a period of political uncertainty and exile from Hindustan in 1544 CE. The rulers are depicted in an interior space. Since the arched window at the center of the scene opens to a landscape of lawn and trees, the space is probably a garden pavilion (and thus a representation of a garden pavilion on the walls of the Chihil Situn, itself a garden pavilion). The Mughal is shown wearing a robe of honor, seated on a dais with the shah, his head slightly lower than that of his host and gazing toward the shah, as befitting his subject status in that moment. Around them swirls a lavish reception with entertainment provided by a group of musicians (on the viewer's left) playing string instruments, mouth and lap harps, and large frame drums (a variety of the *daf*) while two dancers sway to the rhythm. Although it is the political meeting of the two rulers that is the principal subject, the musical entertainment occupies the center foreground, where it invites us to listen to the drumbeat and melodies of the music, the effect of which is performed by the dancers' lithe bodies. Many of the listeners in the audience have their hands raised, in some cases holding cups and plates, but in others demonstrating an enthusiastic response to the music. Even the robed figure standing next to the dancers is swept up in the rhythm, for as she pours wine from a tall-necked vase into a cup, her knee is raised and her robe flows in response to her movement. Other painted murals elsewhere in the Chihil Situn depict receptions for the Chinese delegation and for Nadr Muhammad Khan, exiled from Transoxiana. Instruments such as the drum, lute (*ʿūd*), and angular harp (*chang*) appear often in these murals as well as in Safavid manuscript and album paintings of the period.

Figure 1.3. (a, *top*) Chihil Situn (finished 1647 CE), as it appeared in 2011, Isfahan. (b, *bottom*) Chihil Situn wall fresco. Photographs: D. F. Ruggles.

From India, a well-known late sixteenth-century painting from a copy of the *Baburnameh* shows not musical performance but sound. The garden scene occupies two facing pages in the manuscript, which records the memoirs of the Mughal emperor Babur (*see plates 1 and 2*). Babur is depicted actively directing the construction of one of his many gardens, the Bagh-i Wafa near Kabul. As described in the memoir's narrative, the painting shows the garden teeming with brightly colored oranges, citron, and pomegranates, the latter attracting birds that are shown perched on branches and in mid-flight. It is a scene of vigorous activity, from the man at the door who has just knocked for entrance to the attendants whose hands are raised in a gesture indicating speech and emotion. The vivid colors and trees laden with ripe fruit appeal to the eyes and taste, and it does not require much imagination to conjure up the soundscape as well: the birds chirping and the horses breathing roughly, the clattering of metal tools, the chatter of the assembly, and the commanding voice of Babur himself.

In both the *Baburnameh* manuscript and the Chihil Situn murals, music is presented together with food, luxurious clothing, attending servants, and a magnificent setting as the attributes of courtly life. However, manuscript paintings do more than simply represent the people, animals, and instruments that emit sound; as in Wright's second model of musical "representation," the actual composition of the page can underscore the relation between sound production and words. For example, in a 1648 illustration in the great Persian epic *Shahnameh*, there is a scene of combat between the hero Rustam and his grandson Barzu, whose identity he does not recognize (*see plate 3*).

In the center foreground, the protagonists face off on horseback, youthful Barzu (on the right) attempting to strike the older, bearded Rustam (on the left) with a mace. Overhead, the clashing armies of each protagonist are led by trumpeters whose long golden horns point centrally and slightly upward toward the four blocks of script, as if the horns were giving voice to the text of the manuscript. The formal design of the painting directs our attention to sound and then supplies the script that will presumably be vocalized, word and image cooperating to tell a dramatic story.

In the battle scene, sound is a supplement that enhances the main action, but in a different painting from an earlier manuscript copy of the *Shahnameh* manuscript made between 1525–1535 CE, music is the central theme. The painting illustrates the story of the musician Barbad, who caught the attention of the Sassanian king Khusraw (r. 590–628 CE) by daring to play the lute and sing for him unbidden while hidden in a cypress outside of the garden pavilion where the shah was celebrating the Persian New Year (*see plate 4*).[24]

The shah, whose back is to the tree and who does not see the entirety of the scene as we do, heard the mysterious and beautiful music and ordered a search for its source. When Barbad descended from his branch and revealed himself, he was promptly appointed chief musician. As in the battle scene described above, the cypress in which the musician hid himself playfully insists on vocalization. The slender tree shoots upward and behind the blocks of script, hidden like Barbad himself, and then emerges from behind the frame. It divides the page and is the tallest element, pushing into the gold-flecked margins, rising from its obscured background position to demand our attention, like the voice of the singer himself.

The sounds and sensory experiences of these historic gardens and landscapes can rarely be heard today, with the exception of fountains that at the Alhambra and a few other palaces still play in their original architectural setting. But even there, it is at best a reenactment of a soundscape, a performance of something that is not the original and yet, in reenacting the original, excites our imagination. Our understanding of what the garden sounded like, or smelled like, derives from manuscript painting, sculptural imagery, and literary evocations where the effects of sound and sensory stimulation are described or represented. Thus, although we may go in search of the sensory experiences that exceeded the visual, ultimately we have to return to visual evidence that shows, through pictorial representation of both the production and the effect of sensory stimuli, the ephemeral sounds, scents, and experiences that are no longer present. However, this is a different kind of visual practice than is usually welcomed in art history. It is one that does not insist on vision as the primary or the only way of knowing the history of architecture and the built environment. Instead, it enlists the visual to discover the echoes of other important sensory ways of knowing the world around us, both present and past. To understand Islamic gardens in all their sensory splendor, the eyes want the accompaniment of the nose and ears, indeed, the entire sensate body.

NOTES

1 See Ruggles 2007.
2 See Panofsky 1997.
3 See Lacan 1977. Lacanian theory had a powerful effect not only on the field of psychoanalysis but also on literary, cultural, anthropological, and art historical studies.
4 John Tagg, personal letter to D. Fairchild Ruggles, quoted in Harris and Ruggles 2007, 13.
5 For example, Ruggles 1997a and Ruggles 2007.
6 See Roeder 1994, with thanks to Professor Barbara Mooney for directing me to this source.
7 Roeder 1994, 1116; see also the chapter "Odour and Power: The Politics of Smell," in Classen et al. 1994, 161–179.
8 See Ruggles 2008, 5–7.
9 Wright 2004.
10 See Ibn Khaldun (1332–1406 CE) quoted in al-Maqqari (ca. 1577–1632 CE) 1967, I: 380.
11 See Behrens-Abouseif 1989, 5.
12 See Çelebi (1611–1684 or 1685 CE) 1834–1850 , 49–50.
13 Cited in Pérès 1983, 169.
14 See Ruggles 2000, 123–128.
15 See Ruggles 2008, 82–83. For a brief description of five manuscripts on sonic automata, see Shiloah 1979, 49–50, 63–64, 66–67, 70–71, 96–98.
16 See Ruggles 2008, 78–79, citing the description in al-Khatib al-Baghdadi (1002–1071 CE) 1931, I: 100–104.
17 See Navagero 1563 (translated in Ruggles 2011, 118) and Münzer 1991, 93–95.
18 Ruggles 2000, 170, citing Navagero 1563.
19 Nasir-i Khusraw 2001, 67.
20 See Ibn al-Khatib 1956, 170; translated in Pérès 1983, 209. Ziryab—named after a type of black bird because of his dark skin—came from Baghdad and revolutionized music through his performance, teaching, and the improved design of the *ʿūd*. Less is known about Abu Tammam (not the same as the ninth-century poet who flourished in Syria and Egypt), cited in Ibn Zaydun (1003–1070 CE) 1951, 13; translated in Pérès 1983, 210.
21 Arabic text and Spanish translation in Nykl 1941; for a new translation with reproductions of the images and study of the manuscript see Robinson 2007a.
22 See Denny 1985, 40.
23 These have been studied by Sussan Babaie (Babaie 1994).
24 See Sims 2002, 312; also Welch 1979, 114–115.

PART TWO

The Ottoman Empire and Turkey

CHAPTER TWO

A Sound Status among the Ottoman Elite

Architectural Patrons of Sixteenth-Century Istanbul Mosques and Their Recitation Programs

NINA ERGIN

The architectural form of the mosques built by Mimar Sinan, who served as the imperial master architect of the Ottoman dynasty between 1539 and his death in 1588 CE, clearly reflected to contemporary viewers from within Ottoman culture the status and wealth of the respective buildings' patrons. The majority of these patrons who commissioned and funded mosques were members of the ruling elite and grandees. Not only the quality of construction materials and the level of sophistication in the craftsmanship displayed in the architectural details and furnishings but also the presence and number of domes and minarets established a hierarchy based on a certain "decorum," as expressed by the art historian Gülru Necipoğlu.[1] In addition to these two variables of the patrons' status and the form and size of the mosques' establishment, their correlation to a third variable in the context of this Ottoman architectural decorum deserves closer scrutiny: what has so far not been considered is the role played by Qurʾanic recitation, an integral part of the experience of mosque space. This oversight is surprising, considering that mosques' endowment charters (*vakfiye*) carefully specify the suras (chapters) and *āyas* (verses) to be read, as well as the number and salary of reciters.[2] Based on a survey of fourteen of Mimar Sinan's mosques in Istanbul, this chapter investigates whether there existed a hierarchy in recitation parallel to the hierarchy of architectural form, and if so, in what shape. In other words, how did architectural patrons use sound in order to convey their status among the Ottoman elite? And, given that architectural form was regulated based on rules of "decorum," could small mosques make themselves bigger by housing a richer soundscape with a large number of reciters?

Ottomans availed themselves of a variety of status markers in order to manifest the boundaries between the different social classes within their society. At the very top of the social order stood the sultan and his immediate family, composed of kin related by blood as well as slave-concubines and slaves and servants of either sex. As is common in dynastic states and empires, there was no distinction between the ruler's household and the central organ of the state governing the territory.[3] According to the ideals of Ottoman statecraft, underneath the sultan and his family, the most basic division in sixteenth-century Ottoman society separated the empire's subjects into the flock (*reʿāyā*)—Muslim and non-Muslim peasants and urban dwellers who were required to pay taxes—and the tax-exempt military class (*ʿaskeri*), who served the ruling house in a variety of capacities. The *ʿaskeri* included not only military officials and soldiers but also an elite that can be further subdivided into three career paths: "Men of the Sword" (*seyfiye*), mostly palace-educated military administrators; "Men of the Pen" (*kalemiye*), who performed administrative tasks; and "Men of Learning" (*ʿilmiye*), who provided religious and legal expertise. Between the *reʿāyā* and *ʿaskeri* classes, and also within the *ʿaskeri* between rank-and-file and elite, social mobility was ideally possible based on individual achievements and qualifications, whether intellectual or military in nature.[4]

Naturally, this ideal conception of a society with clearly demarcated groups contributing their expertise to the maintenance of the empire's social and political status quo could hardly be carried over into the real world, and by the second half of the sixteenth century, when social climbing (based not only on merit but also on connections) became prevalent and started to provoke a certain anxiety among the elite, a discourse of decline had emerged.[5] The purported decline and corruption of Ottoman state and society was also cause for repeated lament by the disgruntled scholar and historian Mustafa ʿAli (1541–1600 CE). In his case, social mobility did not occur as he had expected it according to the previously mentioned ideal of a meritocratic Ottoman society: despite his prolific literary and administrative achievements, he could never quite reach the elevated positions to which he aspired.[6]

Regardless of whether society indeed ever functioned along the lines of this idealized conception, the ideal itself is very telling about the ways in which Ottomans imagined themselves as individuals within a collective entity or as having agency within given social, economic, and political structures. Even if these structures could be permeated by persons with the right qualifications (or connections), boundaries mattered a great deal, and material culture, both mundane and spectacular, contributed to their existence and maintenance.

The previously mentioned Mustafa ʿAli, in his *Tables of Delicacies Concerning the Rules of Social Gatherings* (*Mevaidü'n-Nefais fi Kevaidi'l-Mecalis*), offered guidelines for the sixteenth-century Ottoman gentleman, not only about good manners in everyday life situations, but also about many aspects of material culture that demonstrated as much as cemented the gentleman's standing. Among these count clothing, for which he gives a list of different types of cloth and headgear, together with the administrative ranks that are allowed to wear these items; transportation, for which he discusses different types of boats, beasts of burden, and carriages or carts suitable for different ranks; and residences.[7] As to the last, Mustafa ʿAli was even more specific, suggesting the specific number of rooms that the living quarters of functionaries should contain according to their rank. In each case, Mustafa ʿAli emphasized that there needed to be an appropriate relationship between one's status and the status symbols one owned; that is, the quality of one's clothes, weapons, residence, servants, and horses had to be neither so high as to exceed one's means nor so low as to suggest miserliness.[8] The list of objects, goods, and actions by means of which Ottomans demarcated their status could be extended almost infinitely here, from the consumption of foods deemed delicacies and luxuries appropriate for the elite in contrast to staples, to other types of comestibles (including medicines), to book ownership.[9]

Most important in the present context, however, are architectural patronage and, connected with it, the establishment of charitable endowments (*vakıf*).[10] The latter secured the funding for the construction and maintenance of mosque complexes, as well as for the staff employed, the goods consumed, and the (mostly social) services offered in the complexes' various schools, hospitals, inns, Sufi convents, and soup kitchens. Within certain limits, the decision regarding what to include in (or exclude from) a mosque complex remained in the hands of its patron. In this way, the buildings erected and the services offered reflected either the perceived needs of the population in the location of the new construction or the patron's predilections for a specific branch of Sufism or orthodox learning or for ensuring the physical health and well-being of the beneficiaries. The same was true for the hiring of Qur'an reciters for the mosque and for the Qur'anic suras chosen to be recited.

According to Necipoğlu, "[t]he preoccupation with social typecasting informed the typology of Sinan's mosques, which can be interpreted as architectural portraits representing patrons as relatively generic or individualized types."[11] The mosques thus reflected "certain expectations of propriety relative to the rank of the mosque patrons."[12] Although these expectations regarding the architectural decorum of mosques were never written down explicitly, they are implied in the buildings themselves, in textual and archival sources—such as Mimar Sinan's autobiographical treatises, which contain listings of his monuments,[13] and construction progress reports—and in the institutional framework, namely, the imperial guild of architects and the inspection committees consisting of building supervisors, *vakıf* administrators, architects, judges, and other elite members. These ensured that each mosque was appropriate to the rank of the patron in terms of cost, site, functional program, plan type, number and size of domes, number of minarets, façade, construction materials, ornamentation, and epigraphy.

For instance, mosques commissioned by a sultan, crown prince, or royal woman could include a monumental dome on four supports, surrounded by half domes; those sponsored by (grand) viziers, grand admirals, and governors-general had hexagonal or octagonal domed baldachins with exedral half domes; while cubical mosques without a dome—or at most a small one—were deemed appropriate for the mid- to low-ranking members of the elite. This tripartite classification of superior, medium, and low is indicated in table 2.1, which lists the surveyed mosques according to their patrons' rank.[14] However, patrons could and on occasion did breach this decorum; the more high-ranking a patron was, the more possible it became to shape one's commission with innovative elements in order to express one's individuality.[15] In case of someone having the audacity to breach the decorum without sanction, that individual's reputation would suffer swiftly, becoming a subject of slander.[16]

About the eighteenth-century mosque of the Guardian of the Imperial Harem (*darüssade ağası*) Moralı Beşir Ağa in Argos, Hedda Reindl-Kiel has remarked: "It seems that Beşir Ağa's *vakf* activity as a whole was directed not towards monumental buildings bearing his name but employing a sizeable group of people to pray for the salvation of his soul."[17] Indeed, the employment of reciters, who often dedicated the blessings accumulated from their chanting of the Qurʾan to the patron and the dynasty, constituted a significant element of Ottoman mosque architecture, as much as domes, minarets, decorative tiles, and calligraphic inscriptions. This is evident from the extensive space that *vakfiye*s, detailing the conditions and day-to-day operations of the endowment, devote to listing the mosque's reciters, their qualifications, and the suras to be chanted, as summarized in table 2.1.[18] Do these primary sources reflect a decorum or hierarchy in recitation parallel to the tripartite (high-middling-low) hierarchy of architectural form?

The fourteen mosques included in this survey were selected so as to include four commissioned by the sultan and his immediate family, to represent the highest echelon of the elite; eight erected by grand viziers, who at the same time were the sultan's sons-in-law, viziers, grand admirals, and governors-general, to represent the middling category; and two, built by an army judge and a steward to the grand vizier, to represent the lowest rank (see table 2.1). The selection has been restricted to sixteenth-century Istanbul; since there also existed a ranking or hierarchy distinguishing between monuments in the imperial capital and the provinces, including the latter would have added another layer of analysis that is beyond the scope of this chapter. Another important criterion for selection has been the existence and accessibility of the relevant *vakfiye*. While the relatively small number of fourteen examples makes it unwise to extrapolate wide-ranging generalizations from this survey, some preliminary remarks can be made about the particular context of sixteenth-century Istanbul.

Before delving into more general remarks based on quantitative data, an example of how a recitation program as determined by the *vakfiye* unfolded over the time-span of a day will enable readers to visualize and auralize its experiential qualities. The Kara Ahmed Paşa Mosque (fig. 2.1) was completed in 1572 CE for the eponymous grand vizier (vizierate 1553–1555, d. 1555 CE), who was married to Fatma Sultan, a daughter of Sultan Selim I (r. 1512–1520 CE).[19] In terms of its architectural form, the mosque adhered to the decorum established for patrons of Kara Ahmed Paşa's status: within an enclosed garden, a rectangular porticoed courtyard, partially encircled by the cells and the classroom belonging to the complex's madrasa, fronts the prayer hall. The porch leading to the prayer hall consists of five dome-capped bays, and a minaret with a single gallery is inserted in the corner space between the porch and the prayer hall. Mimar Sinan designed the latter over a rectangular ground plan and covered it with a hexagonal baldachin consisting of a

Table 2.1. List of mosques, construction dates, patrons, reciters, and suras recited according to social rank, from highest to lowest*

Mosque (date)	Patron (status)	Reciters employed	Task	Salary†
Süleymaniye Mosque (1548–1559)	Süleyman the Magnificent (sultan)	9 *devirhan*	reciting 10 verses on Fridays	3
		1 *ser-mahfil*	supervising the 9 *devirhan*	5
		116 *cüzhan*	reciting 1 *cüz*	2
		4 *cüzhan*	leaders of the 116 *cüzhan*	3
		41 *en'amcı*	reciting al-En'am at unspecified time	3
		1 *yasinhan*	reciting Ya Sin after morning prayer	6
		1 *tebarekehan*	reciting al-Mülk at unspecified time	5
		1 *'amhan*	reciting Al ʿImran after noon prayer	4
Atik Valide Mosque, Üsküdar (1571–1586)	Nurbanu (wife of sultan, later mother of sultan)	9 *hafız*	reciting unspecified sections of the Qur'an	3
		1 *ser-mahfil*	supervising the 9 *hafız*	6
		87 *cüzhan*	reciting 1 *cüz*	2
		3 *ser-mahfil*	supervising the 87 *cüzhan*	3
		6 *cüzhan*	reciting third of Qur'an for Prophet, Ayşe, and Fatima	2
		1 reciter	reciting al-Bakare's last 2 verses after Friday prayer	2
		1 *ʿaşrhan*	reciting 10 unspecified verses	2
		1 *yasinhan*	reciting Ya Sin after morning prayer	2
		1 *mülkhan*	reciting al-Mülk after evening prayer	2
		1 *ʿamhan*	reciting Al ʿImran after noon prayer	2
Mihrimah Mosque, Üsküdar (1543–1548)	Mihrimah (daughter of sultan, wife of grand vizier)	6 *hafız*	reciting 10 verses on Fridays	1.5
		1 *hafız*	supervising the 6 *hafız*	4
		1 *muarrif*	reciting Fatiha for family of Prophet, Süleyman the Magnificent, and Mihrimah	2
		30 *cüzhan*	reciting 1 *cüz* after morning prayer	2
		2 *duahan*	Ya Sin after morning prayer, Al ʿImran around afternoon prayer	2
Mihrimah Mosque, Edirnekapı (1563–1570)	Mihrimah (daughter of sultan, wife of grand vizier)	10 *devirhan*	reciting unspecified portion of Qur'an	2
		1 *ser-mahfil*	leading 10 *devirhan*	4

Table 2.1. Continued

Mosque (date)	Patron (status)	Reciters employed	Task	Salary†
Kara Ahmed Paşa Mosque (1555, 1565–1572)	Kara Ahmed Paşa (grand vizier, son-in-law of sultan)	1 imam	reciting Ya Sin after morning prayer	1
		7 *hafız*	reciting unspecified sura on Fridays and holidays	2
		1 *hafız*	supervising the 7 *hafız*	3
		1 reciter	reciting 10 verses	1
		1 reciter	reciting Al ʿImran after afternoon prayer	1
		1 reciter	reciting al-Mülk after night prayer	1
		30 *cüzhan*	reciting 1 *cüz* after morning prayer	1
Sokollu Mehmed Paşa Mosque, Azapkapı (1573–1578)	Sokollu Mehmed Paşa (grand vizier, son-in-law of sultan)	1 imam	reciting Ya Sin after morning prayer, Al ʿImran after afternoon prayer	1
		1 of 4 *muezzins*	reciting al-Mülk after evening prayer	[housing]
		6 *devirhan*	reciting every Friday for benefit of Prophet	2
Nişancı Mehmed Paşa Mosque, Karagümrük (1584–1589)	Nişancı Mehmed Paşa (vizier, chancellor)	1 of 2 imams	reciting Ya Sin after morning prayer, Al ʿImran after afternoon prayer	2
		1 of 4 *muezzins*	reciting al-Fath after morning prayer, al-Mülk after night prayer	4
		7 reciters	reciting 1 *cüz* on Friday	2
		1 *ser-mahfil*	supervising the 7 reciters	4
		1 reciter	reciting el-Kahf every Friday	2
Hadım İbrahim Paşa Mosque, Silivrikapı (1551)	Hadım İbrahim Paşa (guardian of the imperial palace, governor-general of Anatolia, fourth vizier, second vizier)	1 *hatip-hafız*	reciting with other *hafız* every day	5
		5 adult reciters	reciting 10 or more verses before Friday prayer	2
		5 young reciters	reciting 10 or more verses before Friday prayer	1
		30 *hafız*	reciting 1 *cüz* each for benefit of Prophet, sultan and patron	2
		1 imam, 4 *muezzins*, 1 teacher, 1 *mekteb* student	reciting al-Enʾam after morning prayer	3
		6 reciters	reciting Ihlas 500 times after morning prayer	2
		1 reciter	reciting 10 verses after noon prayer	1

Table 2.1. Continued

Mosque (date)	Patron (status)	Reciters employed	Task	Salary†
Şemsi Ahmed Paşa Mosque, Üsküdar (1580–1581)	Şemsi Ahmed Paşa (governor-general of Rumelia)	6 *hafız*	reciting 10 verses before Friday prayer	1
		5 reciters	reciting 1 *cüz* for the benefit of the patron	1
Sinan Paşa Mosque, Beşiktaş (1554–1556)	Sinan Paşa (grand admiral)	5 *hafız*	reciting 10 verses on Friday	1.5
		2 *hafız*	reciting Ya Sin and 10 verses at unspecified time	1.5
		1 imam	reciting Ya Sin after morning prayer, al-Mülk after night prayer	‡
		1 *vaiz*	preaching, reciting al-En'am for patron's benefit every day	‡
		2 of 3 *muezzins*	reciting Ya Sin after Friday prayer	1
		1 reciter	reciting Ya Sin before evening prayer	1.5
		2 reciters	reciting 10 verses every afternoon	1
		1 reciter	reciting Al ʿImran after afternoon prayer	1
Piyale Paşa Mosque (1565–1573)	Piyale Paşa (grand admiral)	6 *hafız*	reciting 10 verses on Friday	1.5
		1 *ser-mahfil*	supervising the 6 *hafız*	2
		1 *muarrif*	reciting Fatiha for the deceased	2
		5 *cüzhan*	reciting 1 *cüz*	2
		1 imam	Ya Sin after morning prayer	1
Kılıç Ali Paşa Mosque (1578–1581)	Kılıç Ali Paşa (grand admiral)	1 imam	reciting Ya Sin after morning prayer, al-Mülk after night prayer for benefit of patron	‡
		8 *hafız*	reciting 10 verses after Friday prayer	2
		1 of 8 *hafız*	reciting al-Bakare after Friday prayer	3
		30 reciters	reciting 1 *cüz* after morning prayer	2
		1 reciter	reciting 10 verses after noon prayer	2
		1 reciter	reciting Al ʿImran after afternoon prayer	2
		1 reciter	reciting al-Vaki'a before evening prayer	2
Molla Çelebi Mosque, Fındıklı (1570–1584)	Molla Çelebi (army judge)	1 *muezzin*	reciting Fatiha after every prayer	3
		15 reciters	reciting 1 *cüz* for patron's benefit	2

Table 2.1. Continued

Mosque (date)	Patron (status)	Reciters employed	Task	Salary[†]
Ferruh Kethüda Mosque, Balat (1562–1563)	Ferruh Kethüda (steward to grand vizier)	5 *hafiz*	reciting 10 verses on Friday	2
		29 *cüzhan*	reciting 1 *cüz* each after morning, noon and afternoon prayer, for benefit of Prophet, his daughter Fatima, patron	1.5
		1 *cüzhan*	supervising the 29 *cüzhan*	2
		1 imam	reciting Ya Sin after morning prayer, Al ʿImran after afternoon prayer	2

Sources: The information regarding construction dates and patrons is based on Necipoğlu 2005. The sources from which the recitation programs have been compiled are as follows: Süleymaniye: VGM, Defter no. 52, published in Kürkçüoğlu 1962; Atik Valide Mosque: VGM, Defter no. 1766; Mihrimah Sultan's mosques: VGM, Defter no. 635/2; Kara Ahmed Paşa Mosque: İstanbul Umumi Kütüphane, no. 493, published in Yaltkaya 1942; Sokollu Mehmed Paşa Mosque in Azapkapı: VGM, Defter no. 2104/323; Nişancı Mehmed Paşa Mosque: VGM, Defter no. 572; Hadım İbrahim Paşa Mosque: VGM, Defter no. 574; Şemsi Ahmed Paşa Mosque: Süleymaniye Kütüphanesi, Lala İsmail 737; Molla Çelebi Mosque: VGM, Defter no. 1967; Ferruh Kethüda Mosque: VGM, 2111.

* The middling and lower categories are shaded in lighter and darker tones, respectively.

† Daily salary per person in *akçe*.

‡ No additional salary.

central dome abutted by four exedral half domes. The lateral spaces beyond the half domes are vertically divided through by means of a gallery (*mahfil*).

As to the recitations inside this very proper mosque, which architecturally announced itself as a grand vizier's building commission, the imam began the daily program after the morning prayer by chanting sura Ya Sin (36), considered the heart of the Qur'an because of its explication of the role of the Prophet, the Revelation, and the Hereafter. For this the imam was given one *akçe* (silver coin) in addition to his daily salary. Also after the morning prayer, thirty *cüzhan* recited one-thirtieth (*cüz*; in Arabic, *juz'*) of the Qur'an. From the historical record, it is not clear whether these professional reciters chanted the entire Qur'an (*hatim*) quickly, via simultaneous recitation of its thirty portions, as currently practiced in Egypt,[20] or whether Ottoman practice was to chant the *cüz* one after another, to make for a longer session. Following afternoon prayer, sura Al ʿImran (3), which offers a general overview of mankind's religious history, was chanted by one reciter, who received one *akçe*.[21] Another reciter earned the same amount for chanting after night prayer sura al-Mülk (67), which describes the spiritual in terms comprehensible to humans and compares the earthly world and the Hereafter.

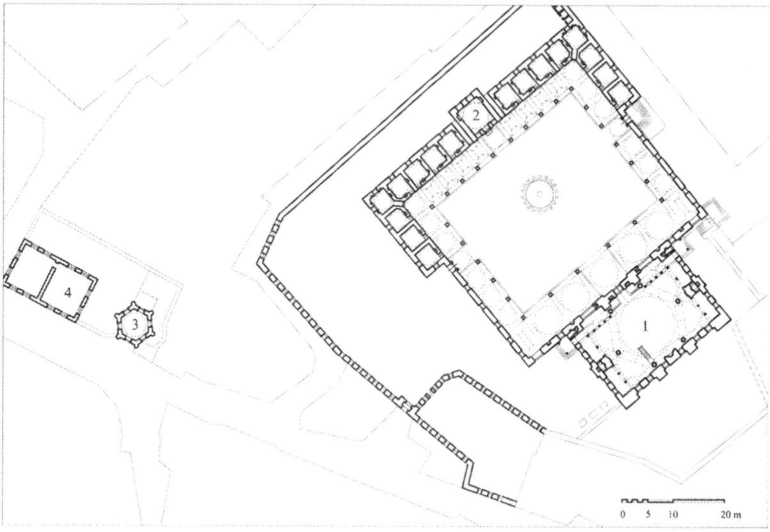

Figure 2.1. (a, *top*) Mimar Sinan, Kara Ahmed Paşa Mosque (completed 1572 CE), Istanbul. Photograph: N. Ergin. (b, *bottom*) Ground plan of Kara Ahmed Paşa Mosque. Source: Necipoğlu 2005, courtesy of Gülru Necipoğlu.

Another reciter read ten Qur'anic verses every day at a time not specified in the endowment deed, while on Fridays and holidays eight *hafız* (persons who had memorized the entire Qur'an) added the recitation of a sura not specified in the endowment deed, hence marking those days as extraordinary. Of these, seven received one *akçe*, whereas their supervisor (commonly called *ser-mahfil*, "head of the tribune or gallery"—the gallery being the site where the reciters congregated) earned a higher salary of three *akçe*. Thus, a total of forty-two persons were engaged in making the Kara Ahmed Paşa Mosque resound with an aural rendition of the Qur'anic text, and the endowment expended fifty-one *akçe* on them daily.

Kara Ahmed Paşa's recitation program was rather generic and conventional in terms of its content, as sura Ya Sin, Al ʿImran, and al-Mülk—which together convey the position of Islam within mankind's history, the responsibilities of Muslims, and the Hereafter[22]—could also be heard as a grouping in a similar temporal order in six of the other surveyed mosques. The employment of thirty *cüzhan*, who then over the course of a day would complete a reading of the entire Qur'an, was also a widespread custom. The recipients of this recitation program—in other words, the mosque visitors and worshipers—may not have been fluent in Qur'anic Arabic, since only highly educated Ottoman Muslims were. However, they would have been able to understand the content due to their childhood training in one of Istanbul's primary schools (*mekteb*), where they would have learned about the most important suras and *āyas* and committed them to memory.[23] The generic nature of Kara Ahmed Paşa's recitation program also ensured that the recipients easily understood the message conveyed through the Qur'anic text, more so than they would have with a more unusual choice of suras and *āyas*. In this case, the *vakfiye* stipulates a recitation program that in both content and quantity appeared as proper and decorum-conscious as the mosque that served as its performance space.

As to the number of persons employed to recite, the mosques surveyed could range anywhere from 7 to 174 (see table 2.2). It should come as no surprise that the Süleymaniye Mosque had the largest number of reciters, employing 174, followed by the foundation of Nurbanu Sultan, wife of Selim II (r. 1566–1574 CE) and mother (*valide sultan*) of Murad III (r. 1574–1595 CE), which employed 111.[24] Particularly noteworthy is the presence of the previously mentioned *cüzhan*: while mosques of high, middling, and low rank can equally be observed to have one group of 30, patrons of the very highest

Table 2.2. List of mosques ranked according to number of reciters*

Rank	Mosque (date)	Patron (status)	Total number of persons paid for reciting
1	Süleymaniye Mosque (1548–1559)	Süleyman the Magnificent (sultan)	174
2	Atik Valide Mosque, Üsküdar (1571–1586)	Nurbanu (wife of sultan, mother of sultan)	111
3	Hadım İbrahim Paşa Mosque, Silivrikapı (1551)	Hadım İbrahim Paşa (guardian of the imperial palace, governor-general of Anatolia, fourth vizier, second vizier)	55
4	Kılıç Ali Paşa Mosque (1578–1581)	Kılıç Ali Paşa (grand admiral)	43
5	Kara Ahmed Paşa Mosque (1555, 1565–1572)	Kara Ahmed Paşa (grand vizier, son-in-law of sultan)	42
6	Mihrimah Mosque, Üsküdar (1543–1548)	Mihrimah (daughter of sultan, wife of grand vizier)	40
7	Ferruh Kethüda Mosque, Balat (1562–1563)	Ferruh Kethüda (steward to grand vizier)	36
9	Piyale Paşa Mosque (1565–1573)	Piyale Paşa (grand admiral)	14
10	Sinan Paşa Mosque, Beşiktaş (1554–1556)	Sinan Paşa (grand admiral)	13
11	Mihrimah Mosque, Edirnekapı (1563–1570)	Mihrimah (daughter of sultan, wife of grand vizier)	11
	Nişancı Mehmed Paşa Mosque, Karagümrük (1584–1589)	Nişancı Mehmed Paşa (vizier, chancellor)	11
	Şemsi Ahmed Paşa Mosque, Üsküdar (1580–1581)	Şemsi Ahmed Paşa (governor-general of Rumelia)	11
12	Sokollu Mehmed Paşa Mosque, Azapkapı (1573–1578)	Sokollu Mehmed Paşa (grand vizier, son-in-law of sultan)	7
13	Molla Çelebi Mosque, Fındıklı (1570–1584)	Molla Çelebi (army judge)	5

* The middling and lower categories are shaded in lighter and darker tones, respectively.

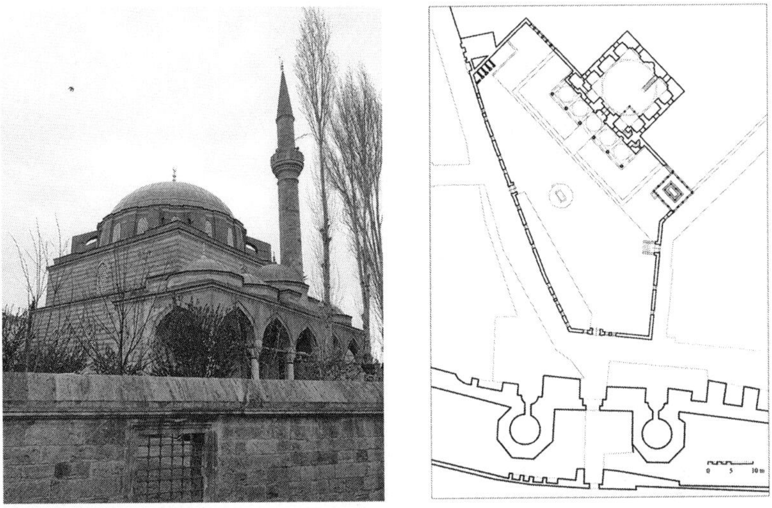

Figure 2.2. (a, *left*) Mimar Sinan, Hadım İbrahim Paşa Mosque (completed 1551 CE), Istanbul. Photograph: N. Ergin. (b, *right*) Ground plan of Hadım İbrahim Paşa Mosque. Source: Necipoğlu 2005, courtesy of Gülru Necipoğlu.

status employed multiples of 30 (see table 2.1). Nurbanu Sultan's *vakıf* provided for 90 *cüzhan*, and Sultan Süleyman the Magnificent's, for 120. In each case, a group of 30 *cüzhan* would congregate after the morning, noon, and afternoon prayer to perform their duty, with an additional, second group after the morning prayer in the Süleymaniye.[25] Spread over the day, the continuity of Qur'anic sound therefore matched the sultan's and the *valide sultan*'s unrivaled status.

Below these most exalted foundations, the ranking based on the total number of persons employed to recite does not always neatly match up with that based on patron status and size and form of the mosque (see tables 2.1 and 2.2). The mosque of Hadım İbrahim Paşa—the chief white eunuch and guardian of the imperial palace under Süleyman the Magnificent, who also concurrently held successive positions as governor-general of Anatolia, fourth vizier, second vizier, and lieutenant-governor of Istanbul—follows Nurbanu Sultan's mosque with fifty-five reciters. This very decorous mosque, which was completed in 1551 CE and consists of a twelve-meter dome on a cubical base (fig. 2.2), befitted the rank of its patron. Yet, by employing a relatively large number of reciters, Hadım İbrahim Paşa, whom Mustafa ʿAli described as possessing unquestionable dignity and propriety,[26] managed to push his way past several grand viziers and even Sultan Süleyman's immediate family. While constructing a larger mosque would have meant breaching the decorum, an act contrary to Hadım İbrahim Paşa's dignified and proper character, recitation may very well have presented an acceptable way to elevate his status. In this respect, financial considerations are much less likely to play a role in the choice of recitation over size of building as status marker. Süleyman's daughter Mihrimah Sultan seems to have put little stake in populating her two mosques with many reciters, as they housed "only" forty and eleven, respectively.[27]

By contrast, Ferruh Kethüda's mosque, which in terms of architectural form was so low ranking that it did not even have a dome, instead boasting only a hipped roof over a rectangular prayer hall (fig. 2.3), employed thirty-six reciters. Of these, thirty were *cüzhan* who recited one *cüz* each after morning, noon, and afternoon prayer, donating the accumulated blessings to the Prophet, his daughter Fatima, and the patron (see table 2.1). The continuity of Qur'anic sound, as found in Süleyman's and Nurbanu Sultan's mosques, was thus ensured here as well, but by a smaller number of staff working longer hours.

As to the lower end of the number of persons employed in this group of mosques, the number of eleven reciters may have constituted a sort of "decorous" minimum requirement, as it occurs three times—in the Mihrimah Sultan Mosque in Edirnekapı, the Şemsi Ahmed Paşa Mosque, and the Nişancı Mehmed Paşa Mosque, where the imams and muezzins were compensated to recite in addition to their regular duties. Was eleven a kind of customary lower limit of persons reciting in Ottoman imperial mosques, only occasionally lowered even further, as in the mosque of grand vizier Sokollu Mehmed Paşa in Azapkapı, which only employed seven? Due to the small number of mosques discussed here, this question cannot be answered presently, but it may serve as a working hypothesis for further inquiries. In any case, the Mihrimah Sultan Mosque in Edirnekapı, as a high-ranking foundation with such a small number of reciters, shows that here status and sound did not entirely match, for the latter fell short. When comparing the size of the princess's mosque and that of the governor-general Şemsi Ahmed Paşa's minuscule prayer hall—the interiors measure around fifty by thirty-six meters and around twenty by twenty meters, respectively—even the latter was relatively better endowed, since it could not have physically accommodated many reciters.

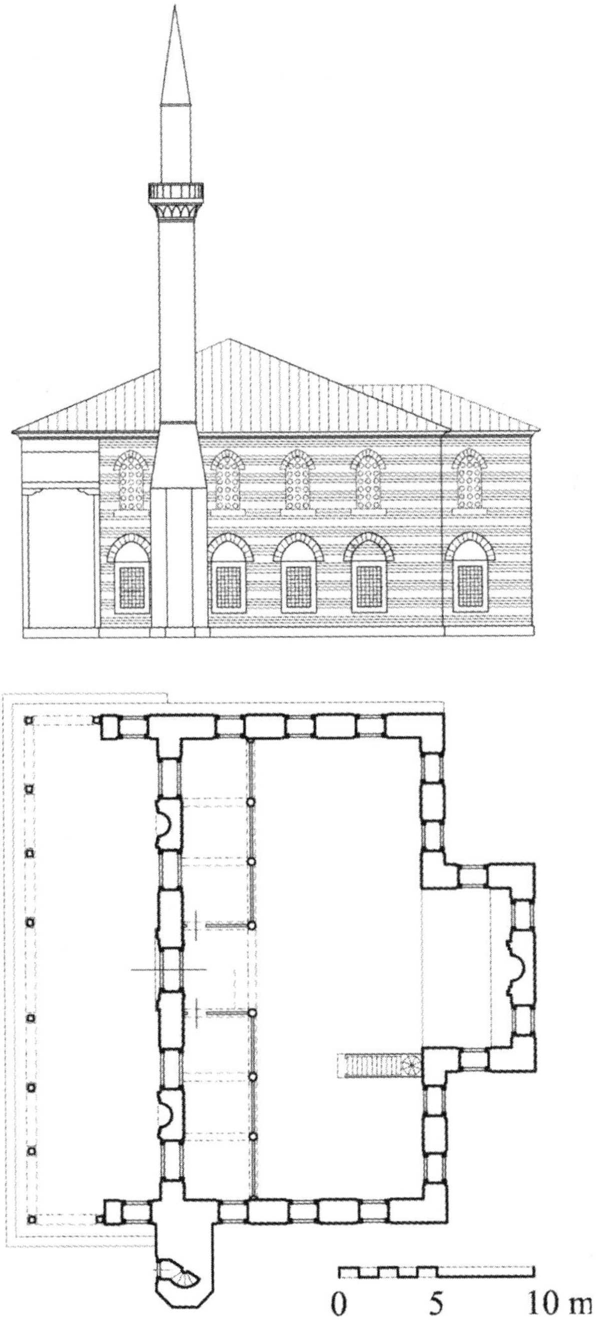

Figure 2.3. Mimar Sinan, Ferruh Kethüda Mosque (completed 1563 CE), Istanbul. Source: Necipoğlu 2005, courtesy of Gülru Necipoğlu.

One issue about which the *vakfiyes* do not allow us to draw any conclusions is the quality of the reciters, though we can infer that the better they were paid, the more qualified they were. The relevant passages generally describe their desired qualifications in stock phrases—such as a beautiful and "soul-caressing" voice, not hurrying when chanting, and familiarity with the rules and traditions of Qurʾan recitation[28]—but there certainly must have been reciters who were more skillful and had voices more "soul-caressing" than others. Indeed, many mosque complexes included a school for recitation (*darülkurra*), where students were trained in the ten canonical readings of the Qurʾan.[29] While impossible to make any claims regarding the reciters' quality as an aspect of a mosque's and hence a patron's status, surely there must have been differences between, for instance, Süleyman's and Şemsi Ahmed Paşa's mosques, just as there are today between mosques located on Istanbul's historical peninsula and peripheral ones in terms of their muezzins.[30] A fatwa issued by Ebussuud Efendi, the grand mufti of Süleyman the Magnificent, also points to such a difference, in that it renders canonically impermissible the attendance of Friday prayer in a mosque other than in one's own residential quarter if the purpose of attending prayer there is to listen to a more beautiful recitation.[31] This indicates that better reciters were drawing worshipers more numerous than the mosque neighborhood's congregation, which must also have accentuated the mosque patron's reputation.

Related to both quality and quantity of recitation is the matter of the salary. One would expect that those patrons who dedicated more funds to reciters' salaries could secure the employment of more skillful ones, maybe even enticing a good *cüzhan* to leave his position at a lower-ranking mosque where he received less compensation. As with the number of reciters, one may also rank mosques based on the averages and total amount of their salaries (see table 2.3; for individual per-diem salaries, see table 2.1). Once again, the Süleymaniye's *vakfiye* stipulated the largest amount with 414 *akçe* (average salary 2.38), followed by the Atik Valide Mosque with 240 (average salary 2.16). And once again, the Hadım İbrahim Paşa Mosque occupies third rank with 114 *akçe* (average salary 2.07), even though it is only of the middling category, and pushed itself ahead of the mosques of Mihrimah Sultan in Üsküdar and Edirnekapı (ranked fifth and tenth, respectively). The code of decorum and his propriety (and probably also fear of negative consequences in case of a breach) may have prevented Hadım İbrahim Paşa from construct-

Table 2.3. List of mosques ranked according to the total salaries paid to persons reciting the Qur'an*

Rank	Mosque (date)	Patron (status)	Salaries Average	Salaries Total
1	Süleymaniye Mosque (1548–1559)	Süleyman the Magnificent (sultan)	2.38	414
2	Atik Valide Mosque, Üsküdar (1571–1586)	Nurbanu (wife of sultan, mother of sultan)	2.16	240
3	Hadım İbrahim Paşa Mosque, Silivrikapı (1551)	Hadım İbrahim Paşa (guardian of the imperial palace, governor-general of Anatolia, fourth vizier)	2.07	114
4	Kılıç Ali Paşa Mosque (1578–1581)	Kılıç Ali Paşa (grand admiral)	1.98	85
5	Mihrimah Mosque, Üsküdar (1543–1548)	Mihrimah (daughter of sultan, wife of grand vizier)	0.51	79
6	Ferruh Kethüda Mosque, Balat (1562–1563)	Ferruh Kethüda (steward to grand vizier)	1.59	57.5
7	Kara Ahmed Paşa Mosque (1555, 1565–1572)	Kara Ahmed Paşa (grand vizier, son-in-law of sultan)	1.21	51
8	Molla Çelebi Mosque, Fındıklı (1570–1584)	Molla Çelebi (army judge)	2.06	33
9	Nişancı Mehmed Paşa Mosque, Karagümrük (1584–1589)	Nişancı Mehmed Paşa (vizier, chancellor)	2.36	26
10	Piyale Paşa Mosque (1565–1573)	Piyale Paşa (grand admiral)	1.71	24
	Mihrimah Mosque, Edirnekapı (1563–1570)	Mihrimah (daughter of sultan, wife of grand vizier)	2.18	24
11	Sinan Paşa Mosque, Beşiktaş (1554–1556)	Sinan Paşa (grand admiral)	1.31	17
12	Sokollu Mehmed Paşa Mosque, Azapkapı (1573–1578)	Sokollu Mehmed Paşa (grand vizier, son-in-law of sultan)	1.86	13
13	Şemsi Ahmed Paşa Mosque, Üsküdar (1580–1581)	Şemsi Ahmed Paşa (governor-general of Rumelia)	1	11

* Mosques of the middling and lower categories are shaded in lighter and darker tones, respectively.

ing a mosque larger than Mihrimah's foundations, but investing in reciters seems to have been one way to circumvent such restrictions. This breach in the context of recitation may have been less immediately noticeable, or it may have been more justifiable because of its pious nature. It may be argued that endowments of mosques with larger numbers of reciters simply had to earmark more funds for their salaries, but that was not necessarily the case, since amounts were not completely standardized and patrons had some leeway regarding how generous they wanted to be. Therefore, the endowment of Ferruh Kethüda, who in terms of his position as steward to the grand vizier ranks lowest among the patrons surveyed, was more generous and devoted 57.5 *akçe* to thirty-six reciters (average salary 1.59), in contrast to grand vizier Kara Ahmed Paşa's endowment, which assigned only 51 *akçe* for forty-two persons (average salary 1.21). If, in addition to the mosque's overall status and that of its patron, salary can serve as indicator for the skill level of the reciters to be hired, then Ferruh Kethüda's slightly more generous salary may have attracted better reciters than Kara Ahmed Paşa's. Still, in spite of these subtle variations in salary across mosques of different ranks, patrons did have to abide by a somewhat standardized salary scale and could not stipulate very high salaries that would have outstripped those given at a sultanic mosque.[32]

Based on the individual salaries (see table 2.1), one can make the following generalizations about the payment scale: the highest-paid reciters (six *akçe*) were found in the highest-ranking mosques and held significant positions, such as chanting the particularly important sura Ya Sin or serving as *ser-mahfil*; *cüzhan* received one to two *akçe*, unless they served as *ser-mahfil* and therefore received anywhere from one half to two *akçe* more than their underlings; reciters chanting a single sura or ten *āyas* received one to three *akçe*; and those patrons who wished to maximize the number of recitations for less money could stipulate that the imam, muezzin, or preacher (*hatip*, *vaiz*) should chant specific suras in addition to their regular duties, but without extra compensation, or that the same thirty *cüzhan* do triple duty.

To conclude, there did indeed exist a hierarchy of recitation programs that reflected the concept of decorum for Ottoman mosques in sixteenth-century Istanbul. Patrons had to adhere to, or at least contend with, mosque prescriptions, both formal-architectural and recitational. The employment of reciters represented a status marker and therefore needed to display an appropriate relationship between the patron's rank and the number of employees and expenditure. If Mustafa ʿAli in his etiquette book had included guidelines for endowing recitation programs to a gentleman's mosque foundation, he might have advised that the expenditure should be neither so high as to exceed the endowment's financial capability nor so low as to suggest miserliness and a disregard for the spiritual benefits of Qurʾanic recitation.

Yet the cases of Hadım İbrahim Paşa, Molla Çelebi, and Ferruh Kethüda suggest that patrons of low-ranking mosques that adhered to the prevailing architectural decorum could nevertheless attempt to elevate their foundation above higher-ranking ones by endowing more funds for a larger number of employees, as well as for higher salaries that likely attracted better reciters. Expressions of individuality via recitation were therefore permitted, within certain limits and as long as one did not challenge patrons at the very top of the hierarchy.[33] The three cases mentioned above also hint that the hierarchy of the recitation programs was not tripartite but rather exhibited a spectrum.

Another way in which mosques could distinguish themselves—a topic reserved for a future study building on the present one—was by means of the call to prayer (*ezan*), as richer endowments could lay claim to the muezzins with the most beautiful voices who then broadcast their mosque's status and position within the urban fabric in an eminently audible manner. Whether in the form of Qurʾanic text chanted inside mosques or the *ezan* emitted from the minarets, without doubt sound represented an integral component of sixteenth-century Ottoman mosque architecture and, much like architectural form, allowed patrons to announce their position within the elite's hierarchy. This is also suggested by Ebussuud Efendi's fatwa, which implies that recitation of a high quality attracted more worshippers to specific mosques, perhaps elevating the respective patron's status socially as much as spiritually.

NOTES

1 Necipoğlu 2005, esp. 115–124.
2 For this argument, see Ergin 2008.
3 See Elias 1983, 41–42. For a more recent discussion of court society, see Duindam et al. 2011.
4 This description of Ottoman society is based on Fleischer 1986, 5–7.

5 On the notion of decline in Ottoman history-writing of the sixteenth century, see Kafadar 1993 and 1997.
6 For Mustafa ʿAli's biography, see Fleischer 1986.
7 For clothing, see Mustafa ʿAli 2003, 137–139. Ottoman sartorial laws, as well as the Ottoman penchant for costume albums cataloguing the appearance of specific professional and ethnic groups within the empire, bespeak a certain taxonomic obsession with class and rank. For both, see the contributions in Faroqhi and Neumann 2004. For transportation, see Mustafa ʿAli 2003, 135–136, 142. For residences, see ibid., 143–144.
8 See Tietze 1982.
9 See Artan 2000; Shefer-Mossensohn 2010; Hanna 2003.
10 For a detailed discussion of endowment-making and charity, see Singer 2002 and 2008. Ottomans established an incredible range and variety of endowments, from small ones feeding animals, to sizeable mosque complexes, meant to endure in perpetuity through a careful balancing of revenue-generating against charitable endowment components.
11 Necipoğlu 2005, 124.
12 Ibid., 115.
13 See Mimar Sinan 2006.
14 This tripartite classification is based on Mustafa ʿAli, who lists these three status levels as "highest" (i.e., sultans), "high" (i.e., viziers, governors, and military commanders), and "middle" (i.e., fiefholders and notables). See Tietze 1982, 580–581; Necipoğlu 2005, 116. The "lowly" are left aside, since they are not able to participate in architectural patronage. Such a tripartite classification also applies to all sorts of goods available in the Ottoman marketplace, which were categorized into first, second, and third grades (superior, medium, and ordinary) in archival documents and ceiling price registers (*narh defter*). An example of the latter, drawn up in the seventeenth century, has been published in Kütükoğlu 1983.
15 On the issues discussed here, see Necipoğlu 2005, 119–120, 124.
16 See Necipoğlu 2005, 115.
17 Reindl-Kiel 2010, 126.
18 To give an example of a relevant *vakfiye* passage: "[T]en persons shall be appointed to this mosque from among the *hafız* [reciters who had memorized the entire Qurʾan] who are known for excellent virtue; who have big skill and capacity in reading the Qurʾan with a beautiful voice. These persons will gather every Friday in the above-mentioned mosque shortly before noon; every one of them will read from the Holy Qurʾan with a soul-caressing and beautiful voice in a way that will awake pleasure in the listener, by closely following the traditions and rules of chanting and reciting; and they will read more blessed verses; and one of them will be the leader, called *ser-mahfil*; and his salary will be six, that of the others will be three dirhem [*akçe*]." *Vakfiye* of Nurbanu Sultan's endowment, preserved

in the Vakıflar Genel Müdürlüğü (hereafter VGM), Ankara, Defter no. 1766; transl. in [Ergin] Cichocki 2005, 357.

19 The mosque was designed in 1555 CE, with the *vakfiye* written in the same year, shortly before Kara Ahmed Paşa's execution. The mosque was built posthumously, between 1565 and 1571/72 CE. For the patron's biography, a detailed building history, and its position within Mimar Sinan's oeuvre, see Necipoğlu 2005, 377–384.

20 I wish to thank Michael Frishkopf for this information.

21 For purposes of comparison, an unskilled laborer on a construction site in Istanbul received a salary of 5 *akçe* per day in 1555, while that year's ceiling price for 1 *okka* (*circa* 1.2 kg) of mutton was 1.9 *akçe*. See Pamuk 2000, 69, 103.

22 See Ergin 2008, 208.

23 Ibid., 208.

24 One may argue that the total numbers should not be equaled to the number of individuals employed due to the possibility of one person occupying more than one position—for example, that of a *cüzhan* while also reciting additional verses on Fridays. Yet, because the endowment deeds list the reciters' tasks and salaries individually (see table 2.1), I will treat them in the same way.

25 For the recitation schedules in the Süleymaniye and the Atik Valide Mosques, see Ergin 2008, 207 and 211 respectively. There may also have been students practicing recitation in the mosque courtyard and other public spaces, but these impromptu recitations have left no trace in the archival sources and therefore cannot be considered here.

26 See Necipoğlu 2005, 392.

27 It is of course possible that the 11 reciters in Mihrimah's mosque in Edirnekapı were expected to recite more, since the number of verses is left unspecified in the endowment deed. Given the sixteenth-century Ottoman penchant for centralization, standardization, and the above-mentioned practice of setting ceiling prices, however, any excessive deviation from the quality and quantity dictated by the specified salary was unlikely.

28 See note 18 for a passage including these stock phrases. An inquiry into the definition and meaning of "soul-caressing" would be an interesting trajectory for a future study.

29 On the ten schools of Qur'an recitation, see Melchert 2008. The reading styles based on the ten authorities are enumerated in detail in the *vakfiye* of the Atik Valide Mosque, where the document specifies the qualifications of the instructor for the *darülkurra*; see [Ergin] Cichocki 2005, 364.

30 At this point, I have not been able to find any information regarding the appointment or recruitment process of reciters in the sixteenth-century Ottoman Empire. To a certain extent it may have paralleled the process by which madrasa graduates were appointed to teach at schools across the empire, and graduates of the most prestigious *darülkurra*s also received positions in higher-ranking

mosques. There are many more questions than answers: did the endowment administrators of the Süleymaniye complex cherry-pick the best graduates of its own *darülkurra* for employment in the mosque? Was there a type of auditioning process, during which an aspiring *cüzhan* had to perform for the *ser-mahfil*? To what extent were clientelism and nepotism factors in the appointment process? Was there a way to circumvent the *darülkurra* system?

31 See Necipoğlu 2005, 57n3; see also Ergin 2008, 213.

32 As mentioned above, the imperial administration set ceiling prices and quality standards for various types of goods and services and deployed market inspectors (*muhtesib*) to control adherence to these. At this point, I am not aware of any archival sources pertaining to the salary scale or "quality control" of reciters.

33 More than by appointing reciters, individuality would have been expressed by selecting suras and verses outside the conventional recitation program of sura Ya Sin after the morning, Al ʿImran after the noon or afternoon, and al-Mülk after the evening or night prayer. Two examples are the Süleymaniye, where forty-one reciters daily chanted al-En'am (6), and the Nişancı Mehmed Paşa Mosque, where al-Fath (48) and al-Kahf (18) occured as rather unusal additions. On the meaning of these additions, see Ergin 2008, 208; and 2013.

CHAPTER THREE

A Concert Platform

A Space for a Style in Turkish Music

JOHN MORGAN O'CONNELL

The relationship between music and architecture is surprisingly understudied in the Muslim world. This lack is especially remarkable given the established study of sound and space in other religious traditions and cultural contexts. In such instances, scholars have either examined spaces designed for sound—studies that range from the analysis of the harmonic proportions in sacred structures (such as Christian churches) to the examination of acoustical principles in secular edifices (such as concert halls)—or looked at the spatial attributes of sound by viewing music as architecture. Here, music is viewed as a sonic construction (e.g., the compositions by Iannis Xenakis, 1922–2001) or as a sound space (e.g., the performances by Karlheinz Stockhausen, 1928–2007). Although other factors (such as ritual convention or technical development) are clearly significant, architecture can be viewed as solidified music or music can be heard as an audible sculpture.[1] That is, sound and space seem to operate in a dialectical relationship, music configuring architecture, architecture shaping music.

In this chapter, I examine the dialectical relationship between one aspect of music (namely, style) and one aspect of architecture (namely, space). With reference to a concert platform in Turkey, I show how one artist (Münir Nurettin Selçuk, 1899–1981; see fig. 3.1) transformed a Turkish style in a non-Turkish space by presenting an "Eastern classical" music (called *alaturka*) in a "Western classical" venue (a concert hall) where a Western classical tradition (called *alafranga*) was usually performed.[2] In this context, he wished

Figure 3.1. Münir Nurettin Selçuk (c. 1939). Publicity photograph made in the Armand Photo Studio (Cairo), and appearing in the program for a concert in Cairo by Selçuk (14 February 1939), sponsored by Odeon Records. The photograph was kindly given to the author by Selçuk's daughter, Meral Selçuk.

to develop a new style of Turkish music that was at once both modern and national.[3] Providing his own solution to the pressing debate about a national music (*milli musiki*) that erupted during the early Republican period (1923–1938), he sought to "alafrangize" *alaturka* by adopting the principles and the practices of *alafranga*. Here, his "first" concert (on 22 February 1930) in the French Theater (Fransız Tiyatrosu) represented a dramatic break with tradition since it provided a new space for presenting an old style.

A Concert Space

Istanbul's Fransız Tiyatrosu offered a physical space for transforming *alaturka*. In contrast to traditional practice, it was a large space for the presentation of an intimate style, *alaturka* typically being performed in upper-class salons (*salonlar*) or in lower-class clubs (*meyhaneler*). In these contexts, vocalists were accompanied either by a small ensemble (called *ince saz takımı*) or an instrumental band (called *fasıl*), a solo arrangement and a choral grouping indicative of a "classical" and a popular reading of *alaturka*, respectively. Of course, *alaturka* was also performed in bigger spaces by larger groups, whether in secular venues (such as the "orchestra" called *küme faslı* in imperial palaces) or in sacred contexts (such as the ensemble called *mutriban* in mystical lodges). Here, a distinction between music for outdoors (such as military parades) and music for indoors (such as state occasions) was especially important, the issue of amplitude in musical practice (among other factors) determining a space for a style.

Selçuk changed this connection between space and style. By presenting *alaturka* with a small ensemble in a large concert hall, he transcended the established distinction between place and practice. Although the Fransız Tiyatrosu at the time staged plays and hosted recitals by French artists, it was principally designed for opera, being home to a large stage and an even larger amphitheater. To adapt his style to this space, Selçuk adopted the performance conventions of a concert artist by standing (rather than sitting) in front of (rather than beside) a select group of instrumentalists. Dressed in tails (*frak*), he employed the musical techniques of a Western vocalist (bel canto) to project his voice from the stage to the auditorium. Unusually, Selçuk did not require a choral backing or use a percussion instrument (a tambourine called a "*def*"). Rather, he sang by himself without technical assistance for more than two hours. For these innovations, his first concert was considered by the renowned instrumentalist Lâika Karabey (1909–1989) to be a courageous endeavor.[4]

The Fransız Tiyatrosu provided a symbolic space for transforming *alaturka*. Since its foundation during the nineteenth century, the theater had attracted a cosmopolitan audience resident in Istanbul that was eager to celebrate the latest developments on the Western stage. As its name suggests, the Fransız Tiyatrosu promoted French acts and rivaled the Naum Tiyatrosu, which promoted Italian works.[5] Following the great fire of 1870, which destroyed many theaters in Istanbul, the Fransız Tiyatrosu became the principal establishment for hosting concerts and for staging operas. By 1930, it still retained its exclusive status, promoting international artists and attracting cosmopolitan audiences. While the theater suffered economically from the demographic transformations that followed the foundation of the Turkish Republic (1923), it benefited socially from its established history and its recognized artistry. That it was French (rather than Italian) was especially noteworthy since French had supplanted Italian in Turkey as the language of music and as the language of culture.

Selçuk was acutely aware of this association between sound and society. As an artist with an aristocratic pedigree, he wished to recover the status of *alaturka* at a time when *alafranga* was favored. In particular, his "alafrangization" of *alaturka* reiterated an established pattern in Turkish history where the Westernization of Turkish culture went hand in hand with the modernization of Turkish society. In this respect, Selçuk represented a male model in time and space. As a "man of the Tanzima" (*Tanzimat adamı*), he characterized historically the intellectual attributes of Turkish enlightenment.[6] As a "gentleman of Istanbul" (*İstanbul efendisi*), he fulfilled geographically the gendered ideal of Turkish masculinity. In both instances, Selçuk accommodated musically a national aspiration toward cultural purity (in terms of musical transmission) with an international recognition of multicultural hybridity (in terms of musical performance) to provide an individual compromise between the past and the present, between the East and the West. Here, his engagement with a French conception of classicism had a peculiarly Turkish dimension.

Selçuk wished to reap the benefits derived from a French understanding of "classical" music. Adopting the French titles "*soliste*" (soloist) and "*artiste*" (artist), he considered his musical performance as a concert (*konser*) and his musical role as a *concertiste* (*konsertist*). In contrast to traditional usage, he rejected the Turkish title "*hanende*" (singer, reader) in favor of the French title "*chanteur*" (*şantör*), now viewing himself as a *virtuose* (*virtuöz*) who provided a unique interpretation of *chant* (*şan*). He even employed French terms in newspaper interviews to discuss his musical innovations and his stylistic strategies. By using a French lexicon in musical discourse, he seemingly presented a scientific basis for his version of a national music. The Fransız Tiyatrosu was the ideal context for expressing a French connection. For Selçuk, it offered a "chic" location for singing to a chic audience. He even used the word "chic" (*şık*) to describe his new style of vocal performance, showing how his musical manner, like his social standing, was chic.

Selçuk employed a nonnational language (namely French) to validate a national music that was Turkish.[7] Here, he also provided his own solution to the development of a national language. That is, he addressed the language reforms instituted by the president of the Turkish Republic (1928), Mustafa Kemal Atatürk (1881–1938).[8] As with music, Selçuk aimed to rid language of its Arabic and Persian influences. As with music, he sought to employ a contemporary Turkish lexicon that was both modernized and Westernized. In this matter, his use of Turkish sat comfortably with his use of French, providing a sonic fusion of the local and the global that was ideologically shrewd yet socially acceptable. In his bid to separate the Ottoman past from the Republican present, he sought to alafrangize language and to Westernize music to circumvent the contemporary antagonism toward the Ottoman language (*Osmanlıca*) and Ottoman music (*alaturka*). For him, the first concert provided an ideal platform for the verbal articulation and sonic presentation of a new art for a new state.

A Concert Style

Of course, the first concert was not the first concert in Turkish music. During the nineteenth century, Turkish musicians and Turkish vocalists regularly performed Western music, or *alafranga*, in concert halls and opera houses.[9] At the time, the Fransız Tiyatrosu and the Naum Tiyatrosu were the chief venues for presenting French artists and Italian musicians. Under the directorship of the competing impresarios Seraphin Manasse (1837–1888) and Michel Naum [Duhany] ([1800]–1868), the two theaters were designed (at different times) in a French manner and an Italian fashion, respectively, the former later featuring an additional gallery in deference to the democratic principle. Because the Fransız Tiyatrosu had fewer boxes than the Naum Tiyatrosu, it had better acoustics, its smaller orchestra and its compact chorus being ideally suited to hosting operettas by French companies. *Alafranga* was also presented in private venues (such as palaces and embassies) and in public spaces (such as gardens and kiosks). In all instances, style and space articulated a social imperative: *alafranga* was chic.

The promotion of *alafranga* to the detriment of *alaturka* must be understood within a wider historical context. Following the abolition of the Janissaries (1826) and the dissolution of the Janissary Band (called "*mehter*") soon afterward, *alafranga* was sponsored by the military (in the form of brass bands) and by the court (in the form of salon soirées). Significantly, *alafranga* was taught in the imperial school (Enderun Mektebi) and was performed by the imperial orchestra (Muzıkay-ı Hümayun). An emergent bourgeoisie, for the most part bureaucrats who acquired wealth and status follow-

Figure 3.2. The Darüttalimi musical ensemble (c. 1930). Publicity photograph, from the archive of Tuğrul Acar.

ing the Westernizing reforms initiated during the Tanzimat era (1839–1876), also supported *alafranga*. While *alaturka* was not ignored at certain moments during the nineteenth century,[10] *alafranga* was increasingly viewed as the appropriate style for a Westernized elite, a style that was institutionalized in music schools and patronized by music societies. *Alafranga* was also presented in concert settings and represented in concert reviews.[11]

Yet *alaturka* was not a silent partner in the triumphant thrust of *alafranga*. *Alaturka* scholars employed *alafranga* terminology when conceptualizing Turkish musical practice (e.g., Haşim Bey 1864) or when theorizing about Turkish musical principles (e.g., Çağatay 1895). *Alaturka* musicians invoked *alafranga* practices when arranging Turkish music (by employing a native understanding of harmonic consciousness) or representing Turkish music (by using a modified version of musical notation). Indeed, *alaturka* enthusiasts began to develop a hybrid compromise between an "Eastern" original and a Western prototype (see fig. 3.2.), Western conventions finding expression in ensemble practice (e.g. the appearance of Western conductors in concert presentations) and Western tastes being featured in musical theater (e.g. the emergence of Westernized genres in theatrical productions). While a number of connoisseurs (e.g., Rauf Yekta Bey, 1871–1935) sought to save *alaturka* from the clutches of *alafranga*, *alaturka* was increasingly viewed as impure and by implication immoral. Unlike *alafranga*, *alaturka* was not chic.

The situation had not changed by the twentieth century. In the climate of musical reform that followed the foundation of the Turkish Republic (1923), Turkish commentators attempted to develop a national music (*milli musiki*) worthy of a nation-state. Either they looked to Western classical music (as did, e.g., the conductor Osman Zeki Üngör, 1880–1958), or they looked to Turkish folk music (as did, e.g., the composer Adnan Saygun, 1907–1991). For them, the polyphonic arrangement of Turkish music represented the purest expression of a national idiom. For them, however, *alaturka* was outmoded and marginalized, being either relegated to the archives of history (now being studied exclusively by scholars in conservatories) or sustained in houses of debauchery, contemporary nightclubs (*gazinolar*) and drinking houses (*meyhaneler*) that presented an inebriated context for the celebration of a degenerate style and for the perpetuation of a cosmopolitan aesthetic. For such critics, *alaturka* represented the cultural capital of the Ottoman Empire and had no place in the Turkish Republic.

The first concert sought to offset the decline of *alaturka* during the early Republican period. In particular, Selçuk wanted to enshrine *alaturka* in an *alafranga* edifice, the concert hall. Although seemingly adopting a hybrid solution to the development of a national music, he actually invoked a Western conception of classicism to position *alaturka* on an equal footing with *alafranga*. By employing the term "classical" (*klasik*) and by avoiding the word "*alaturka*," he hoped to redefine Turkish music as a classical music, and in doing so, he acquired for his Eastern tradition the esteem usually reserved for a Western tradition. For him, "Turkish classical music" (now called "*Türk klasik musikisi*") was distinguished from other styles of Turkish music since it was now presented on the concert stage, using the performance practices and ritual conventions usually associated with Western classical music (now called "*garb klasik musikisi*"). In this way, the classical was extricated from the vernacular. As a classical style, *alaturka* could once again be chic.

The first concert was not the first concert in *alaturka*. Just before the foundation of the Turkish Republic, concerts by *alaturka* ensembles were staged in music theaters and concert halls. Sometimes these performances were directed by a conductor wielding a baton. The period also witnessed the presentation of *alaturka* recitals by renowned instrumentalists. Even Selçuk had already presented a concert performance of *alaturka* in a Turkish hall (the

Türk Ocağı in Ankara) and in an Egyptian theatre (the Azbakiyya Gardens in Cairo). In these performances, however, he (like other *alaturka* musicians) had not developed a concert style of Turkish classical music. Here, Selçuk's 1928 visit to Paris was seminal. While there, the artist took lessons in bel canto (ostensibly at the Conservatoire de Paris), and he also attended performances of Western classical music. Accordingly, he developed the notion of a soloist who performed *alaturka* in a recital using Western techniques and conventions. For him, the first concert was both classical in its style and chic in its staging.

A Concert Hall

Perhaps the Fransız Tiyatrosu (fig. 3.3) was not such a chic venue for a classical style. Founded most likely after 1827, it was reputedly the oldest theater in Istanbul.[12] Like other theaters, it was redesigned and relocated usually as the result of conflagrations that bedeviled the European quarter of Istanbul (called Pera or Beyoğlu). Originally thought to have been designed by a Venetian architect called Bartolomeo Giustiniani (probably in 1831), it was first built in the Italian style as an amphitheater with no gallery or balcony. Like the Naum Tiyatrosu, it featured many boxes and a large parterre. With the accession of Manasse to the directorship of the institution (1864), the stage was expanded and the lobby redeveloped, the addition of a new ballroom with glass doors earning the theater the title of Palais de Cristal. While Manasse was soon seconded to Egypt (1869) for his enlightened approach to theatrical production,[13] the Fransız Tiyatrosu survived the great fire (1870), becoming the principal venue in Istanbul for opera.[14]

Why the Fransız Tiyatrosu relocated from its older location in the Elhamra Pasajı to the newer position in the Halep Pasajı nearby is not clear. Perhaps because of intense competition from other theaters that had been recently constructed, the Nouveau Théâtre Français (as it was now called) replaced a circus arena (called Théâtre Cirque de Pera), whose circular layout informed the design of the theater. While the circus dome was dismantled in 1886, the new theater was little more than an enclosed circus still dark and dank from the legacy of vulgar spectacle. In summer, the situation was so severe that resident artists repaired to the Tepebaşı Tiyatrosu to avoid the stench. To accommodate performances of operettas and plays (again under

Figure 3.3. Fransız Tiyatrosu, interior (2016). Photograph: J. M. O'Connell.

the direction of Manasse), the stage was raised and a pit inserted. However, a fire temporarily interrupted activity (1902). Two years later, the New Fransız Tiyatrosu was refashioned by the entrepreneur Campanaki, who designed a hybrid space informed by an Italian manner and a French style.[15]

Following an Italian precedent, Campanaki built seventy boxes. These were arranged in two levels. They were flanked by twelve loggias placed strategically at either side of the stage, six at the ground level (*baignoires*) and six at the main level (*bel-étage*). As the legacy of an aristocratic desire for social segregation, these loggias were the most costly. However, no royal box was included. Following a French precedent, Campanaki retained the large gallery and the wide parterre. In keeping with similar developments in France, these were divided into the cheapest seats in the balcony and the gallery and the more expensive positions in the seats (*fauteuils*) and the stalls (*stalles*). Critical here was proximity to the stage, seat price now being reflective of a bourgeois aspiration to acquire social status through economic display. To attract a cosmopolitan audience that was resident in the area, Campanaki also redesigned the facade of the theater, widening the entrance to draw in wealthy clients and expanding the lobby to facilitate social ostentation.

However, Campanaki retained the circular configuration of the original circus. Possibly believing that his improvements were temporary, his design enabled different types of activities to be staged. In addition to plays and operettas, more popular acts (such as vaudeville and cabaret) were promoted, and more low-brow shows (such as acrobatic displays and wrestling matches) were scheduled. For this reason, the theater was renamed (in 1906) the Varyete Tiyatrosu (named after the French theatre called Théâtre des Variétés). The theater was one of the first venues to offer film screenings, after 1907 doubling as a cinema under a number of names (including İdeâl Sineması and Royal Sineması).[16] During the First World War, the theater was most notable for hosting productions by Turkish companies, the residence there of the famous actor Muhsin Ertuğrul (1892–1979) being especially noteworthy. Probably in 1929, the theater again adopted its original name, the Fransız Tiyatrosu. As the newspaper advertisements for the following year show, the theater management wished the venue once again to be chic by way of the classical.[17]

In 1930, the Fransız Tiyatrosu hosted solo recitals by international artists. For example, in January it featured two recitals by the French pianist Marcelle Meyer (1897–1958), which probably included (as was her custom) works by contemporary French composers. In February, the German composer Emil von Sauer (1862–1942) performed two piano recitals of romantic works and one of his own compositions. In March, the Hungarian virtuoso Joseph Szigeti (1892–1973) offered a violin recital of twentieth-century works. In the same period, other performances were made at the theater by the coloratura soprano Ada Sari (1886–1968) and by the lyric soprano Ninon Vallin (1886–1961). The schedule published in contemporary newspapers detailed performances by the famous comedienne Marie Bell (1900–1985) and the young film star Charles Boyer (1899–1976). It also showed presentations of a minstrel show entitled *Lou[i]siana*; a staged production of *Anna Karenina*; and a musical comedy entitled *Sapho* and starring the famous actress Cécile Sorel (1873–1966).

Why, then, did Selçuk choose to perform his first concert in the Fransız Tiyatrosu? True, the theater was striving to recover its reputation for classicism in the present despite its promotion of populism in the past. True, too, the theater still attracted a cosmopolitan audience that was more exclusive, even though it had also attracted a local audience that was more humble. Crucial here was the intervention of the theater director, Jean Lehmann

(d. 1933). As manager of the Fransız Tiyatrosu since 1912, he had overseen the survival of the theater during a turbulent period of Turkish history. Here, he astutely sponsored both Turkish artists and non-Turkish performers to satisfy an ideological imperative as well as a social obligation. As an impresario who was known to "appeal to the cosmopolitan audiences of Beyoğlu" (Özdamar 1991, 92), Selçuk accommodated the national and the international dimensions of Lehmann's artistic policy. That Selçuk was aristocratic as well as fashionable clearly helped. Simply put, he had class and he was classy.

A Concert Stage

Was the staging of the first concert in fact so chic? In imitation of the managerial style, Selçuk melded the national (namely, *alaturka*) with the international (namely, *alafranga*) to develop a national music (*milli musiki*). In imitation of the theatrical space, he melded the popular with the "classical" by presenting a diverse program that encompassed the vernacular and the classical styles of Turkish music and that embraced both subaltern and elite tastes of Turkish audiences. Indeed, the artistic policy of the theater reflected the artistic strategy of the vocalist, the theatrical space both visually (in terms of its architectural configuration) and sonically (in terms of its musical programming) implicitly informing the hybrid character of the first concert. This hybridity was expressed in the unique program of Turkish compositions. It was also expressed in the distinctive manner of Turkish performance. It was manifested in the critical evaluation of Selçuk, with music critics articulating either an Eastern or a Western perspective and adopting a traditionalist or a modernist viewpoint.

The program of the first concert was unique (see fig. 3.4 and table 3.1). Divided into five sections (*kısımlar*), it featured classical works (such as a *kâr-ı nev*), light classical compositions (such as *şarkılar*), and folk songs (such as *türküler*). It also included "alafrangized" numbers, *alafranga* arrangements of *alaturka* songs called *fantezi şarkılar.* In contrast to traditional practice, the program was not organized into "suites" (*fasıllar*), a collection of vocal compositions and instrumental works usually collected together according to mode (*makam*) and normally arranged hierarchically according to meter (*usul*). In the first concert, unrelated modes were juxtaposed and uncharacteristic meters were intermingled. In addition, unconventional genres were

FRANSIZ TİYATROSUNDA

Münir Nurettin

Beyin

Konser Programı

Refakat edecek hey'eti musikiye:

MES'UT CEMİL Bey, RUŞEN Bey, NUBAR Ef.

ARTAKİ Ef. ve Mösyö VASİLİEF

22 ŞUBAT CUMARTESİ GÜNÜ

akşam saat tam 21½ ta

Konsere on yaşından aşağı çocuklar kabul olunmaz.

Figure 3.4. Program of the "first" concert in the Fransız Tiyatrosu, from a photograph of the original program to be found in the archive of Münir Nurettin Selçuk (Istanbul), with thanks to Meral Selçuk.

Table 3.1. Program of the concert in the Fransız Tiyatrosu

Genre	Meter	Mode	Title	Composer
First section (*Birinci Kısım*)[a]				
Kar[-]ı Nev	Ağır Düyek	Rast	[Gözümde Daim]	Dede Efendi
Şarkı	Curcuna	Suzinak	Pek Revadır	Ahmet Rasim Bey
Şarkı	Curcuna	Uşşak	Neden Hiç Durmadan	Suphi Ziya Bey
Şarkı	Curcuna	Hüseyni	Feryâd [E]diyor	Suphi Ziya Bey
Divan	Sofyan	Şehnaz	Vardımki Yurdundan	[Nevres Paşa]
Second section (*İkinci Kısım*)[b]				
Şarkı	Ağır Aksak	Hüzzam	Durmasın Aksın	Bimen Efendi
Şarkı	Aksak	Segah	Benim Sen Nemsin	Ahmet Rasim Bey
Şarkı	Değişmeli	N[i]haven[d]	Süzüp Süzüp	Rahmi Bey
Türkü	Çitfte Sofyan	Mahur	Dün Yine Günümüz	Refik Bey
Third section (*Üçüncü Kısım*)[c]				
Şarkı	Düyek	Rast	Senin Aşkınla	[Basmacızade] Abdi Efendi
Şarkı	Curcuna	Kürdili Hica[z]kar	Sana Ey Canımın Cânı	Rahmi Bey
Şarkı	Düyek	Ni[k]riz	Gönül Ne İçin	Ruhi Bey [Faize Ergin]
Fourth section (*Dördüncü Kısım*)[d]				
Şarkı	Semai	Nihavend	Ne Olur	Refik Bey
Fantezi Şarkı	Sofyan	Nihavend	Tereddüt	Ali Rıfat Bey
Fifth section (*Beşinci Kısım*)[e]				
Şarkı	Segin Semai	Hüzzam	Kirpiklerinin	Artaki Efendi
Şarkı	Semai	Ferahnak	Ruhumda Bahar	Artaki Efendi
Dağ[i]	Curcuna	Uşşak	Akşam Olur	Traditional [Urfa]
Halk Şarkısı	Curcuna	Hüzzam	Allı Yemeni	Traditional [Istanbul]

[a] Accompanied by *kemençe* and *tanbur*.
[b] Accompanied by *kanun*, *kemençe*, and *tanbur*.
[c] Accompanied by *tanbur*.
[d] Accompanied by *keman*, pi*[y]ano*, and *viyolonsel*.
[e] Accompanied by *keman*, *tanbur*, and *kanun*.

combined and atypical styles were mixed. It is surprising that Selçuk did not adopt the Western convention of performing a song cycle that was equivalent in character to the Eastern concept of a vocal suite (*fasıl*). It is also surprising that he did not employ the Western notion of tonal organization that was similar in spirit to the Eastern idea of modal arrangement.

The vocal style of the first concert was also unique. In terms of voice production, Selçuk melded an Eastern concern for larynx oscillation and chest register with a Western preoccupation with breath control and vocal projection. As he reminisced in an interview with the journalist Salih Harun published in *Yeni Sabah* on 10 January 1964: "I was able to use all of the sounds available to the head voice [*kafa sesi*] in addition to the sounds available to the chest register [*göğüs sesi*] and to the larynx [*hançere*] which are characteristic of eastern music."[18] His synthesis of East and West was not universally lauded. One critic at the event complained that Selçuk sounded hoarse. Apart from the exceptional duration of the solo performance, the design of the theater may have been unhelpful. Given its circular configuration (inherited from the circus) and the uneven arrangement of the auditorium (combining different interior styles), it was inevitable that the acoustical properties of the performance space were hardly ideal for a solo recital.

The instrumental backing for the first concert was more conventional. In an arrangement reminiscent of a chamber ensemble in *alaturka* (called *ince saz takımı*), Selçuk was accompanied by Mesut Cemil Tel (1902–1963) on the long-necked lute (*tanbur*), Ruşen Ferid Kam (1905–1981) on the pear-shaped bowed lute (*kemençe*), and Artaki Candan (1885–1948) on the trapezoidal plucked zither (*kanun*), a distinguished lineup of classical artists playing classical instruments supremely suited to the historic significance of the classical occasion. However, all commentators bemoaned the diminished status accorded to these venerable artists both in terms of space (being placed behind the vocalist onstage) and in terms of time (not being accorded an instrumental solo or interlude). The problem was exacerbated by the inclusion of Western instruments used to accompany the *fantezi şarkılar*, a cello and a piano being critically assessed in their relationship to the performance of an "alafrangized" *alaturka*. That the pianist was a Russian émigré (a Monsieur Vasilief) of questionable ability was the subject of considerable discourse.[19]

Hybridity in musical practice was reflected in hybridity in musical criticism. On the one hand, the author Peyami Safa (1899–1961) was critical of the hybrid character of musical composition. In the 24 February 1930 issue of *Cumhuriyet,* he characterized the Westernized arrangements of *alaturka* pieces in the following terms: "[t]he two *fantezi* songs that mimicked *alafranga* were least liked and little applauded. The European-styled *fanteziler* were gaudily ornamented like a woman's shoe manufactured by a cheap cobbler." He recommended: "Let us save our musical repertoire from adulterated [*mağşuş*] melodies and from a synthesis of styles [*melez*] in imitation of the worst novels, operas, etc." On the other hand, the journalist Ahmed Vâlâ Nurettin Bey (1901–1967) was critical of the hybrid character of musical performance; in the 24 February 1930 issue of *Milliyet,* he assessed the *Westernized* rendition of *alaturka* in the following manner: "However, M. Nurettin Bey's voice was much too alafrangized [*fazla alafrangalaştırmış*]. The sole flaw of the concert was as follows: his voice emerged sometimes, and with some exaggeration, from his nasal passage."

However, both reviews reflected distinctive conceptions of hybridity. For Safa, the Westernized arrangement of *alaturka* compositions was unacceptable since it detracted from the presentation of a Turkish art music that was dignified and purified. For Vala Nurettin Bey, the Westernized rendition of *alaturka* was intolerable since it undermined the representation of a Turkish folk music that was modern (by way of musical arrangement) and national (by way of musical provenance).[20] Here, the critics presented two readings of a national music, Safa, the revisionist, invoking an "orientalist" perspective to promote a "classicized" Turkish music, and Vala Nurettin Bey, the revolutionary, invoking an "occidentalist" perspective to advance a folklorized Turkish music. Where Safa employed the ambiguous mannerisms of old Turkish to endorse a traditionalist interpretation of Turkish music, Vala Nurettin Bey used the precise style of new Turkish to support a modern understanding of Turkish music. In this way, each critic crafted his own conception of acceptable practice where hybridity in musical composition or in musical performance provided pathways for exploring distinctive understandings of a new music in the new republic.

A Concert Audience

A critical evaluation of Turkish music requires a critical evaluation of Turkish society. Where Safa represented the musical tastes of an imperial tradition, he also espoused the conservative values of an imperial society. Here, his views on music and morality chimed well with the attitudes of an old elite recently sponsored by the Ottoman court. Where Vala Nurettin Bey represented the musical tastes of a republican modernity, he also espoused the radical values of a republican hegemony. Here, his views on music and nationalism reflected the progressive attitudes of a new elite, recently empowered by the republican regime. That Vala Nurettin Bey was a socialist is especially interesting since he employed modern Turkish to combat conservatism in Turkish music and backwardness in Turkish society. Although explicitly critical of Safa's "orientalist" agenda, he was also disparaging about Selçuk's "occidentalist" project. That the vocalist had courtly connections was particularly irksome, his vocal style like his lifestyle inviting unfavorable scrutiny by the journalist.

Yet contemporary accounts of the first concert do not reveal such a social distinction in the concert audience. Most commentators emphasized the elegant character of those assembled in the crowded hall, remarking on their fashionable attire, were they gentlemen (wearing ties) or ladies (wearing shawls). Each member of the audience was termed either "chic" (Turkish, *şık*) (for women) or "well groomed" (Turkish, *tertemiz giyinmiş*) (for men).[21] After the curtains opened, they were hushed into a reverent silence that was unusual in *alaturka* performances. They uniformly remarked on the artist appearing in tails on stage, standing rather than sitting in the manner of a solo recitalist. As I show elsewhere,[22] they also commented on the ways in which the artist did not appear to grimace when singing or to cover his mouth when performing, unfavorable habits employed by *alaturka* vocalists especially in popular locales. Some noted that the vocalist did not bellow, mumble, or nod.[23] They uniformly viewed the first concert as the emancipation of *alaturka*, now "classical" in both style and setting.

However, social uniformity in theory was not matched by social uniformity in practice. When examining the receipts for the first concert (see table 3.2),[24] it is clear that the audience was highly segregated into distinctive seating positions across the auditorium. Only one of the two loggias on either side of the stage on the main floor (*bel-étage*) was occupied, costing its occupants around TL 15.[25] However, the two equivalent loggias on the ground level (*baignoires*) were full, costing their occupants TL 12.25 each. The remaining boxes were priced around TL 10 for the main level and TL 8 at the ground level, sixteen boxes at the higher level and eighteen boxes at the lower level, constituting more than half the boxes available. Most of the audience mem-

Table 3.2. Receipts from the "first" concert in the Fransız Tiyatrosu

Number[a]	Seat	Price	Extras	Stamp	Cost [Kr]	Total [TL][a]
1	box	1,190	239	66	149[5][b]	14.95
2	box	980	201	54	12[2]5	24.50
13	box	790	163	44	[101]7	132.2[3]
3	box	790	163	44	[101]7	30.5[3]
18	box	632	133	35	80[2]	144.3[0]
105	seat	237	49	14	300	315.00
12	seat	237	49	14	300	36.00
130	seat	158	33	9	200	260.00
28	balcony	118	25	6,5	149,5	41.86
21	gallery	79	17	5	101	21.21

[a] The total number of tickets sold = 333; the total net = TL 803.98; the total gross = TL 1,200[60]. A municipal grant at 2.5 percent [TL 25.51] brings the final gross to TL 1,046.11.
[b] The figures in brackets represent miscalculations in the original receipt.

bers were seated on seats (*fauteuils*), where 117 of them paid TL 3, or in the stalls (*stalles*), where 130 members paid TL 2. Another 28 paid TL 1.5 for a seat in the balcony, and 21 paid TL 1 for a place in the gallery (*gallerie*).

Surprisingly, the first concert was not full. In contrast to contemporary accounts of a crowded auditorium,[26] only 333 places out a possible 536 were sold. Of course, this calculation does not include complimentary tickets for friends and critics, who may have filled the vacant boxes. What the receipts do show is the economic benefit of social distinction. As I demonstrate elsewhere,[27] the earnings for the first concert were impressive, with around TL 1,050 taken. However, this figure represents an untaxed total and does not reflect the costs incurred. In terms of taxation, 20 percent was deducted in the form of an excise duty (*istihlak vergisi*) and an additional toll (simply entitled D.A.). In addition, a stamp duty of 5 percent and municipal tax of 2.5 percent were also incurred. This tax burden resulted in a net profit of some TL 780. In terms of the costs, the hall had to be hired (ca. TL 240) and the concert had to be advertised (ca. TL 80). That left only around TL 460 to be distributed among the artists.[28]

Critical here is the issue of profitability. First, Selçuk as the principal artist was widely believed to have benefited economically from his first concert. However, he probably took home only around TL 230 from his Turkish debut,[29] if he was paid (as he was in other instances) half the takings. That would have left around TL 230 to be distributed among the four instrumentalists, each artist earning approximately TL 57.50. Clearly, his aspiration to be a soloist had a financial aspect. Second, Lehmann as the theater director was not so encumbered by the profit motive. As he did in other instances, he agreed in advance to deduct 30 percent from the net total. While this amount was considered to be excessive by other artists, it was considerably less than the hire of concert venues in other theaters, where some managers charged up to 45 percent.[30] However, the concert receipts show that Lehmann was no accountant, since his calculations show many mistakes with respect to income accrued and money subtracted.

In fact, the first concert was organized to advertise sound recordings. Significantly, thirteen out of the eighteen works presented in the concert had already been recorded and catalogued by the recording company His Master's Voice (Sahibinin Sesi). As the relevant catalogue shows,[31] most of the program was available in the public domain. As its principal artist,[32] Selçuk performed a repertoire that was featured on his own artistic label (the FE series), an exclusive selection of recordings advertised at an exclusive price. Here, the social standing of his concert audience translated into the economic power of his record consumers. To maximize market share, Selçuk recorded items that were as varied as his concert repertoire, ranging from the classical to the popular and encompassing the traditional and the contemporary. In this way, Selçuk used the social spaces of the concert platform to disseminate the sound spaces of the media industry to garner an impressive return. As his main sponsor, Sahibinin Sesi played a critical role.

A Concert Series

The first concert was not the last concert. The following month (on 23 March 1930), Selçuk performed another concert at the Fransız Tiyatrosu. As the relevant receipt shows, this concert was better attended, attracting 430 rather than 333 patrons. However, the profit margin did not reflect this increase since the artists took (before costs were deducted) only about TL 820 net this time, in contrast to the TL 780 or so net the previous time. The situation can be explained in terms of seat pricing. In contrast to the first concert, the second concert showed that no loggia in the *bel-étage* category was occupied. However, seven loggias in the *baignoires* category were taken. At this event, the boxes were reassigned "seat I" and "seat II," boxes in the two classes costing TL 5 and TL 4 and being filled with thirty-four and thirty-two audience members, respectively, the cheaper prices ensuring that in this concert, nearly all of the boxes were filled. The remaining concertgoers flocked to the cheaper seats in the auditorium and the gallery.

This decline in the value of concert tickets was reflected in the declining number of record sales. Following the 1929 Wall Street crash, Selçuk sold only some 13,000 records in 1930, whereas he had sold around 28,000 discs the previous year. His income accordingly declined from £650 to £300 over the two years. The reduction was most noticeable in the second half of 1930, when only 3,000 recordings were purchased and £75 was earned.[33] While other factors were also to blame (such as the invention of sound films and the introduction of radio broadcasts),[34] it is clear that his recitals at the Fransız Tiyatrosu were neither profitable (in terms of income earned) nor productive (in terms of discs sold). Recently a husband and newly a father, Selçuk quickly had to adopt an alternative strategy to improve his financial position. Here, Sahibinin Sesi helped. Through the intervention of Candan (who was employed by the company), in 1931, for the next concert series, the artist moved to the Melek Sineması, which had previously been used as a recording studio.[35]

The Melek Sineması ("Angel Cinema") was a very different space from the Fransız Tiyatrosu. Built in 1924, its exterior was modern rather than traditional, and its interior was uniform rather than hybrid. As an excellent example of Art Deco, it emulated the design of contemporary cinemas in Europe and America. It was especially noted for its resonant properties.[36] Here, Selçuk benefited from the juxtaposition of the aesthetic and the acoustic by taking advantage of a neoclassical space to present a neoclassical style. The transformation was immediate. The artist now found it easier to project his voice, and the critics found it harder to criticize his style. For example, Safa considered Selçuk's performance presentation somewhat forced in the Fransız Tiyatrosu but more controlled in the Melek Sineması.[37] His artistic style also had financial substance, since the Melek Sineması (with 875 seats) was considerably larger than the Fransız Tiyatrosu (with 536 seats), with Selçuk acquiring economic as well as cultural capital from his recent move. Significantly, the cinema was sold out.[38]

In 1932, the artist transferred from the Melek Sineması to the Glorya Sineması. Having found a better space for his new style, why did Selçuk move to yet another venue? While the Melek Sineması was ideal for presenting a classical style, it was less ideal for representing a classical repertoire. Because of its acoustic properties, critics could now clearly hear his flaws as well his strengths. While they celebrated his musical technique, they denigrated his linguistic skill, now noting his incorrect articulation of words and his faulty knowledge of texts. This resulted in an acrimonious debate about his "alafrangized" *alaturka*.[39] Surprisingly, Selçuk did not suffer from this public onslaught. In fact, the negative publicity had a positive influence on ticket sales for his concerts and record sales for his recordings. Indeed, record sales for the last half of 1930 and the first half of 1931 showed a dramatic increase, from around 3,000 to 6,000.[40] Here, Selçuk confirmed the old adage: all publicity is good publicity.

Where Melek Sineması was noted for its acoustic properties, the Glorya Sineması was noted for its social standing, a symbolic space ideally suited to the presentation of a classical style. Although the two venues were similar in size, the Melek Sineması represented a socially egalitarian venue (with all seats costing the same price), while the Glorya Sineması represented a socially segregated arena (with different seats costing different prices) for the reception of a national music. The repertoire performed in each context emphasized this social divide. While the pieces performed in the Melek Sineması were popular in character, the works performed in the Glorya Sineması were serious in nature, the four performances presented there each being neatly organized into a classical, a light-classical, and a folk section (*kısım*). Two aspects of symbolic capital are pertinent here. First, the Glorya Sineması replaced the Fransız Tiyatrosu as the chic venue in Beyoğlu.[41] Second, the Glorya Sineması now attracted non-Turkish audiences to Turkish concerts, a fact much celebrated by Safa in his enthusiastic reviews of the relevant performances. For Safa, Selçuk represented the liberation of an Eastern style in a Western state.

The concerts in the Glorya Sineması were extremely important. They set a precedent for the design of future concert programs in Turkish classical music. This design is still found today. The concerts also established Selçuk as the principal architect of a classical style, a national music with an international profile. What is missing here is the commercial factor. In contrast to previous performances, the price of tickets was considerably cheaper, ranging from TL 0.75 to TL 2 (in contrast to TL 1–15 in other venues). Clearly, these concerts were conceived as "artistic" occasions. However, Sahibinin Sesi did not lose the opportunity to advertise the latest recordings by Selçuk.

For the first time, the company advertised the latest discs of the artist in concert programs. Although few numbers were performed in the four concerts, the efforts of Sahibinin Sesi were not in vain. That is, the concerts were not profitable, but the recordings were, the artist selling some 3,500 and 3,750 discs in the first and the second halves of 1933, respectively.[42]

A Concert Platform

The first concert revealed a number of paradoxical positions. In terms of style, it presented a hybrid combination of *alaturka* and *alafranga* to develop a pure tradition, a particular version of a national music that was ideologically astute and financially advantageous. In terms of space, it presented an "alafrangized" *alaturka* in a hybrid space, the heterogeneous style of the musical performance reflecting the eclectic design of the musical space, the Fransız Tiyatrosu. The range of paradoxes encompassed other domains. In terms of society, the first concert was designed to appeal to Turks and non-Turks alike since it attracted a diverse audience to hear both *alaturka* and *alafranga* numbers. It was also designed to appeal to different social classes, the classical and the popular intended to attract an upper-class and a lower-class following, respectively. In terms of economics, the style was replicated in space, since seating position was determined by seating price, the economic reflective of the social in terms of display and distinction.

The first concert also initiated a number of dialectical relationships. In terms of style and space, music and architecture operated dialogically to influence a musical style (at the Melek Sineması) and a musical repertoire (at the Glorya Sineması). In these venues, the acoustical properties were reconfigured and the social attributes of musical production were renegotiated. In terms of producers and consumers, the artist and the critic also operated dialogically, with Selçuk adapting his style to a new criticism, and Safa reconfiguring his criticism to a new style. Here, new spaces allowed for new interpretations by the vocalist and new reflections by the journalist. These two dialectics were informed by two mediators. First, the theatre manager controlled the costs of musical production by means of accounting. Second, the commercial sponsor promoted the benefits of musical consumption by way of advertising. For each mediator, Selçuk represented an ideal that was both fashionable and honorable, attributes that could be displayed on the concert platform as performances and disseminated from the concert platform as recordings.

NOTES

This chapter complements but does not replicate material published in my last monograph (see O'Connell 2013). It is a revised version of a paper presented at the Summer School hosted by the Aga Khan University and Simon Fraser University held at the Institute for the Study of Muslim Civilizations (London) on 3 July 2013. The paper was one of a number of presentations and workshops on the central theme: "Music, Art and Architecture in Muslim Contexts." I would like to thank Dr. Farouk Topan for his invitation to speak at this meeting. I would also like to thank the participants at the Summer School for their insightful comments on the original paper.

1 The literature on the relationship between music and architecture is extensive. In this chapter, I draw upon the works of Grueneisen (2003) and Forsyth (1985) for a general overview of the relevant issues and for a specialist discussion of concert spaces respectively. In particular, I invoke Carlson's (1989) consideration of spatial semiotics as they relate to the design of interior spaces, especially with respect to opera houses and concert halls. While I am aware of the many studies that concern music and architecture from the perspectives of acoustics (for example Beranek 1979) and technology (for example Kronenburg 2012), these publications inform but do not determine my critical evaluation of the dialectical relationship between sound and space.

2 "*Alaturka*" is the Turkish spelling of the Italian term "*alla turca*." Its name literally meaning "in a Turkish style," *alaturka* was employed in Turkey during the nineteenth century to distinguish between an "Eastern" style of Turkish music (*alaturka*) and a "Western" style of Turkish music (*alafranga*). *Alafranga*, whose name literally means "in a Frankish manner," began to replace *alaturka* as the musical style of choice. See O'Connell 2000, 2003, 2005, 2010, 2011, and 2013, among others, for a fuller discussion of the terms *alaturka* and *alafranga* in Turkish music.

3 Münir Nurettin Selçuk is considered to be a major culture bearer of *alaturka*. Having studied with many of the most important composers and performers of the tradition, he represented a singular "line of musical transmission" (*meşk silsilesi*) that was principally associated with the Mevlevi order. In this sense, his musical education represented a pristine path of musical induction, Turkish in essence yet Muslim in character. On the other hand, Selçuk melded his traditional style with a nontraditional manner, performing *alaturka* in the style of *ala-*

franga. Further, he performed compositions by Turkish and non-Turkish composers, and he performed with instrumentalists who were both Muslims and non-Muslims. Here, his recognition of a multicultural dimension in musical practice ran counter to the prevailing trend of performing Turkish music by Turkish musicians, a music that was national, and musicians who were Muslim. See O'Connell 2010 and 2013 for a critical discussion of musical hybridity in Turkish music during the early Republican period.

4 See Karabey 1966.

5 See Aracı 2010.

6 The Tanzimat (English, "Reorganization") was a period of Westernizing reforms in the Ottoman Empire. The usual dates given for this era are 1839–1876, although 1839–1871 are also given.

7 See O'Connell 2013 for an in-depth discussion of music terminology in Arabic and French, in Turkey at the time the use of Arabic being indicative of a conservative perspective and the use of French being reflective of a progressive position.

8 There are many publications that consider the life and work of Mustafa Kemal Atatürk. In English, Kinross 1964 offers a standard account. More recently, Mango (1999) has written a critical study that is both incisive and readable. While the musical reforms and musical debates that occurred in the time of Atatürk have received considerable attention, I provide a summary of the most important sources in O'Connell 2013, 51–77.

9 See Baydar 2010 and Kosal 1999 among others for a general overview of *alafranga* in Turkey during the nineteenth century. See Aracı 2010 and And 1971a for publications on opera and theater respectively during the period. See Aracı 2006 and Spinetti 2010a for excellent studies of Western musicians in Turkey at the time. In particular, see And 1971b and Mestyan 2011 for a coverage of theatrical productions in French at the Fransız Tiyatrosu, among other venues. In addition, see Aksoy 1985, Feldman 1996, and Jäger 1996 for general studies of *alaturka* during the nineteenth century. In particular, see Greve 1995 and O'Connell 2005 for a consideration of the Westernization of *alaturka* during the Tanzimat era and the early Republican periods respectively.

10 See O'Connell 2005.

11 See O'Connell 2013.

12 The history of the Fransız Tiyatrosu is complex and convoluted. In contrast to the Naum Tiyatrosu (see Aracı 2010), it has not received a thorough study. Although And (1971b and 1983) and Mestyan (2011) provide important information, they do not agree on the founding date of the theater, And believing and Mestyan not believing that the theater was the oldest in Istanbul. While neither author provides primary sources to support his arguments (they often rely upon journalistic references), they agree that the Fransız Tiyatrosu went through three stages of development: the first in the 1860s, the second in the 1880s, and the third in the 1900s.

Although I am principally interested in the final stage of this evolutionary trajectory, I think that Mestyan presents the most convincing account of the theater's architectural history. See also Yazıcı 2010 for an introductory overview of relevant publications.

13 See Mestyan 2013.

14 Mestyan (2011, 162–188) provides an informed study of Seraphin Manasse. Noting the rivalry between Michel Naum and Manasse (see also Aracı 2010), he presents a textured reading of a talented impresario who had to negotiate the prejudices of imperial patronage and the professional jealousies of established rivals. Significantly, Manasse advocated a French understanding of civilization (see also Mestyan 2013), a particular reading of enlightenment that was advocated by the director and presented by his artists in Istanbul and Cairo.

15 The Nouveau Théâtre Français (Yeni Fransız Tiyatrosu) was most probably built by Jean Barborini (1820–1891), an Italian architect who also constructed the Glorya Sineması. Although Mestyan discounts And in this matter, Barborini could not have redesigned the theater in 1904 following the conflagration of 1902, as he died in 1891. Like other sources (see for example Gökmen 1991), And 1971b implies that the theater proprietor Campanaki was responsible in part for the refurbishment of the theater in 1904.

16 The first public screening reputedly took place in 1896. Although private sessions had already been organized at court, the first screening in a designated space was organized by Sigmund Weinberg (b. 1868) in association with Pathé Frères. Although some sources argue that this screening occurred in the Fransız Tiyatrosu (then called Varyete Tiyatrosu), Scognamillo (1990, 12–13) argues that the first screening took place the year before in the Glorya Sineması (then called Lüksemburg Apartmanları). However, the quality of screenings and the length of films shown in the Fransız Tiyatrosu were much better and more appreciated, respectively. For an interesting discussion of the relationship between the film industry and the recording industry in Istanbul at the time see Ünlü 2004, 83–94.

17 The information presented here draws on research already published in my recent monograph (see O'Connell 2013, 109–40). For 1930, I accessed this information through a systematic perusal of the following newspapers: *Akşam*, *Cumhuriyet*, *Milliyet*, and *Son Posta*.

18 *Yeni Sabah*, 10 January 1964.

19 See O'Connell 2013, 147–153, for a fuller evaluation of music reviews written after the first concert by Hakkı Süha Gezgin (1895–1963) in *Vakit* (25 February 1930), by Peyami Safa (1899–1961) in *Cumhuriyet* (24 February 1930), and by Ahmed Vālā Nurettin (1901–1967) in *Milliyet* (24 February 1930).

20 See O'Connell (2000) for a fuller discussion of a national style of Turkish music. In this article, I note three distinctive styles representative of three different positions: *alafranga*, *alaturka*, and folk music. For Safa, the performance of *alaturka*

using Western vocal techniques in a concert setting was consistent with his conception of a national style that was Western and modern. For Nurettin Bey, the polyphonic arrangement of folk music conformed to his notion of a national style that was Western and modern. In this sense, Nurettin Bey was invoking an established trend in Europe that envisaged the development of national musics during the nineteenth century. Accordingly, his perspective can be considered to be occidentalist.

21 During the 1920s, "chic" (Turkish, *şık*) was used widely to signify the fashionable, whether it related to sartorial sense or a desirable venue. Selçuk also used the word to describe a new style of vocal improvisation (*gazel*). According to his daughter, Meral Selçuk (b. 1930), he would say with reference to his own performance of a vocal improvisation "*şık bir gazel oldu*" (English, "that was a chic *gazel*") (interview with Meral Selçuk March 1994). For a fuller discussion of Turkish chic, see O'Connell (2013, 36–41).

22 See O'Connell 2013, 150.

23 See ibid., 21–50, for an in-depth discussion of disparaging terminology employed to denigrate vocal exponents of *alaturka*.

24 The receipts for the first concert were obtained from the personal archive of Selçuk. My sincerest thanks to Meral Selçuk for allowing me to review these and other primary sources related to the life and work of the artist.

25 The Turkish currency (called Türk Lirası [TL] where 1 TL = 100 Kuruş [Kr]) underwent a massive devaluation after 1929. The precise exchange rate is hard to calculate accurately, especially for the period after sterling left the gold standard (in 1931). At the time of the first concert, £1=TL 10.50, it represented a huge devaluation from the relevant rate in 1929 when £1=TL 1.15. For comparative purposes, the sterling-dollar exchange rate was £1=$5.00. Interestingly, Selçuk was paid in pounds sterling by Sahibinin Sesi until 1931. For a fuller explanation of the contemporary economic and political issues surrounding this devaluation see O'Connell 2013, 213–214.

26 See for example the reminiscence of the concert by Orhan Nasuhioğlu cited in Kulin 1996, 11. When I interviewed Nasuhioğlu (February 1994), he mentioned that the concert hall was completely full. In his words, the venue was "*tıklım tıklım doluydu.*"

27 See O'Connell 2013, 126–133.

28 See ibid., 132.

29 This amount is consistent with the relevant earnings for concert performances quoted by Selçuk and cited in Saait 1933.

30 See O'Connell 2013, 139.

31 See Sahibinin Sesi 1930.

32 Selçuk was the principal artist for Sahibinin Sesi. Not only was he featured as such in the relevant catalogues (see Sahibinin Sesi 1928, 1929, 1930, and 1934), he

was also sponsored by the company, his trip to Paris (1928) and his first concert (1930) being supported by the company. Further, Sahibinin Sesi advertised Selçuk's recordings on a special artistic label (the FE series). They also featured the artist on a special 12" disc (the FF series). See O'Connell 2013, 247–259 for a complete discography of Selçuk's recordings with Sahibinin Sesi.

33 See O'Connell 2013, 213.

34 See Gronow 1981 and Dinç et al. 2000.

35 Ünlü 2004, 254.

36 See Uluç 2010.

37 In his review Safa noted diplomatically: "In previous concerts his voice had been a little unnatural (*gayri tabii*) and somewhat forced (*cebri*)." In this concert, he confirmed that: "his voice was both natural and in keeping with the original character of our music." Concerning Selçuk's vocal style, he observed: "his voice was more dominating (*fazla hakim*) than before. He was able to conceal more easily the effort that was expended (in vocal production)." (*Son Posta*, 21 December 1931).

38 In the same review, Safa noted that some concertgoers had to be turned away because the concert venue was full (*Son Posta*, 21 December 1931).

39 See O'Connell 2013, 160–167.

40 See ibid., 213.

41 See O'Connell 2013 for an in-depth explanation of this transformation. Generally speaking, Jean Lehmann's aspiration toward a French version of classicism in musical performance was not successful for two reasons. First, the recitals by French artists were not well attended. Second, the Fransız Tiyatrosu no longer received public funding to support its concert activities. Although Lehmann also actively promoted Turkish performers after the first concert by Selçuk, his financial position became untenable. Following his death in 1933, the Fransız Tiyatrosu was amalgamated with the City Theatre (Darülbedayi). Upon restoration (1989), it is now called the "Ses Tiyatrosu," today being home to a traditional style of Turkish theatre (called *orta oyunu*).

42 See O'Connell 2013, 213. Following the financial crash on Wall Street in 1929, there was a major decline in record sales worldwide (see Gronow 1981). Although Selçuk never managed to achieve the sales figures that he acquired for his first recordings (1928–1929), he managed to sell ca. 7,000 discs per annum (1933–1936). All calculations are based on record contracts and record receipts found in Selçuk's personal archive.

CHAPTER FOUR

Articulating Otherness in the Construction of Alevi-Bektaşi Rituals and Ritual Space in a Transnational Perspective

IRENE MARKOFF

I begin by posing a number of questions. Do Muslim rituals require a "formally consecrated or architecturally specific space"?[1] Or is the engagement with the audition of sacred words in poetry and prose of more importance, particularly when the element of music is included as performed by music specialists who can be viewed as "embodiments" of ritual expressions of piety?[2] Are there cases when Muslims feel compelled to name and orient space through religious practice in order to challenge "dominant categories of [a] larger culture" in local or diasporic contexts and thus become empowered?[3]

These questions can certainly be applied to a discussion of Alevi-Bektaşi[4] devotional practices that can be defined by their "portability" and the "neutrality" of the space in which they are found.[5] This harkens back to the past when Alevi religious rituals were (and still are) held in private homes in rural areas without conspicuous exterior architectural markers[6] and in clandestine fashion in order to circumvent repercussions from the Sunni-oriented Ottoman state. Today such rituals, known collectively as *ayin-i cem* or, in short, *cem*, are also held in urban contexts in newly constructed structures that function both as cultural centers and as places of religious ritual (*cemevi*) but, again, are often devoid of recognizable exterior architectural markers.[7] It is these urban structures that the Turkish state persists in defining as cultural institutions where folkloric performances take place, rather than true Islamic worship spaces (*ibadet*), thus perpetuating the marginalization of the Alevi religious minority and denying it "recognition as a distinct community."[8]

Drawing from textual sources and extensive ethnographic research conducted in Turkey, Bulgaria (the eastern Rhodope Mountains and the northeastern Deli Orman regions), and Canada, this chapter sheds light on the persistence, through reconfiguration and revitalization, of Turkish Alevi-Bektaşi- and, to a lesser extent, Bulgarian Bektaşi-Baba'i-oriented spirituality, identity, sacred assemblies, and ritual spaces in a changing sociopolitical climate and through increasing ties to a transnational Alevi-Bektaşi network.[9] More important, it utilizes aspects of a multidisciplinary spatial methodology to analyze the poetics and politics of sacred space[10] and seeks to decode the dynamics of hierarchical situatedness and symbolic performative gestures of ritual participants within such spaces.[11] Here, an essential role is played by poetic-musical expression featuring the long-necked plucked lute known as *bağlama* or *saz* (referred to as the "stringed Qur'an," or *telli Kuran*).[12] It is this instrument that accompanies the sacred movement (*semah*) and mystical sung poetry (both devotional songs, called "*nefesler*" primarily by Turkish Bektaşis and related communities in Bulgaria, and *deyişler*, the sung poetry of Alevi bards) that recalls, reinforces, and helps imagine and dramatize knowledge of religious lineage and primary saints and poets. The poetry also elucidates symbolic nuances of esoteric teachings and theological motifs that reference the belief system of the Bektaşi order of dervishes and reaffirm the values and ethics of the closely related Kızılbaş-Alevi (Turkmen and Kurdish) and Tahtacı communities of Anatolia; Bektaşis in European Thrace; and Baba'is, Kızılbaş, and Bektaşis in the eastern Balkans.

Alevis

Alevis can best be defined as formerly rural-based, nonorthodox, endogamous, and latitudinarian socioreligious communities in Turkey and the Balkans, historically referred to as Kızılbaş, that in the twentieth century began to share in a common transregional identity referred to as Alevism.[13] Considered from a Sunni perspective to be heterodox in their practices, the Alevis draw their worldview from Shi'i Twelver Islam, Sufism (deriving from a close association with the Bektaşi order of dervishes), and pre-Islamic traditions tracing back to Central Asian shamanistic practices and beliefs. Special reverence is paid to the family of the prophet (*ehl-i beyt*) and by extension to the imams of Twelver Shiʿi Islam (*on iki imamlar*) expressed through the practice of *tevella* ("being friends" of Imam ʿAli) and its counterpart *teberra* ("being enemies" of the enemies of ʿAli). Alevis also respect the Qurʾan, the Prophet Muhammad, and his teachings, and firmly embedded in their consciousness is the trinity of Allah, Muhammad, and ʿAli, considered to be the "key" (*anahtar*) to communal worship. The formula *Hak Muhammad ʿAli ulu Hünkār ʿAllah* (Muhammad, Ali, and the *hünkār*, a term frequently used for Hacı Bektaş, the thirteenth-century spiritual founder of the Bektaşi order and patron saint of the Kızılbaş-Alevi) further elucidates religious authority in Alevi-Bektaşi beliefs. Alevis differ from Bektaşis in that membership in the community is a guaranteed birthright. Membership in the Bektaşi order of dervishes, on the other hand, is open to any individual in society who chooses to commit to a variety of obligations and ritual activities determined by the degree of one's involvement in the order and the supervision of a *murşid* (religious guide) who prepares a committed individual for "initiation" (*nasip*) into the order. Alevi communities fall into the jurisdiction of a *dede* (also known as *murşid, pir*), who descends from a holy lineage or caste (*ocakzade, dede soyundan*). This hereditary religious guide not only leads formal (*ayin-i cem*) and informal (*muhabbet/muhabbet cemi*) ritual gatherings but also functions as a "director of conscience," or mediator and judge, in cases of conflicts and immoral behavior that are brought forward and confessed to the entire community and resolved, sometimes with the penalty of excommunication or "shunning," in the Christian sense (*düşkünlük*), during the most important annual rite known as *görgü cemi*.[14] Such rituals are restricted to formally initiated members (*ikrar verenler*; literally, "those who have affirmed the beliefs" during the initiation ceremony) following the ritual establishment of spiritual kinship between two married couples (*musahiplik*) who pledge lifelong support to one another in a bond that is sometimes stronger than that between blood relatives.

Alevism and Bektaşism share common origins, such as an affiliation with the same saintly "lineage" (*silsile*), a similar repertoire of mystical poetry, and a belief system that incorporates underlying features deriving from Babaʾism and Hurufism and favors gender equality, openness to other religious belief systems, and humanitarianism. Morality and rules for *edep/erkān* (ethical behavior and principal attributes of the faith) also figure prominently for Bektaşis and Alevis and are embodied in the simple phrase *Eline, Diline,*

Beline, Sahip Ol (literally, "Pay heed to your hands, tongue, and body"; that is, "Do not steal, do not lie, and do not engage in adultery or immoral sexual behavior").

The following expanded discussion of the origins of Alevi expressive culture, music, and sung poetry will contribute to a deeper understanding of how Alevi heritage is recalled, reinforced, and imagined in sacred space through the expertise and informed contribution of the primary ritual specialists, the *dede* and *zakir* (ritual music specialist) and through the structure, dynamics, and aesthetics of rituals. It will serve to formulate a context for the main analysis that will consist of two main examples drawn from ethnographic data collected from 2004 to 2013.[15]

In Search of Origins: Shamans, Mystics, Minstrels, and Lutes

Strong evidence traces the origins of Alevi-Bektaşi expressive culture to the shamanism of Oğuz and Turkmen tribal culture, the music and poetry of Central Asian minstrels and their folk lutes, and the mystical orientation of folk Islam with its "popular preachers."[16] Links with shamanism include the close proximity of women with men in rituals with music and dance, the imbibing of intoxicating drinks (*dem, bade*), and the "sacrifice" of animals (*kurban*).[17] Another parallel involves the "otherworldly" trance journeys bridging life and death during the initiation process of shamans[18] that recall similar rites of passage experienced by uninitiated Alevi-Bektaşis who, led by a spiritual guide, symbolically "die before dying" (*ölmeden önce ölmek*) and are then reborn as they follow the Sufi "path" (*yol*) that will take them through "four gateways" (*dört kapı*) beginning with the divine law of literal Islam (*şeriat*) and culminating with the immediate experience of God (*hakikat*).[19]

Some scholars suggest that hereditary shamans seamlessly morphed into hereditary holy men (*dedeler*, sing. *dede*) through the influence of wandering dervishes and their propensity toward rituals involving music, movement,[20] and states of altered consciousness.[21] One can now see a tripartite connection that links shamans, minstrels, and *dedes*, and it is interesting to note that many Alevi *dedes* and *zakirs* have also been or are minstrels (*aşıks, ozans*)[22] who contribute to the essentials of Alevism (*Alevilik*), namely, *saz, söz ve muhabbet*,[23] meaning "lute, poetry, and conversation" with an intimate circle of kindred spirits.[24]

Lutes

For the Alevis, the *bağlama*, or *saz*, is a powerful symbol of group identity and creed. It is an anthropomorphic symbol of Imam ʿAli and the tenets of the faith: the resonator is said to represent his body; the neck, his sword *zülfikār*; the twelve frets of the past, the twelve imams of Shiʿa Islam; and the lower course of strings, the prophet Muhammad.[25] The typical Alevi tuning A–D–E (*aşık* and Alevi *düzeni* or Veysel *düzeni*; *bağlama düzeni*) from high to low pitch facilitates the creation of a polyphonic texture featuring movement in parallel fourths and fifths, a distinctive feature of Turkmen and other Central Asian plucked lute performance practice.[26] Shared heritage is clearly discernible when comparing the tunings, playing techniques, and stereotyped motifs typical of Turkish plucked lutes, such as the *çöğür*, *ırızva*, or *ruzba*, with the two-stringed *dutar* of Turkmen and Kurdish minstrels (*bakhshi* or *baxši*) from Turkmenistan and Iranian Khurasan, Karakalpak bards in northern Uzbekistan, and Kurdish Ahl-e Haqq *tanbur*[27] players in Iran and Iraq.[28] Characteristic of these traditions is the open-handed, fingertip (*parmakla*) strumming and plucking of the lutes referred to as *şelpe* and *pençe* by Alevis and other regional performers.[29]

In his poetry, the fifteenth-century Bektaşi mystic Kaygusuz Abdal refers to a two-stringed plucked lute (*iki telli saz*) but also to the *kopuz*, accorded widespread status as the ancestor of the *saz/bağlama* in Turkey.[30] A case in point is the "minstrel's lute" (*kopuz-i ozan*) documented by the fourteenth-century Muslim scholar Abdükadir Maraghi. Traces of this bowl lute with two strings tuned in unison, an interval of a fourth away from the single remaining string,[31] are found in Anatolia today with the *ırızva* or *ruzba*, which is tuned in the same way and utilized by Alevi minstrels such as the twentieth-century Alevi *aşık* Nesimi Çimen (d. 1993).

Alevi-Bektaşi Sacred Poetry

Alevi-Bektaşi poetry traces back to fourteenth-century dervish literature and its themes of dervish life, mystical experience, spiritual intoxication (*mest*, *vecd*), and reverence for Bektaşi saints and early Bektaşi dervish collectives known for their ascetic and antinomian ways. [32] These collectives renounced many aspects of mainstream society and its customs and evinced tremendous love for Imam ʿAli. In a poem (*Beylerimiz elvan gülün üstüne*) that is still sung by Bektaşi in Bulgaria's eastern Rhodope Mountains, the fourteenth- or fifteenth-century mystic Kaygusuz Abdal pays homage to his spiritual guide, Abdal Musa, an important Bektaşi saint whose *türbe* (tomb, shrine) is found in Elmalı, a village close to Antalya in southern Anatolia. The poet refers to the Urum Abdalları or Abdalan-i Rum, the itinerant "deviant" dervishes[33] who wore the sheepskins used during Bektaşi rituals on their backs (*postun eğnine*). He also mentions the *erler* (wise ones), the *nurlar* (those who have seen the light of Imam ʿAli), and the sick (*hastaları*) who make pilgrimages to Abdal Musa's tomb in search of cures. He presents images of ritual ceremonies where the true ones or faithful (*gerçekler*) stand in the *dar* position (*dara durmuş*)—the position that is symbolic of martyrdom and Mansur al-Hallaj[34]—in the center of the ceremonial hall (*meydanında*) in which Bektaşi ritual ceremonies take place and where the "candles of mystical truth" are lit (*Hak cerağın yakarlar*), ritual prayers (*gülbang*) are recited, and the mysteries (*sır*) of the order are revered and protected.[35] In another poem, the poet defends the idiosyncrasies of heterodox groups by asking if he is at fault for "playing the *tanbura* lute" (*ben çalarım tanbura*), and "shaving his beard" (*bu sakalı kırkarım*) in the spirit of Abdalan-i Rum and Kalenderi dervishes.[36]

The epicurean spirit in which this and other esoteric poetry was conceived alludes to the nonconformist tendencies of the Malamatiyya[37] and appears to exhibit outright mockery of orthodox Sunni doctrines, yet succeeds in concealing the secrets of the order.[38]

Proto-Shiʿism, Shah Ismaʿil Safevi, and the Kızılbaş Connection

Strong Shiʿi messages are found in the ecstatic poetry of the charismatic Shah Ismaʿil Safevi (d. 1524 CE), who wrote under the pen name Hatayi, conveying what the Ottoman Sunnis considered to be heterodox concepts such as the manifestation of God in human form (*tecelli*; Arabic, *tajalli*) and metempsychosis (*tenasüh*; Arabic, *tanāsukh*).[39] It has been established that the shah's verses expound portions of both Shaykh Safi's and, later, Imam Jaʿfar's versions of the Alevi holy book known as *Buyruk*, together with the principles of the religious doctrine (*erkan*).[40] It is not surprising that hymns in honor of the twelve Shiʿi imams (*düvazdeh imamlar, düvazlar*) sung during Alevi *cemler* are generally those of Hatayi.

In one of Hatayi's poems, he reminds his Kızılbaş supporters that the true path is that of Muhammad and ʿAli (*Yol Mohammed Ali'nindir*), who are not only sources for exoteric and esoteric knowledge but also defenders of the faith (*Seyf Muhammet Ali'nindir*). A warning follows that strictly forbids fraternizing with Yezid (*Varma Yezidin yanına*), cursing him (*Lanet Yezidin huyuna*), as he will be waiting with an executioner's sword (*Satır Yezit ensesine*).[41] The name *Yezid* refers specifically to the Umayyad Caliph Yazid, who was responsible for the death of Imam ʿAli's son Hussein at Karbala in 680 CE, but also to the Ottoman Sultan Selim (d. 1520 CE), who retaliated against Ismaʿil's attempts to gather converts among the Turkmen population in Anatolia.

Ethnographic Case Studies

The analysis will now proceed to two ethnographic accounts of Alevi-Bektaşi *cems* that will serve to elucidate how poetic-musical and sacred dance forms, binding forces in the collective consciousness of Alevis, contribute to the sacralization of space. I take up two main cases: first, an urban Turkish context where the "reinstitutionalization"[42] of Alevism has resulted in the reconfiguration of ritual practices; second, a rural Bulgarian context where more grassroots rituals reflect a bonding with Turkish Alevism-Bektaşism. I also decode the polysemics and politics of *cemevi* design and ritual performativity, the proxemics of hierarchical situatedness inherent in the *cem*'s spatial organization, and the portability of ritual objects, ritual elements, and ritual specialists that transcend space in the rural-urban, national-transnational "transfer of ritual."[43]

Case Study 1: Istanbul, Turkey

Sacred Space and Ritual Actors Upon entering the large, empty congregational hall (*cem meydanı*; *cem salonu*) for Alevi-Bektaşi devotional rituals (*cemler*) on the top floor of the Kağıthane Hacı Bektaş Cultural and Educational Center (also known as the Nurtepe Cemevi; fig. 4.1) in Istanbul on a summer day in 2013, I was struck by the opulence and sheer size of the mostly carpeted square space and its lack of architectural resemblance to other Alevi-Bektaşi ritual halls in Istanbul, including those with domes (the restored Şahkulu Sultan dervish lodge and shrine complex, the Bağcılar Cemevi, the

Figure 4.1. Interior of the Nurtepe Cemevi congregational hall, Istanbul. Photograph by I. Markoff.

Yeni Bosna Cemevi, and the Kartal Cemevi, for example) and those without domes. Instead, a prominent octagonal, framed steel structure (*kubbe*, the Turkish word for "dome") with internal wedges constituted the roofing for a major portion of the room. This structure was supported by four pillars and marked by a cosmically oriented, highly illuminated oculus-like center, encircled by a smaller octagonal frame.[44] Projecting from the smaller octagon was a sparkling chandelier that towered above the central *dar meydanı*, or *dar-ı Mansur* (symbolic of the gallows of Mansur al-Hallaj), a circular wooden space with twelve triangular segments that is utilized for *semah* (ritual dance) performance, the ritual appearances of the twelve services, and the formal initiation of Alevis into the sect. Omnipresent were the usual prominent visual markers, such as images of Imam ʿAli, the twelve imams of Shiʿi Islam, and Hacı Bektaş, and a portrait of Mustafa Kemal Atatürk, the founder of the secular Republic of Turkey, all reinforcing Alevi-Bektaşi beliefs and identity through the direct experience of art.[45] A huge mural of the twelve imams was positioned on the wall directly above the *post*, the area designated for the primary ritual specialists: the *dede*, who conducts the liturgy with a variety of ritual prayers (*gülbang*, recitations from the Qurʾan and commentary); the *rehber*, who assists the *dede*; and the *zakir*, who sings *nefesler* and *deyişler* throughout the service, accompanying himself on the *bağlama*. This repertoire forms the backbone of *cem* rituals, as two *dedes* I interviewed affirmed that a *cem* is not possible without the sacred and illuminating "words" (*kelām*) of the *dede* or the *zakir*'s repertoire, both of which express Alevi identity and cosmology, thus serving as an educational tool (*ciddi bir eğitim araçtır*).[46] The Nurtepe *dede* I interviewed explained that it is the affect associated with the acoustic phenomenon of music coupled with the informed and "proper" emotionally charged expressivity of the expert *zakir* that serves as a "channel" (*vasıta*) or intermediary transporting the listener into an exhilarating state of consciousness that opens the door to "submitting" (*teslim*) to the true path of spiritual ecstasy (*hal, vecd*) and union with God.[47] From his perspective, music is the inner dimension of *muhabbet*, which allows you to "eat the meal of spirituality."[48] The *dede* also noted that the structure of the *cem* allows for a gradual buildup to the experience of *vecd* through utterances and music that become more and more animated in character, triggering the increased intensity of body posturing and culminating in sacred dance (*semah*).

Ritual: Introduction Before the ritual began, I positioned myself, camera in hand, on a bench for the elderly close to the entrance of the *cem salonu* for the weekly Thursday evening *cem*. The room soon came alive with attendees from the local Alevi community and several guests. Although in village *cems* gender separation is not always typical, in this case a more "orthodox" approach was evident. Following entry through doors separate from men, women without elite ritual status (not one of the twelve services) were seated to the right of the officiating *dede*, the *zakir*, another *dede*, and the *rehber*. These ritual specialists sat at the far end of the room beneath the mural of the twelve imams and on a slightly elevated platform with small lecterns for reading texts in front of them. Men without elite ritual status sat to the left of these officiants. Directly in front of the officiants were three electric candles (replacing the real candles used in the past), symbolizing the trinity of Allah, the Prophet Muhammad, and the Imam ʿAli; microphones were present for the projection of sound in the room that can hold approximately three hundred people. Gender integration was observed in the area for those performing the elite ritual function of the "twelve services" (*oniki hizmetler*)[49] and *semah* "turners," who sat at the perimeter of the circular *meydan* area facing the *dedes*, *rehber*, and *zakir*, an area that is traditionally designated for initiated *musahip*-paired sect members.

As my *dede* informants explained, the noticeable separation of the sexes is a strategy instituted to alleviate potential discomfort that might arise from holding hands with or embracing strangers during parts of the service. On the other hand, this urban-based approach may be related to the anxiety of promoting an image of "the moral and credible 'other' in the eyes of Sunnis."[50]

As a longstanding observer and researcher of such ceremonies in Turkey and the Canadian and Bulgarian diasporas, I soon understood that this particular weekly *cem* was a hybrid, shortened, reformulated, highly scripted, and standardized version of aspects of regional *cems* including the annual *görgü cemi* (rite of purification and integration), but without the initiation segment (*nasip alma*) or the full-fledged ceremony of interrogation (*sorgu*), where disputes are settled and penalties, including excommunication (*düşkünlük*), are issued.[51] The *dede* who presided over the Nurtepe *cem* referred to a printed text, and the musical repertoire chosen was the same as that found in most urban *cemevis* and in some cases associated with popular Alevi artists such as Arif Sağ (b. 1945),[52] *aşık* Daimi (d. 1983), and others. This repertoire is more familiar to the general congregation than the numerous regional varieties of *deyişler* that have not garnered the attention of state media and the recording industry. The *cem* segments were sometimes highly dramatized, as was the case with the running entrances of the twelve services (*on iki hizmet*) along two visibly marked and lengthy, carpeted walkways leading to the central *meydan* and *dar* area below the chandelier and octagonal *kubbe*, where they took their places for ritual bowing (*niyaz*) and prostration (*secde*), and prayers. Although the roles of the twelve services are traditionally restricted to initiated sect members, in the urban setting accommodation is at the forefront, as this duty is also delegated to uninitiated youth as a mechanism for recruitment and commitment through elevated status in the *cem* hierarchy.

Ritual Proper The *cem* proper began with a sermon of sorts given by the *dede*, who briefly synthesized the Alevi belief system but also asked the congregation to ensure that they had arrived in a state of physical and spiritual purity before giving their communal consent (*rıza*) for the ritual to begin. As the *dede* recited a poem, the *zakir* spontaneously improvised on phrases from the Dance of the Cranes, somehow diverting everyone's attention from the power of the lyrics. After those attending were asked to embrace and lightly kiss the cheeks of whomever they were seated beside, each of the twelve services were invited to come forward through specific verses of the twelve services (with poetry by Hatayi) performed by the *zakir*. They later came forward again to execute movements symbolic of their special function in the devotional assembly, with recited formulas (*tercüman*) and prayers interspersed with the dede's *gülbanks*. The segments that followed focused on specific genres of *deyişler*, beginning with those invoking the twelve imams (*düvazlar*) with poetry by Hatayi, Kul Himmet and Virdi Derviş, followed by two examples of the *illallah*, or *tevhid* (statement of monotheism), genre (with poetry by Derviş Ali and Hatayi), suggestive of *zikr*, where everyone joined in singing the refrain, including the phrase *La Illāhe Illallāh*, while striking their thighs in kneeling position to the rhythm of the music.[53] The prayers associated with this genre involved the full prostration (*secde*) of devotees.

The next segment involved the cantillation of the *miraçlama* (poetry by Hatayi), the Alevi version of the miraculous night journey and ascent (*m'irāj*) of the prophet Muhammad when he met with forty saints (*kırklar meclisi*) and recognized the superiority of ʿAli; everyone present became inebriated from the juice of a single grape and rose in imitation of the Prophet to dance the *semah*.[54]

The *semah* movement began as the *miraçlama* concluded, with the *zakir* accompanying young members of the cultural center's *semah* group performing two (one partial and one complete) highly choreographed versions of regional sacred dances. They were dressed modestly, but with only a hint of the designed costumes emblematic of the Alevi cultural revival of the late 1980s and 1990s, which are far removed from the ordinary clothing typical of more traditional ceremonies but standard practice for "folklorized" *semah* performances that occur at festivals outside of the ritual context. In this case, the *semahcılar* (*semah* performers) had tied green strips of cloth (*kemerbest*), symbolic of the prophet's family (*ehl-i beyt*), to their waists [55] and executed their movements with bare feet.[56] Moving in circle formation, they began with slow movements during the *ağırlama* section and increased the complexity of the figures as the music quickened in tempo in the *yeldirme* section. The emotional intensity permeated the room and generated swaying movements from the onlookers, normative practice at *cems*. The last element in the ceremony involved the performance of a lament (*mersiye*) for the martyrdom of Imam Hussein at Karbala; collected by Arif Sağ in his native Aşkale (Erzurum province),"Bugün Matem Günü Geldi, Ah Hüseyin, Vah Hüseyin" ("Today is the day of mourning, O Hussein, dear Hussein"), it generally stimulates weeping through the accounts and imaginings of the tragedy at Karbala and the fate of Imam ʿAli's family but also for the persecution of Alevis at the hands of the Ottomans, Sunnis, and at times the Turkish state.[57] Joining hands and swaying from side to side, everyone sang together in poignant, collective remembrance. Though not a part of long-standing tradition, this physical act of solidarity harkened back to the intimacy of closed village rituals; from my perspective, the physical sense and perception of space diminished, creating a unity of being and community through the power of poetry and the lyricism and rhythmic intensity of the music. The *cem* ended with prayers, the distribution of fruit (*lokma*, meaning shared food during a *cem*), and a heartfelt request for everyone to attend the weekly liturgy.

This contemporary account of an urban Alevi *cem* illustrates how the hierarchical groupings and ritual actions of Alevi confessional groups lend both "design"[58] and an aura of sacredness to a simple architectural space; they accomplish this through the performance of liturgy where they invoke and experience sacred presence through kinesthetic modes of attention and response involving prescribed utterances, symbolic gestures (*niyaz*), and interactions that build in emotional and sensory intensity through the medium of music and poetry.[59] The devotional meeting also reveals that despite their increased visibility during the period of revitalization (late 1980s and 1990s), marked by empowerment through the establishment of a solid network of well-endowed and well-connected local and transnational organizations, federations, and foundations, Alevis in Turkey experience marginalization in a hostile political and increasingly orthodox Sunni sociocultural milieu; this milieu continues to misunderstand Alevi beliefs and practices and denies their religiosity as Islamic. As a result, Alevis have become even more motivated to find strategies that will serve to grant them official acceptance as a religious rather than a cultural group. This may also be one way of explaining not only the canonization of ritual texts, the standardization of religious rituals and sacred ritual repertoire, and the predictable choreography and positioning of certain *cem* segments but also a modicum of orthodox nuances characterized by gender separation, the communal raising of voices, and the proliferation of the full ritual prostrations (*secde*) that occur within newly constructed spaces exuding an elevated sense of aesthetics and visibility.

Case Study 2: Antinomian, Nonorthodox Islamic Communities in Bulgaria

Alevi-related communities in Bulgaria are found primarily in the rural regions of Deliorman (Ludogorie) in northeastern Bulgaria and in the eastern

Rhodope Mountains of southern Bulgaria.[60] They are often labeled as Shiʿa but self-identify as Kızılbaş, Bektaşi (the Çelebi and Babağan branches), and Babaʾi (followers of Kalenderi dervishes, often referred to as Abdalan-i Rum, who were eventually integrated into the Bektaşi order of dervishes, as were the Kızılbaş). They are the descendants of Turkmen and Yörük tribes and Turkmen supporters of Shah Ismaʿil Safevi who were deported from Anatolia in the mid-fourteenth, fifteenth, and sixteenth centuries.[61] Sacred traditions thrive in these close-knit village communities with one or more religious leaders (*baba/boba*)[62] who guide and meet with their *talips* (disciples) in small groups of up to ten initiated married couples known as *gyol* in the eastern Rhodopes. Members of this religious minority share a common worldview, religious doctrine, devotional practice, and musical repertoire and make pilgrimages to shrines, particularly for annual festivals (known as *maaye* in the eastern Rhodopes and *anma töreni* in the Deliorman region) commemorating their beloved saints. These festivals include blood sacrifice (*kurban*), offerings to saints, outdoor festivities, *nefes* performance, auctions (*tırk*) to raise funds for shrine upkeep, and evening *cems*. The term *maaye,* no longer utilized in Turkey, is of particular interest, for a record from Ottoman imperial registers (1572 CE) describes the banning of "deviant" Abdal dervishes from a *mahyā* (religious festival) at the shrine of Seyyid Gazi, close to Eskişehir in western Turkey, because of their appearance and unorthodox practices, which included drumming in the mosque and tomb and playing long-necked lutes such as the *sheshtar* (six-string plucked lute) and *kopuz*.[63] Not only were the Abdals attached to this shrine, but they were also affiliated with two fifteenth-century antinomian Abdal saints: ŞücaʿeddinVeli, whose shrine complex is close to that of Seyyid Gazi, and Otman Baba, whose cult center is located close to Haskovo in the eastern Rhodopes and is a main center of visitation for Bulgarian nonorthodox communities.[64] Of relevance here is that since the 1990s, Bulgarian Babaʾis in particular have made pilgrimages to the Bektaşi shrine complex of Şücaʿeddin Veli, where many *babas* seek authority (*icazet*) from the current *postnişin* (chief *baba* of a *tekke*) and are invited to annual festivals (*anma törenler*) in honor of the saint on a regular basis. At such festivals, Turkish and Bulgarian *semah* groups participate in a communal *cem* and an outdoor concert.

Despite the socialist government's attempts to assimilate Turks by restricting Islamic religious practices and minority rights, during the so-called regeneration process of the mid-1980s,[65] Alevi-related groups in Bulgaria strengthened and further revitalized aspects of their heritage following the fall of communism in 1989. Official associations of Alevis were formed in Deliorman and the eastern Rhodopes in the 2000s, the major Elmalı Baba shrine complex in the south was rebuilt and transformed in 2011, and annual festivals at saints' tombs (*türbeler*) were publicly acknowledged as religious festivals rather than Turkish picnics. Young, uninitiated adults mobilized spiritually and intellectually by immersing themselves in religious doctrines and rites through the agency of frequent communal gatherings of an informal nature known as *muhabbet* or *moabet*, where they sing *nefesler*—referred to locally as "the Qur'an"—and learn to perform *semahs* to the accompaniment of the *saz* (lute) played by *zakirs*, otherwise known as *İmam Cafer* (Ja'far), in honor of the sixth imam of Shi'i Islam. A young, modern, Baba'i *dede* (age thirty-four) in the eastern Rhodopes, for example, organizes bimonthly Saturday evening *muhabbetler* for youth in his village during the winter months. In 2009 I was invited to an *ölüm muhabbet* (ritual gathering for the death of an individual in the community) in the same village, where I witnessed young people, still in the learning stages, performing *semah*. This occurred following a special service that was closed to outsiders.

The term *cem* or *ayin* is used for more formal types of prayer meetings reserved for initiated individuals, such as the *musahip ayini*, the *ikrar verme ayini*, the *ayin-i cem*, and the *görgü cemi*, also referred to as *tarikten geçmek cemi*. The most treasured ceremony is the *kırklar cemi* modeled after the "Assembly of the Forty" (*kırklar meclisi*), held on Nevruz (Persian New Year), on 21 March, which Alevis and Bektaşis consider to be Imam 'Ali's birthday. The *nefesler* and *semah* musical genres in rituals are similar in function and content to the *deyişler* found in Turkey, but there are differences in the terminology and the tune families utilized. Although these gatherings and rituals are still held in private homes (*muhabbet evi, cem evi*), generally those of the religious leaders, they are also held in newly built prayer houses (*dergah evi; cemevi*) of sorts situated close to a number of saints' shrines where, in some cases, dervish lodges also once stood. This was the context for the *kurban adağı muhabbet* (animal sacrifice as a votive offering ritual) that I requested and financed in August 2012 as a token of respect for the Baba'i residents from the mixed Sunni, Baba'i, and Bektaşi village of Sevar (Caferler in Turkish), located in the Razgrad province of northeastern Bulgaria.

The ritual activities began with a visitation to the tomb of a Bektaşi saint, Deniz Ali Baba, in the village of Denizli (Varnentsi in Bulgarian), Silistra

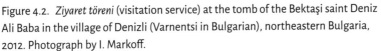

Figure 4.2. *Ziyaret töreni* (visitation service) at the tomb of the Bektaşi saint Deniz Ali Baba in the village of Denizli (Varnentsi in Bulgarian), northeastern Bulgaria, 2012. Photograph by I. Markoff.

province, coordinated by Sevar's female mayor and the president of the Razgrad Cem Association (*dernek*); the activities involved approximately thirty people, including Baba'i *babas* and a *zakir*. Various ritual gestures (*niyaz*) were required for entry into the sacred realm of the simple, rectangular tomb structure, with its framed portraits and calligraphy, and continued inside. These gestures included touching the top of the open door frame, kissing two fingers, and then kissing and touching one's head to the right and left sides of the door frame, followed by touching fingers to the threshold (*eşik*). Similar gestures were observed as everyone paid their respects to the three individual sarcophagi.

We then sat on the carpeted floor for a brief visitation service (*ziyaret töreni*; fig 4.2) that included the lighting of three candles, the recitation of prayers, the unaccompanied communal singing of a *nefes* for the saint Deniz Ali Baba, and a special blessing (*vakitlerin hayırına dua*) for the occasion.[66] As a group of women prepared food for the ritual meal (*lokma*) outdoors, our small group then made our way to the nearby *cemevi*, another simple rect-

Figure 4.3. Interior of the *cemevi* situated next to the tomb of Deniz Ali Baba in the village of Denizli (Varnentsi in Bulgarian), northeastern Bulgaria, 2012. Photograph by I. Markoff.

angular structure with cushions and small stools surrounding the periphery of two sides of the room, its walls adorned with framed images of the twelve imams, plus Hacı Bektaş Veli, Kemal Atatürk, and Şücaʿeddin Veli (see fig. 4.3).

Those attending the *muhabbet* were between the ages of fifty and seventy-five and had participated in such rituals together for many years. The women sat to the right and the men to the left of the *baba*, who, together with two *kafadar* (the term in Deliorman for *musahips*) couples and several prominent sect members, was positioned at the far end of the space. There was no sign of printed materials for the *baba* or *zakir* to refer to, and the ceremony progressed with dignity, reverence, rapt attention, and restrained yet relaxed exultation. The presence of alcohol (*dem*) was something I had experienced in *muhabbets* in the eastern Rhodopes, but in this case, the two *kafadar* (ritually initiated) women, dressed in identical village clothing, poured and then passed small metal goblets of alcohol placed on a tray to everyone at various stages throughout, but initially following the *zakir*'s performance of the "three" (*üçler*) *nefes* sung in honor of Allah, Muhammad, and Ali.[67]

Sung first at all *cems* in Deliorman, this *nefes* is valued as the "key" (*anahtar*) to all rituals, according to a prominent Halife Baba from the region who received his *icazet* from the *postnişin* of the Şücaʿeddin Veli Baba *tekke* in Turkey. In the cycle of formal *cems* performed from late fall until May, this *nefes* is generally followed by others for "the five" (*beşler*, i.e., the family of the Prophet: Muhammad, ʿAli, Fatima, Hasan, and Hussein); "the seven" (*yediler*, i.e., the family of the Prophet plus Hatice-i Kubra and Salman-i Pak); the twelve Shiʿi Imams; and "the forty" (*kırklar*), referring to the *mʿiraj* and the Gathering of the Forty Saints.[68] On this occasion, the *üçler nefesi* was followed by a *kurban* (ritual slaughter) *nefesi*, a *semah nefesi* without dancers "turning *semah*" (*semah dönmek*), and a *nefes* sung in my honor as the guest (*mihman*) who had come from afar to honor the saint and the community. Although the goblets were distributed at least twelve times, the amount of alcohol was insufficient to cause a high level of inebriation, but the devotional resonance that filtered through the space and the ritual gestures of intimacy (embraces, kisses on the cheeks, touching one's neighbors with the fingertips) contributed to the aura and aesthetic of *birlik* ("unity," "oneness," "togetherness") that is the ultimate goal of Alevilik, Bektaşilik, and Baba'ilik.

Conclusion

This chapter serves to illustrate that despite the ever-changing and complex orientations within Alevism-Bektaşism in its broadest, transnational and rural/urban sense, the essence of the belief system is still encapsulated in the *cem* ceremony through a constellation of symbolic, hierarchical relationships that are dramatized in a "habitus" of "collective effervescence"[69] within a seemingly neutral space that functions as a sanctuary from the outside world. Within this sanctuary, the confessional group is transported into sect heritage through the knowledge and ritual duties of the *dede* or *baba*, the ritual assistants (*on iki hizmetler*), the *semah* turners, and the *zakir*. All these components are indispensable elements in the sacralization and aestheticization of space, the renewal and review of religiosity, and the inspiration for spiritual solidarity and cultural identity. But it is the expressive culture of the *zakir* that dominates as an agent that continues to shape, bind, and contribute to an Alevi-Bektaşi collective consciousness, or what might be termed *communitas*.[70] This form of *communitas* persists within the social intimacy of village rituals held in modest structures in the Bulgarian context. It is also present in the Turkish urban context, where new, visible urban spaces serve to accommodate the emergence of an "urban stranger sociability"[71] and the exigencies of the urban ethnoscape that have led to "rationalization and scripturalization," standardization, and in some respects Sunni-ization of the new, demystified Alevism that some fear will lead to the assimilation of Alevis into mainstream Sunni Islam.[72]

NOTES

I would like to thank the many individuals in Turkey, Bulgaria, and Canada who were invaluable in guiding me in my research and also in assisting me with my fieldwork activities. Endless appreciation to Stefan Balashchev and Rumiana Andreeva, Veysel Bayram, Muharem Aliosman, Kamber Kamber, Yıldız Salif, Cafer and Cevriye Cefer, Orhan Has, Galip Sadık *dede*, Kemal Esef Cafer, Emine Hüseynova Cafer, Halil Ibrahim Koz *baba* and *anabacı* Necmiye Halil Koz, and Nesibe Kedikova in Bulgaria; Mehmet Ersal, Songül Karahasanoğlu, Süleyman Şenel, Yusuf Başaran *dede*, Zeynel Şahan *dede*, Mehmet Demirtaş *dede*, Niyazi Parlar, Ozan Akbay, and Güneş Çetinkaya Şerik in Turkey; and members of the Canadian Alevi Association in Toronto.

1 Metcalf 1996, 3, 5.
2 Ibid., 5; see Qureshi 1996.
3 Metcalf 1996, 12.
4 In this chapter, I interchangeably use the terms Alevi (literally, "followers of ʿAli"), Alevi-Bektaşi (due to their strong connection with the Bektaşi order of dervishes), and Kızılbaş-Alevi (due to their renewed identification with Kızılbaş heritage pointing to close spiritual ties with Shah Ismaʿil and the Shiʿi Safavids of Iran). *Kızılbaş* (literally, "redheads") refers to the headpieces with twelve folds worn by the Turkmen military elite who supported Shah Ismaʿil I (1487–1524 CE), founder of the Safavid dynasty in Iran, and also to the Turkmen Kızılbaş located in Anatolia who later identified with the Bektaşi order of dervishes to escape Ottoman persecution and oppression. The term "Kızılbaş" was replaced with the appellation "Alevi" in the late nineteenth and early twentieth centuries because of the former's strong derogatory implications.
5 See Metcalf 1996, 6; Qureshi 1996, 48.
6 See A. Anderson 2014, 63.
7 The Sunni Ottomans conjured up a mythology branding Alevis as irreligious (*ladini*) "heretics who failed to observe the five pillars of Islam, denied the mosque,

and participated in drinking parties (*cem bezmi*) with music and dance where men and women engaged in communal sex after a candle-extinguishing ceremony, *mum söndü*" (Markoff 2002b, 793; see also Mélikoff 1974; Eyuboğlu 1980). Note that the terms "*cem*" and "*ayin-i cem*" are used interchangeably to mean Alevi sacred assemblies, but the term "*cem*" is more commonly used as a cover term and is combined with adjectives to signify different varieties of such rituals.

8 Tambar 2010, 652.

9 Şehriban Şahin (2005) discusses the transnational dimension of the Alevi movement and how the Alevi Manifesto generated by Turkish associations (*dernekler*) and foundations (*vakıflar*) in Hamburg inspired similar associations in Turkey to demand freedom of religion from the state-financed Directorate of Religious Affairs, which caters to the needs of the dominant Sunni majority.

10 The analysis also draws from the anthropologies of religion, cognition, and emotion.

11 See Knott 2005.

12 In Turkey, the Persian term "*saz*" can refer to a musical instrument in general, but also to the fretted, long-necked plucked folk lute of various sizes that is widespread throughout the country, which is more specifically and commonly called *bağlama*.

13 See Markoff 1986; Markoff 1993; Markoff 2002b.

14 See Markoff 2002b, 798.

15 I am indebted to the Social Sciences and Humanities Research Council of Canada for funding fieldwork conducted in Bulgaria (2012) and Turkey (2013).

16 See Mélikoff 1974; Subtelny 1989, 593–595; Ocak 1996.

17 See Dinçer 2004, 167.

18 See Van Deusen 2004, xii; Başgöz 1967; Levin and Süzükei 2006, 171.

19 See Andrews and Markoff 1987, 55.

20 Among the most widespread and important examples of the Alevi sacred dance, the *semah*, are the *Kırklar Semahı* ("Dance of the Forty Saints") and the *Turnalar Semahı* ("Dance of the Cranes"), with their symbolic figures of ascent. In the *Turnalar Semahı*, the image of the elegant crane (*turna*) preparing for flight symbolizes both the ascending soul of Imam ʿAli and the metamorphosis of Central Asian miracle-working shamans into birds. In the *Kırklar Semahı*, the nocturnal ascent of the Prophet Muhammad (*miʾrac*) to heaven leads him to the gathering of the forty saints (*kırklar meclisi*). There he is said to have beheld the manifestation of divine reality in ʿAli and to have recognized ʿAli's possession of the mystery of sainthood, *sırrı vilayet* (see Birge 1937, 266; Markoff 1993; Markoff 2002a).

21 See Van Deusen 2004, 108; Köprülü 2006. There is a possibility that Alevi *dedeler* find their origins in the Turkmen *babalar* who traveled westward from Khwarezm and Khurasan carrying "old pre-Islamic customs under the cloak of Islam" and also functioning as wandering minstrels (Birge 1937, 31).

22 The terms *"ozan"* and *"aşık"* are used interchangeably in Turkey to mean epic singers and poet singers or minstrels.

23 Conversation with *dede* Yusuf Başaran in Istanbul, June, 2013.

24 Turkmen poet-singers (*bagşy/baxši*) are known for their wisdom and knowledge and their healing abilities and magical acts, typical of shamans. More important, religious lineages are prominent in their tribal organizations (Bennigsen and Wimbush 1986).

25 See Markoff 2002b, 796.

26 See Picken 1975, 288; Zeranska-Kominek 1990, 104. "La, re, mi" is the Turkish nomenclature utilized for the tuning, with its fixed intervals of a descending perfect fifth followed by an ascending major second; the actual pitches vary depending on the performer.

27 See During 1998, 123.

28 See Picken 1975, 271.

29 See Birge 1937; Parlak 2000. The term *"pençe"* is more appropriate for usage with Alevi *parmakla* or *şelpe* techniques because of its deeper symbolic meaning of "the family of the mantle" (*pençe-i āl-i-ābā*), referring to the Holy Five, namely, the prophet Muhammed, his daughter Fatima, Imam ʿAli, and his sons Hasan and Husayn.

30 See Gazimihal 1975, 74, 123; Picken 1975, 270; Köprülü 2006, 210–211.

31 See Picken 1975, 266; Bardakçı 1986; Feldman 1996, 177.

32 See Markoff 2009 for a Turkish version of some of the material in this section. See also Karamustafa 2006, 2, 20, 84. Spiritual intoxication is often masked through the use of language and images that describe earthly preoccupations such as drinking, sensuous love, and infatuation that cause the lover (*bülbül*, the "nightingale") to lament and burn up with thoughts of the beloved (*gül*, the "rose") that is hidden under many veils of separation, which are allegories for the relationship between man and God and the spiritual ascent to the perfection of the Divine (see Schimmel 1982).

33 Karamustafa 2006, 4.

34 Mansur al-Hallaj's act of martyrdom in asserting *"ana al-Haqq"* ("I am God") coincides with the Alevi interpretation of Ibn al-ʿArabiʾs *waḥdat al-wujūd* ("Unity of Being") as "the unity of God, man, and nature" or the manifestation of God in the human being (Dressler 2003, 118). Yürekli (2012, 124) comments that "the tenth-century incident epitomizes the incompatibility of antinomian and legalistic interpretations of Islam."

35 See Gölpınarlı 1963, 175.

36 See Karamustafa 2006, 83.

37 See Vryonis 1971, 363.

38 See Yönetken 1963, 42; Markoff 1993, 97.

39 See Roemer 1990.

40 See Karakaya-Stump 2010, 279.
41 See Gölpinarlı 1963, 306, for the full text.
42 Es 2013, 41.
43 Langer 2010.
44 See Akın 1995, 71–72. Despite the presence of dome ceilings in some ritual halls, one does not find the lantern ceiling (*kırlangıç kubbe*) plus an oculus, found in the *meydan* (ritual hall) of the central Bektaşi shrine complex in the Hacı Bektaş village near Nevşehir. This particular design had apparently become "a prototype that was replicated in a number of ritual halls in eastern Anatolia by the late 19th century" (Yürekli 2012, 123). Lantern roofs in eastern Anatolia, however, do display an octagonal shape even though the Alevi civil engineer in charge of the Kağıthane *cemevi* believes that such symbolism was not intended in the *cem salonu*'s ceiling.
45 See Haider 1996, 41.
46 Yusuf Başaran *dede*, pers. comm., June 2013, Istanbul.
47 Zeynel Şahan *dede*, pers. comm., June 2013, Istanbul.
48 Zeynel Şahan *dede*, pers. comm., June 2013, Istanbul.
49 The twelve services consist of the *dede*, *zakir*, and *rehber*, as well as the following: *gözcü* (the primary keeper of order who maintains discipline during the ceremony), *delilci* or *çerağcı* (the keeper of light who lights candles and extinguishes them at the end of the ceremony), *süpürgeci* or *farraş* (the sweeper who symbolically cleans the *meydan*), *sakka* or *saki* (water carrier), *lokmacı* or *kurbancı* (the one who is in charge of animal sacrifice and the preparation of the sacrificial meal), *peyikçi* (the crier who informs the community that a *cem* is going to occur), and *iznikci* (the one who keeps the ritual premises clean). At the Nurtepe *cem*, the *dedes*, *rehber*, and *zakir* remained in the *post* area, and some of the assigned roles were performed by more than one individual, which is often the case.
50 Es 2013, 33.
51 I have witnessed similar rituals (designated as *Birlik Cemleri* or "Rituals of Unity") in Toronto that function as education tools, the *dede* explaining the meaning of each segment in detail for Alevis in diaspora, who have been distanced from rituals.
52 See Markoff 2002a and 2002b. Arif Sağ is a virtuoso, a megastar Alevi *bağlama* artist and singer who not only established his own school of performance practice but was a member of Turkish parliament from 1987 to 1991 and a vocal defender of Alevi rights. The repertoire mentioned has become a canon of *cem* performance practice, its obvious role to create "standardized cem ceremonies" through "unifying different cem practices" (Es 2013, 37).
53 Two popular staples of Alevi sacred repertoire were performed: "Aliye Selman Olasın" (*duaz-ı mam*, poetry by Hatayi), which has become popular through recordings and performances by popular Alevi artists such as Tolga Sağ, Yılmaz

Çelik, Muharrem Temiz, and Erdal Erzincan (CD *Türkuler Sevdamız 3*, *Iber Müziği*, 2005), and a *tevhid*, "Bugün Bize Pir Geldi," whose source is *aşık* Ismail Daimi (poetry by Hatayi).

54 It is this meeting that is considered to be the model for the Alevi-Bektaşi *cem* and the sacred dance *semah*.

55 See De Jong 1989, 13. De Jong suggests that the color green is often viewed as a symbol of the death of Imam Hussein by poison.

56 According to some *dedes*, women should not be barefoot, but this is now typical practice.

57 For the most part, Alevis have enjoyed support from Turkish Republican authorities. For example, the state secularism of Atatürk liberated Alevis from the ulema- and shariʿa-minded Sufi orders and valued Alevis for sustaining remnants of Central Asian Turkic culture through minstrelsy and aspects of their expressive culture. See Markoff 1986; Sözer 2014, 10; and Dressler 2013, 5.

58 Personal communication from Yusuf Başaran *dede*, May 2013.

59 See Berthomé and Houseman 2010.

60 Baba'is and Bektaşis in Bulgaria are born into the faith and maintain endogamy, as do Alevis and Tahtacis in Turkey, although initiation rites and fictive kinship are crucial for legitimate status and full participation in sect rituals. The main difference between these confessional groups in Bulgaria and Alevis in Turkey, however, is that religious leaders (*baba/dede*) are chosen from the community on the basis of knowledge and experience rather than spiritual lineage (*dede soyundan/ocakzade*). Baba'is are more open in allowing outsiders to observe their rituals than Bektaşis are. Bektaşis, in addition, are supervised by a *rehber* (a religious guide's deputy) and a spiritual mother and father who prepare them for ritual initiation (*nasip, ikrar verme*).

61 See İnalcık 1954; Ocak 1994; Zhelyazkova 1998; Gramatikova 2011.

62 The use of the newer term *dede* illustrates influence from Turkish Alevis.

63 See Yürekli 2012, 45.

64 See Yürekli 2012. See Mikov 2005 and Gramatikova 2011 for further information concerning such sacred sites of pilgrimage.

65 See Zhelyazkova 1998; Sözer 2014, 82. Alevis dissimulated (*taqiyah*) easily during socialism, when visits to private homes for rituals were referred to as going to the *maale* (dialect for the Turkish word *mahalle*, meaning another quarter or area in the village).

66 One framed portrait was that of Cemil Hayder Baba, a celibate dervish (Babağan branch of Bektaşi dervishes who follow the *erkān* of Balım Sultan), who served as *postnişin* (officiating head of a *tekke*) of the shrine from 1938 until he died in 1962. I thank Veysel Bayram, president of the Razgrad Cem Association, for offering this and other information and for helping to arrange the *muhabbet*.

67 It is said that the consumption of alcohol is a means of simulating the *kırklar meclisi* (gathering of the forty).

68 Although the numbers three, five, and seven are highly valued symbolic concepts for Alevis, Bektaşis, and related communities in Turkey, I am unaware of specific *deyişler* there that are referred to as *üçler, beşler,* or *yediler.*

69 Becker 2004, 79–82; Berthomé and Houseman 2010, 58.

70 Victor Turner's (1977) concept of *communitas* is used here to mean a feeling of oneness during rituals of cathartic religious experience that also build solidarity in communities on the margins of mainstream society.

71 Tambar 2010, 672. This phrase refers to the heterogeneity of Alevis, who have migrated from various regions of Anatolia, attending *cem* services in urban areas. In Anatolia, the communities were tightly knit and under the jurisdiction of one *dede* who had a personal relationship with his followers and was therefore able to conduct the *görgü* (interrogation) *cemi* with integrity and insider knowledge.

72 See Şahin 2005, 479; Karaosmanoğlu 2013, 588.

Plates 1 and 2. Babur plants a garden at the Bagh-i Wafa, in the *Baburnameh*, ca. 1590 CE, by the painter Bishndas. Victoria and Albert Museum, 276-1913 and 276A-1913. © Victoria and Albert Museum, London.

درختهای انار هم هست گرداگرد حوض تمام سبزه زار
جای عین باغ همین است در وقت زرد شدن نارنجها بسیار
عمل بشنداس چهره نانها

Plate 3. Rustam fights Barzu without recognizing him, in the *Shahnameh*, painted in Isfahan, 1648 CE. Windsor Royal Library Collection, MS 1005014, fol. 279v. Courtesy of the Royal Collection Trust; © Her Majesty Queen Elizabeth II, 2015.

Plate 4. Barbad the concealed musician, *Shahnameh*, made in Tabriz between 1525 and 1535 CE, attributed to the painter Mirza ʿAli. Nasser D. Khalili Collection of Islamic Art, MSS 1030, fol. 713a. Courtesy of the Khalili Family Trust; © the Nour Foundation.

Plate 5. (a, *top left*) Traditional courtyard home (*bayt ʿarabi*), Damascus, 2004. Photograph: J. Shannon. (b, *top right*) Cuarto Dorado, Alhambra Palace, Granada, fourteenth century. Photograph © Oronoz. (c, *bottom*) Interior, Hall of ʿAbd al-Rahman III, Madinat al-Zahraʾ. Photograph: G. Anderson.

Plate 6. Andhrayaki Ragini. Ink, opaque watercolor, and gold on paper. Bilaspur, Himachal Pradesh, India, ca. 1710 CE. Metropolitan Museum of Art online collection (www.metmuseum.org), folio 2006.33; purchase, Friends of Asian Art Gifts, 2006.

Plate 7. Panchama Ragini. Ink, opaque watercolor, and gold on paper. Bikaner, Rajasthan, India, ca. 1640 CE. Metropolitan Museum of Art online collection (www.metmuseum.org), folio 1996.378; purchase, Patricia Phelps de Cisneros Gift, in honor of Mahrukh Tarapor, 1996.

Plate 8. Shri Raga. Ink and opaque watercolor on paper. Bundi, Rajasthan, India, mid-seventeenth century. Metropolitan Museum of Art online collection (www.metmuseum.org), folio 1981.163; gift of Phillips, Gold and Company, 1981.

Plate 9. (a, *top*) The male section of the *kiiz üi*: the imam of Bayan-Ölgii is seated to the left of the place of honor (*tör*). (b, *bottom*) The female section of the *kiiz üi*: lamenters. Ölgii, Bayan-Ölgii, August 2004. Photographs: S. Daukeyeva.

Plate 10. Death of Zahāk. Illustration by Sultan Muhammad in the Shah Tahmasp *Shahnameh*, ca. 1522–1542 CE. Holding of the Metropolitan Museum of Art, OASC.

Plate 11. Young man playing the *kamāncheh*. Painting attributed to Mirza ʿAli, ca. 1575 CE. Holding of the Aga Khan Museum, OASC.

Plate 12. The feast of *ʿĪd al-Fiṭr* begins. Illustration by Sultan Muhammad in the *Divan* of Hafiz for Sam Mirza, ca. 1526–1527 CE. Photograph: Abolala Soudavar.

Plate 13. Lovers' picnic (painting right; text left), illustrated folio from a manuscript of the *Divan* of Hafiz, 1526–1527 CE. Attributed to Sultan Muhammad. Ink, opaque watercolor, and gold on paper. 19 × 12.4 cm (7½ × 4⅞ in.). Image number DDC104092; accession number: 2007.183.2. Harvard Art Museums/Arthur M. Sackler Museum, Gift of Stuart Cary Welch in honor of Edith Iselin Gilbert Welch, 2007.183.2. Photograph: Imaging Department © President and Fellows of Harvard College.

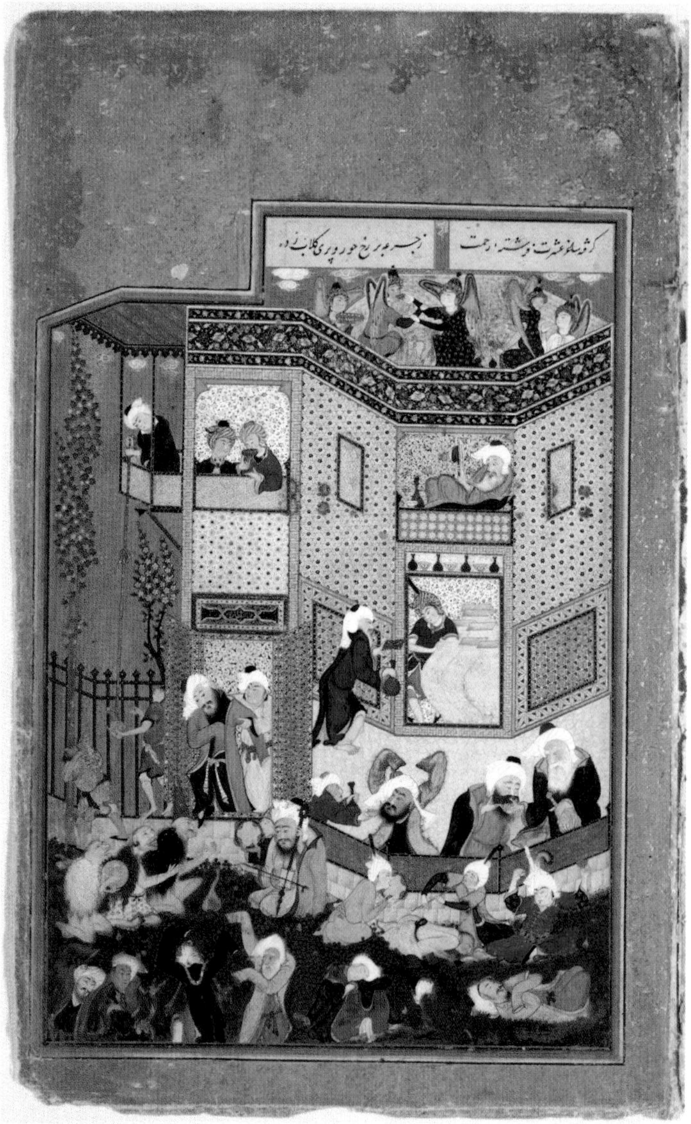

Plate 14. Earthly drunkenness (painting recto; text verso), illustrated folio from a manuscript of the *Divan* of Hafiz, 1526–1527 CE. Sultan Muhammad. Ink, color, gold and silver on paper. 28.7 × 35.5 cm ($11\frac{5}{16}$ × 14 in.). Image number 211711; accession number 1988.460.2. Harvard Art Museums/Arthur M. Sackler Museum, the Stuart Cary Welch Collection, Gift of Mr. and Mrs. Stuart Cary Welch in honor of the students of Harvard University and Radcliffe College. Jointly owned by the Harvard Art Museums and the Metropolitan Museum of Art, 1988.460.2 Photograph: Imaging Department © President and Fellows of Harvard College.

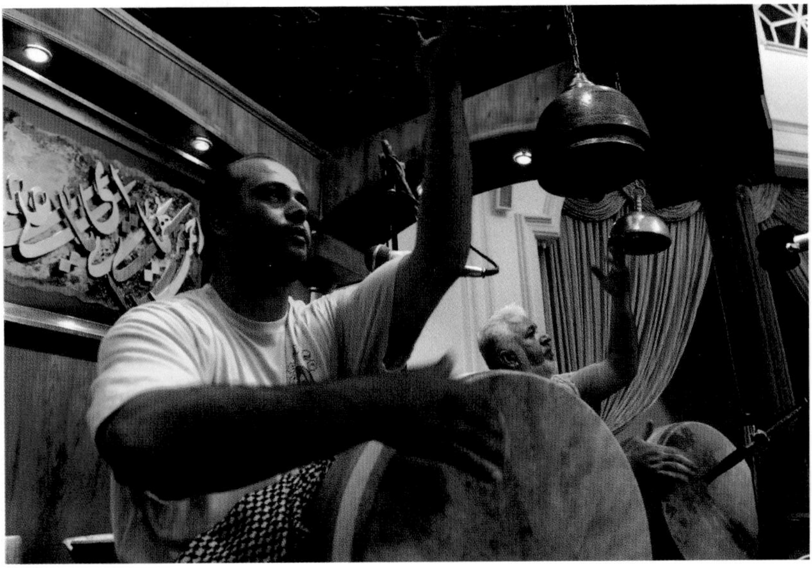

Plate 15. (a, *top*) *Murshid* Alireza Hojjati with *żarb* and portrait of Imam ʿAli. Zurkhaneh Takhti, Yazd, 2006. (b, *bottom*) *Murshidhā* Qasim Qasimi and Murtaza Namayandeh playing *zang* and *żarb*. Zurkhaneh Astan-i Quds, Mashhad, 2006. Photograph courtesy of Stefano Triulzi.

Plate 16. Disposition of athletes in the *gowd* and their relation to the *sardam*. Zurkhaneh Valiᶜasr, Sabzevar, 2006. Photograph courtesy of Stefano Triulzi.

PART THREE

The Arab World

CHAPTER FIVE

Venerating Cairo's Saints through Monument and Ritual

Islamic Reform and the Rise of the Architext

MICHAEL FRISHKOPF

The General Argument

For centuries, Muslims have venerated their saints (*awliyā'*; sing. *walī*) in two primary ways: through construction and maintenance of sacred built environments centered on monuments, especially shrines (*maqāmāt*; sing. *maqām*), and through ritual acts (individual or collective, private or public) centered on what I call "language performance,"[1] especially individual shrine visitation, *ziyāra*, and the collective ritual called *ḥaḍra*. These two ways are frequently connected, symbolically referencing one another, socially and spiritually linked, and collocated in the same physical space. They may harmonize, reinforcing one another, in which case Islam tends to localize at the shrine. Or they may conflict.

In the modern era, the global Muslim community—the *umma*—has weakened dramatically. Reformers (*muṣliḥūn*) have sought to strengthen the *umma*, at nearly any cost—even that of interior faith—through enforced social uniformity. When monumental and ritual practices of saint veneration conjoin harmoniously, they deepen and broaden faith, developing a more proximate, adapted spirituality, centered at the shrine. But this conjunction also diversifies the *umma*. From the reformist viewpoint, such conjunctions must be opposed.

In this chapter, I interpret changes in the relation of sacred built environments and sonic rituals of saint veneration, from harmonization to conflict, in relation to global reformist discourses in the postcolonial period.

I propose that contemporary Islamic reformers—even those who are Sufi in orientation—frequently oppose collective, public forms of performative saint veneration, not essentially for ideological reasons, centered on a quest for spiritual virtue (as overtly stated in their discourses), but rather for pragmatic reasons, centered on a quest for social power. Reconfiguring monuments to attenuate ritual, destroying what I call "ritual resonance," is a means of reforming Islam. Drawing on the social theory of Jürgen Habermas, I interpret these changes as an instance of a broader phenomenon: the systemic colonization of the Muslim lifeworld by what I term the "architext."

A Connected Localization

I argue that Islam fully localizes through a resonant combination of ritualized monument and monument-centric ritual. Yet such localizations remain connected to Islam's global center, producing a connected network of localized sites. Such a network challenges any monolithic definition of Islam and is thus particularly distressing to reformers seeking uniformity. Whence the power of resonant monument and ritual to localize Islam in this way?

For devotees, the saints are alive, interacting with the living, actively present in the rituals that invoke them: *ziyāra* (visitation) and *ḥaḍra* (presence). Intimate individual connections are established through the former; public social presence, through the latter. Saints' bodies are enshrined, and shrines are embodied, both radiating spiritual blessing, or *baraka*. The saint is omnipresent, but this presence is concentrated at the shrine, where it energizes ritual through participation in *ziyāra*, a temporally free, asynchronous, individual sonic practice (visiting and circumambulating the shrine and communing with the saint); and in *ḥaḍra*, a temporally fixed, synchronized, collective sonic practice (chanting and singing). These rituals both invoke and express saintly presence. Hence, shrine and ritual are mutually reinforcing—the ritual invocation of "presence" energizing the shrine, the spiritual body of the shrine energizing the *ḥaḍra*.

Both monument and ritual provide models for venerative behavior, the former materially mediated, carried by the shrine; the latter humanly mediated, carried by ritual. When these models harmonize, Islam gradually localizes over the course of generations. The localizing potential of saint veneration is most powerfully activated in *public ḥaḍra*, a freer, more flexible ritual that adapts more easily and rapidly to its sociocultural and built environment. The public *ḥaḍra* draws on local musical, poetic, and narrative traditions and is well suited to the space of performance and the demographics of its participants. Such adaptation transpires through communicative feedback loops arising among participants, a "resonance" sedimenting a cohesive, affect-laden socio-spiritual network and inculcating a humanly mediated performative model transmitted through performance from one generation to the next. Saints participate actively in this network, providing moral authority and emotional engagement, through the agency of their embodied shrines. Localization revolves around a proximate, ritualized *axis mundi* centered on the saint's shrine, a pale reflection of the global axes at Mecca and Medina, with their celebrated ritual pilgrimages (*ḥajj* and *ʿumra* in Mecca and *ziyārat al-rasūl*, "visiting the Prophet," in Medina) centered on corresponding global shrines (the Kaʿba, and the *rawḍa*, the Prophet's own *maqām*). Indeed the great saints are known as *aqṭāb*—"axes"—underscoring their local centrality. Figuratively, local life turns about them, becoming literal in the circumambulations of *ziyāra*.

But most remarkably (and most distressingly to reformers), this localizing process unfolds *without* sectarian fissioning. The shrine "cult"—flexibly but firmly tethered to the global axes—does not develop as a new religion; the local is empowered precisely through deeply felt embodied linkages to global models. These linkages are at once paradigmatic and syntagmatic: the local shrine and associated rituals replicate atemporal paradigms found at Mecca and Medina as a kind of loving emulation; they are simultaneously connected in temporal sequence (syntagmatically) through the *walī*'s *silsila* (spiritual lineage) and oral transmission in a connected series of feelingful human relationships dating back to the Prophet. Indeed, the Prophet's own presence—lovingly invoked in word and action—is palpably present in every shrine ritual. Localized Islam, linked to the center through flexible embodied relationships, thus necessarily defines what Islam is for everyone; it cannot be simply pruned away.

For centuries, this sort of connected localization underlay Islamic expansion, enabling adaptation to diverse local conditions through performative and architectural connection to local saints. Saint veneration constituted a ramifying process responsible for much of Islam's dramatic success during many centuries of hegemony. But it is precisely this stretching of Islam's boundaries, an inner unity of faith clothed in outward diversity of form, that is most intolerable to reformers concerned to ensure a visibly uniform Islam that conforms to centralized textual and architectural models.

Ritual Resonance, the Built Environment, and the Colonization of the Muslim Lifeworld

In Islam as well as other traditions, sacred architectural interiors tend to be performatively and socially constrained—by traditional convention, official decree, or both—and so freer public rituals of saint veneration typically take place within the more ambiguous, liminal zone of the shrine's proximate exterior space, the *sāḥa*, often a garden or courtyard, where the sacred begins to shade into the quotidian, and strictures (on who can participate and what they can do) are somewhat relaxed. Here, resonance is more possible and its effects are broader. In search of a unified *umma*, reformers oppose such practices. One effective technique is the attenuation of ritual resonance via the built environment.

The built environment is at once a material, acoustic, social, and—at times—spiritual phenomenon, its physicality overlaid with normative conventions and legal conditions regulating usage. What I term "ritual resonance" is the emotional intensification (culminating in ecstasy, *wajd*) resulting from sonic-social interactions, cybernetic feedback loops developing during collective devotional practices, particularly those incorporating flexible, improvisational musical structures in exterior spaces. Through such participatory feedback, rituals adapt to particular locales. Resonance enables Islamic localization by producing durable, affective socio-spiritual networks, including participants and saint, that conform to local sociocultural contexts. The built environment may amplify or inhibit such ritual resonance, depending on its structural properties. In the present study, I interpret the impact of the built environment on sonic practices of saint veneration in Egypt.

In the past, Cairo's built environment, including purpose-built Sufi structures (e.g., the *khānqāh* and the *zāwiya*), mosques (*masājid*), and shrines (*maqāmāt*), served as a resonant sonic-social amplifier for the veneration of myriad local saints, particularly at their shrines, where circumambulatory devotions accompanied *ḥaḍra*, becoming remarkably public, musical, and ecstatic in the shrine's *sāḥa*.

Scholarship documents weekly *ḥaḍra* at the Cairo mosque-shrine of Sidi ʿAli Zayn al-ʿAbidin (the Prophet's great-grandson), dating back to the mid-nineteenth century at least. Around the year 2000, however, Sidi ʿAli's long-standing, vigorous Saturday *ḥaḍra* was displaced and nearly eradicated by the massive rebuilding and expansion of his mosque-shrine. If the *ḥaḍra* did not quite disappear, its resonance was drastically attenuated.

Drawing on Habermas, I interpret this attenuation as an instance of the colonization of the sonic-social Muslim lifeworld by systemic currents of Islamic reform, deploying universal, authoritative material models—what I call the "architext"—to impose normative uniformity, attenuate resonance, and eliminate localized ritual practice, an instrumental strategy of ritual coercion that seeks to impose social unity by suppressing the diversity of Muslim oral tradition, thereby renewing the political power of the *umma*.

Saint Veneration in Islam

Veneration of the *awliyāʾ*—architecturally, through construction, maintenance, and public recognition of a shrine, and ritually, through practices centered on it—has been central to Muslim devotional life in Egypt for centuries.[2] Most Egyptian Muslims understand the *awliyāʾ* (literally, "near ones," i.e., near to God) to include the holy men and women of Islam other than the prophets, including the Prophet's companions (*ṣaḥāba*), select jurists (*fuqahāʾ*), scholars (ʿulamaʾ), martyrs (*shuhadāʾ*), and preachers (*khuṭabāʾ*), but especially the Prophet's immediate family (the Ahl al-Bayt, "people of the house") and assorted mystics (Sufis, *mutaṣawwifa*), ascetics (*darāwīsh*, *fuqarāʾ*), and guides (*shuyūkh*, *murshidīn*) associated with the mystical orders (*ṭuruq ṣūfiyya*; sing. *ṭarīqa ṣūfiyya*). Through such veneration, Islam localizes at the shrine as an affectively charged socio-spiritual network.

Unlike Catholicism, Islam has no formal procedure for canonization. Rather, a former shaykh (spiritual leader) becomes a *walī* via popular consensus, supported by a network of followers who share extraordinary experiences and stories, for instance, tales of *karāmāt* (miracles). Therefore, the social boundaries of the *awliyāʾ* are always somewhat fuzzy and indeed depend crucially on practices of veneration. When a saint's shrine is dilapidated, and rituals subside, the saint is soon forgotten.

Egyptians of all social classes and religious orientations—a group extending far beyond formal members of Sufi orders (*murīdīn*) to include a much broader category of devotees (*aḥbāb* or *muḥibbīn*; literally, "lovers")—adore and venerate the *awliyā'*, communing in prayer, seeking their *baraka* (spiritual blessing), worldly assistance (*madad*), and afterworldly intercession (*shafā'a*).

A long tradition of Muslim thinkers condemned saint veneration as *bid'a* (heresy), or even *shirk* (polytheism), Islam's cardinal sin. But their position, most stridently adopted by the thirteenth- to fourteenth-century scholar Ibn Taymiyya and the eighteenth-century Wahhabiyya movement, has become widespread only in the last few decades. Indeed Ibn Taymiyya himself was persecuted for promoting it.[3]

For centuries, saint veneration was ubiquitous, and it continues today. Defenders interpret Qur'an 10:62 ("Behold! verily on the friends [*awliyā'*] of Allah there is no fear, nor shall they grieve") to sanction veneration, including the shrine itself and the ritual practices performed there, and this verse frequently appears inscribed on shrine walls. New saints are even periodically added to the canon.[4]

Architectural Veneration

Architectural veneration entails the construction and maintenance of the saint's shrine, known in Egypt as *maqām*, sometimes *mashhad*, or *mazār*. The shrine includes a presumed tomb (*qabr*, *ḍarīḥ*) under a cuboid *tābūt* (sarcophogus)—real or symbolic (because the named saint may not actually be buried under it). At one end of the *tābūt* there extends a vertical protuberance, the *'immat al-walī*, decorated as if it were the saint's veiled head—wrapped in cloth and a veil (for women) or a turban (for men). The *tābūt* thus acquires an orientation, a front and a back, and an anthropomorphic presence (*ḥaḍra*): the shrine is embodied. The entire *tābūt* is draped in a *kiswa* (like the covering of the Ka'ba), embroidered with religious inscriptions,[5] often enclosed in a *maqṣūra* (grillwork), and housed within a *turba* (mausoleum), usually a square structure under a *qubba* (dome; the word can also denote the shrine as a whole).[6] The Prophet's shrine at Medina provides the paradigm for many of these features.

Architectural elements—usually reflecting the era of their construction—portal, arch, pendentive, *muqarnas*—combine with surface arts: decorative arabesques and geometrical designs, along with calligraphy—mostly Qur'an or religious poetry—inscribed, painted, or framed and mounted on walls. Traditionally the shrine enables counterclockwise circumambulation around the *tābūt,* though this practice has recently been curtailed—through architectural modifications separating male and female sides—as a *bidʿa* (innovation) that encourages mixing of the genders (though such mixing is permitted at the Kaʿba itself).

The shrine proper is typically coupled with an adjoining structure, such as a mosque (*masjid*) and minaret (*mi'dhana*), all venerating the *walī.*[7] This architectural complex, whether modest or extensive, standard or idiosyncratic, projects *baraka,* praises as well as embodies the saint, attracts and accommodates visitors undertaking this lesser "pilgrimage," and shapes the social interactions that take place within and around it, through ritual participation as a sacred presence, a person.

While scholars classify shrines as funerary architecture, for believers, the saint is alive, spiritually and socially present. His or her active presence is expressed in beliefs: that saints may select their place of burial (guiding pallbearers to a final resting place); that they interact with the living, other saints, and the Prophet; that they communicate with visitors, in *ḥaḍra* and in dreams; and that their bodies do not decay after death.

If interior architectural space defines the shrine's explicit venerative focus, functioning as the center of saintly presence, exterior space surrounding the shrine, especially the open courtyard called *sāḥa,*[8] is crucial for saint veneration, enabling inclusive, collective ritual in communion with the saint. While vulnerable to encroachment (crowded by tombs situated to receive saintly *baraka*), exterior spaces enhance the building's grandeur (and hence attractiveness and power) by offering majestic vantage points and providing capacity to accommodate public ritual and festival.[9] More important, the *sāḥa* provides a liminal zone for the rituals of informal Sufism and the broad community of *aḥbāb,* where socio-spiritual relationships are most malleable. These rituals take place outside the mosque or shrine, structures that impose social strictures on their interiors, as formulated in shariʿa (Islamic law) or the *ādāb* (spiritual etiquette) of affiliated Sufi orders. Yet the *sāḥa* remains within the shrine's corona of *baraka.*

Ritual Veneration

Ritual saint veneration centers on what I have called "language performance," including prescribed action, speech, and sound. The *zāʾir* (plural, *zuwwār*) performs the individual ritual of *ziyāra* at any time. This ritual includes visiting the shrine; greeting the saint; reading the Fatiha; circumambulating the *tābūt*; touching the *maqṣūra* or *tābūt* to acquire imbued *baraka*; uttering supplications (*adʿiya*), often of a personal nature; reciting the Qurʾan or traditional prayers (*ṣalawāt*); and making or fulfilling vows (*nudhūr*)—all means of developing a close relationship to the saint.

The collective ritual of *ḥaḍra* centers on *dhikr* (chanting the Names of God, performed by the *dhakkīra* and led by the *mustaftiḥ*) and *inshād dīnī* (religious hymns, chanted by a *munshid*), sometimes with instrumental accompaniment, along with recitations of the Qurʾan and other sacred texts, and religious speeches. These collective practices take place within the shrine itself; in an adjoining mosque, *khānqāh*, or *zāwiya*; or in the *sāḥa*. The latter allows for greater performative freedom (melodic instruments, in particular, are considered improper within the mosque-shrine) and social inclusion, while remaining within the *riḥāb* (precinct) of the saint's spiritual presence and *baraka*, and thus offers maximal potential for adaptation and resonance. Despite certain universal features, ritual veneration becomes highly localized, centered on the shrine and adapting to its particular environment,[10] including the particularities of place, time, and participants—what the Sufis of old called *makān*, *zamān*, and *ikhwān*.[11]

At the *maqām*, *ziyāra* and *ḥaḍra* are intertwined and complementary. Whereas *ziyāra* is primarily a coming-into-presence through individual, asynchronous action in architectural space defined by the shrine, *ḥaḍra* is primarily a calling-into-presence through collective, synchronous action in architectural time as defined by ritual periodicities (weekly, annually) and the coordinating rhythm of *dhikr*. They are two dimensions of the same localized venerative process, and they synergize through social-spiritual exchange, each ritual supplying participants to the other and raising its emotional level.

The *ḥaḍra*, whose auditory dimension is historically included under the heading *samāʿ* ("spiritual audition," though this term is little used in Egypt today), is a regular feature of the Sufi *ṭarīqa* (spiritual order), typically performed inside its affiliated structure—mosque or *zāwiya*—directed by its shaykh, socially, aesthetically, and emotionally constrained in accordance with his spiritual vision.[12]

The freewheeling public *ḥaḍra* (*ḥaḍra ʿāmma*), occuring in the saint's *sāḥa* and performed in conjunction with a designated *ziyāra* day or *mawlid*, is free from such constraints. The word "*mawlid*" (pl., *mawālid*; "birthday festival," but here implying rebirth, i.e., death) designates both the time and the place of "birth," and hence the *mawlid*, like the *ziyāra*, centers on a shrine. Public *ḥaḍra* is open, enabling the mass of *aḥbāb* to celebrate the saint under direction of the *munshid*, who attempts to raise the emotional level as far as possible.[13]

Public *ḥaḍras* are multiply liminal: performed in the *sāḥa*, open to a range of devotees, drawing on poetry and music with ambiguous sacred-secular interpretations, and often involving ambiguous practices (collection of tips—*nuʾaṭ*—for musicians, selling drinks or tickets for rides and games or to watch dances, copresence of men and women) that may be construed as economic or sensual as well as spiritual within the saint festival context. Yet this flexibility also empowers local adaptation. The word "*ḥaḍra*" (presence) refers explicitly to that of the Prophet, angels (who are said to seek out and attend sincere *ḥaḍra*), and saints, but it can also refer to the participants themselves: "presence" links the human and spiritual worlds tightly.

In each of the *ḥaḍra*'s phases—called "*majlis*" or "*ṭabaqa*"—tempo, melodic mode, and poetic language accelerate and intensify in a steady buildup of emotional energy and dynamic interaction, from a nonmetric prelude toward an emotionally heightened climax (sometimes reaching the point of ecstasy, *wajd*), whose level is an important indicator of mystical school, from "*ṣaḥw*" ("sober") to "*sukr*" ("intoxicated").

In the latter case, much more prominent in the public *ḥaḍra* unfolding outside religious buildings and Sufi orders, participants may achieve rapturous states known as *wajd* or *ḥāl* (ecstatic trance; mystical parallels to secular *ṭarab*), sometimes collapsing, uttering ecstatic phrases (*shaṭḥiyāt*) apparently contradicting shariʿa, or speaking in tongues (*siryaniyya*); a person in such a condition may be described as "*majdhūb*" (divinely mad) or even "*malbūs*" (possessed).

As a liminal ritual performed in a liminal space, the public *ḥaḍra* is thus perfectly positioned to reshape the socio-spiritual relations at the core of Islamic belief and practice in accord with the local social and cultural environment. When spatial, regulative, and communicative factors allow for the *ḥaḍra* to adapt to its sociocultural circumstances and to develop power through regulative and amplificatory feedback cycles of what I term "thought-feeling" (affectively charged concepts and relationships, i.e., "belief"), the *ḥaḍra* becomes a powerful means of Islamic localization.

Cybernetic feedback loops build spiritual thought-feeling in *ḥaḍra* through the dynamic interaction of its participants—including the saint—in a socio-spiritual network assembled during performance and enabled by a critical minimal degree of freedom in movement and expressive communication, a process closely resembling that of the *ṭarab* characterizing secular Arab music.[14] While specialist reciters, singers, and musicians communicate through text and music, others communicate through movement, gesture, dynamics, exclamations, and *dhikr,* sometimes actively calling to performer specialists for repetitions. Some of these communications are metaphysical, transmitted through a spiritual faculty of discernment (*baṣīra* or *firāsa*) located in the *ʿayn al-qalb* (heart's eye). At the other extreme, material communication—for example, the bestowal of *nuʾaṭ*—also contributes to feedback and raises the spiritual level.

Maximizing ecstasy by manipulating performative parameters (texts, tempos, modes) depends on addressing local factors of *makān, zamān,* and *ikhwān* within a broader sociocultural environment. Selecting the right settings cannot be predetermined. Rather, they are adjusted through feedback. Maximizing ecstasy requires a flexible ritual steered by both negative and positive feedback, linking "performers" and "listeners," ritual leaders and ritual practitioners, and humans and spiritual beings. Negative feedback is the process whereby skillful performers locate optimal settings of performative parameters. Positive feedback is the process whereby, those settings having been discovered, the emotional mood is driven upward.

As the *munshid* expresses his inner state through poetry, music, and voice, he scans listeners' responses, enabling his adaptation—through vocal expressivity, selection of couplets, rhythms, and melodic modes (*maqāmāt*)—to address their collective state, bringing it closer to his. These interactions depend critically on a suitable exterior built environment, a *sāḥa* facilitating such interactions. When all factors align, the space develops ritual resonance.

Resonance binds the performing group to spiritual realities and to each other through collective thought-feeling shared across the performative network, forging affective and doctrinal unity and culminating in cries of "*madad!*" (help!) from *munshid* and *ahbāb*, expressing *wajd*, an ecstasy of closeness to the saint, Prophet, or God, a spiritual localization that may proceed to the point of *fanā'*, annihilation of the self. These cries, at first signs, subsequently become triggers, and their resonant amplification spreads to affect others, raising the spiritual-emotional level.

But resonance develops in trajectories beyond the individual *ṭabaqa* as well, over the course of an evening, across the week-long *mawlid*, or year after year, gradually forging a localized Islam centered at the shrine. Each powerful *ḥaḍra* attracts more participants, better musicians, more vendors and cafés, all spiraling upward. Emotional, spiritual, and economic activity are all self-reinforcing. Conversely, *ḥaḍra* decline is self-reinforcing in the same way.

Resonance, combining architectural and ritual veneration, thus creates a localized social solidarity and culture of veneration centered on the *ḥaḍra*, the shrine, and the venerated saint. These processes of resonance, which can be partly inferred from the silent historical record, still characterize Sufi performative interactions today.[15] Resonance localizes Islam by providing salient, deeply affective models for the way Muslims relate to each other, to the saints, and to Islam generally, models well adapted to local conditions.

Models for Islamic Saint Veneration

Monuments and ritual provide models for behavior, sustained over time. Buildings, together with their interior spaces, endure through purely material inertia, requiring only occasional maintenance. As long as they remain fixed, buildings' forms tend to reinscribe the same social patterns on each successive generation that uses them. Architecture thus appears as a materially mediated model for the globalization of Islamic beliefs and practices via widely distributed Islamic architectural elements, such as the shrine's *tābūt* and *maqṣūra* or the mosque's *miḥrāb* and women's section, which consistently orient users in particular ways.

Certainly architectural style can and does localize, in tandem with ritual usage. Much as happens with plates in tectonic movement, when the stresses between material and ritual culture are too great, a building will be transformed or even demolished and replaced by another that conforms more closely to social reality. Yet given the enormous costs—of money, effort, time—the politics (regulation, patronage), and the centralized decision making involved in architectural transformation, delays and distortions inevitably enter the architectural feedback cycle, precluding adaptation. Architecture thus tends to play a constraining role.

Ritual veneration, on the other hand, comprises a flexible set of adaptive social practices leaving (at least until the modern era of audiovisual recording) no material residue, guided by collective memory, and centering on texts that are recited, intoned, and sung—what I have termed "language performance."[16] In public *ḥaḍra*, the feedback cycle is especially short, enabling rapid adaption to sociocultural conditions, as well as to the built environment. Transmitted through performance itself, such models may be lost (when neglected for a generation), or they may endure through the massively parallel transmissive power of oral tradition.

In conjunction with ritual, monumental saint veneration catalyzes a localized form of Islam, centered on the saint (and, after death, the saint's shrine) as "axis." Monumental and ritual forms of veneration may harmonize, especially when the former are built expressly to house the latter. Indeed, architectural veneration may amplify performative veneration, rendering it more emotionally powerful, more socially attractive, and more auspicious. At other times, however, architectural form dampens performative veneration, attenuating or inhibiting resonance altogether. In either case, one may ask how—and why.

During my initial research in Cairo in 1992, I regularly attended the weekly public *ḥaḍra* venerating the Ahl al-Bayt saint ʿAli Zayn al-ʿAbidin (known to devotees as "Sidi ʿAli"), performed just outside his mosque. This vigorous *ḥaḍra*, including *dhikr* and amplified *inshād* with instruments including reed flute (*kawala*), cymbals (*kāsāt*, known among musicians as *tōra*), and drums, mainly the *ṭabla* (single-headed goblet drum), *mazhar*, and *duff* (frame drums), was positioned adjacent to an outdoor café offering refreshments to spectators and participants alike. The ritual lasted some eight hours, from *ʿaṣr* (afternoon prayer) until well past *ʿishāʾ* (night prayer), in a series of increasingly resonant *ṭabaqāt*, each featuring a different *munshid* and building from quiescence to tumultuously ecstatic *madad*. For more than six months, I faithfully attended this *ḥaḍra* every Saturday afternoon, socializing with musicians and *munshidīn*. Most participants were regulars, composing a tightly bound social network, a subculture devoted to Sidi ʿAli—forming and reproducing a localized Islam. I returned occasionally in subsequent years and finally filmed the ritual in 1998, after which I left Egypt for four years.

Returning in 2002, I was shocked to find that Sidi ʿAli's mosque had been torn down. In its place was a gleaming new marble structure featuring extensive staircases in front, which provided direct access to the mosque, enabling visitors to bypass the shrine, housed at the lower level (and perhaps answering those critics who condemn the presence of shrines in mosques altogether). These staircases also served to obliterate the *sāḥa*, formerly site of the weekly *ḥaḍra* and its adjacent café. A small *ḥaḍra* continued, but far from the shrine; shorter, detached from *ziyāra*, and bereft of *dhikr*, it was no longer ritually effective. The network had dispersed. Why did architectural veneration, formerly harmonized with ritual veneration, now oppose it?

Interior and Exterior Ritual

Structures Purpose-Built for Interior Ritual Performance

Today's most socially resonant *ḥaḍras* are performed in the liminal *sāḥa* area *outside* the mosque-shrine, and *outside* the social structures of the Sufi orders as well. Strictures of reformism, impinging on social-architectural interiors and Sufi orders alike, have limited the ritual ecstasy that can take place *within* social or architectural structures.

In the past, however, religious architecture was specifically designed to accommodate *ḥaḍra*, often public, within which localizing resonance was broadly accepted. During Egypt's Ayyubid and especially Mamluk periods, purpose-built structures arose to house Sufi ritual. Such structures—such as the *ribāṭ*, *zāwiya*, and *khānqāh*—typically enclosing shrines and dedicated to specific saintly lines, served to venerate saints and shaykhs through a harmonious blending with resonant ritual. These structures were supported by pious endowments (*awqāf*) from wealthy patrons who carefully stipulated ritual activities and the personnel to perform them. The proliferation of such structures is documented by the medieval Egyptian historian Maqrizi (1364–1442), who lists twenty-two *khānqāhs*, twelve *ribāṭs*, and twenty-seven smaller *zāwiyas*, besides numerous tombs.[17] During the Mamluk period, *ziyāra* to saints' shrines was so common that an entire genre of "pilgrimage guides" emerged.[18] The *zāwiya* (corner), originally designating the location of a particular teacher within a mosque, later came to refer to an independent structure associated with a shaykh and his *ṭarīqa*. Here the shaykh taught and conducted *ḥaḍra*, and here he was typically buried, so that structure and ritual transitioned naturally to promote shaykh as saint after his death.[19] Thus, upon visiting Egypt, Ibn Battuta (d. 1377) wrote that the Sufis "meet in a *qubba* inside the *zāwiya*." There they read the Qur'an and then hold a *dhikr*.[20] Such behavior can still be observed today.

During Egypt's Ottoman period, when the sultans themselves were increasingly involved in Sufism, the *zāwiya* expanded beyond its affiliation with a specific *ṭarīqa*, including a large Sufi meeting place (*qāʿa*). Open to the general population, the *zāwiya* became a locus for popular, resonant Sufi practices. ʿAbd al-Ghani al-Nabulusi (d. 1731), a Syrian writer and traveler, shaykh, and Sufi, describes the Friday *ḥaḍra* held in the *zāwiya* of poet-saint ʿUmar Ibn al-Farid, calling attention to ecstasy via feedback:

> The [Sufis] and all of those attending had read *Sūrat al-Kahf*, and they began to pray for the Messenger—God's blessings and peace be upon him—and for his majesty [the sultan]. Then they sealed the meeting and read the *al-Fatiḥah*. Then all of the Qur'an readers read something from the Qur'an. Next a singer arose and sang from the words of the shaykh ʿUmar—May God be satisfied with him. Everyone sat silently. A singer would rise and another would sit down, and, whenever one of them sang a hemistich of a verse, those present would show ecstasy and be seized by a spiritual state. So the singer would repeat that hemistich, while the people sat jammed together. That congregational mosque was so full that, if someone was seized by a spiritual state, he would get up and throw himself upon the others, and they would all call out together as the inner meaning of that verse of the shaykh ʿUmar's speech pervaded them.[21]

The number of *zāwiyas* increased throughout the Ottoman period; writing in the late nineteenth century, the Egyptian minister and reformer ʿAli Mubarak (1823–1893) noted 225.[22] Interior spaces continued to house ecstatic rituals throughout this period, as is evident from a number of firsthand accounts, such as that of Edward Lane, writing in the 1830s. In his famous *Manners and Customs of the Modern Egyptians,* Lane describes a number of resonant *ḥaḍras* unfolding within the *īwāns* of Husayn mosque, displaying a level of behavioral and musical ecstasy that would never be tolerated today, including ecstatic, musical *dhikr*, full of dancing, whirling, and trance, all centered on *ziyāra* to the shrine.[23]

Given the severity of the Ibn Taymiyya–derived doctrines they adopted, it is unsurprising that the reformist Wahhabi faithful set about destroying saints' shrines in order to eliminate *ziyāra* and related rituals,[24] because everything about the shrine encourages them. It is adequate proof, perhaps, of the close link between architecture and ritual that it was only by destroying the shrines themselves that the detested rituals could be halted. But *Sufi* reformers could also limit localization while preserving shrines, by attenuating resonance through modifications to the built environment.

Ritual Veneration in the Structural Exterior

Today, ecstatic interior scenes are no longer observable because of new ritual norms applied there, part of the rising arc of Islamic reformism, whose branding of activities not clearly articulated in Prophetic Sunna as *bidʿa* has gradually gathered wide approbation. Likewise, rituals in the "interior" of Sufi social structures—the *ṭuruq*—are more limited than those performed "outside" these social organizations.[25] In contemporary Egyptian Sufism, it is the freewheeling *ḥaḍra* unfolding in exterior, liminal spaces, between shrine and street, where adaptive flexibility suffused by *baraka* results in resonance, an emergent order of emotional power and social cohesion forging Islamic localizations. Conversely, when external spaces themselves are lost, resonance is curtailed, adaptive ritual veneration contracts, and localizations are inhibited.[26]

The power of ritual veneration in the exterior space surrounding the shrine exploits three principal freedoms—physical, cultural, and social—supporting resonance, yet without disconnection from sacred *baraka*. First, exterior space enables broader participation and freer interaction. Second, exterior space liberates ritual from sociocultural restrictions generally applied to architectural interiors, especially religious prohibitions on the performance of music, inclusion of women or children, and gender mixing. Third, socially exterior space frees participants from performative control of any shaykh, enabling greater freedom for the buildup of musical emotion.

The saint's annual *mawlid* is the grandest of occasions for such public saint veneration. *Mawlid* features many public *ḥaḍra*s (often simultaneous) in the *sāḥa*, each *ḥaḍra* a succession of *ṭabaqat*, each *ṭabaqa* an ecstatic buildup, each evening (over a series of nights—up to two weeks, for the greatest saints) reaching greater intensity, climaxing in the *layla kabīra* (great night), at which festival intensity—the number, the quality, and the overall dynamic level—attains its peak. The *mawlid* is well documented,[27] especially that of Tanta's famed saint, Sidi Ahmad al-Badawi,[28] and ʿAli Mubarak's *Khitat* contains long lists of *mawlid* dates.[29] Down to the present day (I observed it in 1992), the success of al-Badawi's festival depends in large measure on the availability of a large *sāḥa* proximate to the shrine itself, where public *ḥaḍra* is performed. Several of Cairo's saints are also visited weekly on a designated day (*yawm al-ziyāra*), an occasion celebrated as a miniature *mawlid* in the *sāḥa* area exterior to the shrine.[30] Such rituals are empowered to transform social relations, localized Islamic expressions capable of forging Islamic locality.

Indeed, it seems likely that in many cases, public *ḥaḍra* in exterior spaces is precisely what effected the transformation of religious figures into saints, establishing the complex of what some scholars have called the "cult of the saints" on a solid affective and socially cohesive basis. *Ḥaḍra* provided the impetus to build shrines—while shrines provided the impetus to hold *ḥaḍra*; both supported popular canonization. Thus Homerin, while stressing literary and hagiographic factors in the poet Ibn al-Farid's sanctification, also recounts the powerful and populous experience of *ḥaḍra* at the poet's shrine.[31] Michael Winter, writing of the Ottoman period, is more explicit: "The tomb of the departed shaykh . . . was the focus of veneration, visitation (*ziyāra*), and ritual, and as such was the center of the order, the site of the annual celebration on the shaykh's birthday, and an assurance of the continuity of the order. The tomb often established the shaykh as a saint."[32] Fernandes argues that during Egypt's period of Ottoman rule, Sufi shaykhs acquired tremendous social influence, disbursing food and economic opportunities through weekly *ziyāra* or annual *mawlid* festivals. Shaykhs were even regarded as carrying political power, in direct competition to the rulers, as a kind of state-within-a-state.[33] After death, the shaykh's shrine would continue to radiate *baraka*, his reputation depending on the ritual performance of *ḥaḍra*, alongside *ziyāra* or *mawlid*. The saints were regarded as forming a hidden spiritual government (*ḥukūma bāṭiniyya*), invoked in the course of *ḥaḍra* performance through *madad* and even overt statements of this doctrine.[34] The saint's power was gathered and displayed at the *mawlid* in social, spiritual, emotional, and economic forms.[35]

But if the tomb established the shaykh as a saint, a localized Islamic center, it could do so only via resonant ritual performance, confirming the power of saintly presence through personal experience. Resonant collective ritual not only elevated the shaykh to sainthood but also forged durable, affective social connections among saint and the participating *aḥbāb* who supported that status.

Architectural and Ritual Veneration of the Ahl al-Bayt in Cairo

Among all the *awliyāʾ*, the Ahl al-Bayt associated with Cairo shrines, being directly connected to the Prophet and architecturally proximate, are the most widely venerated in Cairo today, most present as a living force in the spiritual life of the people. The roots of such veneration can be traced to the rule of the Fatimids (969–1171), Egypt's only Shiʿi dynasty. Shiʿi Islam centers on devotion to the Ahl al-Bayt, whose members include the imamate. Despite two centuries of Shiʿi government, the general Egyptian population never turned substantially to Shiʿism.[36] But loving devotion for the Ahl al-Bayt percolated and persisted among Sunnis, and the custom of their *ziyāra* was thereafter lovingly maintained.[37] Such devotion is both expressed and kindled through *inshād*, especially in *ḥaḍra*, where *dhikr* (remembrance of God) is counterpointed by poetic devotion to the Prophet and Ahl al-Bayt.[38]

The Ahl al-Bayt of Cairo—as saints, as shrines—are quintessentially "exteriorized" with respect to sociocultural or architectural structural interiority, since their living presence transcends the *ṭarīqas*, representing saint veneration in its broadest sense: beyond their shrines and *sāḥas*, Cairo's Ahl al-Bayt define and name entire neighborhoods—al-Husayn, Sayyida Zaynab, Sayyida ʿAisha, Sidi ʿAli—enjoying the bounty of the saint's precinct (*riḥab al-walī*) and a broad swath of the general population (including Christians) flocks to their shrines for communion and assistance.[39] Such public saints are both more influential and more vulnerable than more hidden, structurally interiorized saints closely associated with specific *ṭarīqas*: on the one hand, they are venerated by many more people; on the other, their devotees are not formally organized, and their public veneration is more widely condemned as heresy (see fig. 5.1.)

In Cairo today, the *aḥbāb* continue to perform weekly *ziyāra* to certain Ahl al-Bayt shrines, as they have for centuries. Alongside *ziyāra* is *ḥaḍra*, includ-

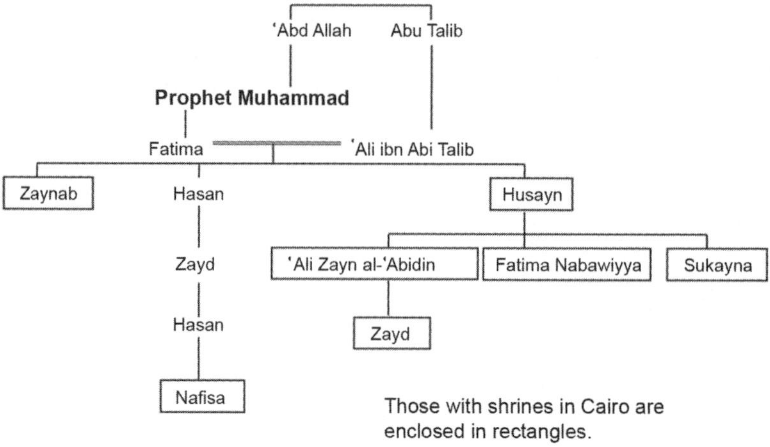

Figure 5.1. The most prominent figures of the Ahl al-Bayt in Cairo. Those with shrines in Cairo (outlined in rectangles) include the Prophet's grandchildren, Sayyida Zaynab and Imam al-Husayn; al-Husayn's children, ʿAli Zayn al-ʿAbidin, Fatima al-Nabawiyya, and Sayyida Sakina; and Sayyida Nafisa, Hasan's great-granddaughter.

ing musical performances of religious poetry (*inshād*) and chant (*dhikr*).[40] For example, Friday is *ziyāra* day at the *maqām* of Sayyida Zaynab, the Prophet Muhammad's granddaughter (see fig. 5.2).[41] Likewise, Friday and Tuesday are recognized *ziyāra* days for the Prophet's grandson, the Imam al-Husayn, Sunday for Sayyida Nafisa, and Monday for Fatima al-Nabawiyya, with public *ḥaḍras* in each saint's *sāḥa*.[42] Such gatherings, often ecstatic, also catalyze economic activity, including a café, food stalls, itinerant vendors of food and drink, and entertainments for the children. The whole complex of spiritual, social, and economic activity resonates . . . or did.

Architectural Veneration of ʿAli Zayn al-ʿAbidin

The Prophet Muhammad's great-grandson ʿAli Zayn al-ʿAbidin ("Ornament of the Worshipers," 658?–713?), colloquially known as "Sidi ʿAli," ranks among the most prominent of Cairo's Ahl al-Bayt.[43] His architectural and ritual veneration centers on a mosque-shrine marking what the general population

Figure 5.2. (a, *left*) Friday is *ziyāra* day at the *maqām* of Sayyida Zaynab, Cairo. (b, *right*) Visitors recite prayers and touch the silver *maqṣūra* (lattice), obtaining *baraka* (blessing). Circumambulation is now precluded, as at other shrines, by a division between men's and women's areas. Photographs by M. Frishkopf.

holds to be his burial site, not far from the shrine of his aunt Sayyida Zaynab (see fig. 5.3). Because renovating a shrine constitutes an act of veneration, attracting numerous wealthy devotees to the task, and because such acts are poorly documented, reconstructing shrine histories can be complex. However, it is possible to hazard a history of Sidi ʿAli's shrine so as to demonstrate how monuments may constitute a form of localized veneration harmonizing with ritual.

Most scholars deny that ʿAli Zayn al-ʿAbidin is buried at his Cairo *maqām*.[44] Following Maqrizi, some say the site marks the burial place of his son Zayd (694–740), founder of Zaidism, who led an insurrection in Kufa against the Umayyad caliph Hisham in 740 and was later captured and crucified.[45] Others claim that both are buried in Medina.[46] But popular sentiment—and shrine epigraphs—hold that both father and son rest in this shrine, whose history traces to the pre-Fatimid period. Evidently such differences are not new. According to Maqrizi,

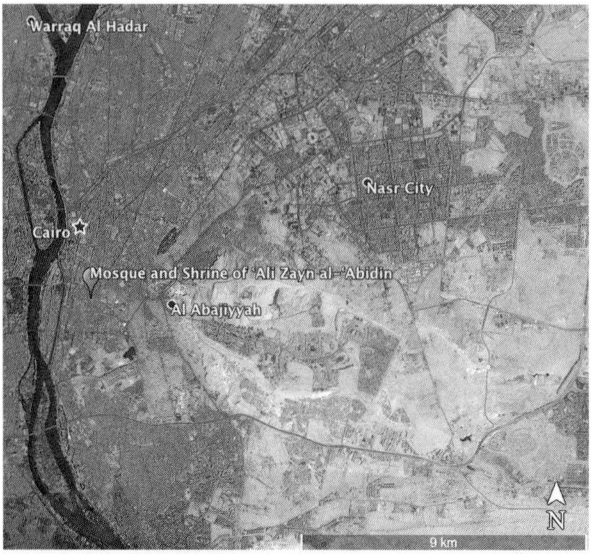

Figure 5.3. Location of Sidi ʿAli Zayn al-ʿAbidin's mosque-shrine in Cairo, near that of Sayyida Zaynab. Sidi ʿAli's shrine is located in an extension of Cairo's southern cemetery, adjoining the *madhbaḥ* (slaughterhouse) district. The gleaming new mosque squeezes into a densely packed built environment, its exterior stairways eliminating the *sāḥa* where *ḥaḍra* was formerly held. Map data © 2015 ORION-ME, © 2015 Digital Globe, © 2015 Google.

> This *mashhad*, lying between the ibn Tulun mosque and the city of Misr [i.e., Fustat], the people call Zayn al-ʿAbidin, but this is a mistake, as it is the *mashhad* of the head of Zayd ibn ʿAli.... In the old times it was known as the mosque of Muharras the Eunuch, who built it in the time that Hisham ibn ʿAbd al-Malak took [Zayd's head] to Egypt... then the people of Egypt stole it and buried it in this place. Al-Kindi wrote that it came to Egypt in the year 122 AH.[47]

Maqrizi claims that al-Afdal (1066–1121 CE), son of Fatimid minister Badr al-Jamali,[48] found Muharras's mosque in ruins, located the head, and honored it with a new shrine in 525 AH (1131 CE). (The timeline is problematic: al-Afdal died in 515 AH; possibly the credit for rebuilding should go to his son, al-Afdal Kutayfat.)[49] A new dome was added in the Mamluk period (fifteenth century),[50] and the shrine was again renovated in the early nineteenth century, under Ottoman rule.[51]

A report from the international Comité de Conservation des Monuments de l'Art Arabe mainly confirms these data, indicating that little remained of the original Fatimid structure: "The tomb of Zayn al-ʿAbidin was founded by Badr al-Jamali at the end of the fifth century Hijri (eleventh century CE) and was reconstructed by ʿUthman Agha Mustahfazan in 1225 AH (1810 CE). It hasn't retained its original construction except for a Fatimid arch in the interior and its entryway door. These were classified under the Comité's program of renovation."[52] In the late nineteenth century, a new Ottoman *maqṣūra* was added, dated 1863. A plaque (*lawḥa*) located at the entrance to this mosque proclaims: "this is the *mashhad* of the Imam ʿAli Zayn al-ʿAbidin."[53] In this form, the mosque-shrine appears to have endured until the very end of the twentieth century.

Reconstructing *sāḥa* history is more difficult, but there are clues suggesting the continuous availability of an open exterior space until the mosque was entirely rebuilt in 2000. Thus Maqrizi writes: "All around the shrine of Zayd, what the ordinary people know as ʿAli Zayn al-ʿAbidin, are gardens, extending to the east and west."[54]

Ostensibly, the Comité did not authorize extensive renovation of the ʿAli Zayn al-ʿAbidin mosque because of its perceived lack of historical significance, aside from the aforementioned Fatimid arch and door. Yet, Comité reports suggest at least a passing concern for maintenance of ritual, beyond historical and aesthetic criteria. For instance, at the mosque-shrine of Sayyida Sakina (daughter of Husayn, also known as Sukayna), "the Comité declined to conduct large scale conservation activities[;] . . . because it was of little or no 'merite artistique,' it deserved only limited restorations that were necessary to maintain the cultic activities practiced there."[55]

As a result of this combined policy of conservation, renovation, and neglect, the mosque-shrine and *sāḥa* of ʿAli Zayn al-ʿAbidin appear to have been left relatively undisturbed for centuries as a site for traditional rituals of *ziyāra* and *ḥaḍra*. While the surrounding area no doubt filled with tombs during this period, the *sāḥa* in front of the mosque, where a weekly Saturday *ḥaḍra* was performed at least from the late nineteenth century, remained available.

Ritual Veneration of ʿAli Zayn al-ʿAbidin

I visited Sidi ʿAli every week from fall 1992 until spring 1993. On Saturdays, the usual trickle of shrine visitors would coalesce into crowds that also patronized the adjacent café and participated in festive activities around the mosque and throughout the district. Vigorous musical *ḥaḍras*, beginning in early afternoon and continuing into the evening—with short breaks for *ʿaṣr*, *maghrib* (sunset) and *ʿishāʾ* prayers—took place in the *sāḥa* adjoining the mosque's entrance.

Heralded by the crackling of speakers and warmup of musical instrumentalists, the *sāḥa* would crowd with *dhakkīra* (performers of *dhikr*) and *muḥibbīn*, many gathering in the adjoining café, threaded by steady streams of devotees flowing to and from the shrine's interior. The *ḥaḍra* was solemnly launched by an elderly shaykh (the *mustaftiḥ*) who recited prayers and then clapped his large, sonorous hands to set the tempo. After a few minutes, the amplified *munshid*, supported by a traditional music ensemble comprising reed flute and percussion, took over as de facto *ḥaḍra* leader. Tips (*nuʾaṭ*) enhanced the mood as the *munshid* uttered supplications in the donor's honor. Musicians responded to feedback, lifting the emotional level by gradually raising tempo and tonal center, while the *munshid* did the same with the text, culminating with praise of Sidi ʿAli at the climax of the hour-long *ṭabaqa*, as the *sāḥa* was resounding with resonance. By this time, someone would inevitably enter a trance state, *wajd*. Reaching its peak, the music and *inshād* ceased, and with it the *dhikr*. After a short break, the *ḥaḍra* resumed with a new *ṭabaqa* featuring another *munshid*. All the while visitors streamed in and out of the shrine, performing *ziyāra*. Both men and women participated in all activities.

Sidi ʿAli's weekly Saturday *ziyāra* and *ḥaḍra* was documented long before I arrived in Egypt. Already in the nineteenth century—shortly after what appears to have been the final renovation to the old mosque—ʿAli Mubarak noted that devotees venerated Sidi ʿAli with a *ḥaḍra* performed every Saturday afternoon and evening.[56] In 1976, de Jong published an ethnographic survey of Cairo's *ziyāra* days as he had observed them while residing in Cairo from 1972 to 1973. He too describes Sidi ʿAli's Saturday *ḥaḍra*:

> The *ḥaḍra* starts after the *ʿaṣr*-prayer in the square before the mosque, which is surrounded by tombs. During the *ḥaḍra*, musical instruments such as *dufūf, kāsāt,* and various kinds of flutes may occasionally be used. After the *ʿishāʾ* prayer a *ḥaḍra* is held until about two o'clock in the morning, generally preceded by a political speech delivered by one of the members of the local executive committee of the Socialist Union for this quarter. *Munshidūn* and musicians all belong to a relatively new *ṭarīqa*, the Awlād Abū al-Qāsim or Qāsimiyya, who have virtually monopolized this *ḥaḍra*.[57]

From these two brief accounts, we may infer the continuity of this particular *ḥaḍra* over more than a century, though given what is known about the flourishing of Sufism and saint veneration in Egypt from the thirteenth century to the nineteenth, and the establishment of the shrine even earlier, ritual veneration at Sidi ʿAli's shrine is likely far older.

We can also establish a trajectory of decline. Criticism of saint veneration may be long-standing, but this critique did not flourish in practice until recent decades. De Jong records informants to be "generally of the opinion that *ziyāra* days were not what they had been in former times and that the number of participants had declined." Indeed, he discerns a connection to the exterior built environment and its implications for economic exchange and devotion, noting the impact of tomb building on *ziyāra*—but also deliberate attempts to preserve the *sāḥa*: "The space available for the *ziyāra*-day near the mosque of Sidi ʿAli has been considerably reduced in recent times because of the random burying and building of memorials here, since for its *baraka* it is a favourable site in burial. Lately, however, certain limitations were set on this and the local executive committee of the Socialist Union in this quarter initiated the sanitation of the mosque and its surroundings."[58]

By the time I witnessed it, some twenty years later, Sidi ʿAli's *ḥaḍra* was shorter and less orderly than the one de Jong had observed. Musicians were not all from a single *tariqa*. Many participants appeared desperately poor, not the sort of group that might appeal to politicians, and indeed there were no political speeches. Tombs continued to encroach from all sides.

Yet the *sāḥa* directly in front of the shrine was still cleared for *ḥaḍra*, which vigorously unfolded more or less exactly as de Jong had described it. The venerable mosque was dilapidated but featured a localized patchwork of architectural styles—Fatimid, Mamluk, Ottoman—uniquely referencing its history, and the *ḥaḍra*, if diminished, remained spirited and crowded, adapted to its sociocultural and built environments. Resonance continued to flourish (see fig. 5.4).

Architectural and Ritual Renovation at ʿAli Zayn al-ʿAbidin

In 2000, Sidi ʿAli's idiosyncratic mosque-shrine was torn down. An imposing, standard-issue twenty-first-century mosque, in gleaming marble, was erected in its place, with the shrine on a lower level and the mosque above. The shrine room was divided into male and female sides, preventing mixed-gender gatherings and making circumambulation—a key moment of *ziyāra*, during which the saint's axial centrality is deeply experienced—impossible. Extensive exterior stairways built above the old *sāḥa* eliminated this open exterior space, forcing *ḥaḍra* into side alleys far from the shrine, while enabling reform-minded worshipers to enter the mosque at the upper level, without encountering the *maqām* at all. A massive iron gate was constructed between alleys and stairways, blocking the former free flow between *ziyāra* and *ḥaḍra*. While *ziyāra* continued, its energy was depleted by disconnection from *ḥaḍra*, and resonance declined sharply (see figs. 5.5, 5.6, and 5.7).

This transformation cannot be interpreted as anti-Sufi: the new ʿAli Zayn al-ʿAbidin mosque was unequivocally erected to venerate the saint in a grand fashion. Rather, by attenuating resonance of the public *ḥaḍra*, replacing a localized monument with a standard architectural form, and capitulating to reformist antipathy toward worship alongside a shrine, the renovation appears as reformist and pro-Sufi yet anti-localization. This interpretation is supported by the following narrative, related to me by an Egyptian architectural historian:

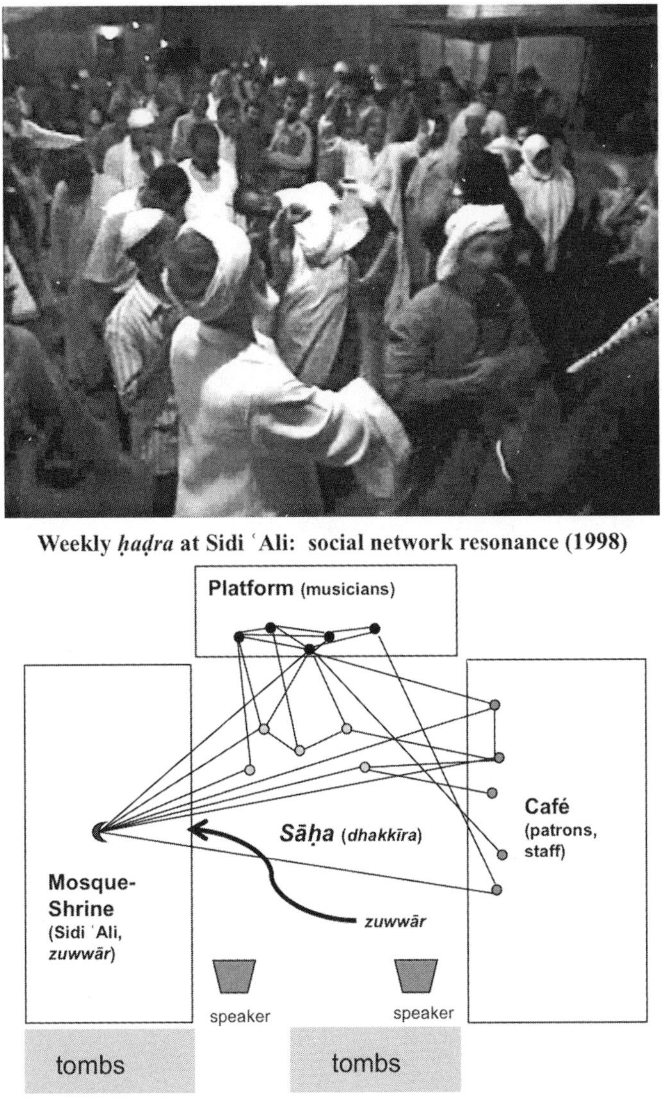

Figure 5.4. (a, *top*) Ecstasy: a resonant scene from Saturday *ziyāra* and *ḥaḍra* at the mosque-shrine of Sidi ʿAli in 1998. The Ottoman-era mosque appears in the background (*top right*); the *sāḥa* is in the foreground, full of *dhakkīra*, with the *mustaftiḥ* leading (clapping; *bottom center*); the *munshid* appears at right. From video by M. Frishkopf. (b, *bottom*) *Ziyāra* and *ḥaḍra* schematic: resonance at Sidi ʿAli's shrine, 1998. The *ḥaḍra* remained active and energetic, even if it had declined since de Jong described it.

Figure 5.5. The mosque-shrine of Sidi ʿAli in 2015: a monumental ritual silence: (a, *top*) A banner announces "*maqām* Sidi ʿAli Zayn al-ʿAbidin"; the main stairway is visible, with the mosque behind it. (b, *bottom*) An iron fence blocks direct access to the surrounding cemetery area, including the new *sāḥa* on the other side of its gate. The small dome marks the *maqām* of another saint (Sidi Khurshid). Photographs: M. Frishkopf.

Figure 5.6. The mosque-shrine of Sidi ʿAli in 2015: a monumental ritual silence (continued): (a, *left*) The top of the stairway levels off in an extended landing providing direct access to the prayer area, avoiding the *maqām*, and eliminating the old *sāḥa*. Photograph: M. Frishkopf. (b, *right*) The *maqām*, located on the lower level, is isolated from the main prayer area; a barrier separates male and female sides, precluding circumambulation. Photograph: Walid Ibrahim, 2014.

During the 1970s ʿUmar al-Faruq served as Egypt's Minister of Housing and secretary of Egypt's largest construction company, The Arab Contractors. Personally he was devoted to the Ahl al-Bayt, serving on the boards of several of their mosques. In this way the Arab Contractors became involved in rebuilding mosques and shrines, a confluence of money, politics, and spiritual devotion.

After the 1992 earthquake, there was a competition between the Ministry of Culture and the Ministry of Housing to restore damaged historic mosques. While the former adopted a holistic conservation approach, balancing engineering with historical preservation and concern for local cultural context, the latter were more concerned with applying scientific principles, regardless of history or culture. Both Ministries used the Arab Contractors to carry out renovations. The more secular Ministry of Culture was commissioned to renovate

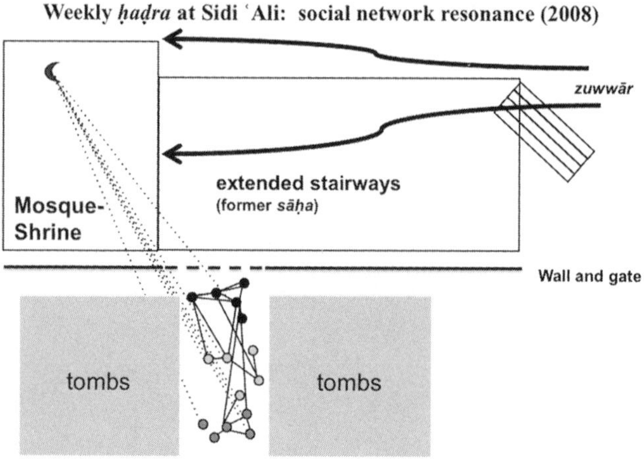

Figure 5.7. *Ḥaḍra* in the new *sāḥa*, 2015: (a, *top*) Supported by his ensemble, the *munshid* performs for his café audience; the mosque of ʿAli Zayn al-ʿAbidin is bathed in green light behind the iron gate. (b, *middle*) The *munshid* turns to perform for *aḥbāb* (*zuwwār*) on the other side of the gate. (c, *bottom*) *Ziyāra* and *ḥaḍra* schematic: Sidi ʿAli's shrine, 2008. Displaced from its customary *sāḥa*, *ḥaḍra* squeezes in side alleys, distant from the shrine's *baraka*, from which it is also socially and symbolically blocked by an iron gate. The two rituals of *ziyāra* and *ḥaḍra* are separated. Photographs: M. Frishkopf.

> historic sites of touristic interest, while the Ministry of Housing was given the task of renovating Ahl al-Bayt shrines, thanks to a push from then Minister of Housing, Ibrahim Sulayman, with funding from the Ministry of Religious Endowments (*Awqāf*). They carried these out without consideration for the urban fabric.[59]

ʿAli Zayn al-ʿAbidin's new mosque is simultaneously a monumental act of veneration and a reformist act of the Egyptian state, performed without concern for local history or culture. It serves *ziyāra* in a manner less likely to contravene contemporary Islamic sensibilities, including injunctions against mixing of men and women, circumambulating a shrine, or praying in a mosque containing a shrine. Most strikingly, the new design inhibits *ḥaḍra* resonance, thereby weakening support for Islamic localization in saint veneration. While it is hard to attribute intentionality without further confirmation, the Comité was at least somewhat concerned with ritual practice, perhaps in the manner of its successor, the Ministry of Culture. But the Ministry of Housing harbored no such concerns.

While the *ḥaḍra* continues to be held each Saturday, it is now far from the *baraka*-radiating shrine, squeezed into irregular side alleys between tombs and separated from the mosque by the iron gate. Presence of enshrined body and embodied shrine in *ḥaḍra* is far weaker, the iron gate physically obstructing resonance. On one occasion, I witnessed the *munshid* turn and try to perform for *aḥbāb* trapped on the other side of these iron bars, as if imprisoned there (see figs. 5.5, 5.6, and 5.7a and b). When *ḥaḍra* pauses for prayer, most participants no longer even pray in Sidi ʿAli's mosque; instead, they worship in an adjacent mosque dedicated to another saint (Sidi Khurshid). I asked one *munshid*—whom I had known since 1992—about the changes we had both witnessed. He told me the new *sāḥa* is officially sanctioned; they are not allowed to perform *ḥaḍra* any closer to Sidi ʿAli's shrine. What does he think of this new situation? He merely shrugged, muttering "*tagdīd*" (modernization, renewal).

Separated from the *maqām* and *ziyāra*, *ḥaḍra* attendance has markedly declined, its resonance inhibited (see fig. 5.7c). What remains cannot even be called *ḥaḍra*, properly speaking: all *dhikr* has ceased; there is no shaykh; *munshidin* privilege popular song and *nuʾaṭ* over the messages of religious *inshād*; café patrons laugh and talk, sometimes moved to stand and dance, but spiritual emotion is limited. Listeners exclusively consist of patrons of these makeshift alley cafes; the *ḥaḍra* is no longer attractive to the spiritually minded, appearing instead as a form of low-class entertainment. As another longtime *ḥaḍra* attendee, a middle-class woman whom I had known since 1992, wistfully told me, "there's no more *ḥaḍra*, just dance and money." The weekly event has ceased to play an effective role in Islamic localization at Sidi ʿAli's shrine.

The Rise of the Architext: The Suppression of Resonance and Delocalization of Islam

Resonance, resulting from cybernetic loops of thought-feeling flowing through communicative channels (musical, verbal, economic, spiritual) established among *ḥaḍra* participants (including the saint himself) and adapting to local conditions centered on the shrine, injects local relations with common affect, supplying a Durkheimian "effervescence" (e.g., *wajd*) that forges local solidarity, an affective socio-spiritual unity. Sequences of shrine-centered *ḥaḍra ṭabaqat*, exhibiting longer-term amplificatory feedback cycles across hours, weeks, or years, bind together entire communities of participating *aḥbāb*, sharing belief in the saint and stories of his life and miracles.

But this embodied, localized Islam, centered on the shrine, never detaches from the global: the *aḥbāb* continue to perform universal Islamic rituals and hold universal Islamic beliefs. Rather, the local is connected to the global—paradigmatically and syntagmatically--through embodied connections, supporting Islamic universals with local roots. Such an Islam can be characterized as externally diverse but internally unified. Unlike purely global Islam, defined and carried primarily by fixed material models—universal texts (Qurʾan, Sunna) and structures (the mosque or minaret) oriented in a fixed direction (*qibla*) toward a globally fixed point (the Kaʿba)—localized Islam develops through humanly mediated models, constituting an oral tradition whose adaptation and transmission occur in conjunction with performance, centered on, supporting, and empowered by the shrine.

In this chapter I have focused on how monumental and ritual saint veneration may support resonance, and thus a socially, ritually, and doctrinally localized Islam, or—conversely—may oppose it, depending on the particular configurations of the built environment, which thereby appears as a powerful factor shaping the nature of Islam itself.

Until the nineteenth century, interiors of purpose-built architecture were crucial for providing protected spaces where resonance could thrive. Ritual critiques, however, developed in the medieval period and rose to prominence with nineteenth-century reform movements, becoming more widely activated since the 1970s. Following accusations of *"bidʿa,"* new spatial and social configurations of the built environment attenuated resonance in interior spaces.

But localizing resonance, evicted from interiors of mosques, *zāwiyas*, and shrines, continued to thrive in socially and architecturally exterior spaces of liminality: in the *sāḥa*, situated between shrine and street; among the *aḥbāb*, situated between *ṭarīqa* members and non-Sufi Muslims; among the Ahl al-Bayt, situated between the Prophet and ordinary saints. Resonance had always been more socially and emotionally powerful in these exterior structural positions. Now they became the principal stage for enactment of resonance and social localization. Here, outside the formal jurisdiction of religious authority, resonant ritual was empowered, more exposed and more vulnerable, but also more difficult to control via religious discourses and more powerfully maintained via mass oral transmission.

Governments could still impose controls, through regulation enforced by state power. Samuli Schielke has recently written about police interventions in *mawālid* through spatial reconfigurations aimed at ensuring a more orderly, "rational" festival. In the case of Sidi Ibrahim al-Dasuqi's *mawlid*, as examined by Schielke, police barriers occluded the main square where festivities were traditionally held, resulting in displacement to side alleys and a corresponding reduction in economic value (and hence, in my terms, resonance).[60]

Yet I argue also that these "reformist" spatial reconfigurations, preserving architectural veneration while suppressing ritual veneration, cannot—at the system level—be interpreted as "rationalizing" or "modernizing" Islam, even if informants make such claims. Religion is never entirely rational, and Islam is never entirely "modern." Nor do they oppose saint veneration; despite centuries of anti-Sufi polemic, reformers are not, on the whole, anti-Sufi.

Rather, in my view, such spatial reconfiguration is—again, at the system level—dedicated to the evisceration of Islam's localized social-spiritual solidarities of public exterior space in favor of an externally unified, global *umma*. Such solidarities are created by resonant public *ḥaḍras* conjoined with *ziyāra*, but not by *ziyāra* alone, which does not forge social solidarities on its own, or by a monument itself.

Localization is repressed by attenuating resonant performance, replacing ramifying, humanly mediated adaptive models with universal, static, materially mediated models precluding adaptation. I call this collection of static, material models the "architext," literally "prime text." This neologism,[61] also combining fixed forms of "architecture" and "text," references those material structures stubbornly insisting on their own hegemony, resisting all adaptation, localization, or ramification.

Why this rise of the architext at this particular historical juncture? Islam has always existed as both system and lifeworld in Habermas's sense.[62] The lifeworld provides meaning, while the system aims at coordination, extending power by colonizing the former. All that has changed is the means by which power has been acquired, and this change can be understood by reference to historical conditions.

During the period of Islamic hegemony, from the seventh up until the nineteenth century, Islamic globalization proceeded via localization, extending deep roots by embracing adaptive resonant practices that incorporated local performative types and structures. Converts could join the *umma* while retaining most of their familiar lifeworld, freely combining local culture with the essential Islamic message of *tawḥid* (monotheism). Such syncretism was sanctioned by local scholars and norms (e.g., in West Africa via the so-called Suwarian tradition).[63] Rituals, such as *ḥaḍra*, drawing on local music, poetry, and other practices, provided an essentially localizing force. Connecting global essence and local form, Islam quickly established itself in the hearts and minds of Muslims around the globe, emphasizing inner feeling over outer uniformity, gathering all into the *umma* via an inner unity belying outwardly ramified diversity.

But then calamity struck. Europe prevailed over Islam, first in outlying areas and then at its very core. With the fall of the Ottoman Empire and the end of the *khilāfa*, this process was complete. Muslim thinkers sought an explanation. The rapid fall from power had to be attributed to Islamic malpractice. Suddenly, localized socio-emotional structures were understood as a point of weakness rather than strength. The formula "globalization via localization," inner unity through outer diversity, was inverted. Henceforth outer unity was to be privileged, at the cost of inner diversity. Even hypocrisy could be tolerated, as long as all Muslims were—literally and metaphorically—praying in the same way and in the same direction. Saint veneration, a universal practice, could be tolerated, but not ecstatic rituals with the capacity to fragment the *umma* through formation of local solidarities. The system seized ground from the lifeworld in an attempt to reconstitute its power.

These processes are exemplified in the Egyptian case, where saint veneration enjoys support from the highest official sources of political and religious authority, yet architectural renovations of a shrine squelch longstanding ritual resonance that had forged localized communities for centuries. In the case of Cairo's Ahl al-Bayt, the domination of the engineering-oriented Ministry of Housing over the more culturally sensitive Ministry of Culture is symptomatic of this broader shift in the balance from lifeworld to system. Sidi ʿAli's old idiosyncratic shrine, reflecting and supporting a long, diverse history of community veneration, from Fatimid to Ottoman times, is gone. At his glorious new shrine, veneration continues, but disconnected from locality. Resonance is suppressed, as deeply localized spiritual-social meaning is sacrificed for global unity and power.

NOTES

1 See Frishkopf 1999, 2013.
2 Lane 1842, 209–221; Goldziher 1971; Gilsenan 1973; de Jong 1976; Williams 1985; Waugh 1989; Hoffman 1995; Reeves 1995; Johnson 1996; Christopher Taylor 1998; Winter 2004, 163–178.
3 See Laoust 1962; Christopher Taylor 1990, 128; Fierro 1992, 231–232.
4 See Iskander 2001.
5 Christopher Taylor 1990; Winter 2004, 165–166.
6 El Sandouby 2008, 90.
7 *Baraka* does not require the saint's physical presence, and many shrines are not burial sites at all, at least not of the whole eponymous saint. On the one hand are a number of "head shrines" (*mashāhid al-ruʾūs*), putatively containing only the saint's head. On the other are "vision shrines" (*mashāhid ruʾya*), established through dreams. Egyptian Sufis frequently told me that every saint has 40 shrines. Finally, many shrines are misattributed.
8 Chih 2007, 25.
9 Christopher Taylor 1990, 90.
10 See Frishkopf 2000.
11 For example, Abu Hamid al-Ghazzali (d. 1111) or al-Junayd. See MacDonald and al-Ghazzali 1902 (January), 1–2.
12 See Frishkopf 1999.
13 Lane 1842; McPherson 1941; de Jong 1976; Frishkopf 2001; Winter 2004, 170–178.

14 Racy 1991; Shannon 2003b. For links between *ṭarab* and *wajd*, see Frishkopf 2001.
15 Frishkopf 2001.
16 Frishkopf 1999, 2013.
17 Schimmel 1965, 376.
18 Schimmel 1965, 371; Winter 1982, 109; 2004, 164–178; Christopher Taylor 1990, esp. 7–16 (guides), 100–137 (*ziyāra*); Ohtoshi 1995, 2006.
19 Fernandes 1980, 41.
20 Fernandes 1980, 130.
21 Homerin 2001, 80. "Spiritual state" translates *wajd* and *ḥal* in the original. See Fernandes 1980, 130. *Sūrat al-Kahf* and *al-Fatiḥah* are Qur'anic chapters (18 and 1, respectively).
22 See Fernandes 1980, 44; 1983; Behrens-Abouseif and Fernandes 1985, 120.
23 Lane 1842, 432–433, 459, 458–463.
24 Wensinck and Ansari 2012.
25 Frishkopf 2001.
26 Compare El Sandouby 2008, 86–90.
27 Schimmel 1965, 371.
28 Lane 1842, 219–220, 239–240; Schimmel 1965, 371; Reeves 1995; Winter 2004, 128; Çelebi et al. 2011, 397–415.
29 Mubarak 1886; McPherson 1941; Christopher Taylor 1990, 104.
30 De Jong 1976; Christopher Taylor 1998.
31 Homerin 2001, 83.
32 Winter 1982, 109.
33 Fernandes 1983, 14–15.
34 Reeves 1995.
35 Fernandes 1983, 15.
36 Lapidus 1988, 287; Winter 2004, 167.
37 Lane 1842; de Jong 1976; Christopher Taylor 1990; Hoffman-Ladd 1992, 617 ff.
38 Hoffman-Ladd 1992, 629; Frishkopf 2000.
39 Reeves 1995, 310.
40 Frishkopf 1999.
41 Abu-Zahra 1997.
42 De Jong 1976.
43 For Shiʿi Muslims, ʿAli Zayn al-ʿAbidin is the fourth Imam; however this status is not generally recognized in predominantly Sunni Egypt.
44 Kohlberg 2012.
45 Raghib 1970, 27–28; Muhammad 1971, 105–106; de Jong 1976 (but he miswrites "Zayn" for "Zayd"); Williams 1985, 52.
46 Madelung 2012.
47 Maqrizi n.d., 1202. See also Williams 1985, 52–53.
48 Badr's architectural contributions to Cairo are legion; see AlSayyad 2011, 70.

49 Williams 1985, 53.
50 Muhammad 1971, 106.
51 Rogers 2012, citing Ali Mubarak.
52 Misr Lagnat Hifz al-Athar al-ʿArabiyya al-Qadima 1933, 128.
53 Muhammad 1971, 106.
54 Maqrizi n.d., 799.
55 Misr Lagnat Hifz al-Athar al-ʿArabiyya al-Qadima 1887, 41; Ibrashy 2005, 243; El Sandouby 2008, 183–184.
56 Mubarak 1886, 91.
57 De Jong 1976, 30.
58 De Jong 1976, 39; see also Taylor 1990.
59 The source remains anonymous out of privacy concerns. Ironically, these were the very funds originally linked to the maintenance of particular shrines and their rituals, which had been seized by the Egyptian government in the early nineteenth century, under Muhammad ʿAli Pasha, in order to assure centralized control—an early step toward eradication of the local, in the service of power.
60 Schielke 2008, 543.
61 In his study of poetics, Gérard Genette (who acknowledged his neologistic debt to Louis Marin) distinguishes five forms of "transtextuality," of which "architext" is one; Genette defines it as "the entire set of general or transcendent categories ... from which emerges each singular text." Nebahat Avcioğlu applies this literary concept to the architecture of Istanbul. Both use it in a completely different sense from mine. See Chabrol and Marin 1974; Genette 1997, 1; Avcioğlu 2008.
62 See Habermas 1987, 113–198, especially 118.
63 Samwini 2003, 37, drawing upon Ivor Wilks and others.

CHAPTER SIX

Nightingales and Sweet Basil

The Cultural Geography of Aleppine Song

JONATHAN H. SHANNON

Listening Architecturally

This chapter explores the resonances between naturalistic metaphors and the modern built environment in Aleppo, Syria, through analysis of what I call the cultural geography of Aleppine song, focusing on the resonance of the *qudūd ḥalabiyya* genre within the built environment of the old city of Aleppo. Drawing on ethnographic and phenomenological investigations of the relationships among space, place, and sound, I propose a way of listening to Aleppine song architecturally, as well as of viewing Aleppine architecture, both classical and vernacular, acoustically. I do so by outlining the "acoustemology" of urban Aleppo (*ḥalab*), and the cultural geography of the popular Syrian song form called the *qudūd ḥalabiyya* ("the Aleppine *qudūd*").[1] The preponderance of naturalistic images in these songs—especially of birds, plants, and gardens—speaks volumes about the society that created and consumes them, as well as the anxieties and contradictions of a society undergoing rapid change. For this reason, the cultural geography of the *qudūd* offers an ear onto the fault lines between past and present understandings of place in Syrian society.

I argue that performance of the *qudūd* today expresses more than a deeply romantic or nostalgic impulse among Syrians. Rather, the contemporary interest in these songs resonates with a longing (*ḥanīn*) for a disappearing past as a means of redefining "development" and "modernity" to be more in tune with local and regional cultural values. In this way, performance of the *qudūd* engages with revivalist and preservationist discourses in the spatial realm (especially architectural renovation projects in the old city of Aleppo) but also resonates in the musical and auditory realms (e.g., in movements to standardize the call to prayer, *adhān*, in the city). Musical performance thus promotes a type of cultural engagement that blends nostalgia for the past and critical engagement with the forces of modernity in order to create the grounds for a social revival. In this way, the songbirds sing of a nuanced modernity, and the aromatic plants announce a complex relationship to cultural authenticity in an urban environment. This chapter analyzes the acoustic ecology of the old city of Aleppo in the decade prior to the outbreak of the Syrian rebellion in March 2011. The relationships I discuss between the urban soundscape and landscape of Aleppo are now disrupted and likely will not return to what they were in the late twentieth and early twenty-first centuries.

The Sonorous Built Environment

Anthropology, ethnomusicology, and cultural geography offer productive ways of analyzing the relationships among sound, the built environment, and social formations.[2] A key insight of recent studies has been that the built environment—human-made structures and forms that organize social and cultural life—both expresses existing social forms and helps construct and refashion them anew.[3] For example, gender, class, and other social hierarchies are simultaneously reflected in and constructed through household forms, interior decoration, urban design, and landscape architecture.[4]

Moreover, the physical form both reflects and reproduces the distribution of power in society,[5] so that one can read the built environment as a manifestation of power and also understand power as responding to specific complexes of physical form. The distribution of social power within the built environment also structures the cultural life of that space, including its acoustic properties, opening spaces for what de Certeau (1984) called "tactics" of subverting this power through creation of new spaces or appropriation of existing ones. Thus the urban soundscape reverberates with the power and social dispositions (or habitus) of its inhabitants, and, to extend de Certeau's analysis, one might analyze not only the tactics and strategies of "walking in the city"[6] but also those of listening to it.[7]

We should not assume, however, that the relationships between built environment and social and cultural forms are either uniform or simple. Rather, the construction of place and the spatial structuring of subjectivities are contested processes. As Stokes (1994b), among others, has remarked, musical performance is intimately tied to the production of modern subjectivities and the politics of place-making. It is through these complex interactions among place, subjectivity, sound, and politics that acoustemologies arise.

Analysis of Aleppo's built environment must begin with the physical and cultural distinction of the city into three basic but contrasting zones: the old city, the new city, and the peri-urban exterior spaces.[8] The old city (*madīna qadīma*) refers to the premodern intramural residential and commercial areas of Aleppo that surround the Citadel;[9] the central areas date mostly to the medieval and early modern periods but in many instances bear traces of Roman and even pre-Roman design. Like Damascus, Aleppo claims to be the oldest continuously inhabited city in the world. The new city[10] comprises the wide variety of neighborhoods outside the intramural city limits, including those dating to the late Ottoman era (c. 1875–1915) and those of more recent construction. Finally, the peri-urban spaces mark the liminal borderland between the urban zones and the countryside (*rīf*), both spatially and in terms of their sonic properties, as I explore in the following pages.

Recent developments have targeted both the preservation and renovation of the old city, the modernization and development of the new, and the planning for projected urban growth into peri-urban zones.[11] Regarding the old city, demographic shifts have led to the relative overcrowding and impoverishment of most old city neighborhoods in the last half of the twentieth century due to the relocation of the merchant classes to the newer quarters and the influx of rural migrants.[12] Recent decades have seen the gradual transformation of the old city into a zone for nostalgic consumption through the renovation of historic buildings (mosques, caravansaries, Qur'anic schools, and numerous traditional courtyard homes, which have been transformed into restaurants and boutique hotels). These projects are a consequence both of the old city's designation as a UNESCO World Heritage site, with its attendant privileges and restrictions, and of the rise of a new comprador capitalist class eager to profit from increased tourism and consumption of heritage. As a result, the old city has enjoyed not only renewed investment, critical attention to infrastructural development, and rising tourism but also increasing class divisions and even "gentrification."

The new city neighborhoods are diverse architecturally, socially, and sonically. Tony upscale neighborhoods house the established merchant classes, many elites, and the small population of foreign diplomats, while emerging and aspiring middle-class residents flock to newer developments on the outskirts of town. The new city also features quarters housing majority Kurdish and Christian populations, with a mixture of socioeconomic classes and diverse soundscapes: wedding songs and funereal chants, church bells, and other markers of ethnicity and sect resound in these enclaves. The newer quarters remain the most densely populated zones and, as a result, the most diverse in terms of their social and sonorous properties.

Finally, the peri-urban zone marks transitional areas along Aleppo's rural fringe, where exploding population growth and increasing in-migration have led to the construction of new residential neighborhoods as well as the development of light industrial and agricultural facilities. It is mostly in these areas where Aleppo retains a distinctly rural character, in terms of both its built environment (housing styles and uses) and its dominant soundscapes.

The tripartite urban geography maps social and cultural distinctions that reveal fault lines in the distribution of socioeconomic power and its attendant cultural manifestations. While the old city falls under the patronage of UNESCO and other NGOs eager to curtail development and to direct resources to the preservation of historic sites, the newer neighborhoods outside the old city walls, as well as the growing peri-urban and rural periphery, are less subject to regulation and standardization. As a result, each zone resonates as a soundscape echoing the contradictions and anxieties of the communities that inhabit it, and each reverberates with the sounds of a society undergoing transition. In the following pages, I outline these soundscapes for each zone, focusing on the acoustemology of the old city.[13]

An Acoustemology of Sounds Resounding in the Old City of Aleppo

By "acoustemology" Steven Feld refers to sonic ways of knowing and the production of knowledge in acoustic environments. An acoustemology therefore privileges a sonic sensibility that complements other modes of attention—visual, kinesthetic, olfactory, tactile, gustatory—and links them in a particular hierarchy of senses.[14] An acoustemology of urban space opens our ears to the ways sounds—ambient, natural, industrial, musical—resonate with deeper cultural patterns and social distinctions within a given social and ecological space, whether the rain forest of New Guinea, the villages of Europe, the coast of Ghana, urban Syria, or anywhere else humans inhabit.[15]

A given physical space implies an acoustic environment because built environments promote particular soundscapes. A home interior, a patio, a street, a neighborhood—these spaces comprise acoustic spaces as well. Moreover, these acoustic-physical spaces are laden with social meanings, carry particular cultural histories, and construct and reproduce subjectivities.[16] In this manner, architectural spaces can be analyzed as "extension[s] of the musical or vocal art form performed within [them]."[17] We might add other forms of sonic activity that transcend codified music and song forms—ambient noise, natural sounds, and others that constitute a given acoustic environment.

While numerous recent studies have focused on song in the Arab world, including Syria,[18] less attention has been paid to nonmusical sonic phenomena within the Arab world's urban environments—the rich acoustic fabric that constitutes the sonic background to everyday life activities—and to the interactions of musical and nonmusical sonorities in these places. Yet the acoustic ecology of urban Syria offers an important domain for critical analysis of the complex interactions between musical performance, economic development, and social trends, on the one hand, and the sonorous built environment, on the other. While Western academic scholarship has largely been silent on these relationships, Syrian scholars and performers have made the explicit connection between the built environment and the soundscapes of modernity. For example, Saadallah Agha al-Qalaa, a prominent Syrian academic, television producer, musician, and former politician, claimed that a strong correlation exists between built environment and vocal style in Syria. In his 1997 program *Nahj al-Aghani* (The course of songs: A second book of songs), al-Qalaa analyzed the 100 most important songs in the twentieth century, basing his analysis on the same standards used by the tenth-century al-Isbahani in compiling his *Kitab al-Aghani*.[19] In one episode from 1997, al-Qalaa explored the relationship between architectural line and vocal style in the Arab world across the twentieth century. Through analysis of dominant architectural and vocal styles from the early to the mid-twentieth century in Syrian song, including the transition from traditional to modern styles, al-Qalaa argued that the highly melismatic phrasing of early singers like the late Sabri Moudallal (1918?–2006) corresponds with the sinuous alleyways

Figure 6.1. Old City, Aleppo, 1997. Photograph: J. Shannon.

and ornate architectural forms of the old city. By contrast, the clearer, refined voice of modern singers like Sabah Fakhri (b. 1933) corresponds with the rectilinear lines of the modern city (see figs. 6.1 and 6.2).

Al-Qalaa demonstrated this thesis with selections of songs from these and other artists along with corresponding depictions of architectural features from the old and new cities. In addition, he demonstrated this proposed relationship through performance of the *qānūn* (plucked zither), an instru-

Figure 6.2. New City, Damascus, 1997. Photograph: J. Shannon.

ment on which he is a recognized expert, and a computer-generated graphic display that he claimed interacted with the sounds of the instrument. When he played melismatic, older-style phrases, the computer graphics were winding and sinuous. When he played in a less ornamented style, the graphic lines were more rectilinear.

The suggestions of such relationships are very old, like those claiming a close tie between the arabesque in the visual domain and the art of improvisation in the musical.[20] While al-Qalaa's demonstrations were more suggestive than definitive, and he offered little analytical proof of his thesis, subjectively I found that many Syrian listeners and quite a few performers made the connections between the older musical styles and the older architectural forms. One artist performing in al-Matbakh al-ʿAjami, a renovated twelfth-century palace near Aleppo's Citadel, argued that his music sounded better in older buildings because of the implicit association of the place with the sounds (it didn't seem to matter that the organizers nonetheless erected a sound system for the largely acoustic concert). In a similar manner, an Aleppine architect once discoursed with me at length about the mystical associations of the arabesque in architectural form and the flow of music in Islamic countries. Like others, he complained about not only the relatively poor acoustics of the large halls and sports arenas where concerts are often held but also of their lack of social intimacy, such a critical aspect of Syrian performance practice.[21] Likewise, a friend remarked to me during a concert at the Aleppo Citadel's amphitheater (see fig. 6.3), which requires amplification because of its being *en plein air* atop the fortified hillock, that "this is how the music was meant to sound!" His remark implies that there is an elective affinity between the place and the sounds, that the authenticity of the architectural space endows the music with a certain added authenticity, despite the need for modern amplification. In this fashion the musical forms and spatial forms authenticate one another.

These explicit and implicit associations between place and sound arise less from fundamental structural similarities in the domains of music and architecture, even when they may exist, than from the metonymic role of the old city as an index of tradition and cultural authenticity.[22] Affectively, the older songs and styles evoke an older way of being in the world, one associated more with quarters of the old city than with the new. This relationship must also be understood as a nostalgic view of both Syrian music and the old city. It reflects a common sentiment of longing for a lost past or Golden Age, especially among scions of bourgeois families and those (including al-Qalaa's)

Figure 6.3. Aleppo Citadel amphitheater, 2004. Photograph: J. Shannon.

with roots in Syria's Ottoman history, for whom the older songs and places index a time of relative openness, economic prosperity, inter-communal harmony, and peace. For these cultural actors the transformations of the twentieth century have engendered a certain anxiety over modernity and its aftermath; while they have largely profited from these changes, the transformation of the old city (especially its earlier impoverishment and decline, then its renovation, and now its destruction) promote the refashioning of traditional gender and class regimes that they experience as embodied in the architecture and associated acoustic forms as well.[23] Therefore, nostalgic attachments to the old city can be analyzed as a means, not for escape from modernity, but for the active construction of modern subjectivities.

The most important context for this sort of nostalgic longing has been the decline and later revival of the fabled old cities of Damascus and Aleppo. The old cities hold the majority of Syria's urban patrimony, including mosques, markets, and other distinctive buildings, and were the primary locus of musical performance in pre- and early modern Syria.[24] More than a collection of buildings, the old city is a soundscape that resounds with the life force of the inhabitants and resonates with rich and complex histories. For current and past inhabitants, as well as for many tourists in search of authenticity, the old city inculcates a type of authentic "auditory spatial awareness";[25] that is, it reverberates with the affective, spatial, and cultural values of the inhabitants (as I indicated was the case with the Aleppo Citadel's amphitheater). As an auditory space, the old city resonates with physical and social distinctions of traditional urban space: the division of residential from commercial zones; the definition of distinct neighborhoods (*ḥārāt*) via narrow streets and alleyways; often an implicit or explicit division among religious communities into loosely defined Muslim, Christian, and, until relatively recently, Jewish neighborhoods; and the existence of particularly functional buildings, such as mosques and warehouses (*khāns*), as well as an identifiable domestic architectural style, the *bayt ʿarabī*.

The *bayt ʿarabī* (the "Arab house," or courtyard home), is the primary locale of domestic life as well as musical performance in the modern era (*see plate 5a*). Divided into public and private domains (each with well-known gendered associations) the *bayt ʿarabī* constitutes in popular memory a veritable garden of paradise, replete with aromatic plants, citrus and jasmine trees, and often small vegetable gardens, offering a lush counterpart to the commercial space of the streets and marketplace.[26] Eulogized in numerous memoirs and poetic texts,[27] the *bayt ʿarabī* serves as a prime index of authenticity, and a referent for nostalgic reminiscence as well as present and future development; for these reasons it has been the object and target of the majority of renovation projects in the old cities of Aleppo and Damascus. An engineer friend lamented the fact that his family had abandoned their former *bayt ʿarabī* in Aleppo's old city and relocated to a modern apartment in the new city along with so many aspiring social climbers. His small balcony was laden with plants and bird cages which, in his words, "bring him back to his old home, to a time of innocence and authenticity (*aṣāla*)."

In addition, the courtyard home must be understood as an acoustic space promoting a distinctive soundscape. Sequestered from the public space of the street and *ḥāra*, the *bayt ʿarabī* echoes the sounds of domestic life. Itself divided into inner and outer spaces, the courtyard may resound with the sound of a fountain, of songbirds in trees or cages, as well as the sundry noises of daily life. A sound walk through any old city *ḥāra* will reveal a mixture of domestic sounds irrupting into the street—silverware clattering on plates, a radio or television sounding from a room, voices. Meanwhile the sounds of the street may filter into the courtyard—motor scooters and delivery vehicles zooming down the alleyway, food sellers shouting their calls, donkeys braying from their carts, voices of passing children, and so on. The use of its large courtyard and expansive patios (*īwāns*) as sites for musical performance is well-documented in recent memoirs and television serials, such as *Khan al-Harir* (The silk bazaar).[28] This function remains important as the larger of these homes have in recent decades been converted into restaurants and hotels that often feature musical performances.[29]

Beyond the *bayt ʿarabī*, the individual neighborhoods are served by mosques, churches, smaller markets, and larger thoroughfares that lend a rhythm and timbre to the sounds of daily life. One marker of the old city and its spatial-cultural organization is the density of the call to prayer (*adhān*) as it reverberates five times a day, every day, in the alleyways and courtyards from the numerous small mosques in the *ḥāra*. These are usually accompanied in the early morning hours by predawn supplications (*tasbīḥ*), and, depending on the *ḥāra*, the sounds of church bells. In addition to providing "soundmarks"[30] of their physical locations, the regular sounding of the call to prayer marks the time of day, just as the ringing of church bells in the Christian quarters marks particular prayer cycles and days of the week.

Adjacent to the residential quarters, the *sūq*, or "marketplace," provides a complementary soundscape of its own: a mix of the buzz of commercial activity, sounds of music emanating from radios and CD players in small stands and sidewalk carts, the rush of small vehicles, the occasional horn blast, and the sounds of voices and often animals in the small streets, overlaying the previously described domestic and religious soundscapes. Mixed in with all of these sounds are mediated musical sounds issuing from kiosks and shops. In public spaces the most commonly heard songs are the latest pop songs, some classic pan-Arab stars like Umm Kulthum or ʿAbd al-Halim Hafiz, and also Syrian performers like Sabah Fakhri and the Lebanese diva Fairouz; one often hears recordings of Qurʾanic recitation, especially from small shops and food stands. The interspersing of music kiosks throughout the old city commercial zones means that a sound walk will invariably be an exposure to song. The farther one moves from the commercial and residential centers the less likely one is to hear these songs, so that in the peri-urban neighborhoods the songs are less frequently heard, and other sounds prevail.

Music floats from circulating minibuses, taxis, and private cars, and the occasional open window. A young boy sings a song learned in school on his way home for lunch, while a woman in the privacy of her courtyard home blasts a Nancy ʿAjram (b. 1983) hit on the radio. A young laborer shouts across the rooftop to a colleague to bring a tool, while a large military bus rumbles past the city gate. Thus over the course of a day, the various soundscapes will interact—the din of commercial activity commencing in the early morning hours as the world comes to life, and waning with the onset of the afternoon prayer, followed by lunch and siesta, then the recommencing of commerce and its sounds through the evening, over and over again, marking the hours and days of the week. In this way, the old city offers a particular sonic environment with a mixture of regularized, codified sounds, and more aleatory, found sounds.[31] It is in this overall acoustic environment that the songs known as *qudūd ḥalabiyya* assume their importance as markers of authenticity.

The Cultural Geography of Popular Aleppine Song: The *Qudūd Ḥalabiyya* as Sonic Markers of Authenticity

The *qudūd ḥalabiyya* form a genre of song that is today among Syria's most popular.[32] Although their origins are a matter of debate, many of the *qudūd* were most likely composed in Aleppo and other Syrian cities, especially Damascus and Homs, and in neighboring countries such as Turkey, Iraq, and Egypt.[33] Because of Aleppo's role as a meeting place and collecting place of different traditions, they came to be attributed to "Aleppo" (*ḥalab*, hence the adjective *ḥalabiyya*, "Aleppine" or "from Aleppo"). The word *"qadd"* in Arabic means "equivalent," and in the *qudūd*, religious lyrics were set to the melodies of popular folk songs, and vice versa, in a form of contrafactum composition; new words were set to "equivalent" melodies. Properly understood, the *qudūd ḥalabiyya* are composed in standard Arabic (*fusha*), not colloquial (*dārija*), though in general use today any of the light songs in *dārija* performed at the end of the Syrian *waṣla*, or "musical suite" (and usually termed *"aghānī shāʾiʿa"* or *"aghānī shaʿbiyya"*), are classified among the *qudūd*, even if technically they are not. For the purposes of this essay *qudūd* refers to this broader category of light classical songs in standard and colloquial Arabic.

Structurally the *qudūd* are similar to the *muwashshaḥāt*, a genre of sung poetry of Andalusian origin, but are usually much simpler. Where the *muwashshaḥāt* often follow complex rhythmic and modal patterns, the *qudūd* tend to have simpler rhythms and melodic structures; as a result, some scholars and performers have suggested that the *qudūd* are in fact second-rate *muwashshaḥāt*.[34] The *qudūd* treat themes common to Arabic poetry and song in both classical and popular registers. These include love and longing for the beloved (*ghazal*), religious faith and praise (*madīḥ*), and descriptions of historical events (such as the return of heroes, or notable events in the region's history).

In the context of performance, the *qudūd* serve to lighten the atmosphere of a concert, which is why they typically occur at the end of a *waṣla*, when audiences may dance and the mood is joyful. The lightness at the end of the *waṣla* is, I have suggested elsewhere,[35] modeled on the structure of the *dhikr* and the religious *fāṣil*, which also begin with slow and heavy rhythms and end in quick, often ecstatic rhythms and dancing, creating a sense of release. For this reason the *qudūd* are very popular, not only among older aficionados—the famed *sammīʿa* (listening connoisseurs) and lovers of the older, "classical" Arab music—but also among youth and others having less of a bond with the older songs. Both because many of the *qudūd* are composed in colloquial and not standard Arabic, and because of their lightness, they tend to speak to the popular sentiments of urban, modernizing classes, old and young, as well as "defenders of tradition" or anyone sharing a desire for lightness and fun.[36] While such songs cannot compete in terms of sheer volume and popularity with contemporary Arab and international pop music in the overall Aleppine and Syrian soundscape, they nevertheless maintain a certain popularity among Aleppines, especially those residing in the old city, where these songs can still be heard not only in performance but from cassette and CD players in many areas of the city. Along with the *muwashshaḥāt*, they also form a corpus of standard songs that aspiring performers master.

A significant number of the *qudūd* (and the other traditional light songs classified as such) feature naturalistic referents. Various plants and trees, lush gardens, songbirds and messenger birds, animals, water sources, wells, fountains, the sun and moon, and the wind and rain all feature in a number of the commonly performed *qudūd*. Among the best-known songs performed at the end of the *waṣla* in the melodic mode *ḥijāz* is "al-Bulbul nāghā ʿalā ghuṣn al-full" (The nightingale sang from the branch of the jasmine tree). A loose English translation of the Arabic lyrics is as follows:[37]

> The nightingale sang from the branch of the jasmine tree, [1]
> Ah anemone flower [2]
> I intend to find my beloved, [3]
> Between the jasmine and the sweet basil. [4]
>
> My heart became ill, O my promise. [5]
> I need a doctor to heal me. [6]
> The doctor's medicine does me no good. [7]
> The sight of my beloved will cure me. [8]
>
> The beggar came to the door of the house. [9]
> The beautiful one told him, "Rely on God." [10]
> He told her, "I'm no beggar. [11]
> Give me a kiss, by God." [12]
>
> We were six at the spring. [13]
> The beloved came, then we were seven. [14]
> He asked for a kiss, I didn't give it. [15]
> I told him, "It's forbidden on Friday." [16][38]

"Al-Bulbul Nagha" is a light song about flirtation and longing, set in a garden or natural spring where people gathered to collect water or seek respite from work and the heat of the day. One notes the use of the masculine pronoun *maḥbūb* and *ḥabīb* to refer to the beloved (as in lines 3 and 8), common to classical Arabic poetry and much Arab song, though the feminine is used in line 10 (*al-ḥilwa*/beautiful one), thus reinforcing both the traditional gender associations of the song and the gendered division of space and social labor of the traditional home. The beloved is referred to as a flower (*shaqīq al-nuʿmānī*, anemone, line 2) to be found among other garden plants (*yāsmīn* and *rīḥān*, line 4). The flirtations occur in a home in what is possibly a peri-urban or even rural setting ("The beggar came to the door of the house"), but in any case in an environment infused with vegetation and natural imagery, like the gardens of traditional courtyard homes. Lovers gather near a spring, birds sing from the branches, and love is in the air.

While very few contemporary urban Aleppines have experience seeking water from a spring, the themes resonate both with older residents who do (for example in the well of a traditional courtyard home or in jaunts to rural and peri-urban spaces such as gardens and farms), and with younger listeners, who may pine nostalgically for a life they have only known through song, lore, and mass media programming. Indeed, the younger listeners I interviewed about this and other songs appreciated the lyrics and catchy melody as meaningful symbols of joy and of "the olden days" (*ayyām zamān*). Attending Sabah Fakhri concerts in Aleppo, Damascus, Beiteddine, Cairo, and Fes, during which he performed "al-Bulbul nagha," revealed to me the enormous popularity of the song and its role as a "crowd pleaser." In addition to Fakhri, numerous other contemporary performers in Syria include this song in their repertoire, including Sabri Moudallal, Omar Sarmini, Hamam Khairy, Mayada Bisilees, and the group Salatin al-Tarab, among many others both well known and obscure.

Other *qudūd* draw on the well-known use of animal metaphors to refer to the beloved or to carry messages to the beloved, including songbirds (as in "al-Bulbul Nagha"), gazelles, doves, and so forth. In the collection of *qudūd ḥalabiyya* edited and notated by ʿAbd al-Rahman al-Jabaqji (n.d.) I counted no fewer than 25 out of 168 songs that directly feature natural referents, not including reference to the night, the wind, and gazelles, as these are so common as to be found in many if not all renditions of most of the songs of the genre. For example, "Sayd al-ʿasari" (The fishmonger) compares the movement of the beloved to the playful movements of fish (*"āh yā samak yā bunī,"* "O fish o *bunī* [a type of fish]"). Others refer to plants or birds commonly found in courtyard gardens, including:

jasmine (*yāsmīn, full*): "*al-Full wa-l yāsmīn*," "*ʿAlā waraq al-full*";
rose (*ward*): "*ʿAmā yā bayāʿ al-ward*";
fruits: "*al-Qaraṣiyya*" (a type of citrus), "*ʿalā bayāʿīn al-ʿainab*" (referring to sellers of grapes);
trees in general: "*Yā māyla ʿal-ghuṣūn*" (O swaying on the branch);
nightingales (*bulbul/bulābil*): "*al-Bulābil fī-l rawḍ*";
birds (*ṭīr, ṭuyūr*): "*ʿA-ṭīr ʿaīnī*," "*Yā ṭīr yā gharīb*";
gardens (*rawḍa, janīna*) in general: "*Bayn al-janāyin*."

This is hardly an exhaustive list, and it omits the vast repertoire of *muwashshaḥāt*, many of which draw on similar themes.

A few songs in the *qudūd*/light song repertoire refer specifically to neighborhoods in Damascus or Aleppo, though particular spatial referents are rare. For example, "Ya tira tiri," by the Damascene composer Abu Khalil al-Qabbani, refers to a messenger dove carrying a lover's note to the resort areas of Dumar and Hama (now residential suburbs of Damascus). "Zawalif ya bu z-ziluf," a popular song often performed along with *qudūd*, refers to someone asking to be taken to Khan al-Harir (the silk bazaar) in Aleppo to have a look around and buy a bracelet for his beloved, which she would then wear on her chest and say, "have a look." The folkloric song "ʿAla al-yamma" refers to Aleppo, "all of it olive trees." Several well-known songs reference Syria in general, or Damascus through the metonymy of Syria with Damascus in the term *al-shām*, which in Syria refers to Damascus, but outside of Syria and in other contexts refers to the whole of Syria, even Greater Syria, depending on the context.[39]

While these songs do not in general reference specific neighborhoods or places in the old city (with the exception of Khan al-Harir), and indeed many of the song lyrics were composed elsewhere and utilize generic themes, listeners in Aleppo nonetheless manifest strong affective associations of the songs with the old city, in popular narratives, mass media images, and musical performances in Syria. The *qudūd* and similar genres of "light," "popular" songs (the *aghānī shāʾiʿa* and *aghānī shaʿbiyya*) are frequently used in the soundtracks to television serials depicting the old cities of Damascus and Aleppo, for example, in the thirty-episode serial *Khan al-Harir* (The silk bazaar), based in 1950s Aleppo, or in the fifteen-episode *Ayyam Shamiyya* (Damascene days), based in Damascus in the late Ottoman period.[40] In many ways they serve as sonic icons of the old quarters, though in everyday life they are typically only heard as a sonorous current beneath the usual sounds of daily life. Nonetheless, even when they found the pan-Arab pop songs to be more popular or entertaining, the urban youth I polled on the relative value of the old and the new songs typically acknowledged the high prestige value and authenticity of the older traditional songs relative to the newer pop songs;[41] these associations pertained in very diverse contexts: a bus ride chock-a-block with young military conscripts, a falafel stand in the old city, a bakery in the new city. For a large swath of Aleppines, the *qudūd* reverberate as deep markers of their identities.

Consuming Sounds: Nostalgia and the Anxieties of Modernity in Aleppo

What might account for the persistence of older songs, replete with naturalistic metaphors and even rural associations, among residents of a large metropolitan center (technically Syria's largest) that has undergone significant transformation in recent decades? What are the cultural dynamics of listening to the soundscapes of the old city in an era of global cultural flows? What about Aleppo's built environment allows for such songs to resound and interact with the existing sonorous environment?

No doubt the inherent nature of the songs themselves—playful lyrics, catchy melodies, and light rhythms—make them easily amenable to preservation as an archive of cultural memory even when at great temporal-spatial remove from their internal reference points. They are fun to listen to and to perform. However, I argue that the songs not only resonate with popular sentiments couched in a centuries-old poetic-musical tradition; they also resonate with a built environment marked by deep divisions as a result of dislocations and transformations of the last half century. The *qudūd* and other popular songs serve as an archive of collective memory, sonorous dimensions of a pastoral vision of their city that, along with other forms of popular culture, orient local, regional, and national subjectivities. This pastoral (even utopian) vision is closely identified with older regimes of value (as captured in popular culture representations as well as in recent renovation projects in the old cities) based in traditional gender, class, ethnic, and sectarian hierarchies and distinctions.

In recent decades, as Syria has undergone rapid transformation, the dominant regimes of value and attendant social formations have transformed, leading to new visions of gender relations, a reformulated labor force, and altered landscapes of hope and desire; the onset of civil strife in 2011 and the destruction of much of historic Aleppo since 2014 has fundamentally altered the physical and social landscape in wide swaths of Syria.[42] The *qudūd* in these contexts serve as soundmarks of authenticity in a changing social and acoustic environment; in the hustle and bustle of daily life, these songs and related soundmarks (such as the call to prayer) stand out as points of repair, sonic indexes of a longing for authentic culture, and (somewhat paradoxically) deep signifiers of modernity.

As I have argued elsewhere,[43] this longing (*ḥanīn*) is not (merely) an escape from harsh realities. Rather, Syrian *ḥanīn* engages with and embodies the anxieties and contradictions of a society undergoing change, and thereby is a hallmark of Syrian modernity. Aleppo's soundscapes (including the *qudūd* and also the broader sonorities of everyday life) reflect these struggles and contradictions, and at the same time offer Aleppines an acoustic vehicle for constructing notions of personhood and communal identity through discourses of sentiment and affect that are at the heart of Syrian modernity.[44]

In this way these songs and sounds link visions of a utopian past with those of a dystopian (and even heterotopian)[45] present and future. In the context of the current crisis, when the population and much of the urban infrastructure have been destroyed or are under threat—many thousands of refugees and internally displaced, cherished landmarks destroyed or damaged—these songs also sound the prospects for the future.[46] Indeed, if (to use Jameson's famous formulation) modernity is a form of nostalgia for the present,[47] then performing and listening to the *qudūd* announce a past-oriented longing for a present when the associations internal to the songs (their referential regimes of value) are rapidly fading away. Thus the *qudūd*, rather than standing apart as an aesthetic form divorced from daily life, participate in the construction of modernity through a sonorous engagement with nostalgic longing in the present.

Conclusions: Architectural Listening

To listen to songs architecturally, and to behold architecture sonically, we must understand song forms contributing to the construction of the built environment, and the built environment as reverberated with a particular soundscape. That is, we should listen to spaces as acoustemologically significant environments for the production of social difference and the enactment of power. Through their rich engagement with the acoustic and physical environment of Aleppo's old city, the *qudūd ḥalabiyya* teach us how to listen architecturally and also how to look at and inhabit space acoustically. The old city offers a particular sonic environment with a mixture of regularized, codified sounds and more aleatory, found sounds from the built environment. The sonorous environment of Aleppo invites us to "listen to" and not merely "walk in" the city as an echo chamber of a complex urban acoustemology. The *qudūd* resound in courtyard homes and kiosks within an architectural and acoustic environment rich in associations with authenticity and the contradictions of modernity.

What the future holds for Aleppo—for Syria, its peoples, and its musical legacies—remains unclear. As scholars we need to attend to the broader acoustic environment beyond the restricted realm of musical sounds and cultivate ways of listening to the cultural logic of the built environment—the cultural geography that the songs and other sonic artifacts help to construct. When the time comes to rebuild or refashion the city, these affective, acoustic, and architectural associations may promote a deeper appreciation of the social forces at play.

NOTES

1 The term "acoustemology" comes from Feld 1996.
2 In this essay I do not review the literature on the status of music and song in Islamic societies, nor the numerous possible relationships between architectural forms and musical forms, such as the arabesque. Such information can be found elsewhere (see Shannon 2006 and Frishkopf 2011, among others). Rather, I focus on the social life of song in the contemporary Aleppine built environment.
3 See Feld and Basso 1996; Lawrence and Low 1990; Low and Lawrence-Zúñiga 2003.
4 See Lawrence and Low 1990, 467; see also Bourdieu 1979; Stewart 1996.
5 See Lefebvre 1991.
6 de Certeau 1984, chapter 7.
7 See also Bourdieu 1979; Connell and Gibson 2003; Leyshon et al. 1998; Thibaud 2003.

8 The same distinctions pertain to Damascus and the other ancient walled cities of Syria.

9 Aleppo's Citadel (*qalaʿ*) is a large fortified palace lying on a hill at the heart of the old city. It has been used and rebuilt since at least the third millennium BCE, and its general appearance owes much to construction in the thirteen to the fifteenth centuries CE (see Bianca 2007). It has suffered damage during the Syrian civil war.

10 Unlike in North African cities, the French term "*ville nouvelle*" is not used to describe extramural urban developments in Syria, and "*medina*" or "*madīna*" does not refer exclusively to the older quarters, usually the walled city.

11 See Ayad 2011; Abdelkafi 2012; Balbo 2012; Busquets 2005; Salamandra 1998; Totah 2006.

12 See Zenlund 1991; Shannon 2006, 88–89.

13 I hasten to add that since the outbreak of the Syrian uprising in March 2011, these acoustemological properties have shifted dramatically as Aleppine society struggles through unprecedented challenges to its human, social, and physical environments.

14 Feld 1996; see also Howes 2005.

15 On the acoustemologies of New Guinea, European villages, and Ghana, see, respectively, Feld 1990 and 1996; Corbin 1998; and Feld 2004; Feld 2012.

16 See Blesser and Salter 2007, 3.

17 Blesser and Salter 2007, 11.

18 See Danielson 1997; Marcus 2007; Racy 2003; Shannon 2006; Touma 2003.

19 The series *Nahj al-Aghani* was broadcast on television and cable in 1997 and, along with previous documentaries on the music of Muhammad ʿAbd al-Wahab, Umm Kulthum, and Asmahan, forms the basis for al-Qalaa's ambitious *Second Kitab al-Aghani*. See the website of his production company for more information: http://awj-production.com. Accessed 30 April 2012.

20 See Shannon 2006, 178–179; Leaman 2004, 114; Al Faruqī 1978.

21 See Shannon 2006.

22 See Shannon 2005.

23 For more on these contradictions in the parallel case of Damascus, see Salamandra 2004 and Totah 2006.

24 See Marcus 1989, 43–44, 233–234; and Shannon 2006, 87–89.

25 Blesser and Salter 2007, 11.

26 See Totah 2006.

27 For example, Terjeman 1993; Qassab Hassan 1995; Qabbani 2000 [1983].

28 Haqqi 1996; see Salamandra 1998.

29 For more on the courtyard home in the Arab and Islamic worlds, see Edwards et al. 2006.

30 Schafer 1977, 10.

31 Due to limitations of space, I limit my remarks to the acoustic ecology of the intra-

mural or old city of Aleppo but make reference to the other urban, peri-urban, and rural soundscapes that interact with those of the old city.

32 See Qalahji 1988.

33 See, for example, ʿAli al-Darwish cited in Shannon 2003a, 91.

34 See Shannon 2006 for more discussion of the social location of this music.

35 See Shannon 2004.

36 These songs tend to be called "widely spread songs" (*aghānī shāʾiʿa*).

37 Arabic lyrics taken from al-Jabaqji, n.d.

38 I thank the Syrian scholar and artist Muhammad Qadri Dalal for pointing out this song to me. Some versions of this song substitute Damascus for Aleppo, and the provenance is likely Latakia. Full lyrics can be found at www.zamanalwasl.com, forum thread 1483, accessed 15 May 2013.

39 The same phenomenon is found in the use of "*maṣr*" to refer to both Egypt and to Cairo, depending on the context.

40 See Haqqi 1996; al-Malla 1993. For more information on these serials, see Salamandra 2004, 105–124; Shannon 2005.

41 See Shannon 2006, 48–50.

42 See Borneman 2007; Gallagher 2012; Rabo 2005, 82–84.

43 See Shannon 2006.

44 See Shannon 2005. See also Foster 2002 for the concept of "bargains with modernity."

45 See Charles Taylor 1999 and Gaonkar 2001.

46 As the Syrian conflict has evolved, music has played an important role in articulating frustrations, rallying defiance, and expressing hope for the future. The dominant aesthetic frame has been a mixture of global hip-hop mixed with traditional chants known as *ʿarāda* (on similar practices in Egypt, see Colla 2012). However, a few songs that have circulated since 2011 have altered the lyrics of popular *qudūd* to comment on the changes taking place inside Syria. Examples of these and other musical responses to the conflict in Syria form part of a collectively edited video project called "Songs of the New Arab Uprisings" (http://bit.ly/snarvid). Analysis of these songs is beyond the scope of this essay.

47 See Jameson 2003, 279.

CHAPTER SEVEN

Aural Geometry

Poetry, Music, and Architecture in the Arabic Tradition

SAMER AKKACH

Beauty's glamour appears in two things:
A line of poetry [*bayt al-shiʿr*] and a tent of hair [*bayt al-shaʿar*].

Wa-l-ḥusnu yaẓharu fī shayʾayni rawnaquhu
baytun mina-l-shiʿri aw baytun mina-l-shaʿari
—Cited by al-Nabulusi in *Hullat al-Dhahab al-Ibriz*[1]

In the *Republic,* Plato expressed his profound dislike of poets. He was highly suspicious of their creative abilities, considered them to be the bad citizens of the republic, and was bent on banishing their delusory practices from his state. He recognized the immense power poetry can exert on the human soul but saw in that a dangerous manipulation of emotions. "We may assume, then," he wrote, "that all the poets from Homer downwards have no grasp of truth but merely produce a superficial likeness of any subject they treat, including human excellence."[2] Plato sought in every human act a truthful core grounded in rigorous reasoning, and poetic *re-presentations* were, in his view, incapable of delivering that. For him, the poet is like a painter who paints an object's lookalike, but neither the painter nor his audience knows the reality of that object; everyone engages merely with "colour and form." The nature of the painter's work is mimetic, and mimicked reality lacks truthfulness and vitality. "In the same way," Plato explains, "the poet can use words and phrases as a medium to paint a picture of any craftsman, though he knows nothing except how to represent him, and the meter and rhythm and music will persuade people who are as ignorant as he is, and who judge merely from his words, that he really has something to say."[3] "So great is the natural magic of poetry,"[4] Plato admits—yet only to argue that, if one strips it of its poetic coloring and reduces it to plain prose, one will discover how little it amounts to.

In total contrast to Plato's position, and despite his influence on early Islamic philosophy, the Arabs prized "the natural magic of poetry" and celebrated the irreducible power of persuasion inherent in its rhythm and music. They excelled in it and took great pride in their poetic skills. In pre-Islamic Arabia, they even wrote the finest poems in gold and hung them on the cover of their most sacred sanctuary, the Kaʿba. These became known as the "hung" or "golden odes" (*muʿallaqāt* or *mudhahhabāt*), and their authors enjoyed a high social status.[5] By honoring poetry in this way, the Arabs recognized the sacredness and transcendental beauty inherent in poetry's "natural magic," maintaining their admiration for poetry and their attachment to it, despite the Qurʾan's indirect belittling of its merit.[6] For them, this magical quality was an expression of the human poetic creativity, which was recognized in the poet's ability to construct (*inshāʾ*) metrically measured, rhythmical, rhymed, and meaningful compositions.[7]

The celebrated fourteenth-century historian Ibn Khaldun, in his *Muqaddima*, remarked on a fundamental connection between nomadism and the gift of poetic eloquence. He said that for the Arabs, the art of poetry was the most noble of all literary arts, and that was why they made its content the register of their sciences and news, the testimony of their rights and wrongs, and the source to which they returned for knowledge and wisdom.[8] In terms of form, however, Ibn Khaldun describes Arabic poetry as being "unusual in tendency, and difficult in method" (*gharīb al-nazʿa, ʿazīz al-manḥā*). He explains why this is so:

> Because it is a form of articulated speech that is divided into verses, which are equal in meter [*wazn*] and united in the last letter of each verse [i.e., rhymed]. They call each of these verses *bayt*, the rhyming letter that unites the composition *rawiyya* and *qāfiya*, and the whole speech, from beginning to end, *qaṣīda* and *kalima*. Each verse of poetry [*bayt*] is individual in its constructed elements and meaning, as if it is an isolated speech independent of what is before or after it. So if a verse is taken alone, it would be complete in its own right.[9]

For centuries, the Arabs composed and perfected their poetry by astute hearing, until, in the eighth century CE, a brilliant Iraqi linguist, grammarian, and literary scholar from Azd (Oman) known as al-Khalil bin Ahmad al-Farahidi (d. 791 CE) was able to codify the complex variety of classical Arabic poetry through the discovery of its unique metric system.[10] Al-Khalil, who must have been skilled in mathematics and geometry, analyzed the structure and rhythms of Arabic poetry and came up with fifteen original meters (to which one was added later), according to what he termed *"dawāʾir al-ʿarūḍ,"* which might be rendered into English as "metric" or "prosodic circles."[11] *Al-ʿarūḍ*, from the verb "*ʿaraḍa*," "to display" or "expose," is the prosody or scale (*mizān*) by which poetry is measured. *Al-ʿarūḍ* is called this, says al-Khalil in his *Kitab al-ʿAyn*, because poetry is "displayed over it," or "exposed to it" (*yuʿraḍ ʿalayhā*), in order to be measured.[12] It is, in other words, the matrix of Arabic poetry. He identified five such circles, with each determining the rhythmic order of a set of meters. Since al-Khalil's codification, *al-ʿarūḍ* became a science, and numerous works were written to elucidate his complex metrics.[13]

Medieval Arabic sources considered the rhythmic structure of classical Arabic poetry to be the basis of both singing and music; thus an understanding of the underlying geometry of al-Khalil's prosodic circles provides insights into the rhythmic structure of classical Arabic music. This is one aim of the present chapter. The other is to discuss the architecture-infused discourse of classical Arabic poetry, that is, the metaphors inherent in Arabic poetry's technical terminology and related conceptualization of order and structure. The discussion of these two aims reveals aspects of the aesthetic sensibility that governed the poetic, musical, and architectural expressions in premodern Islamic cultures, imbuing them with a unifying sense of identity.[14]

Poetry and Music

In his famous *Kitab al-Aghani* (The book of songs), Abu al-Faraj al-Isbahani (d. 967 CE) reports the Abbasid Caliph Harun al-Rashid's desire to identify the best three voices (*aṣwāt*; sing. *ṣawt*), meaning sung poetry, out of the best hundred known in the Islamic world.[15] He also refers to the differences

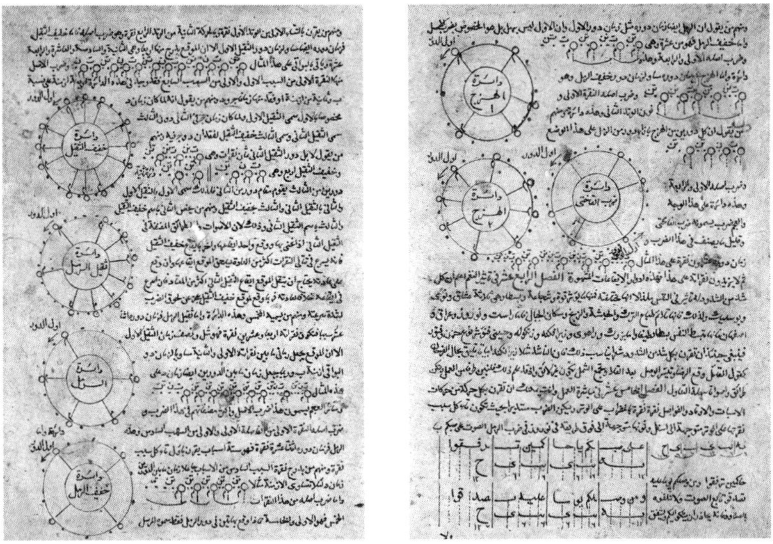

Figure 7.1. Folios from the thirteenth-century renowned musician Safi al-Din al-Urmawi al-Baghdadi's *Kitab al-Adwar fi al-Musiqa* (Book of modes). These show the close correspondence between prosodic circles and musical cycles, revealing how poetry and music are united in terms of metric structure and rhythm. Lawrence J. Schoenberg Collection, Kislak Center for Special Collections, Rare Books and Manuscripts, University of Pennsylvania, LJS 235. Courtesy of the University of Pennsylvania Libraries.

among the selectors over who uses the best "melodies" (*alḥān*; sing. *laḥn*) to sing certain lines of poetry, as the chosen *laḥn* has to correspond with the music embedded in the rhythm of the poem.[16] The renowned philosopher and music theoretician al-Farabi (d. 950 CE), in his *Kitab al-Musiqa al-Kabir* (The great book of music), explains this relationship in a highly detailed and theoretically sophisticated way, using well-developed disciplinary idioms. He shows how the early theory of Arabic music and singing was based on the metric order (*mīzān*) of classical Arabic poetry (see fig. 7.1).[17]

Al-Farabi's contemporary group of anonymous philosophers, the Ikhwan al-Safa' (Brethren of Purity), in their tract on music, also elucidate the fundamental connection between these forms of artistic expressions. Conflating music (*mūsīqā*) with singing (*ghinā'*), they write,[18] "We may now say that *al-mūsīqī* [music][19] is *al-ghinā'* [singing], *al-mūsīqār* [musician] is *al-mughannī* [singer], and the *mūsīqān* is the *ālat al-ghināʾ* [singing instrument]; that singing [*ghināʾ*] is harmoniously composed melodies [*alḥān muʾtalifa*], a melody is successive notes [*naghamāt mutawātira*], notes are vibrating, sustained sounds [*aṣwāt mutarannima*], and sound is an impact [*qarʿ*] occurring in the air from the collision of bodies against each other." Following the classical Greek tradition, the Ikhwan and other medieval Muslim philosophers, such as al-Kindi and Ibn Sina, list their tracts on music among the mathematical sciences (*al-ʿulūm al-riyāḍiyya*).[20] Beyond imitating the Greek model, they did this because the fundamental order in music derives from numbers and proportion. The Ikhwan see the great variety of music, found around the world, as reflecting cultural differences. Different musics, they say, correspond with peoples' natures, as expressed in different habits, languages, and practices. Yet despite the great differences, they add, various forms of music have a shared structure and common regulating principles, these being the principles of singing (*uṣūl al-ghināʾ*) and the rules of melodies (*qawānīn alḥān*). Singing (*ghināʾ*), they say, is made up of melodies (*alḥān*); a melody, of notes (*naghamāt*); the notes, of attacks and rhythms (*naqarāt wa īqāʿāt*). The basic principles of all these are "motions and rests" (*ḥarakāt wa sukūnāt*). The same applies to poetry. Verses of poetry are made up of hemistichs (*maṣārīʿ*); hemistichs, of verbal units (*mafāʿīl*, i.e., prosodic feet); and verbal units, of syllables of varying length and emphasis (*asbāb*, *awtād*, and *fawāṣil*), all of which are based on unvocalized and vocalized letters, which are described in Arabic as being either in motion or at rest (*ḥarakāt* and *sukūnāt*).[21]

Motion and Rest: Al-Khalil's Prosodic Circles

The starting point of al-Khalil's metric system is the contrast between motion and rest, which is specific to the nature of the Arabic script and which calls for some clarifications. Unlike the Latin-based alphabets, the Arabic alphabet does not, properly speaking, contain letters that are designated as vowels. The twenty-eight letters of the Arabic alphabet are in principle unpronounceable on their own. The letters *alif* (*a*), *wāw* (*w*), and *yāʾ* (*y*), which are referred to as "long vowels" in certain situations, are in Arabic *ḥurūf al-ʿilla*, literally, "the letters of weakness," of "deficiency," or of "cause" (the philosophical expression *al-ʿilla al-ūla* means "prime cause"). There are countless words in Arabic in which these letters form no part; hence, they cannot be regarded as vowels. Instead, there are six *harakāt*—literally, "motions" (two corresponding pairs of three, *ḥarakāt al-binā'* and *ḥarakāt al-iʿrāb*)—marked on words in the form of diacritical signs that play the role of vowels in Arabic.[22] These diacritics are not treated as letters (*ḥurūf*), however, although sometimes they are referred to as "small letters" (*ḥurūf ṣighār*), nor are they usually written.[23] In a word such as "*ḌaRaBa*," "to strike," for example, the only letters that are written are those of the root, *ḌRB*, while the lowercase *a* represents a phonetic motion, *ḥaraka*; to put this same verb in a passive form, *DuRiBa* (is struck), changes nothing in the word's spelling. The only things that change are the unwritten "phonetic motions" (*ḥarakāt*), without which the root is unpronounceable, meaningless, or "dead," so to speak. Utterance that causes a word to exist, to assume a presence, to be alive, is effected through the application of the *ḥarakāt*.[24]

Thus viewed, a letter is unpronounceable if not mobilized by one of the vocalizing motions. When a letter receives one of the three vocalizing marks—*fatḥa* (*a*), *ḍamma* (*u*), and *kasra* (*i*), and thereby assumes one of the corresponding states of *naṣb*, *rafʿ*, or *khafḍ*—it is referred to as being in motion (*mutaḥarrik*), while a letter that does not receive a vocalizing mark is referred as being at rest (*sākin*), and the diacritical mark used to identify the state of rest is called *sukūn* (stillness).[25]

Classical Arabic poetry, as Ibn Khaldun explains, consists of sets of complete and independent lines or verses, which are normally divided into two equally proportioned halves or hemistichs (*maṣārīʿ*; sing. *miṣrāʿ*). In al-Khalil's system the verses are reduced to set sequences of vocalized and unvocalized letters to form three different primary combinations, forming the basic structural elements, which are, in turn, combined to form eight different verbal units (*tafʿīlāt* or *mafāʿīl*). The three basic structural elements are referred to as *sabab*, *watad*, and *fāṣila*. The meaning of these terms will be discussed later; here, however, they can be viewed as representing three distinct syllabic sequences of letters in motion and at rest (i.e., vocalized and unvocalized letters). In fact, as there are two variations of the *sabab* and the *watad*—light and heavy *sabab*, and joint and split *watad*—the total number of basic structural forms is five. Representing the vocalized consonant by a circle (O) and the unvocalized consonant by a vertical stroke (|),[26] the five structural elements are represented as follows, reading from left to right:

sabab khafīf (light *sabab*):	O|	S
sabab thaqīl (heavy *sabab*):	OO	Ṣ
watad maqrūn (joint *watad*):	OO|	W
watad mafrūq (split *watad*):	O|O	Ẉ
fāṣila (separator):[27]	OOO|	F

Verbal Units

The two structural elements, identified above as S and W (for *sabab* and *watad*), along with their variants (Ṣ and Ẉ) are combined to generate eight "verbal units" (*tafʿīlāt*), or prosodic feet,[28] which are in turn used in different combinations to generate the fifteen meters of classical Arabic poetry, known as *buḥūr al-shiʿr* (literally, "seas of poetry"). These units are represented by eight abstract words derived from the Arabic verb "*faʿala*," literally, "to do" and "to act," and combining sequences of the three structural elements as shown in the following two examples (see table 7.1). Here, a consonantal letter followed by a long vowel (as formed by the combinations "u + *wāw*" = ū; "I + *yāʾ*" = ī; and "a + *alif*" = ā) is treated as O|—in other words, a vocalized consonant (carrying a short vowel) followed by an unvocalized consonant (*wāw*, *yāʾ*, or *alif*).

The eight verbal units are: *Fāʿilun, Faʿūlun, Mafāʿīlun, Fāʿilātun, Mustafʿilun, Mufāʿalatun, Mutafāʿilun,* and *Mafʿūlātu*. These Arabic words have no meaning other than being verbal expressions of certain sequences of vocalized (in motion) and unvocalized (at rest) letters, as shown in table 7.2. Here, they are presented not as transliterated above but as metrically written, that is as sequences of motions and rests: *ḥarakāt* are in light gray, and letters are in black. Dividing (*taqṭīʿ*) a line of poetry into structural elements follows the

Table 7.1. Representation of *Faʿūlun* and *Mafāʿīlun*

Fa ʿu w lu n		Ma fa a ʿi y lu n
O O | O |		O O | O | O |
W S		W S S

Note: In this representation of *faʿūlun* and *mafāʿīlun*, vocalizing "motions" (*ḥarakāt*) are shown in light gray in order to distinguish them from proper letters and to illustrate how the verbal unit works as a sequence of letters in motion (O) and letters at rest (|). Here verbal units are written as metrically considered, that is, as pronounced and not as normally written in standard transliterations.

Table 7.2. The eight verbal units (prosodic feet)

Letter Label	Verbal unit	In-motion/in-rest pattern	Structural elements
A	*Faaᶜilun*	○| ○○|	S W
B	*Faᶜuwlun*	○○| ○|	W S
C	*Mafaaᶜiylun*	○○| ○| ○|	W S S
D	*Faaᶜilaatun*	○| ○○| ○|	S W S/**Ẉ** S S[a]
E	*Mustafᶜilun*	○| ○| ○○|	S S W/S **Ẉ** S[b]
F	*Mufaaᶜalatun*	○○| ○○ ○|	W Ṣ S
G	*Mutafaaᶜilun*	○○ ○| ○○|	Ṣ S W
H	*Mafᶜuwlaatu*	○| ○| ○|○	S S **Ẉ**

[a] This verbal unit has two forms, the second of which begins with *watad mafrūq* and is used in the *Muḍāriᶜ* meter, see below the fourth prosodic circle, *dāʾirat al-Mushtabih.*

[b] This verbal unit also has two forms, the second of which is used in *al-Mujtath* and *al-Khafīf* meters, see below the fourth prosodic circle, *dāʾirat al-Mushtabih.*

way in which words are pronounced and not as they are written.[29] The verbal units are assembled in certain repetitive combinations to generate fifteen different meters. The meters are structured by either the alternating repetition of two different verbal units or the repetition of a single verbal unit, as shown below. The generation of the meters is based on the geometrical divisions of the circle, hence the name *dawāʾir al-ᶜarūḍ* (prosodic circles). The geometrical divisions of the circle create the cyclic order of the meters, which are three-, four-, or fivefold. Thus the number of divisions on the circle, the distribution of the structural elements (*watad* and *sabab*) over the divisions, and the chosen starting point of the cycle are what set the "rhythm" (*īqāᶜ*) and speed of a metric cycle. The threefold division, for example, is faster than the fivefold division. The technical distinction between the function of the *watad* and that of the *sabab* defines the geometrical characteristics that unify the set of meters belonging to a particular prosodic circle. The *watads*, which set the rhythm, function as the fixed or rigid structural elements of the meter, which cannot be changed without altering the meter's rhythmic character. By contrast, the *sababs* are, as it were, the changeable or malleable structural elements, which allow for variation without changing the distinctive rhythm of the meter. Accordingly, the distribution of the *watads* on the prosodic circle establishes, as it were, the geometrical character of meters.[30]

In *al-ᶜIqd al-Farid* (The unique necklace), the tenth-century Andalusian literary scholar Ibn ʿAbd Rabbih (d. 939 CE) presents a poetic elucidation together with diagrammatic illustrations of the prosodic circles.[31] Although his illustrations, as they appear in the published version of the book, are rather basic and rough, they nonetheless illustrate the basic geometrical principle upon which the prosodic circles are based. The following elaborate geometrical representations of the geometry of the prosodic circles are based on Ibn ʿAbd Rabbih's simple diagrams. According to Ibn ʿAbd Rabbih, the five prosodic circles that dictate the rhythmic patterns of classical Arabic poetry and its meters are named and structured as follows (see chart 7.1).

1. *Dāʾirat al-Mukhtalif*, The Circle of Alternating Sequence
   Rhythmic structure: Fourfold.
   Speed: Ten divisions, marking four alternating non-equal intervals, two short and two long.
   Meters: *al-Ṭawīl*, *al-Madīd*, and *al-Basīṭ*.

   al-Ṭawīl

B	**C**	**B**	**C**	**B**	**C**	**B**	**C**
WS	**WSS**	**WS**	**WSS**	**WS**	**WSS**	**WS**	**WSS**

   al-Madīd

D	**A**	**D**	**A**	**D**	**A**
SWS	**SW**	**SWS**	**SW**	**SWS**	**SW**

   al-Basīṭ

E	**A**	**E**	**A**	**E**	**A**	**E**	**A**
SSW	**SW**	**SSW**	**SW**	**SSW**	**SW**	**SSW**	**SW**

The geometrical structure of the First Circle allows for five possible starting points that can produce five different meters, all of which share the same rhythmic structure and speed.[32] According to Ibn ʿAbd Rabbih, only three of these starting points were used in classical Arabic poetry, forming the three longest meters, *al-Ṭawīl*, *al-Madīd*, and *al-Basīṭ*.[33] As the metric cycle of a poem is determined by the verbal units sequence of a hemistich, the temporal cycle does not always translate spatially into a full turn around the circle. The circle sets the rotational order, but the sequence is considered in a linear way, as shown below, which means a metric cycle can theoretically start and stop anywhere on the circle. In the first circle, for example, each one turn around the circle counterclockwise forms one half of the *Ṭawīl* and *Basīṭ* meters and two thirds of the *Madīd*.

Table 7.3. The linear sequencing of the three meters of the First Circle according to the used/unused starting points; constants: 24 metric letters[a] (per full turn); *Mutaḥarrik/Sākin*: 7/5; *Watad/Sabab*: 2/3

Meter	Linear sequencing[b]												
1. *al-Tawīl*	▼	●	▼	●	●	▼	●	▼	●	●			
2. *al-Madīd*		●	▼	●	●	▼	●	▼	●	●	▼		
3. *al-Basīt*				●	●	▼	●	▼	●	●	▼	●	▼

[a] By metric letters, I mean the letters that count metrically; see endnote 27.
[b] Triangles = *Watad*; circles = *Sabab*

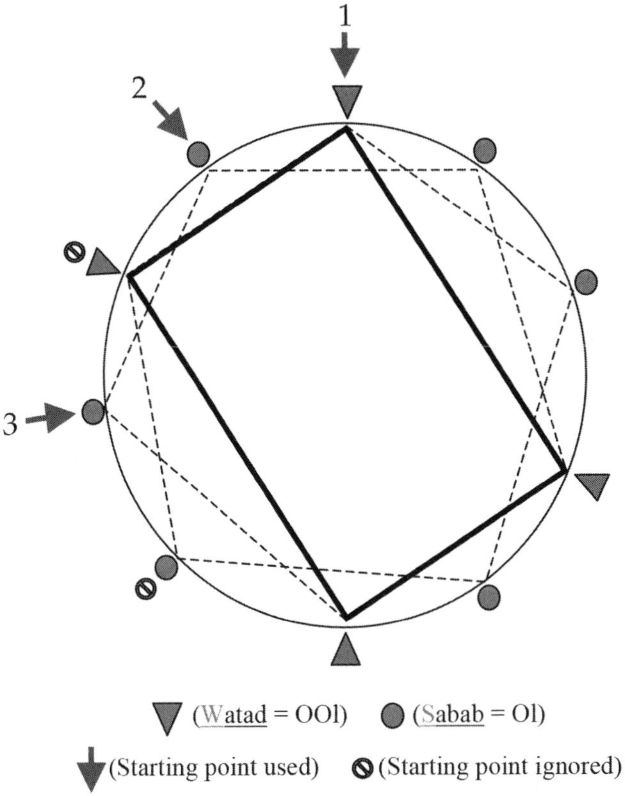

Chart 7.1. The first circle: *Dā'irat al-Mukhtalif.*

2. *Dāʾirat al-Muʾtalif*, The Circle of Concordant Sequence
Rhythmic structure: Threefold.
Speed: Nine divisions, marking three equal intervals.
Meters: *al-Wāfir, al-Kāmil.*

al-Wāfir

F	**F**	**F**	**F**	**F**	**F**
WṢS	**WṢS**	**WṢS**	**WṢS**	**WṢS**	**WṢS**

al-Kāmil

G	**G**	**G**	**G**	**G**	**G**
ṢSW	**ṢSW**	**ṢSW**	**ṢSW**	**ṢSW**	**ṢSW**

The geometrical structure of the Second Circle allows for three possible starting points that can produce three different meters, all of which share the same rhythmic structure and speed. According to Ibn ʿAbd Rabbih, only two of these starting points were used in classical Arabic poetry. These form the two meters of *al-Wāfir* and *al-Kāmil*. Each turn around the circle counterclockwise forms one half of the *al-Wāfir* and *al-Kāmil* meters.

3. *Dāʾirat al-Mujtalab*, The Circle of Collected Sequence
Rhythmic structure: Threefold.
Speed: Nine divisions, marking three equal intervals.
Meters: *al-Hazaj, al-Rajaz, al-Ramal.*

al-Hazaj

C	**C**	**C**	**C**
WSS	**WSS**	**WSS**	**WSS**[34]

al-Rajaz

E	**E**	**E**	**E**	**E**	**E**
SSW	**SSW**	**SSW**	**SSW**	**SSW**	**SSW**

al-Ramal

D	**D**	**D**	**D**	**D**	**D**
SSW	**SSW**	**SSW**	**SSW**	**SSW**	**SSW**

The geometrical structure of the Third Circle allows for three possible starting points that produce three different meters, all of which share the same rhythmic structure and speed. According to Ibn ʿAbd Rabbih, all of

Table 7.4. The linear sequencing of the two meters of the Second Circle according to the used/unused starting points; constants: 21 metric letters (per full turn); *Mutaḥarrik/Sākin*: 5/2; *Watad/Sabab*: 1/2

Meter	Linear sequencing										
1. *al-Wāfir*	▼	○	●	▼	○	●	▼	○	●		
2. *al-Kāmil*		○	●	▼	○	●	▼	○	●	▼	●

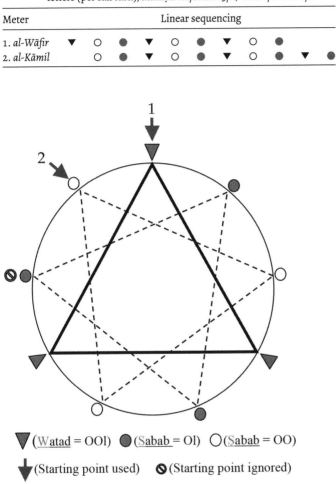

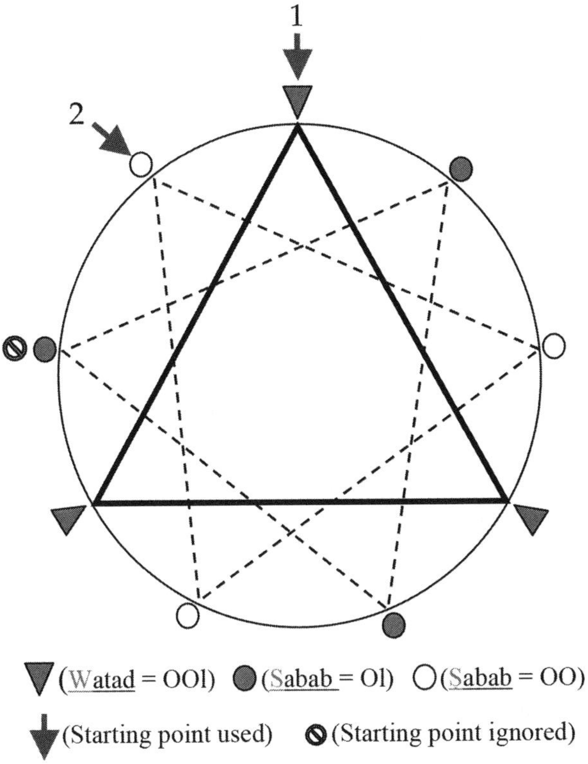

Chart 7.2. The second circle: *Dāʾirat al-Muʾtalif.*

Table 7.5. The linear sequencing of the three meters of the Third Circle according to the used/unused starting points; constants: 21 metric letters (per full turn); *Mutaḥarrik/Sākin*: 4/3; *Watad/Sabab*: 1/2

Meter	Linear sequencing											
1. *al-Hazaj*	▼	●	●	▼	●	●						
2. *al-Rajaz*		●	●	▼	●	●	▼	●	●	▼	●	
3. *al-Ramal*			●	▼	●	●	▼	●	●	▼	●	●

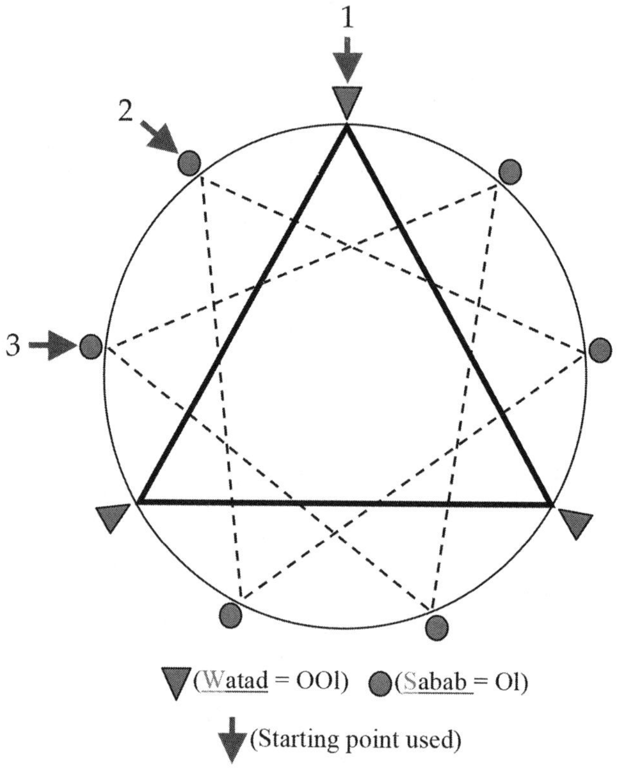

Chart 7.3. The third circle: *Dā'irat al-Mujtalab.*

the three starting points are used in classical Arabic poetry, forming the three meters of *al-Hazaj, al-Rajaz* and *al-Ramal.* Each turn around the circle counterclockwise forms three-fourths of the *Hazaj* and one half of the *Rajaz* and *Ramal* meters.

4. *Dāʾirat al-Mushtabih,* Circle of Analogous Sequence
   Rhythmic structure: Threefold.
   Speed: Nine divisions, marking three equal intervals.
   Meters: *al-Muḍāriʿ, al-Muqtaḍab, al-Mujtath, al-Sarīʿ, al-Munsariḥ, al-Khafīf.*

al-Muḍāriʿ

C	**D**	**C**	**D**
WSS	**ẈSS**	**WSS**	**ẈSS**[35]

al-Muqtaḍab

H	**E**	**E**	**H**	**E**	**E**
SSẈ	**SSW**	**SSW**	**SSẈ**	**SSW**	**SSW**

al-Mujtath

E	**D**	**E**	**D**
SẈS	**SWS**	**SẈS**	**SWS**[36]

al-Sarīʿ

E	**E**	**H**	**E**	**E**	**H**
SSW	**SSW**	**SSẈ**	**SSW**	**SSW**	**SSẈ**

al-Munsariḥ

E	**H**	**E**	**E**	**H**	**E**
SSW	**SSẈ**	**SSW**	**SSW**	**SSẈ**	**SSW**

al-Khafīf

D	**E**	**D**	**D**	**E**	**D**
SWS	**SẈS**	**SWS**	**SWS**	**SẈS**	**SWS**

The geometrical structure of the Fourth Circle allows for nine possible starting points that can produce nine different meters, all of which share the same rhythmic structure and speed. According to Ibn ʿAbd Rabbih, only six starting points were used in classical Arabic poetry, forming the six meters of *al-Muḍāriʿ, al-Muqtaḍab, al-Mujtath, al-Sarīʿ, al-Munsariḥ,* and *al-Khafīf.* Each

Table 7.6. The linear sequencing of the six meters of the Fourth Circle according to the used/unused starting points; constants: 21 metric letters (per full turn); *Mutaḥarrik/Sākin*: 4/3; *Watad/Sabab*: 1/2

Meter	Linear sequencing																	
1. *al-Muḍāriʿ*	▼	●	●	▽	●	●	▼	●	●									
2. *al-Muqtaḍab*		●	●	▽	●	●	▼	●	●	▼	●							
3. *al-Mujtath*			●	▽	●	●	▼	●	●	▼	●	●						
4. *al-Sarī*					●	●	▼	●	●	▼	●	●	▽					
5. *al-Munsariḥ*								●	●	▼	●	●	▽	●	●	▼	●	
6. *al-Khafīf*									●	▼	●	●	▽	●	●	▼	●	●

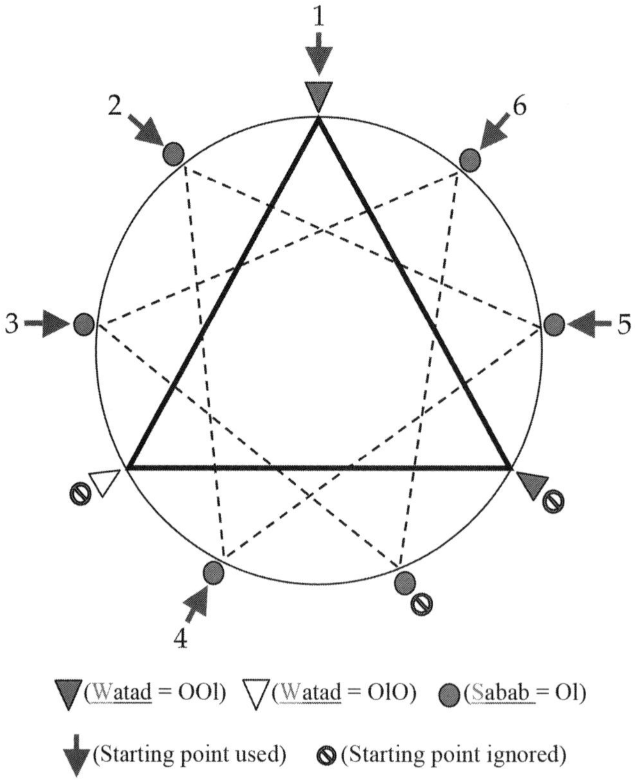

Chart 7.4. The fourth circle: *Dāʾirat al-Mushtabih*.

turn around the circle counterclockwise forms three-fourths of the *Muḍāriʿ* and *Mujtath* and one half of the *Muqtaḍab, Sarīʿ, Munsariḥ*, and *Khafīf*.

5. *Dāʾirat al-Muttafiq*, Circle of Resonating Sequence
   Rhythmic structure: Fourfold.
   Speed: Eight divisions, marking four equal intervals.
   Meter: *al-Mutaqārib*.

al-Mutaqārib

B	**B**	**B**	**B**	**B**	**B**	**B**	**B**
WS	**WS**	**WS**	**WS**	**WS**	**WS**	**WS**	**WS**

The geometrical structure of the Fifth Circle allows for two possible starting points that can produce two different meters, which share the same rhythmic structure and speed. According to Ibn ʿAbd Rabbih, only one starting point was used in classical Arabic poetry, forming the meter of *al-Mutaqārib*. Each turn around the circle counterclockwise forms one half of the *Mutaqārib* meter.

The above diagrammatic representation of al-Khalil's original fifteen meters, according Ibn ʿAbd Rabbih, reveals, as it were, the "aural geometry" of classical Arabic poetry. The metaphor of aural geometry describes how an auditory poetic experience can be presented visually. It translates into visual terms the underlying sonic order of a verse as well as the aural pattern of the cyclic repetition of a poem.[37] Aural geometry also reveals the rotational symmetry and constant ratios on which the prosodic circles were based. It shows how the music of a poem can be visually understood through the distribution of its structural elements on a regularly divided circle. Once the rhythmic structure is set, a poem becomes a continual re-manifestation of this matrix in an ever-changing colorful display. This underlying cyclic repetitiveness, while continually manifesting different meaning and imageries, resonates with the ways in which the music unfolds and geometrical patterns work.[38] While major premodern Arabic sources provide detailed exposition of the close correspondence between prosodic circles and musical cycles,[39] the correspondence of these to the geometric patterns and spatial structures of Islamic architecture remain speculative and conjectural (figs. 7.2 and 7.3).[40]

Table 7.7. The linear sequencing of the single meter of the Fifth Circle according to the used/unused starting points; constants: 20 metric letters (per full round); *Mutaḥarrik/Sākin*: 3/2; *Watad/Sabab*: 1 (equal)

Meter	Linear sequencing							
1. *al-Mutaqārib*	▼	●	▼	●	▼	●	▼	●

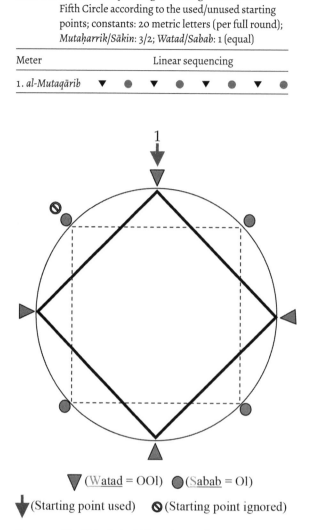

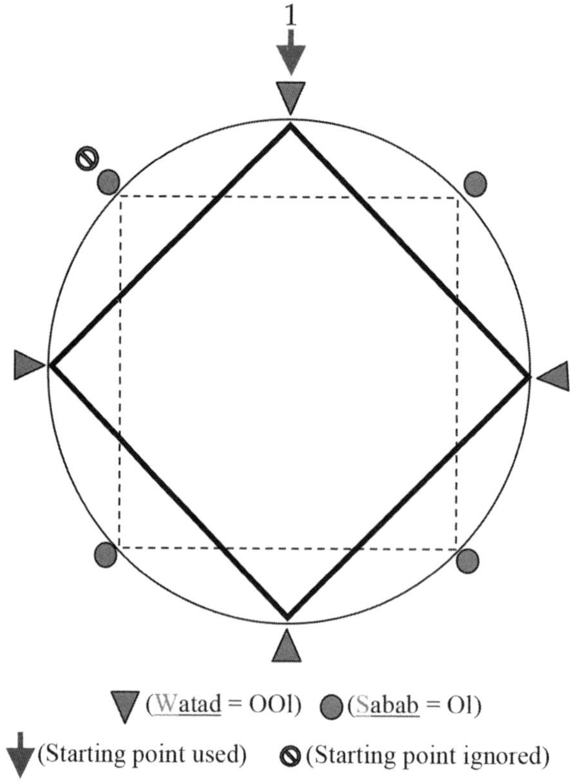

Chart 7.5. The fifth circle: *Dāʾirat al-Muttafiq*.

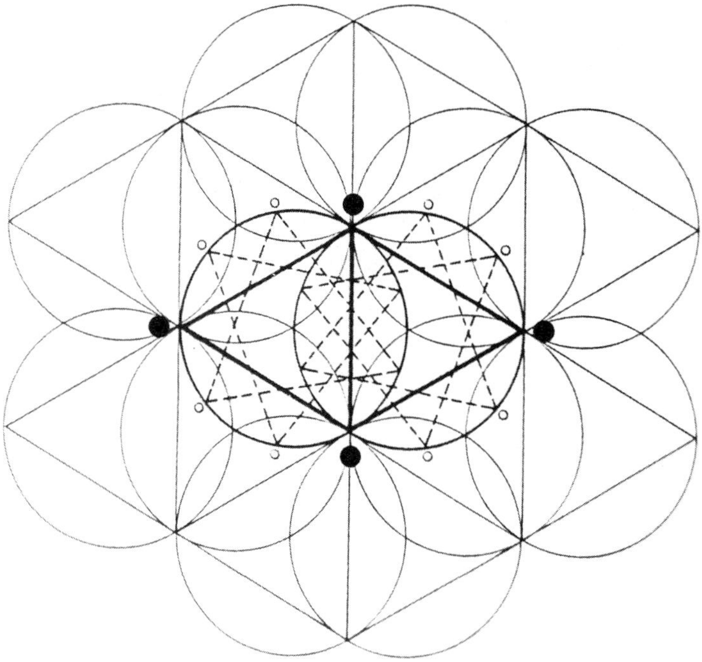

Figure 7.2. A spatial representation of a poem showing the recurrence of a threefold prosodic circle. Each circle represents a hemistich, while each pair of overlapping circles represents a verse. As with a poem, the unfolding of a pattern may extend indefinitely.

Poetry and Architecture

The verse quoted at the beginning of this chapter, "Beauty's glamour appears in two things: / A line of poetry [*bayt al-shiʿr*] and a tent of hair [*bayt al-shaʿar*]," plays on the phonetic resonance of two Arabic expressions, *al-shiʿr* and *al-shaʿar*. Yet the resonance has more to it than just form. In fact, it introduces a conceptual correspondence between poetry and architecture that is consciously articulated and remarkably profound. Although this correspondence would naturally extend to music because of its inextricable affinity with poetry, the analogy between music and architecture remains rather basic and meaningful only through the mediation of poetry. The analogy is based on structural similarity between what might be called "aural" and visual geometry, underpinned by spatial metaphors tying poetic and archi-

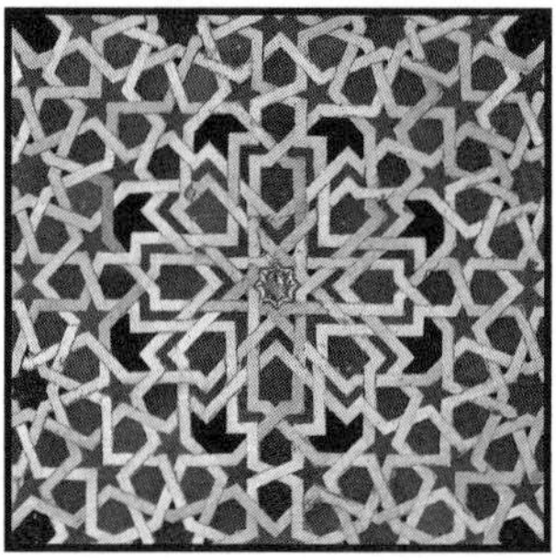

Figure 7.3. Spatial (two- and three-dimensional) expressions of the rotational symmetry of regular geometry. The dome is from the great mosque of Córdoba in Córdoba, and the pattern is from Alhambra in Granada. Photographs: S. Akkach.

tectural compositions. This is as far as the analogy goes, however, as these parallels cannot be generalized into an Islamic essence that dictated artistic production always and everywhere in premodern multicultural Islamic societies.

To start with, the term "*bayt*" (literally, "house"/"dwelling") has several applications in Arabic, the most conspicuous of which, as the quotation suggests, are to a large Bedouin tent as well as to a verse of poetry. The eminent thirteenth-century lexicographer Ibn Manzur (d. 1311 CE) says that *bayt al-shiʿr* (a verse of poetry) is derived (*mushtaqq*) from *bayt al-khibāʾ*, that is, *bayt al-shaʿar* (tent of hair, i.e., made of animal skin), showing that the correspondence is consciously constructed.[41] The prosodic principles of Arabic poetry (*ʿarūḍ*), discussed above, elaborate further the "architecture" of classical Arabic poetry. As already shown, the structural forms of a poem create the music of poetic compositions. According to Ibn Manzur, the three structural elements, *sabab, watad,* and *fāṣila,* were so named because of their architectural connotations. He explains: "The *bayt* in poetry is derived from *bayt al-khibāʾ*, which applies to the small and the large, like al-Rajaz and al-Ṭawīl, and this is because [a line of poetry] embraces the words in the same way a house 'embraces its family' [*yaḍummu ahlahu*], and it is for this reason that they called its structural elements [*muqaṭṭaʿātihi*] *asbāb* and *awtād,* analogically comparing them with the houses' *asbāb* and *awtād.*"[42] Citing al-Azhari's (d. 980 CE) *al-Tahdhīb,* he further elaborates: "a line of poetry is called *bayt* because it is an 'ordered composition of words' [*kalāmun jumiʿa manẓūman*], thus it became as a house composed of 'rooms' [*shuqaq*], 'cover' [*kifāʾ*], 'porch' [*riwāq*], and 'columns' [*ʿumud*]."[43] "*Sabab*" means "rope"; "*watad,*" "peg" or "pin"; and "*fāṣila,*" "separator." The constructed analogy here is that a poem, like a tent, is ordered by the layout of the pegs and adjusted by the stretching and tightening of the ropes that are spaced out by separators. Thus a "house" of poetry is conceptually similar to a "house" of hair, with both being experienced through various modalities of motion and rest.

Lexicographers elaborate this analogy further by explaining that a poem is imaged on a house because a verse of poetry brings together a family of words as a house would bring together its resident family members. Metrically, the pegs (*awtād*) are the fixed and stabilizing components that define the structural rhythm of a meter; they therefore cannot accommodate any variations without losing the identity of the meter.[44] Similarly, the Qurʾan refers to mountains as "pegs" (*wa-l-jibāla awtādan*), presenting them, according to medieval sources, as the necessary structural elements that were used to stabilise earth and stop it from swaying. By contrast, the ropes (*asbāb*) are the flexible and adjustable components, which can accommodate variations without losing the identity of the meter.[45] Furthermore, Ibn Manzur, in his definitions of *ʿarūḍ,* says that the term is used to refer to both the middle of a verse of poetry (*bayt al-shiʿr,* i.e., end of the first half of a verse) and the middle of an "inhabited house" (*al-bayt al-maskūn*), because "a verse of poetry is established, in utterance, upon the [principles of] the building of the Arab's habitable house [i.e., the tent]. The structure of the house in utterance is its middle [ʿarūḍ], just as the structure of the house of fabric [*bayt al-khiraq*] is the pole that stands at its centre: it is the strongest element of the fabric house."[46] This shows how closely the conceptualization of classical Arabic poetry was to the architectural principles of the Bedouin tent.

This metaphorical relationship between poetry and architecture acquired symbolic dimensions in mystical literature. In his *Futuhat*, the celebrated Andalusian mystic Ibn ʿArabi (d. 1240 CE) considered the fundamental principles of classical Arabic poetry to be four: two types of *sabab* and two types of *watad*. He saw this as a reflection in the world of poetic compositions of the fourfold architecture of the natural world, and especially that of the human body. Referring to the four prosodic principles of a house of poetry (*bayt al-shiʿr*), Ibn ʿArabi explains that the "house" is based on these principles just as the body is based on the four humors. He adds: "They are the two *sababs* and two *watads*: light and heavy *sabab*, and split and joint *watad*. The split *watad* represents decomposition while the joint *watad* represents composition; the light *sabab* represents the spirit while the heavy *sabab* represents the body. And with the whole there exists the human being [*al-insān*]."[47] Other elements of conceptual correspondence come from the "science of rhetoric" (*ʿilm al-badīʿ*), which is concerned with the forms, techniques, and elegance of poetic expressions. According to this science, an important form of elegance in a poem is *taṣrīʿ*, which refers to the principle of rhyming the two halves in the opening verse of a poem. A classical poem would consists of many verses (*abyāt*), each of which is divided symmetrically into two metrically equal halves, and the *taṣrīʿ* principle demands that the opening two halves must be rhymed in addition to the standard rhyming of all verses. Such symmetry is not required for the rest of the poem. *Taṣrīʿ* comes from *miṣrāʿ*, which is the single leaf of a double door. With this embellishing technique, the house analogy is further elaborated to include a symmetrical doorway, marking, as it were, the entry into the poem, just as a house would allow access to its interior through a well-crafted, symmetrical, double door.

Furthermore, the Arabic term "*ansha'a*" adds yet another dimension to the conceptual correspondence. The Qur'anic term "*al-nash'a*" and its link to the structure of the human body are of relevance here. Etymologically, it derives from the root "*N.SH.'*," "to grow," "to be alive," of which "*ansha'a*" means "to create," "to invent," "to produce," and "to compose." The Qur'an says: "He brought you forth [*ansha'akum*] from the earth" (11:61). "*Ansha'a*" also means "to begin," "to start," and "to commence doing something." Hence the verse, "He it is who produces [*ansha'a*] gardens trellised and untrellised" (6:141), means that "he invented them and commenced their creation." The term "*ansha'a*" has many applications in poetry and architecture. In poetry, the word means "to compose a poem" and "to commence reciting it"; in architecture, it means "to commence setting up a structure," and "*inshā'*" is used to describe the structure of a building.

Related to the concepts of *nash'a* and *inshā'* is the way in which the addition of the vocalizing motions to the consonant letters of the alphabet was understood. The act of adding these phonetic motions to the letters is called in Arabic "*tashkil*," literally, "giving shape, morph, or figure," and "forming." It derives from "*shakl*," literally, "shape," "morph," and "figure." Just as the consonant letters of the Arabic alphabet were viewed as the word's lifeless body while vocalizing was the animating spirit, the act of transforming the unvocalized letters into pronounceable words through the articulation of the exhaled breath was seen as the act of forming or shaping; in other words, vocalization gives sonic-audible forms to the alphabetic substance, just as breathing the divine spirit into the human body animates the body and imbues it with spatial identity.[48] This forms the cosmological basis for seeing harmony and beauty inherent in poetry and music as being expressed in all creations, and especially in the formation of the human body.[49]

Music and Architecture

The inherent connections between poetry and music, on the one hand, and poetry and architecture, on the other, lead us to consider the mediatory role poetry plays in the relationship between music and architecture. In premodern times, this relationship was based on two principles: that tone can be represented and measured in space and that both music and architecture can be reduced to numbers and proportions (see fig. 7.4). This understanding was conspicuous more in the Western than in the Islamic tradition. The notions of architecture as a frozen music and music as a singing of architecture are common in Western literature. Although their roots can be traced back to Pythagoras, who is credited with laying down the foundations of the science of music, who spoke about the music of the spheres, and most importantly, who discovered that tone can be measured in space, these notions owe their wide popularity to the works of Renaissance architects. Reducing both music and architecture to sets of numbers and proportions in search of a harmonic correspondence between seeing and hearing was a fundamental preoccupation of Renaissance architects.[50] In his canonical text, *De re aedificatoria*, the celebrated Italian architect Leon Battista Alberti (1404–1472 CE) wrote: "The very same numbers that cause sounds to have that *concinnitas*, pleasing to the ear, can also fill the eyes and mind with wondrous delight."[51] And his contemporary, the architect Andrea Palladio (1508–1580 CE), reiterated, "The proportions of the voices are harmonies for the ears; those of the measurements are harmonies for the eyes. Such harmonies usually please very much, without anyone knowing why, excepting the student of the causality of things."[52] During the Renaissance, many scholarly treatises were written on the topic, and numerous works were conceived to reveal its merits.[53]

Although it is possible to trace a similar conception in some Islamic works, such as the Ikhwan's *Rasāʾil*, for example, the lack of writing on architecture in the Arab-Islamic tradition makes it difficult to move beyond conjecture and speculation. It is remarkable that in their encyclopedic work, the Ikhwan devoted separate treatises to geometry, numbers, ratio and proportion, theoretical arts, practical arts, and music, but none to architecture. It is even more remarkable that the discussion of the proportions of the human body, which was a core architectural theme in Vitruvius's canonical text, *The Ten Books on Architecture*, was presented by the Ikhwan in their tract on music.[54] Whereas Vitruvius related the proportions of the human body directly to the architecture of the temple, the Ikhwan related it to the "architecture" of music and poetry. The image we know from Leonardo da Vinci as the Vitruvian man, which has been upheld in the West as a tribute to architectural imagination, was seen by the Ikhwan, long before da Vinci, as an evidence of the harmony and beauty inherent in music.[55]

The correspondence between hearing and seeing that is based on the same harmonic proportions was not zealously followed by Arab-Muslim thinkers. Despite the geometrical and mathematical imagination that lay at the heart of classical Arabic poetry and music, their relationship to architecture, as we saw, was articulated conceptually and metaphorically and not formally. Early on, al-Farabi dismissed outright, on rational-scientific ground, the Pythagorean idea of the music of the spheres, which formed the cosmological reference to the correspondence between hearing and seeing, the aural and the visual.[56] The Ikhwan, while supporting the idea,[57] spoke

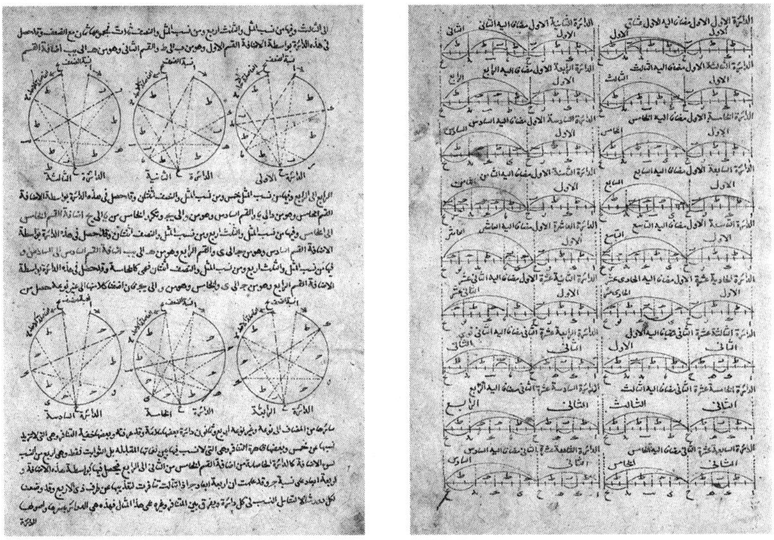

Figure 7.4. Two folios from Safi al-Din al-Urmawi al-Baghdadi's *Kitab al-Adwar fi al-Musiqa* (Book of modes). These show the spatial representations and measurements of modes in linear and circular forms. The principle that tone can be measured in space forms the very basis of the correspondence between music and architecture. Lawrence J. Schoenberg Collection, Kislak Center for Special Collections, Rare Books and Manuscripts, University of Pennsylvania, LJS 235. Courtesy of the University of Pennsylvania Libraries.

about the ephemerality of sounds in contrast to the durability of space and explained the diversity of music with reference to people's differences that are generated by different languages, natures, moralities, and habits.[58] They compared visual and aural perceptions, and presented a view that contrasts seeing and hearing on the basis that the eye perceives through straight lines, while the ear through circular lines.[59] The renowned eleventh-century Ibn al-Haytham (d. 1040 CE), on the other hand, in his celebrated work on optics, *Kitab al-Manazir,* described the numerous conditions and factors that interact in what makes an object visually pleasing. The object being "well proportioned" was only one aspect.[60] Even this may differ according to cultural differences. Thus in the Arab-Islamic tradition, the correspondence between what pleases the ear and the eye was never as simple and straightforward as a numerical and proportional correspondence.

Some modern scholars of Islamic art and architecture have sought a unifying spirit, or essence, that underlies all artistic expressions in the Islamic tradition, including music and architecture.[61] Titus Burckhardt, for instance, in his introduction to El-Said and Parman's book *Geometric Concepts in Islamic Art*, wrote: "In the Islamic perspective, this method of deriving all the vital proportions of a building from the harmonious divisions of a circle is no more than a symbolic way of expressing *Tawḥīd*, which is the metaphysical doctrine of Divine Unity as the source and culmination of all diversity."[62] This idea of *tawḥīd*, "unity," formed the central theme of a discourse aimed at revealing a unifying divine principle in various forms of artistic expressions. It is anchored in the philosophical idea of "unity and multiplicity" (*al-waḥda wa-l-kathra*), discussed by many Muslim philosophers and mystics, which views the great diversity of forms, colors, and meanings, as unity revealing itself in multiple modalities. From this perspective, poetry, music, and architecture meet through the perpetual manifestation of a primary cosmological order, just as the perpetual unfolding of a prosodic circle or a musical cycle produces ever new forms and meanings.[63] Probable and inspiring though it might be, the lack of textual evidence confines this view to the realm of conjecture. Seeing the correspondence between poetry, music, and architecture through the common, though less precise, frame of harmony and beauty is more in line with the documentary evidence currently available.[64]

Harmony and Beauty

Although Plato was suspicious of poets and their abilities to influence people and manipulate emotions, he nonetheless was keen on including music in the early education of his republic's guardians, for he believed that the right mode of music would help to set the soul in harmony rather than discord; hence its necessity. To set music apart from poetry, however, he distinguished between three elements: words, mode, and rhythm. Words have their own disciplining criteria, according to which poets would be ordered either "to portray good character in their poems or not to write at all."[65] Likewise, Plato stresses, all artists and craftsmen must be prevented "from portraying bad character, ill discipline, meanness, or ugliness in pictures of living things, in sculpture, architecture, or any work of art, and if they are unable to comply they must be forbidden to practice their art among us."[66] In Plato's republic, beauty and harmony are set as the goal of all artistic endeavors, as they are the foundations of goodness. And in an environment edified by harmony and beauty, mode and rhythm can enhance the effect of good poetry, "for rhythm and harmony penetrate deeply into the mind and take a most powerful hold on it."[67]

On this ground, medieval Islamic and classical and Neoplatonic Greek thoughts converge. Harmony (*iʾtilāf* and *tanāghum*) is agreed upon as an immediate prerequisite of beauty. A composition or a design is considered beautiful only when its parts are harmoniously put together, and accordingly, beauty becomes no more than harmony manifesting its own intrinsic nature in the world of form. Harmony is anchored in the "science of ratios" (*ʿilm al-nisab*), which is, according to the Ikhwan, "the most noble science, and which is known as the science of music."[68] The science of ratios, they add, is needed in all forms of the arts (*ṣanāʾiʿ*); however, it has been specifically identified with music, which is the harmony of melodies and notes, because harmonious ratios are most conspicuously expressed in its form. When the old sages discovered the principles of melodies and notes through knowledge of the numerical and geometrical ratios, they further explain, they combined them together and there revealed the musical ratio.[69]

Harmony is traced in the natural world, which is seen to have been made up of opposing forces, contrasting natures, and disparate forms. If it were not for the well-considered ratios, the Ikhwan write, these contrasting elements would not have been synthesized together in united, well-identifiable, beautiful forms. For artists and craftsmen to be able to reproduce beauty in their works of art, they have to employ the "virtuous ratio" (*al-nisba al-faḍila*), which is a loose concept the Ikhwan introduce as a guide. The virtuous ratio is not one specific mathematical formula, such as the golden ratio known in Europe,[70] but rather a set of ratios, or even any set of ratios, that combines elements in well-proportioned and well-balanced compositions that suit people's natural dispositions and please the soul. A "metered speech" (*al-kalām al-mawzūn*) is one example, the Ikhwan write. If it is composed according to the virtuous ratio, it will be more pleasurable to the ear than unmetered prose because of the set of ratios that underlie metered speech.

> An example of that is the structure of the long meter [*ʿarūḍ al-ṭawīl*]. It is made up of 48 letters, 28 of which are in motion [*mutaḥarrika*], and 20 are at rest [*sākina*]. The ratio of those at rest to those in motion is $5/7$. And so likewise is half of a verse, which has 14 letters in motion and 10

> at rest, and so is the quarter of a verse, 7 in motion and 5 at rest. It is also made up of 12 *sababs*, which are made up of 12 letters in motion and 12 at rest, and 8 *watads*, 8 of which letters are at rest and 16 are in motion.[71]

The Ikhwan give numerous other examples for the necessity of ratios from diverse fields, such calligraphy, painting, medicine, chemistry, the human body, and of course the world of nature, to demonstrate the effect of good balance on the making of things. The ultimate purpose of all this is expressed in the title of their sixth epistle: "On the Numerical and Geometrical Ratios for the Edification of the Soul and Reformation of Character." As for poetry and verse in particular, which the divine sages used to intone in temples and houses of worship, it is an effective way to employ the natural magic of music "to soften hard hearts and to awaken heedless souls from neglectful sleep and spirits idling and ignorant slumber, in order to make their spiritual world, their radiant domain, and their abiding home enticing to them, and to free them from the world of generation and corruption, save them from drowning in the sea of materiality, and rescue them from the trammels of nature."[72]

NOTES

1 ʿAbd al-Ghani al-Nabulusi, *Hullat al-Dhahab al-Ibriz fi Rihlat Baʿlabak wa-l-Biqaʿ al-ʿAziz*, in al-Munajjid and Wild 1979, 61.
2 Plato 1955, 429.
3 Ibid.
4 Ibid.
5 See Ibn ʿAbd Rabbih 1983, V:269.
6 Referring to the Prophet Muhammad, the Qurʾan says: "And We have not taught him poetry, nor is it suitable for him" (36:69). In his *Muqaddima*, Ibn Khaldun wrote that the Islamic revelation did not prohibit poetry. However, he acknowledged the changing attitude toward it after the advent of Islam, and explained why the notables of later times tended to despise it (Ibn Khaldun, n.d., 581).
7 Aristotle's attitude toward poets and poetry resonated better with the Arab's poetic sensibility. See Ibn Rushd 1986.
8 Ibn Khaldun, n.d., 570. Unless otherwise stated, all translations from Arabic sources are by the author.
9 Ibid., 569.
10 For a short biography of al-Khalil, see al-Hanbali 1998, I:442–444.

11 Little is known about al-Khalil's life and education. Although he is known through his unique dictionary *Kitab al-ʿAyn* as one of the earliest Arab lexicographers and philologists, his ingenious articulation of the meters of classical Arabic poetry reveals, albeit by inference, his skills in mathematics and geometry.

12 al-Farahidi 1984, I:275.

13 See, for example, al-Nahawi 1989 (tenth century CE); al-Mahalli 1991 (thirteenth century); ʿAtiq 1987 (twentieth century); and ʿAbdun 2001 (twenty-first century).

14 On the role of geometry in traditional Islamic art, see El-Said and Parman 1976. On the unifying Islamic sensibility that underlies artistic expressions, see Nasr 1987 and Ardalan and Bakhtiar 1973.

15 For an introduction to the history of music in the Islamic tradition, see Wright 1993 and Shiloah 1992. For a detailed study, see Shiloah 1995 and Touma 2003.

16 al-Isbahani 1952, I:7–8.

17 See al-Farabi, n.d.

18 The following translation is based on Wright 2010, 84–85. Here the Ikhwan equate *mūsīqā* (music) with *ghināʾ* (singing), in terms of nature and principles; however, their discussions show that they are not identical. I, therefore, preferred to adhere to the literal meanings of the terms in order to allow for the shades of differentiation.

19 According to Wright, the term "*mūsīqā*," "music," as is commonly known today, was first "*mūsīqī*." See Wright 1993.

20 In the *Shifaʾ*, Ibn Sina (d. 1037 CE) dedicated the third part of the art of mathematics to the science of music (*ʿilm al-mūsīqā*). See Ibn Sina 1984.

21 Ikhwan al-Safaʾ, n.d., I:196–197. See Wright 2010, 98–99. My translation is guided by Wright's; however, I have attempted to remain closer to the literal meaning of the text.

22 *Ḥarakāt al-bināʾ*, lit., "motions of building," are *fatḥ*, *ḍamm*, and *kasr*, while *ḥarakāt al-iʿrāb*, lit., "motions of expression," *naṣb*, *rafʿ*, and *khafḍ*. On their symbolic and spatial significance, see Akkach 2005, 105–107.

23 See Ibn ʿArabi, n.d., I:130–137.

24 This has formed the basis of the mystical symbolism of the Arabic alphabet. See Ibn ʿArabi, n.d., I:94–137; Akkach 2005, 95–111.

25 This aspect of the Arabic language has been the subject of sustained mystical reflections and acquired cosmological dimensions. For detail, see Akkach 2005, 95–111.

26 Some modern sources use the vertical stroke for *ḥaraka* and the circle for *sukūn*. This seems to make more sense to the native Arabic speakers as the *sukūn* is represented by a small circle. Here I followed the Ikhwan's model; see Ikhwan al-Safaʾ, n.d., I:219; Wright 2010, 116.

27 While the Ikhwan consider the *fāṣila* as an independent structural element, Ibn ʿAbd Rabbih in *al-ʿIqd al-Farid* considers it as a synthesis of two *sababs* and ignores

it (see Ibn ʿAbd Rabbih 1983, V:425). In most sources only *sababs* and *watads* are used in delineating the meters, and that is why it is not referred to in the analyses of the prosodic circles.

28 The dots underneath these letters are not diacritics, but only signs used to distinguish the two types of *sababs* and *watads*.

29 See Ibn ʿAbd Rabbih 1983, V:424–425.

30 In *al-ʿIqd al-Farid* Ibn ʿAbd Rabbih (Ibn ʿAbd Rabbih 1983, V:425) says that the *sabab* was so named because it is unstable, sometimes it holds and sometimes it falls, whereas the *watad* was so named because it always holds and never falls.

31 For the discussion of the meters of classical Arabic poetry, see Ibn ʿAbd Rabbih 1983, V:424–518; for the prosodic circles, V:439–432.

32 The dotted lines in the circle show the fivefold rotational symmetry. The fourfold rhythmical structure of the *watads* interlocks the rotating octagons to create the alternating sequence.

33 It seems that several possible meters in this as well as other circles were ignored for aesthetic reasons. These were noted on Ibn ʿAbd Rabbih's metric circles as *muhmal*.

34 Ibn ʿAbd Rabbih (Ibn ʿAbd Rabbih 1983, V:440) indicates that the original form of the *Hazaj* is six verbal units, two of which have been omitted.

35 According to Ibn ʿAbd Rabbih, this meter originally had three pairs of verbal units (i.e., six units), one of which has been omitted. This explains the missing part in the cycle. The same applies to the *Muqtaḍab* and *Mujtath*. I have shown the complete form of the *Muqtaḍab* as commonly presented in the sources.

36 Although the original form of this meter is D D / D D (reduced to four units by omitting two Ds), having a *watad mafrūq*, as shown in the circle, changes the meter to E D / E D. See Ibn ʿAbd Rabbih 1983, V:473–474.

37 There are many complex variations involved, including the omission of certain verbal units in *al-Hazaj*, *al-Muḍāriʿ*, and *al-Mujtath*, as shown above. The complex variations are not of concern to us here since they do not change the fundamental geometrical structure of the meters. For a detailed treatment of these variations, see Ibn ʿAbd Rabbih 1983, V:424–818.

38 See El-Said and Parman 1976.

39 See Owen Wright's English translation of the Ikhwan's treatise on music as well as his introductory study in Wright 2010.

40 For a detailed discussion of the relationship between music and visual art in the Islamic world, see Owen Wright 2004.

41 Ibn Manzur, n.d., I:292.

42 Ibid.

43 Ibid.

44 See Ibn Manzur, n.d., s.v. "*WTD*."

45 For details of the allowed variations, see Ibn ʿAbd Rabbih 1983, V:426–439.

46 See Ibn Manzur, n.d., s.v. "ʿ*RD*."
47 Ibn ʿArabi, n.d., II:272.
48 For more on this, see Akkach 2005, 105–107.
49 See Ikhwan al-Safaʾ, n.d., I:223–225.
50 See Wittkower 1988, part IV.
51 Alberti 1989, 305.
52 Palladio, cited in Trachtenberg 2001, 741.
53 See Wittkower 1988, Part IV.
54 See Vitruvius 1960, Book III.
55 See Ikhwan al-Safaʾ, n.d., I:223–225.
56 See al-Farabi, n.d., 89.
57 See Ikhwan al-Safaʾ, n.d., I:225. The fifteenth-century music theoretician Muhammad b. ʿAbd al-Hamid al-Ladhiqi acknowledged the Pythagorean idea of the music of the spheres in his brief outline of the history of the science of music. See al-Ladhiqi 1986.
58 See Ikhwan al-Safaʾ, n.d., I:196.
59 Ibid., I:236.
60 See Ibn al-Haytham 1983, 307–316.
61 Searching for the unifying "Islamic" spirit that can be traced in aural and visual art forms involves many theoretical problems and has been subject to intense criticism (see Necipoğlu 1995). Speaking of an Islamic aesthetic or spatial sensibility that shaped the artistic production in certain periods or places can present a viable alternative (see Akkach 2005).
62 El-Said and Parman 1976, ix–x.
63 For sources that adopted the concept of *tawḥīd*, see Nasr 1987; El-Said and Parman 1976; Ardalan and Bakhtiar 1973; Burckhardt 1976; Bakhtiar 1976.
64 See Behrens-Abouseif 1999.
65 Plato 1955, 162.
66 Ibid.
67 Ibid., 163.
68 Ikhwan al-Safaʾ, n.d., I:255.
69 Ibid.
70 See Lawlor 1982, part V.
71 Ikhwan al-Safaʾ, n.d., I:252.
72 Ibid., I:209–210, trans. Owen Wright, in Wright 2010, 123.

PART FOUR

Andalusia and Europe

CHAPTER EIGHT

Tents of Silk and Trees of Light in the Lands of Najd

The Aural and the Visual at a Mawlid *Celebration in the Alhambra*

CYNTHIA ROBINSON

In a memoir entitled *Nufadat al-Jirab fi ʿUlalat al-Ightirab* (Dust from the traveler's knapsack: consolation in exile), the minister, historian, poet, and Sufi Lisan al-Din Ibn al-Khatib (d. 1374 CE) offers a detailed narration of a celebration of the *mawlid*, the Prophet Muhammad's birthday, held at the court of Nasrid Sultan Muhammad V in Granada in December 1362 CE (*rabīʿ al-awwal*, 752 AH).[1] The text was first brought to the attention of scholars by Emilio García Gómez, one of whose primary interests was the determination of the exact area of the Alhambra, iconic palatial seat of the Nasrid dynasty, in which the festivities were held.[2]

García Gómez settled on the so-called Palace of the Lions,[3] but, after decades of discussion, current scholarly opinion favors the proposal recently put forward by Antonio Orihuela and Ángel López, which situates these activities in the more public spaces surrounding the area where official audiences were conducted, known as the *mishwār*—specifically the patios preceding the so-called Cuarto Dorado and the tower reception room known today as the Torre de Machuca (figs. 8.1 and 8.2; *see also plate 5b*).[4]

Other aspects of Ibn al-Khatib's text, however, have largely been overlooked. It is, for instance, of great interest for our knowledge of just how such festivities were organized,[5] given that it allows at least a partial reconstruction of who was present, and how various groups—the royal family; the *shurafāʾ* or descendants of the Prophet;[6] high-profile courtiers; powerful religious scholars; merchants; members of various local Sufi orders;[7] Sufis visiting from as far abroad as Persia—interacted, and their experiences of

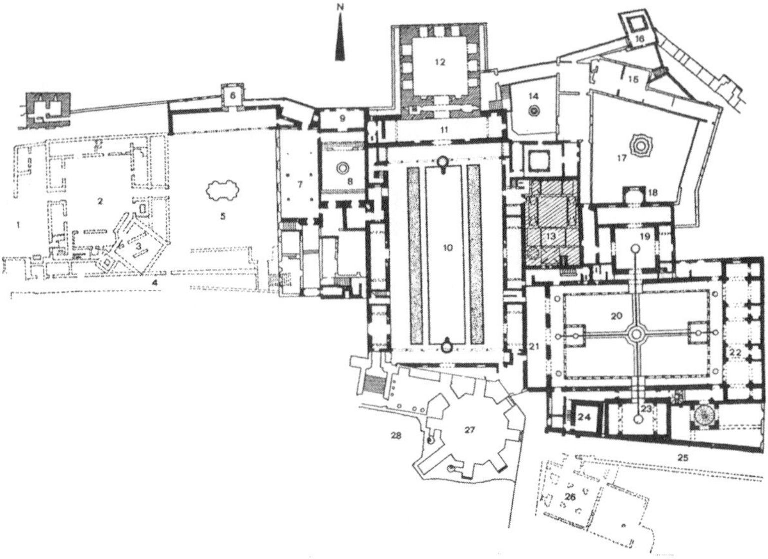

Figure 8.1. Plan, Alhambra Palace, Granada. After Contreras. Courtesy of the Aga Khan Documentation Center, MIT.

both spaces and the events orchestrated in them. One passage that has escaped scholarly notice almost entirely is the section in which Ibn al-Khatib describes the elaborate illumination of a patio, with a pond or pool at its center:

> Encircling[8] the stone borders of the pool was *a thorny maze*[9] *of candelabras of crystal and bronze,* more numerous than any other royal house possesses, more even than the treasuries of the caliphs. Candle-sticks with wide trays, tall columns and feet of ivory, hung with a multitude of receptacles for candles, were also placed about the open space; *[both] trees of wood and sculptures of copper,* the arrangement of whose many pieces had occupied artisans for days. The result elicited stupefaction and confounded thought. The candles were placed into the thorny bodies of the candelabras, of a shape between beveled and turned, minbars for the *trunks* [*j-dh-ʿ*] of wax.[10] Countless sorts of lighting devices must also be listed: niche lamps, oil lamps, torch lights, large candles, and small lamps, according to the [space offered by] places, corners and nooks.

Figure 8.2. Esplanade leading to the Cuarto Dorado and then to the Palace of Comares, past the Torre de Machuca, visible on the left, Alhambra Palace (fourteenth century), Granada. Photograph © Oronoz.

> The intricate display of waxy columns and stumps was ministered to by the hands of the priests of the houses of God, as the large solar disks of wax were arranged, and wicks were ignited with fire.
>
> *Thus did those interlaced branches bloom and illuminate* [azhara]*, and the marvelous spectacle delight.*[11]

The patio, pool, and lights formed part of the setting for an elaborate series of *mawlid* rituals and ceremonies that occupied patrons, participants, and attendees literally from dusk to dawn. The event opened with a candlelit procession, following which the sultan entered the pavilion in which he would receive and greet his guests, seated in state upon a throne. The throne appears to have been placed in the *bahw,* or reception room, of the tower now known as the Torre de Machuca, before which had been erected an elaborate ceremonial tent, made of priceless textiles of silken brocade.

Following the sovereign's entrance, the most distinguished groups of guests, referenced above, were arranged on either side and in front of him, and verses from the Qur'an, prayers, blessings, and sermons were pronounced, after which songs (unfortunately, these are not specified) were performed to the "moans of the hollow wooden flute."[12] The stage for the sumptuous banquet was then set, and all those present, down to the lowliest lackey, feasted amply on the bounty provided by the sultan. Once the main meal had been cleared, desserts were served, and a table of sweets and nuts was set, so that no one would go hungry during the lengthy series of events that followed.

These centered largely on the performance, by a gifted professional singer and reciter of poetry (*musmiʿ*) named al-Marini, who hailed from Mossul, of some twenty-five *qaṣīdas*, or "odes," composed expressly for the occasion. His cadences were frequently accompanied, in an order and fashion not clearly specified by Ibn al-Khatib, by shouts of approval and enthusiastic dances of members of various Sufi confraternities (and perhaps by others as well), and they were punctuated by the recitation of one of the eleven "Poems of the Hours" (intended, as their name implies, to mark the passing of each hour of the *mawlid* celebration) that Ibn al-Khatib himself had authored. These compositions were inscribed onto slips of paper and placed within individual compartments of an ingenious clocklike device; they were emitted, one by one, from one of the twelve "minbar-like" doors of the clock, which opened as the candle that governed its movements reached the end of the quantity of wax allotted for a given hour. As Ibn al-Khatib states, the recitation of the wistfully nostalgic eleventh poem coincided exactly with the appearance of the first rays of dawn in the morning sky, which also constituted the signal for a lavish breakfast to be served, after which the guests began to depart.[13]

Most of Ibn al-Khatib's account consists of a fairly straightforward (if occasionally somewhat hyperbolic) narration of the order of events, and his account of the open courtyard and pool, around which had been artfully arranged a large number of various lighting devices assembled (indeed, perhaps even manufactured) for the occasion, would not initially appear to be any different. The passage ends, however, with a sentence of a notably different tone, containing the phrase, "Thus did those interlaced branches bloom and illuminate." A rather prosaic description and a somewhat rote enumeration, in other words, have suddenly been transformed into *waṣf,* or "poetic description," a genre to which Arab poetic theorists frequently ascribed powers bordering on the transformative, since the objects of "description" were subjected to subtle, ingenious, and often difficult comparisons in order to elucidate and communicate their qualities to an audience that was frequently a listening one.[14] This concept, moreover, is crucial to a reconstruction of the message(s) encoded into the material setting of Muhammad V's *mawlid* celebration.

The verb I have rendered as "bloom and illuminate" is *"azhara,"* fourth-form infinitive of the root *z-h-r,* and the point of the double translation (that is, "bloom *and* illuminate" rather than "bloom" or "illuminate") is to communicate an idea or image that is probably ultimately untranslatable: the concept of flowering branches that are at the same time brilliant, flashing bursts of light. For the English-speaking reader, the double translation most likely conjures two separate images, which it is then her or his task to fuse. For the Arabic-speaking reader, however, especially if he or she were a member of, or visitor to, Muhammad V's court and thus formed part of a social group that highly prized poetic capacity and knowledge, the image conjured is likely to be that of the fusion of those two concepts—indeed, that image would be appreciated and prized precisely *because* it was one of fusion.

Trees and light constitute two of the most common topoi treated in the thousands of verse compositions in a myriad of genres penned or improvised by poets writing in Arabic since the pre-Islamic days of the *jāhiliyya,* or "period of ignorance," and the poet-heroes of the *Muʿallaqat,* or the "Hanging Odes."[15] In the pages that follow, however, I will argue that these two images, especially when fused, as Ibn al-Khatib has done, constitute important elements of a poetics that, in effect, both dictated and recorded how those present at the *mawlid* celebration would (or could, depending both on the sincerity of their devotions and the level of preparation with which they approached both the visual and aural dimensions of the celebration) have perceived the spectacle of what were, in effect, "trees of light."

The late-thirteenth-century poet and theorist Hazim al-Qartajanni (d. 1285 CE; he was born in al-Andalus, though he later immigrated to Tunisia) opined that the most felicitous objects of extended description (*waṣf*) for the poet—those that would best display his imitative capacities—included images (*taṣwīr*) of the glittering of "stars, candles, and incandescent lamps on the pure, still surfaces of the waters of brooks, rivers, canals, and small bays or coves." Similarly appropriate were full, leafy trees, their branches laden with blossoms, as were their reflections, "for the union achieved between a stream's banks and the leaves reflected in its crystalline water is among the most marvelous [*aʿjab*] and pleasurable [*abhaj*] sights to be seen [or, to behold]."[16] These concepts are manifested throughout the famed verses inscribed onto the walls of the Nasrid palace, penned by the most respected Nasrid littérateurs, not least among them Ibn al-Khatib himself, often for the express purpose of their placement where we find them today.[17] They are also, as I have argued elsewhere, embodied by the building itself and by its ornamental program.[18] Most important for this chapter, they appear to have been incarnated, quite literally, by the spectacle of light, crystal, bronze, and pond described by Ibn al-Khatib.

Trees and light are also central to Sufi cosmologies, which would have been familiar to anyone who had studied or taught, for example, in Granada's public madrasa or in those in any other North African capital, whether public or royally sponsored.[19] Indeed, they frequently constitute direct symbolic references to the Prophet Muhammad. The thirteenth-century Murcian mystic Ibn al-ʿArabi, for example, conceived of God's Chosen One as the "Tree of Creation" (*shajarat al-kawn*), a concept with Qur'anic foundations that highlighted his continuous and active role in the processes of the creation of the heavens, heavenly bodies, the earth and all earthly creatures, as well as the continued existence of all of these.[20]

The symbolic resonances, in addition to a direct and unequivocal symbolic association with the Prophet, contained by the "tree-candelabra" for those in attendance at the *mawlid* celebration are numerous. Trees play a multivalent symbolic role throughout the repertoire of *mawlūdiyyāt*, or poems composed in honor of the Prophet's birthday, connected to Muhammad V's court.[21] One miracle included with great frequency among the litanies of the Prophet's *muʿajizāt* that appear in these compositions is that of a tree trunk (*jidhʿ*, the same word used by Ibn al-Khatib in reference to the blocks of wax placed in the candleholders around the pool) that had been made into a bench on which the Prophet sat. As Muhammad, now rested, stood up to leave, the tree suddenly spoke, breaking into eloquent pleas and begging him to stay. The Prophet responded with a promise that it would be restored to its original, leafy, verdant state in Paradise. In the words of Nasrid court poet Abu Ishaq ibn al-Hajj (fourteenth century CE/eighth century AH):

> And tho' the tree trunk burst forth into leaf from pure joy,
> Greening as it saw him [the Prophet], so that he would stay,
> In Paradise it will [truly] green,
> Returning to its former state![22]

Likewise, the tree represents a place, generally a sacred or beloved place, that is now lost to the poet. For example, in a *qaṣīda* about Sufism composed by the Málagan Sufi and poet Ahmad ibn Ibrahim ibn Ahmad ibn Safwan (d. 763 AH/1373 CE) and dedicated to the traditionist Abu ʿAbd Allah al-Tanjali, whom the author calls the "*khaṭīb* and friend of God," we find the following lines:

> The intimate companion has departed—there is no waystation or sacred willow tree
> That can cure those whom the beloved ones have abandoned.[23]

The implicit association of a tree with an absent (divine) beloved evoked by Ibn Safwan, in a *mawlūdiyya* composed by Ibn Zamrak for Muhammad V, becomes much more extended and explicit, appearing amid a veritable cascade of symbols that serve to evoke the union once experienced by, and now lost to, the poet:

> If my plea for a meeting with you had been granted,
> I would not have taken the cloud's lightning flash as my messenger.

Or if, in meeting you, I had seen my hopes realized,
I would not have entrusted my sorrows to the eastern and
southern winds.
But the breeze brings [love] sickness along on its
night journey—
Quite enough to keep the love-sick one occupied!
At the crossroads where the souls used to meet is a thicket of trees
with widespread branches;
I pulled them down, breathing in their fragrance as the wind blew.
I keep a faithful memory of her shade as it spread over me;
For my part, I spread deep shade over my youth.
There, nearby, gazelles grazed to their hearts' content,
And I took pleasure and joy when I halted there.[24]

Here, though, it is the lightning bolt, rather than the tree, that symbolizes the Prophet in his capacity as messenger (here taken literally, as one who acts as go-between between a pair of separated lovers).

The Prophet Muhammad was likewise conceptualized by mystics as the embodiment of one of the most beloved of divine attributes, *nūr* (light), which, when manifested in God's Beloved, served, as in the case of the "Tree of Creation," as one of the generative motors that brought all of creation into existence. Throughout the later Arabic Middle Ages moreover, as Sufi devotions focused ever more intently on the Prophet and his person, exegetes and poets alike linked the light produced by celestial bodies to trees and flowers, which were then placed in symbolic relationship to him,[25] as seen in this *bayt* from a *qaṣīda* composed by Ibn al-Khatib himself in honor of the Prophet's birthday and dedicated to Sultan Muhammad V:

Were it not for you and your light, the stars would not have
appeared,
white blooms that never fade![26]

In the introduction to his (understudied) mystical treatise *Rawdat al-Taʿrif bi al-Hubb al-Sharif* (The garden of knowledge of noble love), Ibn al-Khatib offers a passage of rhymed prose that fully develops the blossom-light fusion motif with which he described the spectacle of lights around the pond. Here, in his dense rhymed prose, trees and lights are inseparably intertwined, producing an image that appears to evoke the Prophet himself:

> May God bless his servant and Prophet, our Lord Muhammad, pearl in the necklace of His well-ordered lovers, merchant of the most coveted goods of His unity, girded with refulgent and radiant proofs and blinding miracles, like the bursting forth of celestial branches which, like the sun, appear on the horizon, adorned with most excellently brilliant flower of all flowers [*zahr al-azhār*], like the restive thunder that leads the cloud-caravan, while the ardent breezes urge the forms of its branches into an embrace.[27]

The association of these two motifs, when fused, with the Prophet is confirmed in the *aljamiado* (that is, Castilian written in Arabic characters) version of the *Libro de las luces* (Book of lights).[28] María Luisa Lugo Acevedo has identified a thirteenth-century Arabic copy of the text that appears to have been used in Aragón; though no specific manuscript has yet been linked to the Nasrid court, it is very likely that the *Libro de las luces* was also read aloud at *mawlid* celebrations during the Nasrid period, as it was in Muslim communities elsewhere throughout the Iberian Peninsula. The Prophet's birth is accompanied by miraculous events and portents, and Muhammad literally emanates a blessed light that he has inherited from the illustrious line of prophets who have preceded him, to whom the final Prophet's coming is announced through a series of miraculous visions and divine revelations. The concept is evoked using the Spanish word for branches (*ramos*) in this passage describing the entrance of Muhammad's forebears into Yathrib (Medina):

> The brightness entered the houses and the people peered out of their doorways at the light, believing it to be flashes of lightning, and they saw the *branches of light* that rose up to the skies. . . . And they said to them, "Who are you, oh, sirs? For we have never seen people more beautiful of face than you, nor more refulgent than they, and especially he from whom *that light, with its bright branches of light*, emits."[29]

The spectacle of lights and flowering branches presented by Sultan Muhammad to his guests at the *mawlid* festivity was thus ultimately a prophetic one. This symbolic relationship, moreover, also formed part of a complex discourse of symbols manifested in both visual and sonic terms, which, as I will argue in the following pages, ultimately also communicated a sense of place.

Sound

Mawlid festivities such as those orchestrated by Muhammad V were intimately intertwined with the interests of powerful Sufi confraternities; indeed, as Ahmed Salmi notes, it is likely, both in some of the celebration's earliest instances at Ayyubid courts and in the *andalusī-maghribī* context, that both the idea for the celebration and its organization were directly appropriated from practices at the most popular and powerful local *zāwiyas*.[30] In other words, such a gesture on the part of a sovereign could be interpreted as constituting a public and carefully orchestrated—and, for some, even cynical—attempt to divert public fervor for and loyalty to popular Sufi institutions and personalities toward the sovereign and thus to secure for the ruling house a perception of legitimacy among social groups that might otherwise not have been so easily convinced.[31]

It is important to remember, however, that whether or not the public celebration of the Prophet's birthday is ultimately owed to a desire on the part of Sufis (and, later, to the acceptance of this desire by members of the religious scholarly elite) to offer a powerful alternative to Christian devotion to Christ—thus overriding deep-seated Muslim reservations concerning devotion to the Prophet's (or to anyone's) person—those devotions, once established, were for the most part sincere. Likewise, it is important to remember that the elaborate candle-lit procession with which Muhammad V's *mawlid* celebration opened—whether or not it was initially inspired by "Christian influence," as some early critics of the practice had it (and as later scholars have been prone to repeat)—would have been interpreted by Muslim attendees in a manner that added value and dimension to their own (Muslim) experience of the occasion.[32] Indeed, according to Ibn al-Khatib himself, many if not most of those in attendance experienced mystical ecstasy (*al-wājid*) during the festivities:[33] the multisensory stimulations offered by gardens, palace, candles, lights, textiles, and perfumes, coupled with the rhythmic sounds of *dhikr* and the musical cadences of poetic recitation, had, at least for some, exactly the effect they were intended to have, doubtless also the effect that devotees wished them to have.

Perhaps the most important among all the stimuli acting on the senses of those present was the aural: it is clear from Ibn al-Khatib's account that words and sounds heard, rather than sights seen, provoked shouts of joy and dances of ecstasy. The sounds and words heard throughout the evening were varied, and by this relatively late date, it was generally accepted that at least two of them—*dhikr*, or the rhythmic repetition of devotional phrases and prayers, and *samāʿ*, or listening to song or musically cadenced recitation of poetry as part of Sufi practices—habitually produced the sort of ecstatic reactions described by Ibn al-Khatib. Nina Ergin, for example, notes that many Anatolian schools of Sufi practice believed that it was possible to attain mystical union only through the sense of hearing and that *samāʿ*, the musical cadences of which assured that the words pronounced reached the hearts of listeners disposed to receive them, offered a path toward mystical understanding.[34] Indeed, al-Qashani, the devoted disciple of Ibn al-ʿArabi, opens his mystical commentary (*taʾwīl*) on the Qurʾan with the following phrases:

> All praise belongs to God whose arrangements of His [Qurʾanic] speech He has made to be the manifestations of the beauty [*ḥusn*] of His attributes and the rising stars [*ṭawāliʿ*] of His attributes [to be] the rising points [*maṭāliʿ*] of the light of His essence. He has purified the channels of audition in the hearts of His elect [*aṣfiyāʾ*] so that the audition may be realized. He has refreshed the sources of the sensory faculties of His friends [*awliyāʾ*] so that the beholding may be certain. He has made their innermost hearts sensitive to [the divine] subtleties by the irradiation of rays of love within them. He has made their spirits yearn to witness the beauty of His countenance, [only possible] by means of their annihilation [*fanāʾ*]; but when He cast upon them [His] speech they found spiritual comfort in it by morning and by evening. Through that [speech] He brought them closer and closer to Him so that they became in near communion with Him. Thereat He purified their souls with Its manifest aspect [*ẓāhir*] so that It became like gushing water and he replenished their hearts with Its inner aspect [*bāṭin*] so that it became like a surging sea.[35]

Al-Qashani, in other words, would likely have believed that the words and phrases sung or chanted during a session of *samāʿ* that entered the hearts of those present achieved a (celestial) effect similar to that achieved by the rhythmically chanted words of the Qurʾan itself.[36]

The study of *andalusī* Sufism—with the complex and somewhat fraught exception of Ibn al-ʿArabi—is still in its infancy, but for the present purposes, it is reasonable to suppose that attitudes toward these matters largely reflected those manifested in other contexts where Islam was the dominant religion, particularly in North Africa.[37] Though earlier jurists had condemned these practices, the rhythmic, almost songlike recitation of both Qur'an and prayers was widespread among Sufis both in al-Andalus and elsewhere and was widely accepted, even by a number of Maliki jurists, in Nasrid Granada. Though the ever-strict al-Shatibi (d. 1388 CE) comes down firmly against these practices, especially if the gatherings at which they took place included ʿulamaʾ, or religious scholars, both Ibn Lubb (d. 782 AH/1381 CE) and Abu al-Barakat al-Balafiqi (d. 773 AH/1372 CE) not only do not condemn them but give favorable opinions of them in their fatwas, or legal opinions. Ibn Lubb states that both *dhikr* and (implicitly rhythmic) Qurʾanic recitation are beneficial if done with sincerity,[38] even calling them the "garden of Paradise" (*riyāḍ al-janna*), a comparison that, though it might seem clichéd on first consideration, indicates that, as for al-Qashani, images that remained imprinted on the heart were primarily spun of words.[39] For his part, according to Ibn al-Khatib, al-Balafiqi, one of the most esteemed religious scholars in Muhammad V's entourage and among Ibn al-Khatib's most revered shaykhs, was himself an expert in *naghma*, or the rhythmic—melodious—recitation of the Qurʾan.[40] It is thus hardly surprising that al-Balafiqi condemned neither rhythmic recitation of the Qurʾan nor *dhikr* (which, along with *samāʿ*, was clearly practiced regularly, given what we know of the Sultan's *mawlid* celebration). It is, however, both somewhat curious and presently without explanation that Ibn al-Khatib, given the esteem in which he held al-Balafiqi, makes only the briefest of mentions of *dhikr* and Qurʾanic recitation in his narration of the *mawlid* festivities. Similarly, he mentions only in passing the singing of songs immediately preceding the banquet (which, as noted previously, he does not quote or even list) to the "moans" of the wooden flute. There is a good chance, given that the powerful confraternity of the Banu Sidi Bono were almost certainly among those performing *dhikr* at the festivities, that the songs performed included verses composed by the ninth-century Baghdadi mystic al-Hallaj: we know, thanks to Ibn al-Khatib himself, that such performances were included among the devotions habitually practiced by this group in their *zāwiya* located in the neighborhood across the Darro River from the Alhambra, known today as the Albaicín.

None of this, however, is openly acknowledged or treated in his account of the official royal festivities. Ibn al-Khatib's attitude toward *dhikr*, in fact, might best be summed up as conflicted. Though he habitually speaks highly of figures revered as Sufis, mystics, or ascetics, and even occasionally of poets who were talented at the execution of *dhikr*,[41] his description of these activities as practiced by the Banu Sidi Bono is at best dispassionate. On occasion, it even reads as disapproving: he notes, for example, that members of the confraternity "created problems" and opines that their practices of *dhikr* induced them to "behave like beasts."[42] Nonetheless, he does acknowledge that the spontaneous session of *dhikr* that erupted at the end of the *mawlid* festivities, which he describes as a "tumultuous noise . . . that bounced off the walls, made louder by the new construction," and in which "experts competed with the vulgar populace," "ended up producing ecstasy."[43]

Much more prominent in Ibn al-Khatib's account, however, is the state of heightened and even ecstatic sensibility attained by those present as they listened to the beautiful cadences of the *musmiʿ*'s performance of *qaṣīda*s (concerning which practice Ibn Lubb had also pronounced favorably, providing the content was suitable)[44] produced for the occasion:

> As regards the reciter [*musmiʿ*], he was especially sought-after for royal gatherings, distinguished both by the excellence of his pronunciation of *iʿrāb* and the perfection with which he read poetic compositions. He was known as al-Marini. Born in Mosul, he was a most worthy representative of his trade in all manner of emotionally moving song. Each time his throat emitted a particularly passionate, ardor-inducing phrase, the Sufis and *fuqarāʾ*, both those who were truly enraptured and those who pretended to be so, received it—following the example of their leaders—with great fervor; things got wild, there was non-stop dancing, mystical ecstasy triumphed throughout, and noisy shouts were raised.
>
> This singer [*musmiʿ*] combined song with the reading of the Poems of the Hours and with the recitation of the *qaṣīda*s [composed for the occasion] in praise of God's Prophet (may God bless him and save him), extolling his birth and narrating his miracles, before continuing with panegyric dedicated to the Sultan, the description of his raiments and throne, and praises of his hospitality and of the occasion. That night the number of *qaṣīda*s [recited] was over twenty-five, which indicates how deeply rooted this art is in Arabic-speaking countries, as well as its elevated status [among those who speak this language]—clearly, there are still embers among the ashes! Among the poets were excellent ones, as well as others held to be of lesser status, according to the

manner in which the experts in this art habitually evaluate its products and categorize them according to levels of excellence.[45]

The *qaṣīda*s whose performance inspired such passionate responses among the Sufis (and perhaps among other attendees as well) were of the genre known as *mawlūdiyyāt* (literally, "compositions in honor of the *mawlid*"; sing. *mawlūdiyya*). As Ibn al-Khatib notes, they generally contain a lengthy enumeration of the Prophet's qualities and miracles, followed by a section of *madḥ* (praises) of the patron (in this case, the Nasrid sultan). They also include a substantial introductory *naṣīb*, or amatory prelude (frequently of thirty lines or more), in which the poet laments love lost and expresses nostalgia for the Arabian lands and landscapes that witnessed its original flourishing.[46] Although Ibn al-Khatib does not state this, it is probable that the enraptured cries, ecstasies, and spontaneous eruptions of dance he records were elicited by the first two sections, rather than the third, of these compositions—the experience of this elevated emotional state would thus have been oscillating (that is, in alternation with a state characterized by the *absence* of ecstasy) and cyclical, rather than stable and teleological, throughout the evening, night, and predawn hours.

Sources indicate that some type of poetic performance in honor of the Prophet was typical of *mawlid* celebrations from their earliest recorded days in Fatimid and Ayyubid contexts. Nevertheless, the genre of the *mawlūdiyya* appears to have truly come into its own under the patronage of *andalusī* and North African dynasties during the fourteenth century CE/eighth century AH; indeed, Salmi notes that, though these compositions were undoubtedly produced both before and after these dates, the vast majority of preserved examples were composed between 1360 and 1367 CE (761 and 768 AH).[47] Though Ibn al-Khatib attests (albeit rather academically and dispassionately) to the emotive potential of these compositions, as well as to the notable quality of some of them, modern critics have not been so kind in their assessments. García Gómez, for example, even though he includes full editions and translations of the "Poems of the Hours" among the texts he selected, dismisses the *qaṣīda*s as "interminable" and neglects to translate a verse.[48] For her part, Bush, although she purports to reconstruct attendees' experience of the *mawlid* festivities through use of the poetry produced for the occasion, also neglects to mention them.[49]

Indeed, the entire poetic corpus of the Nasrid kingdom has long been characterized by scholars as derivative, encyclopedic, ossified, and even nostalgic *avant la lettre*:[50] in sharp contrast to the famed love-and-wine lyrics of late-medieval Persia, verses composed by Nasrid poets have not traditionally been perceived as either interesting or novel. Celia del Moral has offered a thorough and useful synthesis of the poetry of the Nasrid period, and a selection of the large number of verses attributed to Sufi poets by Ibn al-Khatib have been translated by Fernando Velázquez Basanta.[51] Many more poets and compositions, however, await the attention of scholars. Almost no attempt, moreover, has been made to evaluate these compositions as functioning and integral components of courtly gatherings, official celebrations, royal audiences, informal literary *majālis* (séances), religious rituals or observations, or mystical experiences.[52]

Unless we were direct participants in the belief systems commemorated and reinforced by the festivities, the recitation of the twenty-five *qaṣīda*s in their entirety would indeed probably have seemed "interminable" to most of us: if only because of their number and average length (most are longer than sixty verses, and some considerably more), they must certainly have formed the focal point of the evening. Logic, moreover, would dictate that, given the effect we are told that particular verses produced on those most "invested" in the more devotional or mystical aspects of the occasion (i.e., the Sufis and the *fuqarā*ʾ), these words and the musical cadences in which they were pronounced in some way dictated or inflected their experiences, and—almost perforce—their perception of their surroundings, of which the pond and its luminary ornament described at the beginning of this chapter formed a part. Before we return to the visual surroundings and to visitors' experience of them, however, a few words concerning the content of some of the verses are in order.

As noted by Salmi, del Moral and Velásquez Basanta, these compositions do indeed owe a great deal to the early odes known as the *Muʿallaqat*: the amatory *naṣībs* are filled with references to abandoned desert campsites, departing caravans bearing the beloved away from the anguished poet, and the ensuing anguish of longing, absence, and lovesickness. Fleeting references to the lush, well-watered gardens that witnessed past passion abound, often evoked as the poet laments their metaphorical destruction at the hands of separation. The "shaykh, *faqīh, kātib*, and *qadi*" Abu Ishaq ibn al-Hajj, for example, grieves over the torn petals of "blooms of beauty" and the cruelty of his beloved's rejection:

The blooms of beauty in the garden
    Were ripped asunder by their howdahs, as they took them for
        their sleeves;
She bewitches, she can, if she wishes, on the day of defamation,
    Throw a lance that will make shudder [as it hits its mark].
For her, man's reason is booty,
    That of those who died honorably from love's swiftness.
Whenever she wills our drunkenness,
    She gives us a draught of bad omens, instead of wine . . .
Among that which love had left to me is a flash of lightning—
    They imagined it glimmering from between the teeth of a
        smile,
And the breath of a breeze, coming from the armor . . .
    From the caravan, where they die of thirst.[53]

Ibn al-Khatib, in the first of the twenty-five *qaṣīdas* he records in the *Nufadat al-Jirab*, opens by lamenting the departure not only of his beloved but also of the morning breeze, which has deprived him even of the memory of her breath:

What matters such a crime to the heart, after you?
    What if it does seem a bird with no wings?
And what [matters it], to longing, if it burns when the morning
        breeze
    Has departed, taking your breath with him?

He continues, despairing of ever attaining solace, as the night abandons him to the cruel rays of dawn:

Do you see consolation taking hold of my heart after you?
    No, and the dawn is beginning to appear on the horizon.

Implicitly likening himself to a bird, the eternal and eternally polyvalent symbol of the lover, beloved, and love, Ibn al-Khatib evokes his desolation through a reference to his broken wings:

They concealed desire, though it was on fire,
    And the veil stayed drawn despite the gale-force winds.
They left me behind after them,
    My gaze lowered and averted, heavy of step, my wings broken.[54]

The far-off lands of Najd are frequently invoked in these amatory preludes; such references appear to serve, in the context of the Nasrid *mawlūdiyya*, as a stand-in or a substitute for the Hijaz, the region associated with the Prophet's birth and with pilgrimage. The place of memory and desire thus becomes, so to speak, a poetic one rather than a specific geography.[55] Abu Ishaq ibn al-Hajj, for instance, opens his *naṣīb* thus, summing up in a few lines the group of topoi and emotions with which these compositions are habitually introduced:

> May God water the lands of Najd and preserve their tents,
> even though they have despised my infatuated heart,
> And irrigate them, with two springs, with my tears
> and the heart of the clouds that hang in front of my dwelling place.[56]

Most scholarly evaluations of such combinations of motifs, precedent to the equally felicitous appropriation of the central *raḥīl*, or "traveling" section of the *qaṣīda*, converted into an imagined journey to Najd (again and somewhat puzzlingly, rather than to the Hijaz) as precedent to the evocation of the Prophet's qualities and miracles, relegate them to the routinely derivative. Salmi even opines that the *naṣīb* seems overly long and disconnected from the "traveling" and panegyric sections and wonders aloud whether the first two sections of *mawlūdiyya* compositions might not simply be an excuse for the offering of yet one more overblown set of praises to the sovereign.[57] Nevertheless, given the ecstatic reactions described by Ibn al-Khatib to what must certainly have been phrases similar to those quoted previously (indeed, some of these very phrases might have inspired those reactions), it appears that, however self-serving the act of composition might have been (most of the compositions recorded by Ibn al-Khatib were written by men known to have been in the employ of the court, so such a possibility cannot be entirely discounted), the ecstatic effect produced was at least in some cases a very real one. In other words, descriptions of lost desert encampments, fleeting glimpses of equally lost gardens, memories of cruelly departing beloveds (and breezes), and evocations of anguished hearts, when sung, produced in their hearers an effect of *ṭarab*, that is, of simultaneous joy and anguish, a sentiment widely prized among patrons, poets, and audiences alike throughout the history of medieval Arabic poetry and, when activated in the proper context, universally recognized as offering a portal onto the experience of the mystical.

And the fact that the words and phrases were ordered according to the conventions of the classical ode, rather than arranged in the form of the more "catchy" and popular *muwashshaḥa* or *zajal*, does not seem to have been an impediment to the production of this effect—rather the opposite, in fact.[58] Indeed, this latter appears to have been achieved through the judicious deployment of the *waṣf*, or poetic description, of these most "classical" of places, personages, and emotions, familiar to poets, patrons, and audiences since the days of the *jāhiliyya*—in fact, Salmi signals the quantity and quality of *waṣf* habitually included in *andalusī mawlūdiyyāt* as one of their few "original" qualities.[59]

When we remember that every one of these compositions was composed for recitation in musical cadences, many specifically for occasions such as Muhammad V's *mawlid*, it becomes possible to imagine the degree to which the repeated invocation of such a repertoire or symbolic register would have had on its fourteenth-century *andalusī* audience. Indeed, I believe it to have directly influenced the conception of the mise-en-scène for these festivities: the lighting display around the pond together with the elaborate pavilion-tent where the sovereign greeted his guests and from which he observed the proceedings constituted a very literal embodiment of a number of the topoi central to the symbolic repertoire of the *naṣīb*.

Jaroslav Stetkevych has demonstrated the context-specific adaptability of the amatory prelude as it evolved over the centuries, both as part of the formal tripartite structure of the *qaṣīda* (as in the case of our *andalusī mawlūdiyyāt*) and independently of it.[60] Though the *naṣīb* remained a poetic constant throughout the Islamo-Arabic middle ages and beyond, it was hardly ossified or static, and neither its use nor the invocation of the set of topoi most representative of it necessarily implied an exercise in archaism for its own sake. Of particular interest for this chapter is the way in which the *naṣīb* was effectively molded to mystical purposes in the thirteenth century by such luminaries as Ibn al-Farid and Ibn al-ʿArabi.[61] The amatory preludes of our *mawlūdiyyāt*, in other words, do not merely reference an "archaic" poetic tradition but rather participate in a living, mystical one. Long before the date of Muhammad V's *mawlid* celebration, this tradition had absorbed those "archaic" references into its own symbolic register and imbued them with a multivalent complexity that made of the spring breeze (sometimes) an allusion to the Prophet; of the Bedouin beloved (usually) or of the gazelle (frequently) a stand-in for the divine Beloved; and of that beloved's departure or absence (almost always) an expression of yearning for mystical union. When Nasrid court poets invoked the lands of Najd, Bedouin caravans, deserts suddenly in flower after generous rains, or inconsolable sorrow over an abandoned campsite, much more than expressing a simple and uncomplicated nostalgia for the lands of the Prophet's birth, as Velásquez Basanta and del Moral appear to imply, they in fact signaled to those who were prepared to receive such marching orders—and Ibn al-Khatib's account of the *mawlid* festivities would appear to indicate that most of those present were quite prepared to do so—a collective setting-out toward the mystical ascent represented by the caravan's departure.[62]

Just as do Ibn al-Farid's and Ibn al-ʿArabi's compositions, these Nasrid *naṣībs* both prescribe and document mystical experience, an experience that is not linear but circular, not stable but oscillating. But this experience is also located in a specific place—the lands of Najd. Stetkevych argues persuasively that Najd, by the eighth century and in the context of the (neo-)classical *qaṣīda*, had morphed from a specific geographic reference into an idea and an object of diffuse longing.[63] I instead suggest that in the case of the *mawlūdiyyāt*—owing both to the particular nature of the occasion for which they were commissioned and to a general intensification of devotions to the Prophet after the days of Ibn al-Farid and Ibn al-ʿArabi—for most of those present at Muhammad V's *mawlid* festivities, Najd represented a very specific place, one to which they themselves had access through the lens offered by the vivid images that composed the symbolic repertoire of the *naṣīb*.

Many of these images, moreover, combine to compose an imaginary landscape that was supposed to have been literally brought to life by the Prophet. In the particular context of the *mawlūdiyyāt*, many of the "classical" topoi from the *naṣīb*'s earliest days, which had acquired a mystical semantic field at the hands of an Ibn al-Farid or an Ibn al-ʿArabi, are deployed in order to make of the Prophet an intermediary both in the "creation" of the symbols of which the landscape is composed and in the mystical experience offered—through the recitation of the words and the manipulation of the images they conjured—to all those present. Just as Sufi cosmology conceived of the Prophet as an indispensable intermediary in the very process of creation, Ibn al-Khatib, for instance, following a litany of luminous epithets that evoke the Prophet as a manifestation of divine light, refers to him as *nuqṭat al-kawn*—"the point from which all creation emanates"—and praises him thus:

Before existence existed,
before the dark phantasms were dispelled by his light,
The earth was illuminated by the light of your birth,
and it was shaken with vibrations of joy.
And fertility infused that which was withered—
dried teats filled with the softness [of milk].[64]

That is to say, just as the arid lands of Najd await God's bringing of the spring rains—such hopes were expressed by Abu Ishaq ibn al-Hajj in the opening lines of his *mawlūdiyya*, quoted previously—so does the earth await the Prophet's coming so that its fertility may be renewed. Now let us spend a few moments considering what attendees at the 1362 *mawlid* festivities held at the Alhambra actually *saw*.

Sights

In his account of Muhammad V's *mawlid* festivities, Ibn al-Khatib spends a good deal of time describing the architecture and ornamentation of the throne room and *mishwar* of the palatial structures erected by his patron immediately prior to the celebration. These were ample, spacious rooms, adorned with the finest tile and woodwork, boasting fabulously intricate cupolas and platforms of the most exquisite workmanship.[65] As he begins to narrate the actual festivities, however, it becomes clear that Muhammad V had selected the courtyard *between* these structures for the celebration (possibly owing, at least in part, to the unfinished state of the architectural constructions at the time of the celebration), at the center of which was erected an enormous and elaborate ceremonial tent made of brocaded textiles: [66]

> Embroidered upon them were leaves of more varied colors and subtle details than those displayed by valley meadows well watered by the loosening of the strings of the dark clouds' water-skins, when the clouds incline tenderly over them, heavy with rain, more even than those displayed by gorgeously arrayed gardens embellished by puddles and inlets, all turned into brocades by the rain clouds.[67]

Just as was the case with Ibn al-Khatib's description of the courtyard and patio, ablaze with the light of a myriad of candelabra-"trees," this passage contains an abrupt departure from the register of matter-of-fact description and rote enumeration into the multilayered symbolic landscape of *waṣf*. Though the implicit comparison of textile to garden is more than common throughout Arabic poetry, it seems that something a bit more complex is at work here, for this garden is not the enclosed, carefully cultivated, precious pleasure garden of so many a courtly *ghazal*.[68] Rather, it is found amid the breathtaking brilliance of a barren, rugged plain suddenly covered with new blooms thanks to a generous rainstorm. In the final phrases of the account, Ibn al-Khatib, consummate poet that he was, thickly layers his description with terms—the text includes references to valley meadows and to dark, water-heavy rainclouds (mentioned several times); a brief, archaic wink toward wineskins; and the image of the sudden glimmer of puddles and inlets—directly appropriated from the *naṣīb* repertoire. He is signaling to himself and to his readers, using the stylized and coded language of the *naṣīb*, that this *is* Najd, the same Najd evoked and described over and over in the extensive *naṣībs* with which Nasrid poets opened their *mawlūdiyyāt*. Ibn al-Khatib himself, for example, dedicates forty-three of the eighty-two verses of one composition to the evocation of a thunderstorm in Najd:

> [The flash of lightning] crowned the tops of the hills with
>   blossoms [*nuwwār*];
>   He wound rings of white flowers around the tender branches.
> Oh, but how quickly this garden is scattered by the eastern wind,
>   Where once the bright smile of the white blooms flashed and
>   the roses showed their confusion!
> O land in whose valleys I passed my boyhood,
>   Where now our pact is not honored,
> When the breeze weakens over her vacant courtyards,
>   It takes up aromas of willow, wormwood and myrtle.[69]

Ibn al-Khatib's is a garden conjured in an instant by the flash of lightning playing among the trees on the plain (note the use of the term "*nuwwār*," which exists in obvious intertextual relationship with "*nūr*," "light"), only to be immediately and capriciously dissipated by the blowing of the eastern wind. His is a valley, moreover, that reflects, with striking exactitude and feature by feature, Stetkevych's description of the actual place: "The most obvious characteristic of Najd is that it is the centrally located high plateau of the Arabian Peninsula. It is flanked by mountain ranges on the west and east and by inclement deserts on the north and south. There are only seasonal streams in Najd, as well as several springs that form oasislike ponds surrounded by vegetation, but even these are not stable in their water level."[70]

The actual ceremonial tent occupied by Muhammad V and his most esteemed courtiers would surely have called to the minds of all those who saw it the mythical tents whose occupants had so cruelly disdained Abu Ishaq ibn al-Hajj but whom, hopeless with lovesick longing, he blessed anyway. The tent, in turn, with its heavy panels of silk brocade densely embroidered with deep green leaves and flowering branches, as described through the conventions of *waṣf* by Ibn al-Khatib, is fused with the fleeting beauty of the desert garden suddenly burst into flower after a torrential rainstorm, as shimmering and delicate as the gardens evoked in the verses by the same poet cited above, just before their blooms were thoughtlessly trampled by the departing caravan. The patio, with its shimmering pool surrounded by a dense thicket of wax trunks and bronze branches ablaze with white flower-lights, for whose generous irrigation Abu Ishaq ibn al-Hajj had likewise prayed, could be none other than the "oasislike ponds" referenced by Stetkevych, surrounded by verdant vegetation. These visual references, thanks to the oscillating effect achieved through the fusion of light with branches, of brocaded tent flaps with leaves and blossoms, would indeed be fleeting, shimmering ones for those who contemplated the spectacle in the dark of night and by candlelight as they listened to songs and recitations and perhaps performed *dhikr*.

These images, however, are also strikingly literal incarnations of those that devotees' hearts had been trained to replicate, surely functioning in a manner similar to that conceived by al-Qashani for the heart's reception of the recited words of the Qur'an. Culled directly from the symbolic repertoire, they were endlessly repeated in recitations of the *naṣīb*, heard collectively as *samāʿ* in a context in which reaching a state of mystical ecstasy was not only a desideratum but a very real possibility. Rather than inspiration for devotions, the royal tent and pond surrounded by light-trees are their products. They offer something of a point of departure for the night voyage (*masran*), which, as Ibn al-Khatib's "Poems of the Hours" indicate, was the conceptual equivalent, in mystical terms, of the passage of the hours during which the *mawlid* celebration took place. As the caravans departed for Najd, in other words, the souls of those present and capable of undertaking the arduous voyage journeyed upward toward the heights of mystical union.

One of the suburbs immediately adjacent to the Sabika hill, on which the Alhambra was built, was named Najd; it roughly comprises the neighborhood known today as the Realejo. According to Ibn Battuta's descriptions of Granada and its surroundings, the Granadan Najd was home to one of the Nasrid kingdom's most venerated and powerful *zāwiyas*, known as al-Lijam. During Muhammad V's reign, it was administered by a jurist named Abu al-Hassan ʿAli ibn Ahmad al-Mahruk, known as the "shaykh of the *fuqarāʾ*" who earned a modest living through trade (*mutasabbibūn*).[71] This is a group whose presence is specifically mentioned by Ibn al-Khatib as having been among those invited to Muhammad V's *mawlid* celebration in 1362. Its members, marked by particular practices and attitudes that the sovereign and his courtiers themselves may have appropriated for the occasion, would have been well attuned to the ritual, aural, and visual aspects of the mise-en-scène offered by the sultan. And they were likely among those whose jubilant shouts indicated that the words sung by the *musmiʿ* had reached their hearts, that the journey had begun, and that they perceived, as Ibn al-Khatib states in his "Poem for the Eleventh Hour," that,

> Truth witnessed with his presence; he did not hide his face, and
> His account was sweet to the taste.
> We removed our sandals, unfurling, as a carpet, the presence of union,
> And the Beloved was the Cupbearer.

They would have genuinely lamented, along with him, the departure of the night's intimacy, as he again evoked the symbolic tent—

> You have gone, O Night, like the years of my youth,
> Black of wing, the hasty flapping of your tent-flaps ominous

—before bidding farewell to those who continue their voyage upward toward the mystical heights:

> May God preserve them, wherever they go, those travelers who,
> As they pass [*s-r-y*], perfume the horizons
> The companions, O bidder of farewell, depart on their night-voyage![72]

With recitation of the final *bayts* of Ibn al-Khatib's eleventh poem, the first rays of dawn appeared on the horizon.[73] The light-flowers on the branches surrounding the pond faded against the brightening of the sky, and the shimmering gardens of Najd vanished into the darkness between heavy folds of brocade.

NOTES

1 Ibn al-Khatib 1968, 275–289. On Ibn al-Khatib's life, infamous death and writings, see Knysh 2000; Lirola Delgado 2002; and Robinson 2009.

2 See García Gómez 1988. For such festivities in general in the Nasrid kingdom, see ʿAbbadi 1965–1966.

3 The structure was actually known to its fourteenth-century audience as *al-Riyad al-Saʿid*, or "The Garden of Delights," a detail that, as I and others have argued, has significant implications for that structure's interpretation. For the name, see Puerta Vílchez 2001, 79n12. The title was used by Yusuf III in his *dīwān* of Ibn Zamrak; see Ibn Zamrak 1997, 124 (citation from Puerta Vílchez 2001). For some of its implications for the structure's interpretation, see Robinson 2008.

4 See Orihuela and López López 1990, with ample discussion of the debate ignited by García Gómez's theory. Olga Bush's recent interpretation of these spaces is based on their rereading of Ibn al-Khatib's text; see Bush 2006, especially 291–330. Also of interest for this discussion is Ruiz Souza 2004. Useful introductions to the Alhambra and the scholarship surrounding it are found in Grabar 1978 and Puerta Vílchez 1990.

5 The widespread impression of Nasrid culture as "encyclopedic" and derivative has doubtless contributed to scholars' unthinking acceptance of the derivative nature of the *mawlid* festivities organized at the Alhambra by Muhammad V: given that the Nasrid sovereign had spent time at the Marinid court during his period of exile (1359–1362 CE, during which time he was deposed), it is assumed that the celebrations of December 1362 represented a rote imitation of similar festivities witnessed at the North African court. García Gómez (1988) repeats this observation numerous times throughout his study, and it has been taken up more recently by del Moral and Velásquez Basanta (1994).

6 The role(s) possibly played by members of this group, whose importance for late medieval and early modern North Africa was capital, have barely begun to be considered as regards al-Andalus. See Fierro 1996, as well as García Arenal 2012, for a summation of what is presently known concerning the *shurafāʾ* during the Nasrid period, as well as their importance to *morisco* devotional culture.

7 It should be noted that these last four groups frequently overlapped, as demonstrated by a perusal of the biographies contained in Ibn al-Khatib 1973 and Boloix Gallardo forthcoming.

8 "*Dāra bi*" can also be translated as "revolving around," and though Ibn al-Khatib makes no further reference to the use of mechanical devices in the mise-en-scène, this is a possibility that should probably be born in mind.

9 The word used here is "*ḥasak*," which translates as "thorns," "spines," or "prickly herbs." As will be seen, fundamental to my argument will be Ibn al-Khatib's comparison of these lighting devices to various sorts of vegetation.

10 A minbar is a pulpit. This comparison of the blocks of wax to stumps is also, I believe, quite deliberate, and the importance of this root, which references trunks or stumps (the pun will have to stand) will be discussed in greater detail in the ensuing pages.

11 Ibn al-Khatib 1968, 277; García Gómez 1988, Arabic 127–128, Spanish 148–149, emphases mine. All translations, unless otherwise noted, are my own.

12 García Gómez 1988, Arabic 129, Spanish 150.

13 For a complete and detailed narration of the festivities, see, again, Ibn al-Khatib 1968, 275–289 and García Gómez 1988, 123–169.

14 For the transformative powers of *waṣf*, or descriptive poetry, in a variety of ritual and ceremonial contexts in medieval Arabo-Islamic civilization, see the seminal study Hamori 1974. For its implications for *andalusī* contexts, see Robinson 2002 and 2008.

15 The literature on these is truly vast, but a useful introduction, as well as superb English translations, may be found in Sells 1989.

16 Ibn Muhammad Qartajanni 1986, 127–128; text translated into Spanish and discussed in Puerta Vílchez 2001, 77.

17 For the Alhambra verses, see García Gómez 1996; Rubiera Mata 1970, 1976, 1984. For inscriptions in general throughout the Nasrid palace, see the fundamental study by Puerta Vílchez in Puerta Vílchez 1990, 2007, and Puerta Vílchez and Nuñez Guarde 2010.

18 See Robinson 2008.

19 See Puerta Vílchez 2002.

20 See Ibn al-ʿArabi 1998a. For the importance of Qurʾanic trees to the ornamental program of the throne-room of the Hall of Comares, constructed during the early decades of the fourteenth century, see Cabanelas 1988. I have also explored these concepts as points of encounter, negotiation, and dispute between Nasrid and contemporary Castilian Christian and Jewish devotional cultures (see Robinson 2006).

21 The tree is a notably multivalent symbol in Nasrid art and literature, both in contexts that are obviously devotional and others that are less obviously so. Ibn al-Khatib also links it, in the *Rawdat al-Taʿrif*, to concepts such as wisdom and nobility, and suggests for it a feminine incarnation. Another interesting and unexplored source is offered by the palm tree (*nakhla*) at the center of the *risālat al-nakhla* composed by Abu al-Hasan ʿAli ibn Abi Muhammad Abd Allah ibn

Muhammad ibn al-Hasan al-Judhami al-Balafiqi al-Malaqi (d. 794 AH/1391 CE), in which the palm both symbolizes the dynasty itself and calls forth discussion of important devotional and mystical concepts. See Robinson 2006 and 2013, and SLE (San Lorenzo del Escorial) Mss. Ar. 1653, *Kitab Tuhfat al-Basa'ir wa-l-Absar.*

22 Ibn al-Khatib 1968, 303–304.

23 Velásquez Basanta 1995, 632; Ibn al-Khatib 1973, I:221–238.

24 Salmi 1956, Arabic 392, French 393.

25 See Schimmel 1985, 123–143, 290–294.

26 Salmi 1956, Arabic 398, French 399.

27 Ibn al-Khatib 1970, 79–80.

28 See Lugo Acevedo 2008, esp. 23–33, and López-Morillas 1994. See also Barletta 2005, chapter 5.

29 Lugo Acevedo 2008, 455: "entaraba la kalaredad en lash kashash, i-y-ashomabanshe lash gentesh a lash puwertash mirando la luz, cuidando ke-eran relámpagos, y veían losh *ramosh de la luz* ke shubiyan a losh siyelosh.... I deziyanlesh Kiyen sois, ya shennoresh, ke nunca vimos mash fermosha yente ke boshotorosh de karash ni mash rrelunbara[n]tesh k-ellos, i mash akel ke shalle d-el *akella luz con ramos de kalaredad*?" (emphasis mine).

30 See Salmi 1956, 340–356. Concerning the Banu Sidi Bono, one of the better studied and most powerful confraternities active in Granada during the Nasrid period, see Calero Secall 1987 and Sánchez 1992. On the earliest celebrations of the *mawlid* in al-Andalus and the Maghrib, see Boloix Gallardo 2011.

31 Many thanks to Amalia Zomeño for valuable and ongoing interchanges concerning the broader social implications of these festivities. Much of what follows is, in one way or another, fruit of our very fruitful discussions.

32 For the origins of *mawlid* celebrations, including early influences, see Salmi 1956, 345–350, where possible "Christian influence" on the procession of lights is discussed; the idea is repeated in del Moral and Velásquez Basanta 1994, 84n3. All authors here rely substantially on de la Granja 1969 for this assertion. While I do not deny that the witnessing of Christian festivities could have inspired a sort of ceremonial "one-upsmanship" on the part of Muslim clerics and patrons, I maintain that the experience of such festivities would have been much more complex on the part of participants than a simple realization of connections to Christian precedents.

33 Ibn al-Khatib 1968, 278–279; García Gómez 1988, Arabic 132–133, Spanish 155–156. Ibn al-Khatib's own position concerning the "sincerity" of the emotions of those who entered a state of ecstasy (or, as he implies, claimed to do so, or perhaps even faked it—*al-wājid wa-l-mutawājid*) is a bit difficult to read and could, indeed, constitute the focus of an entirely different essay. Much of scholarship's doubts about Ibn al-Khatib's own "sincerity" as regards Sufism and its tenets and practices, indeed, appears to be based on the presence of *al-mutawājid*—the least kind trans-

lation of which would be "the fakers"—in this passage. Kenneth S. Avery, however, has argued for a more nuanced understanding of this term on the basis of its use in numerous Sufi treatises (see Avery 2004, 26–28). In such contexts it would designate an aspirant, a devotee, or even an apprentice, all of which would make perfect sense in the context of Ibn al-Khatib's *mawlid* narration.

34 See Ergin 2008, 212.

35 al-Qashani, n.d., 1.

36 *Tafsīr* and *taʿwīl* in general—not to mention in the context of al-Andalus—constitute understudied topics for students of Arabo-Islamic culture. I am thus not even able to venture a guess as to whether al-Qashani's commentary was known in al-Andalus, or what its distribution was (we are not even, at present, able to answer such questions concerning such major figures as Ibn al-ʿArabi himself!), or to describe or discuss the works of *tafsīr* produced or preferred during the Nasrid period, whether by Sufis or non-Sufis. This is a topic that requires urgent attention (there are numerous manuscripts throughout Spanish and European, and doubtless Maghrebi, collections that might serve as a point of departure). On *tafsīr* in general, useful publications include Nwiya 1970 and Part IV of Rippin 2006, with essays by Walid Saleh, Marianna Klar, Alan Godlas, Jawid Mojaddedi, and Diana Steigerwald. As for al-Andalus, the only recent study of which I am aware is González Costa 2009. Prof. González Costa is currently at work on an edition and Spanish translation of Ibn Barrakhan's *Idah al-hikma*. See also the introductory study to López-Morillas 1994.

37 A good start is offered in González Costa and Lopez Anguita 2009. For attitudes toward *dhikr* and *samāʿ* in North Africa, see ʿAmri 2009.

38 Ibn al-Khatib's *Ihata* is replete with references to those whose talents in Qurʾanic recitation were widely appreciated. See, for example, the biography of Ahmad ibn ʿAbd al-Nur ibn Ahmad ibn Rashid (d. 702 AH/1312 CE), known to contemporaries as "Ibn ʿAbd al-Nur, of Málaga. Expert in *fiqh*, the composition of poetry, the art of calligraphy, and *ʿubbadaʾ*" ("acts of devotion"), he was also an excellent reciter of the Qurʾan, gifted with a beautiful voice (Ibn al-Khatib 1973, I:196–202).

39 For the information concerning these legal opinions, I have relied on Arcas Campoy 2006. See also ʿAmri 2009.

40 Ibn al-Khatib 1973, II:144–145.

41 Ibn al-Khatib 1973, II:287; the poet in question is Ahmad ibn Muhammad ibn ʿIsaʾ al-Amwaʾ, known to his contemporaries as al-Zayyat (d. 765 AH/1375 CE).

42 Ibn al-Khatib 1973, I:459–463; see also Lévi-Provençal 1950, 218.

43 García Gómez 1988, Arabic 132–133, Spanish 156–157.

44 See Arcas Campoy 2006, 43.

45 García Gómez 1988, Arabic 132–133, Spanish 156–157.

46 The classic study on the *naṣīb* remains Stetkevych 1993.

47 Salmi 1956, 356; Salmi also gives an excellent introduction to the genre, including

its style and themes. See also Makki 1991, and del Moral and Velásquez Basanta 1994.

48 García Gómez 1988, 155–156.

49 See Bush 2006, 291–330.

50 García Gómez has been instrumental in cementing this prejudice. See García Gómez 1996, an edition and translation of the famed verses inscribed onto the walls of the Alhambra, which is—in my opinion, inexplicably—peppered with patronizing and dismissive assessments of the very compositions over which he has labored.

51 See, for example, del Moral 1997 and Velásquez Basanta 1995.

52 Such scholarship in general has been wanting in the field of Islamic art history. When such interpretation has been attempted, it has almost always been concerned with the courtly (and implicitly largely profane) sphere of culture. See, for example, Robinson 2002. A recent article by Nina Ergin, however, has attempted to relate Qurʾanic recital to the perception of sixteenth-century mosque architecture in Istanbul (see Ergin 2008).

53 Ibn al-Khatib 1968, 301.

54 Ibid., 292.

55 The substitution is an intriguing (and hardly obvious) one, particularly given that the Nasrids were, at this time, engaged in promoting the idea of a Nasrid caliphate (see Rubiera Mata 2008) and this propaganda also finds its way into the *madīḥ* sections of the *qaṣīda*s in question for this study. One strategy for legitimation assiduously pursued by the Nasrids to this end was to claim descent from Saʿd ibn Khazraj, one of the companions of the Prophet (*anṣār*) and a native of Yemen; see Boloix Gallardo 2006. I hope to consider this particular deployment of Najd in greater detail in a future study.

56 Ibn al-Khatib 1968, 301.

57 See Salmi 1956, 360.

58 For the (supposedly) more "popular" register of mystical lyrics, see, for example, Ibn ʿAbd Allah Shushtari 1988. In fact, Ibn al-Khatib offers us assurance that similarly "classical" mystical *qaṣīda*s on similar themes, which were not necessarily composed for the occasion of the *mawlid*, and which thus could have been recited any number of occasions, were habitually memorized by professional reciters, at the instances of such well-known religious figures as Abu ʿAbd Allah al-Tanjali, and performed before large assembled crowds. See Velásquez Basanta 1995.

59 See Salmi 1956, 365.

60 See Stetkevych 1993.

61 See ibid., esp. 79–102. For Ibn al-ʿArabi's lyrics, see Ibn al-ʿArabi 1998b.

62 See del Moral and Velásquez Basanta 1994. Ibn al-Khatib, in his poem for the second hour, readily acknowledges that the celebrations would have served many as

just such a "point of departure" (see García Gómez 1988, Arabic 134–135, Spanish 158–159).

63 See Stetkevych 1993, 114–115.

64 Ibn al-Khatib 1968, 293.

65 See García Gómez 1988, Arabic 123–127, Spanish 142–147. Given their unfinished state in December of 1362 CE, it is likely that much of Ibn al-Khatib's knowledge concerning the ornamental programs of these spaces was attained during the months and years following the *mawlid* celebration, prior to his own definitive immigration to the Maghreb (where his account was written) in 1372 CE.

66 For a detailed discussion of the tent and its antecedents, see Bush 2006, 291–330.

67 García Gómez 1988, Arabic 127, Spanish 147.

68 Even though this latter is most certainly descended from the *naṣīb*, as noted in Stetkevych 1993, 57.

69 Salmi 1956, 410, French, 411. This *qaṣīda* is not among those included by Ibn al-Khatib in the tenth chapter of his *Nufadat al-Jirab*.

70 Stetkevych 1993, 121.

71 Lévi-Provençal 1950, 216; García Gómez 1988, Arabic 128, Spanish 151. The term employed by Ibn al-Khatib is *fuqarāʾ*.

72 García Gómez 1988, Arabic 140, Spanish 167.

73 See ibid., Arabic 141, Spanish 168–169.

CHAPTER NINE

Aristocratic Residences and the *Majlis* in Umayyad Córdoba

GLAIRE D. ANDERSON

On Yawm al-ʿAnṣara, the Day of Pentecost, in an unspecified year during the ninth-century reign of the Umayyad emir Muhammad I (r. 852–886 CE), a *majlis* (pl., *majālis*) was held in Córdoba. The host, ʿUthman (d. 910–911 CE), was a son of the emir himself. As was his habit, ʿUthman had invited a group of local writers and poets into his reception hall (for which the term *majlis* is also used) on that day to enjoy a meal and a musical performance. Seated within earshot of the assembled men, but screened from them by a curtain, was Baziʾah, ʿUthman's slave, a singer so famous in her day that she was called "the Imam." Upon the unexpected arrival of the host's elder brother, ʿUthman asked Baziʾah to honor the unexpected visit and the assembly with her best song.[1]

This anecdote, which Ibn al-Qutiya (d. 977 CE) relates in his history of Umayyad Córdoba, introduces some of the main themes on which this chapter focuses. Musical performances would have occurred within the semiprivate and private spaces of residences of the ruler and court notables of Córdoba within the city walls, in suburban estates, or at the royal city of Madinat al-Zahraʾ, founded around 938 CE by ʿAbd al-Rahman III (r. 912–961).[2] Taking as a departure point the dual meaning of *majlis* as the performance itself as well as the physical setting in which performance took place, this chapter discusses *majlis* architecture as it has been revealed by archaeology in recent decades. It investigates the interplay between art and architecture and the social dimensions of occasions that brought together men and women of differing legal status as audience, patrons, and performers.[3] The chapter attempts to integrate the material as well as the social aspects of Córdoban Umayyad *majālis* and, in doing so, to illuminate the centrality of musical performance to the function and character of reception space and the objects that were displayed and used in Córdoban court residences.

Majlis Architecture

Only scant physical traces remain today of the old Umayyad urban palace complex, which was situated adjacent to the Great Mosque of Córdoba, where the Episcopal Palace now stands.[4] There are numerous textual references to its various spaces; the musicians who lived there, notably the celebrated Umayyad courtier and Baghdadi emigré Ziryab; and the performances held within its confines.[5] Ibn Hayyan notes that Ziryab's residence was directly connected to the palace by a door installed especially for that purpose. The same author alludes to the small musical gatherings that took place for the benefit of the ruler, such as one that occurred in the chamber known as "the Blessed" (*al-Mubarak*), in which the three famous slave singing women (*qiyān*) known as "the Medinese" sang and played *ʿūd* for the emir and Ziryab.[6]

Given the general bias against music held by most members of the religious establishment, we might assume that music in Umayyad Córdoba would not have been performed in official reception spaces.[7] However, al-Isbahani (d. ca. 967 CE) indicates that in the Abbasid court, panegyric poetry was in fact sung in praise of the ruler on even the most prominent official occasions, such as caliphal investitures, because singing was favored over recitation of poetry because of the greater emotional expressiveness of music.[8] On such occasions, the song emphasized themes such as the religious qualities of the new ruler, thus validating his political legitimacy.[9] The recitation of panegyric poetry during major official occasions in Córdoba is well attested. Given the reported enthusiasm with which the Umayyad court adapted Abbasid musical and other court practices beginning in the ninth century, it is therefore possible that the Hall of ʿAbd al-Rahman III (datable to 953–957 CE) at Madinat al-Zahraʾ, the sole surviving official reception hall of the royal city, could have been a setting for musical performance, such as the singing of panegyric poetry composed by Ibn ʿAbd Rabbihi.[10]

Barceló and others have discussed the space as a setting for court ceremonial, notably the *ʿId* ceremonies of 968 CE described by al-Razi, focusing on the disposition of participants named in the text as an expression of court power hierarchies.[11] However, the spatial arrangement of the hall certainly could have lent itself to musical performance. A wide rectangular hall creates a preliminary entrance space from which one enters into the reception hall proper through the central triple-arched arcade that leads to the central nave, or through flanking double arches that access the lateral aisles flanking the central nave. Within, the nave is separated from the flanking aisles by horseshoe arcades whose columns, featuring white-marble carved capitals and bases and shafts of an alternating blue and pinkish color, add further richness to an interior whose surfaces are lavishly decorated with carved marble and limestone panels depicting dense vegetation (*see plate 5c*). In the place of honor, at the center of the far wall of the central nave, the caliph and those privileged few seated in his immediate vicinity would have had an uninterrupted view of the central aisle and any poets, singers, and musicians present there. Likewise, an audience seated in the two flanking aisles, on mats or perhaps cushions, as was the practice of the time, would have been able to both see and hear the performance in the nave through the arcades that visually demarcate the central space of the hall from the lateral aisles.

Although the Central Pavilion that once faced the Hall of ʿAbd al-Rahman III across a square water pool does not survive as a standing monument (fig. 9.1), the similarity of its plan to the main reception space of the Hall of ʿAbd al-Rahman III suggests the structure could have served as an additional court performance space.[12] The presence of additional smaller square pools on either side of the pavilion suggests an airier architectural setting than the larger hall, open perhaps to the views of water and the surrounding gardens. In addition to the pavilion's main reception area, on its south side an additional suite of rooms (including latrines) arranged around the perimeter of another small pool would have offered an additional more private space for small gatherings. While the pavilion's main basilical plan would have offered the same benefits, in terms of situation of performers and audience as the Hall of ʿAbd al-Rahman III, the pavilion would have provided a rather different atmosphere for the enjoyment of musical performance. Its smaller scale, and especially the visual effects of framed views and reflection that would have accompanied the interplay of architecture, water, and gardens, would have provided the pavilion with an intimate atmosphere quite distinct from the official reception hall that it faced.

Figure 9.1. Remains of the Central Pavilion opposite the Hall of ʿAbd al-Rahman III, Madinat al-Zahraʾ. Photograph: G. Anderson.

The remains of several houses of Umayyad Córdoba unearthed by archaeologists indicate that residences varied in size and elaboration but were commonly arranged around courtyards and almost always incorporated a main hall, the *majlis,* which would likely have served as the main indoor setting for musical performances.[13] Rectangular in plan, these halls were usually arranged transversally and sometimes incorporated square chambers flanking each end of the main space. Excavations in and around Córdoba as well as reconstructions at Madinat al-Zahraʾ offer testimony to the character of tenth-century elite residences. Overall, they give an impression of well-built luxury. Floors were paved in terra-cotta tile with geometric borders inlaid in contrasting white marble or limestone, or else entirely in white marble or purple stone. Walls were sturdily constructed of limestone and decorated with dados painted with red-and-white geometric or floral schemes. Arcades and important doorways were further embellished with richly carved panels of limestone or white marble, similar to those that cover the surfaces of the Hall of Abd al-Rahman III. Fine stone column shafts supporting deeply drilled white marble capitals supported the ubiquitous Umayyad horseshoe arches.

The House of the Pool at Madinat al-Zahraʾ, one of the luxurious resi-

Figure 9.2. Triple-arched façade, House of the Pool, Madinat al-Zahra᾽. Photograph: G. Anderson.

dences excavated in the palace city to date and the only one organized around a garden, incorporates two simple rectangular reception halls situated at the two ends of an east-west axis.[14] Each of the halls faces the interior garden featuring two rectangular planting beds and a square pool situated in front of the western hall. Triple-arched arcades centered in each of the two garden façades would have provided views of the garden within each of the two reception halls (fig. 9.2). The host of musical performances at the House of the Pool would have been able to choose from the interior setting of the hall, which would have been open to views of the interior garden, or the garden itself. Such an environment for the *majlis* is evoked in the paintings from *Bayad wa Riyad*, the only known illustrated manuscript that survives from the medieval Islamic West.[15] One of the paintings depicts a group in a small grassy garden; the architectural setting is suggested on either side of the composition through two towers whose screened windows frame an *ʿūd* player and the audience seated on the grass and enjoying drinks (fig. 9.3).[16]

The presence of a previously unknown reception hall at the western end of the residence, with square chambers flanking a wide central hall, was revealed during a recent campaign led by the German Archaeological Institute at the *munya* (villa) site known as al-Rummaniyya (fig. 9.4).[17] Excavated in

1911 by the archaeologist Velázquez Bosco, al-Rummaniyya's residence was situated on the uppermost of four rectangular terraces that, like the nearby royal city, ascend the slopes of the Sierra Morena mountain range. A visualization of this *majlis*, based on the plan and the archaeological evidence for its decorative program, illustrates the airy pavilion-like quality of the space, and the connection to the villa's exterior spaces that defines this particular hall. Looking south, a viewer within enjoyed panoramic views of the villa's garden terraces and the fertile countryside beyond the *munya*'s stone walls (fig. 9.5a). To the north, the west pavilion opened to a walled courtyard containing a monumental pool surrounded by a perimeter walkway suspended over the water on massive stone buttresses (fig. 9.5b). The archaeologists discovered evidence of white marble pavement, columns, and fragments of carved wall panels that indicate the *majlis* was sturdily constructed and luxu-

Figure 9.3. Garden scene, *Bayad wa Riyad*. Vatican manuscript 368, fol. 19R. 28.2 × 20 cm. Biblioteca Apostolica Vaticana, Vatican City; Album/Art Resource.

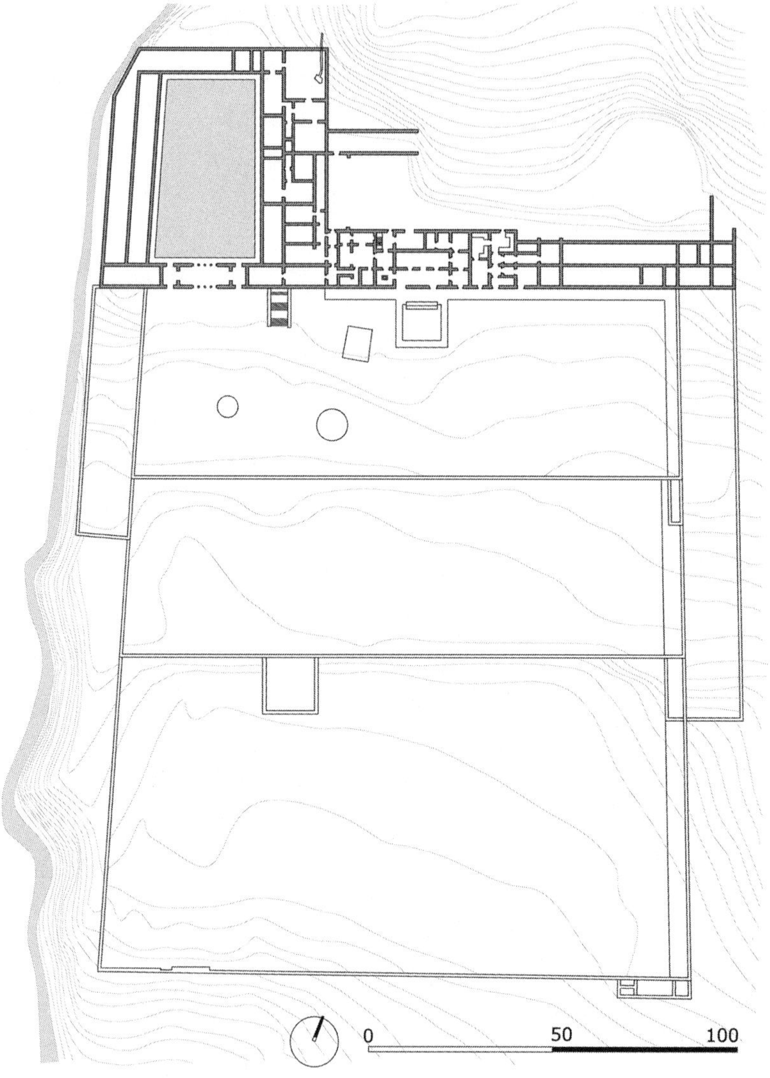

Figure 9.4. Plan, al-Rummaniyya (by Philippe Saad, after Felix Arnold).

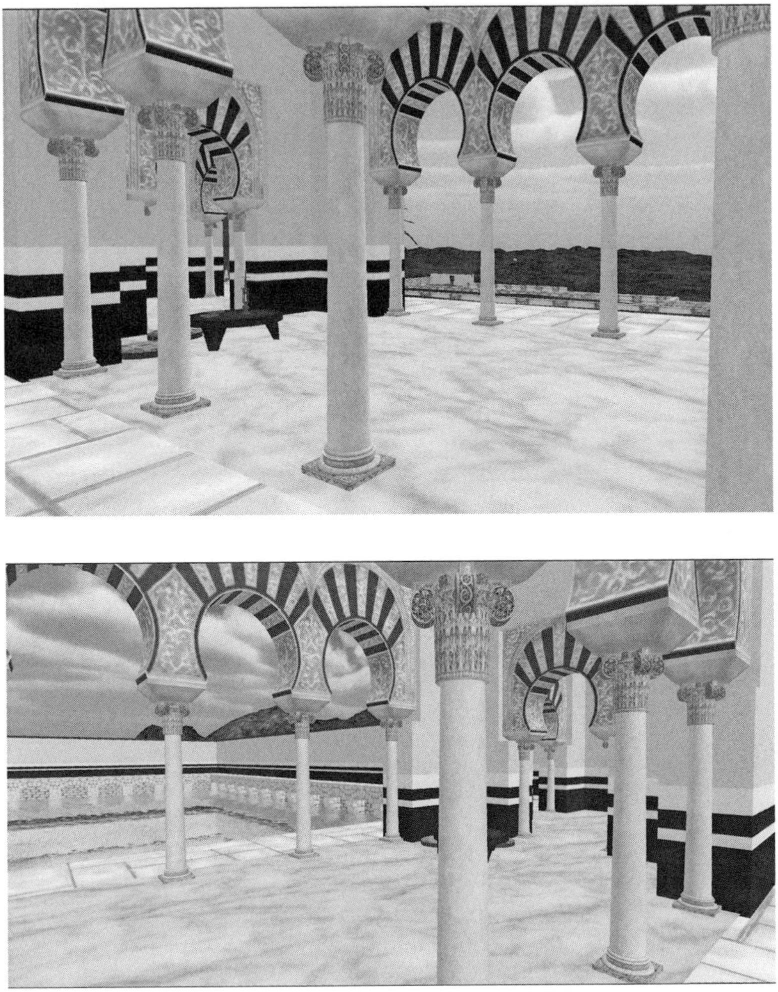

Figure 9.5. Hypothetical visualization, al-Rummaniyya, western reception hall. (a, *top*) View south over garden terraces. (b, *bottom*) View toward monumental pool (*below*). Digital model: G. Anderson, Nate Dierk, Anselmo Lastra, Ariel Li, Ben Parise, Philippe Saad.

riously decorated using materials and a visual language similar to those of the Hall of ʿAbd al-Rahman III at Madinat al-Zahraʾ.[18]

Scenery informed the content of songs performed for the Abbasid court in outdoor settings.[19] The abundant references to garden imagery and other features of landscape and the natural world in Umayyad Córdoban poetry points to a similar impact that architectural and landscape settings such as those that created the aforementioned *majlis* at al-Rummaniyya would have had on musical performance in al-Andalus. Thus, the well-known prominence of garden imagery in the poetry of al-Andalus may not merely be attributed to poetic conventions but seems likely to be partly grounded as well in the ubiquity of garden and landscape as part of the potential settings for Córdoban court *majālis*.[20]

Al-Rummaniyya's residence incorporated a second reception space, this one situated to the east of the one described above, at the center of the residence's overall architectural composition. This second *majlis* has a distinctive plan that finds its only parallel in the so-called Dar al-Mulk at Madinat al-Zahraʾ. This *majlis* type, comprising the core of al-Rummaniyya's residence as well as the Dar al-Mulk, essentially doubles the single hall with the flanking-chambers type. At al-Rummaniyya, the second *majlis* consists of a unit combining two rectangular halls, each measuring approximately fifteen by five meters and with square flanking chambers, connected with a triple doorway in the partition wall. While the front of the hall opens onto a terraced walkway and a small square pool, it is clear that the connection between the innermost reception area and the exterior was not sought. Instead, the exterior doorways were situated to obstruct the sightline between the rear interior *majlis* space and the exterior, shielding the inner hall from extremes of hot and cold and thereby creating a sheltered interior reception area for use (fig. 9.6).

At the Dar al-Mulk, the double-hall *majlis* consists of two wide rectangular halls, each measuring seventeen meters wide by five meters deep, with an area of eighty-five square meters, flanked by smaller square chambers, each twenty-five square meters in area (fig. 9.7). The two halls connect via a triple-arched opening centered in the partition wall. A raised terrace, approached from the lower terraces by two flights of stairs, provided panoramic views of the lower sections of the royal city and the landscape beyond. In pleasant weather, those seated within the Dar al-Mulk's double-hall *majlis* could have enjoyed views of the terrace, the garden parterres, official reception halls,

Figure 9.6. Imaginative visualization, al-Rummaniyya. (a, *top*) Eastern pavilion double hall, rear chamber. (b, *bottom*) Front chamber. Digital model: G. Anderson, Ariel Li.

Figure 9.7. Interior view, Dar al-Mulk. Photograph: G. Anderson.

and other aristocratic residences situated on the lower terrace, as well as the landscape of the river valley beyond the walls of the royal city. If the weather were inclement, wooden doors would have shielded the hall within.

The prominence of the double-hall plan, given its use at the Dar al-Mulk and as the core of the residence at al-Rummaniyya, points to the importance of this distinct *majlis* space. The lateral disposition of space in the rectangular halls lent itself eminently to the seating practices of reception as conducted in medieval Islamic residences. The place of honor would have been at the center of the long wall of the rear reception hall, where the host or guest of honor would have sat with back against the wall, on a carpet or mat, with or without cushions. The width of the hall would have provided ample space for other guests to sit in straight or curving rows flanking the position of honor.

Material Spatiality of the *Majlis*

I have so far focused on the bare outlines of the architectural frameworks that potentially served as settings for *andalusī* Umayyad musical performance. But a discussion only of the architectural framework of a Córdoban *majlis* conveys just a fraction of the rich backdrop against which musical performance took place.[21] Based on more than just the architectural setting, the *majlis* experience would have encompassed a whole array of furnishings and objects and, as we have seen, in some cases views of the surrounding gardens and landscape. All these elements would have combined to contribute to the atmosphere and would have informed, as well as been informed by, musical performance.

Although the furnishings of residences in al-Andalus, as elsewhere in medieval Islamic lands, were relatively few, they would have done as much to establish the character of a space as its architectural elements. In the account of Ziryab's arrival in Córdoba in 822 CE, the house that was provided for him and his family is described as having been furnished with everything necessary, namely, carpets, curtains, utensils, and containers, with storerooms filled with foods, comestibles, and condiments, not to mention eunuch servants responsible for all the household matters.[22]

As Golombek has observed, the role of textiles in the appearance of medieval Islamic buildings would have been paramount.[23] Carpets, mats, curtains, wall hangings, and cushions were indispensable both as furnishings and as part of the overall decor. The visual effect created by the use of textiles within an interior space is conveyed by the visualization of the double-hall *majlis* at al-Rummaniyya, which offers an interpretation of the architectural and decorative evidence with textiles as an integral part of the interior decor. The visualization illustrates the prominence, in the overall effect, of curtains covering doorways as well as used as wall coverings, functions that are attested in Geniza documents (fig. 9.6).[24] Commonly used fabrics for interior textiles were wool, linen, and brocade; red, white, and blue appear to have been popular color choices. Some curtains, for instance, are described as red brocade lined with white and with blue ornamental bands. The model for the textile that decorates the surface of the rear wall of the double hall in the visualization is a dyed wool and linen fragment in the David Collection in Copenhagen, attributed to Egypt and dated to the ninth or tenth century (fig. 9.8).[25] Such curtains seem likely to have had an acoustic function, ameliorating the harsh reverberations of stone walls.

Other furnishings that would have appeared in the reception halls of a well-appointed *andalusī* residence were small round tables (of wood, metal, or stone), as well as chests, boxes, cases, racks, and wall recesses. The *majlis* visualization in figure 9.6 (above) incorporates small, portable round tables, used by diners seated on the floor, which could be easily removed from the room when the meal was finished. Likewise, it includes round cushions, which were often covered with choice materials such as silk and which might be stacked and folded for the greater comfort of the diner.[26]

To textiles and other furnishings we should also add ephemeral effects that would likewise have "set the mood" for musical performance—the fragrance of incense and perfumes, for instance, which were integral to court culture in Córdoba as in the other courts of the Islamic empire. We can get a sense of how pervasive the use of luxurious clothing and fragrance was to the aristocracy of Umayyad Córdoba by Ibn ʿAbd Rabbihi's anecdote in which a man seeks guidance on the permissibility of personal adornment from the hadith transmitter Muhammad ibn al-Munkadir (d. 747 CE).[27] The man seeks out Muhammad in his home and is taken aback to find him seated on doubled cushions while being sprayed with perfume by a slave girl, apparently engaging in the very practices about which he had come to seek Muhammad's advice. Perfumes were an indispensable part of the etiquette of dining in Umayyad Córdoba, used to cleanse the hands and mouth following

Figure 9.8. Tapestry, dyed wool and undyed linen, H: 56; W: 43 cm. Egypt, ninth–tenth century. David Collection, Copenhagen. Inv. no. 1/1989. Photograph: Pernille Kemp; courtesy of the David Collection.

a meal. Ibn Hayyan recounts that after eating with the Umayyad ruler, Ziryab and his son were perfumed with the emir's own fragrance.[28]

The subject of fragrance recalls the celebrated ivory boxes whose function in part was to hold such perfumes. Common visual motifs, including musicians, are discernible in both the carved ivories and carved marble architectural decoration from Madinat al-Zahra˒, al-Rummaniyya, and generally

Figure 9.9. (a, *left*) Pyxis of al-Mughira, seated figures with musician. Probably Madinat al-Zahraʾ, 968 CE (dated AH 357). Inv. OA4068, Musée du Louvre; photograph: Hervé Lewandowski. © RMN–Grand Palais/Art Resource, NY. (b, *right*) Davillier Pyxis. Late tenth century. Inv. OA2774, Musée du Louvre; photograph, Raphaël Chipault. © RMN–Grand Palais/Art Resource, NY.

associated with Umayyad Córdoba.[29] Depictions of musicians occupy an important thematic category in the figural art of Umayyad Córdoba. *ʿŪd* players seem to have pride of place in such representations. For example, a standing *ʿūd* player and an "audience" of two seated courtiers are depicted in the celebrated Pyxis of al-Mughira, dated 967–968 CE and made at either Madinat al-Zahraʾ or Córdoba (fig. 9.9a).[30] Seated *ʿūd* players appear on two other ivories ascribed to Córdoba: the Louvre's Davillier Pyxis (ca. 970 CE) (fig. 9.9b) and the largest and most spectacular of the surviving *andalusī* ivories, the ʿAmirid ivory chest known as the Pamplona or Leyre casket of 395 AH/ 1004–1005 CE (fig. 9.10a).[31]

The incorporation of the *ʿūd* among the instruments in Umayyad musical performance is suggested by the depiction of instruments carved in the surface of ivory objects or painted on objects (such as a ceramic bottle on which the figure blows a horn) and in the interior decoration of the reception hall itself, as an unusual architectural fragment in the Museo Arqueológico y Etnológico de Córdoba attests.[32] A large white-marble capital unearthed near Córdoba and ascribed to the late tenth century, it combines figural imagery with the abstracted vegetal forms standard in Córdoban capitals and other architectural decoration of this period (fig. 9.10b). The Musicians Capital is comparable in size to, although slightly larger than, the marble capitals that likely decorated the single reception hall at al-Rummaniyya, which also suggests the setting for which the capital was made. The drilled vegetal interlace that decorates the surface of the Corinthian capital is in keeping with the other marble capitals that have been unearthed at Madinat al-Zahraʾ and dated to the reign of ʿAbd al-Rahman III and al-Hakam II.

To this standard form, however, the artisan added to each of the capital's four sides the figure of a musician. Substantial in size, their bodies taking up approximately three quarters of the capital's height, each figure is shown with a foot supported on a curling leaf that together protrude to form a ring near the capital's base. Although their faces have been effaced, their draped garments are clearly depicted, as are the instruments that three hold in their hands: an *ʿūd,* a flute, and a three-string fiddle.[33] Likewise, in the musician's roundel on the Pamplona casket, the seated *ʿūd* player is flanked by musicians playing (on the left) a double oboe and (on the right) a horn fitted with a reed. Might these be early representations of the *būq* and *zulāmi,* two popular types of instruments described by Ibn Khaldun (d. 1406 CE)? The *būq,* he notes, is "a trumpet of copper (brass) which is hollow, one cubit long, widening toward the opening, the diameter of which is less than the palm of a hand in width. It has the form of a nibbed calamus. One blows into it through a

Figure 9.10. (a, *left*) Detail with musicians, Pamplona (aka Leyre) casket. Probably made in Córdoba. Ivory, dated 395 AH/1004–1005 CE, Museo de Navarra. (b, *right*) Musicians Capital, *ʿud* player. Museo Arqueológico y Etnológico de Córdoba, Inv. No. D/133. Photographs: G. Anderson.

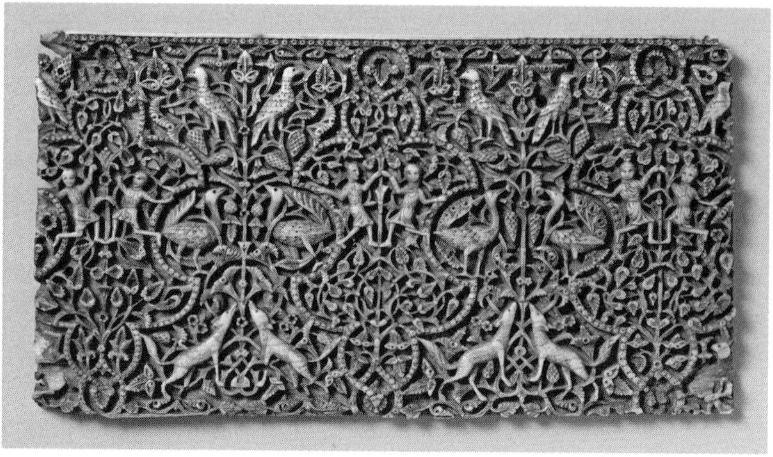

Figure 9.11. Ivory, carved and inlaid with quartz and pigment. H: 4¼ in. (10.8 cm); W: 8 in. (20.3 cm). Probably Córdoba, tenth to early eleventh century. Metropolitan Museum of Art, Inv. No. 13.141. Courtesy of ArtStor Images for Academic Publishing.

small reed which conveys the wind from the mouth into it." He describes the *zulāmi* as having "the form of a reed, with two wooden parts carved [hollow], hollow but not round, because it is made of two pieces put together. . . . One blows into it through a small connected reed." [34] The fourth figure, whose hands appear empty and whose clothing is distinct from that of the other figures, may represent a singer.

In addition to the Córdoban ivories, with their depictions of musicians and their audiences, an ivory panel in the Metropolitan Museum of Art, which may have originally adorned a chest or other item of furniture, provides a rare, if not unique, representation of *andalusī* dancers (fig. 9.11).[35] The panel offers a material counterpoint to Ibn-al-Qutiya's allusion to both music and dancing taking place at the Córdoban residence of a son of al-Hakam I (r. 796–822 CE). While figures are not in themselves unusual in the context of the *andalusī* ivories, the lively movement represented by the artist who carved this panel is a striking departure from the static figures of other Córdoban ivories. Three couples, the women with hair veiled, are arranged against a lush field of vegetation across the middle register of the panel. Perhaps what are depicted here are the movements of a dance carried out by one couple. If we view the image as we would read an Arabic text, beginning at the far right of the panel, the couple begin the dance holding hands. In the center they have executed a complete turn, as the man and woman appear on opposite sides from their starting position at the right end of the pane. At the far left, the further movement of the dance is suggested by the figures' separation, having accomplished a second turn, their hands raised as if having only just separated. Read in this way, the composition gives an impression of lively motion, encapsulated in the figures' bent knees and raised arms, and perhaps in the folds of their garments as they appear to swing around their knees. The dance that this couple (or couples) is performing across the surface of the panel may offer a visual testament to a tradition of *andalusī* dance that may have given rise to the *samra* (Sp., *zamra*), a lively dance specifically associated with al-Andalus and whose popularity in the fifteenth-century Castilian court Reynolds has pointed out.[36]

The reflexive qualities of a *majlis* setting—the potential mirroring of musical themes present in aspects of the architectural decor, the material culture, and the functional use of the space for musical performance—are striking. Furthermore, the poetry itself would have mirrored the musical performance, not as lyrics to be sung, but as deploying metaphors of music and singing. Rosser-Owen has commented on the relationship between poetry and objects during the ʿAmirid regency, which for specific political reasons they adapted from precedents established during the Umayyad reign.[37] The combination of rich materials in decor and material culture must have been intended to please the eye of the beholders as they sat within the *majlis*, surrounded by music making and its representation, viewing and handling precious objects on which were depicted the musical performances in which they themselves were participating at that very moment. We can begin to imagine the effect that the display of expensive luxury objects must have exercised, underscoring the power of the display of material culture as a strategy for establishing or underscoring elite status. The ivory caskets themselves, as is often noted, were among the most prestigious objects made for or distributed among members of the Umayyad court. The function of carved ivory boxes as containers for the fragrances, which advertised status while simultaneously creating a particular atmosphere and mood, points also to how the use of such objects during *majlis* was part of the conspicuous consumption of expensive commodities, a category that encompasses the musicians and the musical performance itself.

Gender and Legal Status in the *Majlis*

A discussion of the spatial dimensions of musical performance in Umayyad Córdoba must also take into account the people engaged with the material world of the *majlis*. Who appeared in the cast of characters participating in musical performances in Umayyad Córdoba, and how were they situated in relation to one another and to these architectural and material surroundings? The audience for musical performances included the ruler or patron; guests, including family members and friends; and the musicians themselves. The musicians were both men and women, as well as Muslims, Christians, and Jews. Some had come to Córdoba from outside the city; some, from northern Iberia; and some, from as far away as Baghdad and Medina. Women are prominent in the texts as singers and *ʿūd* players, and their presence in the *majālis* of Umayyad Córdoba underscores its function as a social framework that brought together men and women of differing legal statuses, backgrounds, and ethnicities as audience, patrons, and performers.[38]

The best-known representation of a musician, the standing *ʿūd* player on the Pyxis of al-Mughira, may be female. The gender of the *ʿūd* player and the two seated figures is ambiguous in that all are depicted without beards and share the same distinctive hairstyle, bangs cut straight over the brow. While the seated figures are very likely court eunuchs, the *ʿūd* player may in fact be female, given that Ibn Hayyan states that this hairstyle was worn not only by eunuch servants but also by the finest singing girls and other slaves (but not, as Reynolds points out, necessarily by their owners).[39] According to Ibn Hayyan, following the arrival in Córdoba of Ziryab and his family, who wore their hair in this style, the people of refinement had their male and female servants adopt the hairstyle but may have continued to wear their own hair combed, parted in the middle, and hanging loose over their temples and eyebrows, according to court fashion before Ziryab's arrival. References to female *ʿūd* players and singers in texts such as the aforementioned anecdote relayed by Ibn ʿAbd Rabbihi occur often enough that a female identity for the al-Mughira *ʿūd* player seems just as likely as a male identity.[40]

It may be that one of the figures on the Musicians Capital is also female. Gender distinction might be conveyed by the difference in the clothing represented on the figure whose hands are empty and that may therefore represent a singer (fig. 9.12a). This empty-handed figure wears a garment with an undisturbed diagonal drape, similar in fact to that of the al-Mughira *ʿūd*

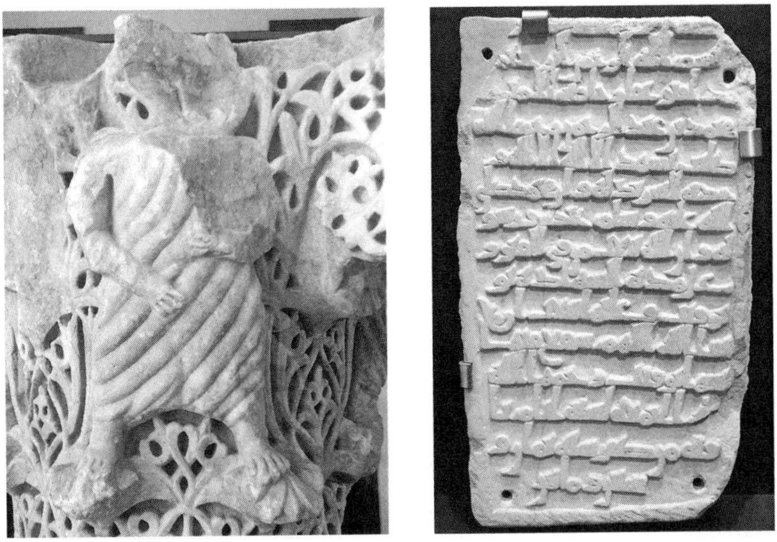

Figure 9.12. (a, *left*) Musicians Capital, female (?) figure. Museo Arqueológico y Etnológico de Córdoba, Inv. No. D/133. (b, *right*) Marble tombstone of Umayyad *jariya* ʿUqar. Museo Arqueológico y Etnológico de Córdoba, Inventory number 11: 355. Photographs: G. Anderson.

player, while the other three figures, who hold instruments, wear garments that appear divided up the middle to form what might be some type of pantaloons. Perhaps, then, the Musicians Capital gives us a representation of a female singer and three male instrumentalists; certainly such mixed-gender musical groups, along with orchestras composed exclusively of women, are attested in Ibn Hayyan.[41]

The tombstone of a female slave, one ʿUqar, in the Museo Arqueológico y Etnológico de Córdoba, offers further testimony to the presence of enslaved women musicians in the Umayyad court (fig. 9.12b). ʿUqar does not appear in Ibn Hayyan or other court texts from Córdoba, to my knowledge, but her tombstone, which bears the date 268 AH/ 881 CE, identifies her as a slave (*jāriya*; pl., *jawāri*) of the emir Muhammad I (r. 852–886 CE).[42] Ibn Hayyan uses the term "*jāriya*" to refer to female slave singers, along with the term "*qayna*" (pl., *qiyān*), with which it appears to have been interchangeable in Córdoba.[43] The quality of the white marble of the tombstone itself, its size (51 cm × 30 cm), and the style of its Kufic epigraphy compare favorably to those of the Tombs of the Banu Marwan, unearthed in the Campo de la Verdad in Córdoba, and to the tombstone of an Umayyad governor of Pechina, a reflection of ʿUqar's position as a member of the inner court circles of the Umayyad court, despite her unfree legal status.

Anecdotes in Ibn ʿAbd Rabbihi's text mention notables sitting in private with female slave musicians. For example, Ibn ʿAbd Rabbihi recounts how the Syrian Umayyad caliph Muʿawiya visited a man who had been ill and found him sitting with a slave girl, the latter holding an *ʿūd*. When questioned about her by the caliph, the man responded that he taught the girl to recite good poetry and that she improved it through the beauty of her singing. At the caliph's invitation, the girl sang; Muʿawiya tapped his foot to the music and noted to the surprised host that "every noble-hearted man is prone to be thrilled by music."[44]

The prominence of other *jawāri* in Umayyad court life is certainly discernible in the select subset of women musicians who attained a prominent status at court as concubines of the rulers, in some cases as *umm walad* (pl., *umm awlād*), "mothers of royal sons," and as active patrons of architecture and important political players at court.[45] Tarub and Mutʾah are two notable examples of women who were known for their musical skill as well as their beauty and who subsequently rose to great prominence at court as mothers of royal sons and patrons of architecture.[46] Mutʾah's status as a singer and musician can be inferred from the reputation of her teacher, none other than Ziryab himself. Ibn Hayyan notes that she founded a mosque and cemetery in the western suburbs of Córdoba, "along with many other [works] for pious and charitable purposes, because she was one of the most generous of women."[47] Indeed, Ibn Hayyan suggests a flourishing of such female patronage during the reign of ʿAbd al-Rahman II (r. 822–852 CE).[48]

Many other unfree women musicians appear in Ibn Hayyan's texts, giving the impression that they were a ubiquitous presence in the extended households of the rulers and other notable figures at court. For instance, Ibn ʿAbd Rabbihi himself is said to have been an admirer of the singing of one Masabih, a slave girl who was trained by Ziryab and belonged to an Umayyad secretary. On learning of Ibn ʿAbd Rabbihi's admiration for her singing, the secretary invited him to his home, where Ibn ʿAbd Rabbihi listened, with great enjoyment, to her performance. The role of these women in Córdoba was not unusual in the Dar al-Islam at this time. Musical women were equally prominent, if not more so, in the social life of the Abbasid court.[49]

According to Ibn Hayyan, Ziryab, who was himself a freedman client of the Umayyads, had some thirty-four or thirty-five women musicians among his extended household, of which two *ʿūd* players, known as Ghizlan and Hunayda (two of the three of Ziryab's well-known students collectively called "the Medinese"), were particularly notable for their command of his repertoire and entered the service of the Umayyad court to teach singing girls following Ziryab's death. Ziryab's daughters, Hamduna and ʿUliyya, inherited their father's skill in music. Hamduna, according to Ibn Hayyan, was said to have been "the pinnacle of skill in singing," and ʿUliyya, as the last surviving member of this famous musical family, lived into old age with a reputation as an important transmitter of musical knowledge.[50]

Sight, Sound, and *Majlis* Plans

The rationale behind the doubling of the single *majlis* plan has been somewhat elusive. However, if we take the musical-performance function of the *majlis* into consideration, we can begin to understand the role that the double-hall *majlis* plan played in court life. The anecdote with which I began the chapter suggests the purpose of the double plan. It might in fact have been in part a functional response to the desire for a *majlis* space that could accommodate the separation of men and women in the *majlis* when such a division was desirable, such as social occasions like the one described at the beginning of this chapter, involving male guests from outside the home. Often such separation of men and women was not deemed necessary, however, as anecdotes like those mentioned above indicate.

In considering the conjunction of architecture, material culture, and music, it is notable that Ibn Khaldun speaks very clearly to the importance of visual aspects of the *majlis* to the overall experience of musical performance. This connection is first made in his characterization of singing as one of the three noble, as opposed to necessary, crafts—so judged because they call for practitioners to consort with rulers "in their privacy and at their intimate parties."[51] While his discussion of architecture tends to the pragmatic, his discussion of music asserts the centrality of beauty as perceived visually as complementary to musical harmony in producing pleasure in an audience:

> Pleasure is the attainment of something that is agreeable. Agreeable sensations of vision and hearing are caused by harmonious arrange-

> ment in the forms and qualities of the thing [things seen or heard]. ... If an object of vision is harmonious in the forms and lines given to it in accordance with the matter from which it is made ... that [object of vision] is then in harmony with the soul that perceives [it], and the soul, thus, feels pleasure as the result of perceiving something that is agreeable to it.[52]

Such pleasure, in Ibn Khaldun's estimation, is derived from the physical senses, is positive and natural, and indeed affects the very soul itself. The reference to harmony in form and line implicates the architectural and landscape settings and associated material culture of the *majlis* as factors in the process by which music produces pleasure. If art and architecture's importance is implied, Ibn Khaldun explicitly acknowledges that the sight of musicians offered the potential to heighten the audience's pleasure in a musical performance: "The object that is most suited to man and in which he is most likely to perceive perfect harmony, is the human form. Therefore, it is most congenial to him to perceive beauty and loveliness in the lines and sounds of the human form ... *every man desires beauty in the objects of vision and hearing, as a requirement of his nature.*"[53] The sight of the musician, along with the visual effects of architecture, landscape, and material culture, could thus heighten the pleasure—sensory but also spiritual—the audience experienced in the performance. The reception-hall plans from Córdoba offered patrons a certain flexibility in defining *majlis* spaces according to the degree of visibility desired. The configuration of architectural space to hide or veil the musician(s) from the audience's view would have been easily accomplished through the use of curtains to cover the doorways of adjacent square chambers situated at either end of the rectangular halls. Textiles used in this fashion would have screened the musician, or a small ensemble of musicians, from view without preventing those in the hall from hearing the music. In a double-hall *majlis,* such as at al-Rummaniyya and the Dar al-Mulk, textiles could also have been used in the arcade separating the two rectangular halls, creating visual but not necessarily aural separation between the two areas. The visualization of the interior double hall illustrates the spatial and visual flexibility, as well as the aesthetic effect, of textiles used in this way. The visualization of the single *majlis* at al-Rummaniyya also conveys how, despite being in a separate chamber, the musician(s) had access to the same views enjoyed by the guests assembled in the main reception space:

the water pool and mountains to the north and garden terraces and river valley to the south. Such an arrangement would have created an ideal environment for the kind of extemporizing expected of medieval Islamic poets and musicians, as the audience in viewing the same scene could gauge the poetic skill of the performer in evoking the subjects that inspired the extemporized poem or song.[54]

In the case of the doubled reception hall at al-Rummaniyya and the Dar al-Mulk, the potential to screen the view between the two reception spaces would have functioned particularly well for musical performances by an ensemble of musicians rather than a single or smaller group of musicians. This too has implications for the gendered space of the *majlis*. The term used in Ibn Hayyan's text to refer to a private orchestra composed entirely or predominantly of women, *sitāra* (literally, "curtain"), derives from the practice of having female musicians perform behind a curtain to separate them from male guests.[55] According to Ibn Hayyan, the emir al-Hakam had just such a private orchestra, composed of enslaved female musicians (*qiyān jawāri*).[56] We might perhaps think of the *sitāra* as an architectural parallel to the use of the veil as article of clothing, one that enabled broader musical uses of spaces.

Conclusion

By attempting to visualize the totality of court residential spaces in Umayyad Córdoba, including taking into account the human actors and their material accessories, we move somewhat closer to understanding a function of reception halls in the elite residences of Umayyad Córdoba that provides a precedent for the key connections between the architectural and musical dimensions of *majlis* gatherings in al-Andalus.[57] By considering the material remains from a *majlis* perspective, we can begin to envision what the reception halls of Umayyad Córdoba may have been like for those who experienced them as patrons, guests, and performers of mixed gender and legal status. Integrating architecture and material culture from the perspective of musical performance may therefore point the way toward an enhanced understanding of how architecture and landscape worked in concert with material culture and social behavior in the context of the *majlis* in Umayyad Córdoba.

NOTES

The research leading to these results has received funding from the European Research Council under the European Union's Seventh Framework Programme (FP7/2007–2013), ERC grant agreement no. 263036, Reassessing the Roles of Women as "Makers" of Medieval Art and Architecture (PI, Therese Martin).

1 Ibn-al-Qutiya 2009, 141. My thanks to Dwight Reynolds for sharing in advance of publication his article entitled "Song and Punishment" (now Reynolds 2017a), in which he discusses this specific female performer and events that ensued from her performance on this occasion.
2 See Vallejo Triano 2006 and 2010, and Rosselló Bordoy 1995.
3 The female performers of al-Andalus are the subject of an essay by Dwight Reynolds entitled "The Qiyan of al-Andalus" (Reynolds 2017b). My thanks to him for sharing this essay in advance of its publication.
4 See Marfil Ruiz 2000.
5 The Arabic references to the urban palace are compiled in Arjona Castro 1982, 250, s.vv. "Alcazar de Cordoba." On Ziryab, see Davila 2009, 121–136; Reynolds 2008, 155–168; Ibn Hayyan 1937, 38–39; Lévi-Provençal et al. 1990, 246.
6 My sincere thanks to Dwight Reynolds for sharing his English translation and commentary on Ibn Hayyan's biography of Ziryab in advance of publication, as it stimulated many of the points I have made in this discussion. For the Arabic see Ibn Hayyan 2003. I have cited here the Spanish translation of Makki and Corriente, which henceforth appears as Ibn Hayyan 2001.
7 On relationships between texts and oral performance traditions see Davila 2004.
8 See al-Isbahani and Harun 1927, V:203, qtd. in Sawa 1985, 76–77.
9 See Sawa 1985, 76–77. Also see Pinckney Stetkevych 1996.
10 See Vallejo Triano 1995; Safran 2000; Monroe 1971.
11 Barceló 1998. See the diagram reproduced in Prado-Vilar 2005, 155 fig. 81.
12 Vallejo Triano now interprets the Central Pavilion as the western reception hall (*majlis al-gharbi*) mentioned in the Arabic texts, built by ʿAbd al-Rahman III as a ceremonial space for his son and heir al-Hakam II. Personal communication, 2016.
13 See Almagro 2007, 30–33; G. Anderson 2007, 60–61.
14 See Vallejo Triano 2006, 145–147; Ruggles 2000, 72.
15 Rome, Vatican, Biblioteca Apostolica, MS. Arab. 368. See D'Ottone 2010 and 2013, and Robinson 2007a. This painting is discussed in D. Fairchild Ruggles's chapter in this volume.
16 For information on such towers (Sp., *mirador*), see Ruggles 2000, 106–109.
17 For a recent discussion, along with relevant bibliography, see G. Anderson 2013, 50–61.

18 On the decoration see G. Anderson 2013, 72–75.
19 See Sawa 1985.
20 See Jayyusi 1992a and 1992b.
21 See Lavan, Swift, and Putzeys 2007.
22 See Ibn Hayyan 2001, 198–199.
23 See Golombek 2007.
24 See Goitein 1967, VI:1; Hinz 2012.
25 Although the fragment itself measures only 56 × 43 cm, the visualization utilizes a sizing derived from dimensions attested in the Geniza documents, of curtains 5.5 cubits long × 3 cubits broad.
26 The model textile used for our silk cushion is David Collection 58.85.1.
27 See Ibn ʿAbd Rabbih and Boullata 2006, 181. The anecdote appears in a section on "Excess religiosity" (179–180).
28 See Ibn Hayyan 2001, 199.
29 On shared motifs in Córdoban ivories and marble decoration see G. Anderson 2013, 87–96. Also see Fernández Manzano 1995.
30 Musée du Louvre, Paris, inv. No. AO 4068. See Folsach and Meyer 2005, catalogue number 11, 314–318, esp. 315.
31 Musée du Louvre, Paris, inv. No. OA 277-4, and Museo de Navarra, Pamplona, inv. No. 1360-B. See Folsach and Meyer 2005, catalogue numbers 13 and 20, 321–322, 328–329. See also Robinson 2007b.
32 Viguera and Castillo Castillo 2001, catalogue, 135–136. See Dodds 1992, 248.
33 On the significance of these figures and their instruments for the history of medieval music see Reynolds 2009, 252–253. Also see Fernández Manzano 1997, 101–136.
34 Ibn Khaldun 1958, II:396.
35 Metropolitan Museum object number: MMA 13.141. Mariam Rosser-Owen, personal communication, November 2012. Also see Folsach and Meyer 2005, catalogue number 24, 333; Dodds 1992, 203.
36 See Reynolds 2009, 244–245.
37 See Rosser-Owen 2007.
38 For unfree elites in the Umayyad court, see G. Anderson 2012, 635–639.
39 Reynolds, personal communication, 2010. Makariou proposes a specific identity for the woman, interpreting the scene as part of a visual allegory with specific religious and political valence linked to the issue of Umayyad succession. See Makariou 2010, 323–324. An alternative interpretation of the scene is offered in Prado-Vilar 2005 and 1997.
40 See Ibn ʿAbd Rabbih and Boullata 2006, II, 181. Córdoba fits within a broader Islamic context in this respect. Caswell notes in his recent study of Abbasid female musicians that the lute was the "master of the musical instruments" by the ninth century, particularly well suited for playing indoors with seated guests and for female instrumentalists. See Caswell 2011, 232–233.

41 The eminent seventh-century Umayyad singer Jamila is said to have had as many as forty female musicians playing at a time. See Caswell 2011, 232.

42 Museo Arqueológico Provincial de Córdoba (Inventory number 11:355). The tombstone was found, with others, in the Sagrada Familia quarter of Córdoba in 1951. See Viguera and Castillo Castillo 2001, 97–99.

43 See Reynolds 2017b.

44 Ibn ʿAbd Rabbih and Boullata 2006, 311.

45 See G. Anderson 2012, 637, 642.

46 See ibid., 642–646.

47 Ibn Hayyan et al. 1999, 116, and Ibn Hayyan 2001, 93.

48 For an overview and the secondary literature see G. Anderson 2012, 644–647; Calvo Capilla 2011.

49 See Ibn al-Saʿi, Toorawa, and Bray 2015; Caswell 2011; Gordon 2004.

50 Ibn Hayyan et al. 1999, 208ff; Reynolds 2008, 157.

51 Ibn Khaldun 1958, II:355–356, 397–398.

52 Ibid., II:397.

53 Ibid., II:398 (emphasis added).

54 The political valence of such views and the relationship between *andalusī* architecture and poetry are explored in Ruggles 1993, 1997b, and 2000.

55 See Ibn Hayyan 2001, 194.

56 Ibn Hayyan uses these terms interchangeably in his text. Reynolds, personal communication. Also see Marín 2000, 125–40.

57 See notably Robinson 2002.

CHAPTER TEN

Sounds of Love and Hate

Sufi Rap, Ghetto Patrimony, and the Concrete Politics of the French Urban Periphery

PAUL A. SILVERSTEIN

I planted jasmine this morning in my public housing project. And I asked myself what I needed to do for France to love me. For France to love me.[1]

—Abd al Malik, "Jasmin et Chrysanthèmes" (2012)

In a poignant scene from Matthieu Kassovitz's award-winning, albeit highly controversial, 1995 film *La haine* (*Hate*), two of the principals, Saïd and Vinz, are wandering through the tower blocks of their home housing project (*cité*) on the periphery (*la banlieue*) of Paris in the aftermath of what is termed in the film to be an antipolice "riot" (*émeute*) when they stop and listen to the music. A resident DJ—the iconic Cut Killer playing himself—has propped two speakers in an upper-story window and is blasting a live cut-and-mix of the American rap artist KRS-One's "Sound of da Police," local hip-hop sensation Suprême NTM's "Police," and Edith Piaf's "Non, je ne regrette rien."[2] Rapt with attention, Vinz glows with appreciation: "He kills; he really kills it." It is a moment of calm in a torrid day of life-changing events, a splash of musical color in an otherwise austere audiovisual environment that Kassovitz films with documentary-like realism.[3] But the very words of praise that Vinz uses already foreshadow the speaker's eventual fate as a victim of police brutality.[4]

The juxtaposition of seemingly incompatible musical genres—chanson and gangsta rap—in Cut Killer's composition underlines the film's portrayal of a hybrid, urban, postcolonial France. The film's narrative architecture precisely relies on such contrasts and collisions of the seemingly incommensurable, on unexpected (and ultimately violent) encounters across the divides of race, ethnicity, class, space, religion, gender, and generation.[5] At the same time, the audio mash-up translates the various differences the film exposes into commensurable forms of belonging and performance. Piaf, NTM, and KRS-One harmonize precisely because of their overlapping themes of getting by, by any means necessary, in the face of institutionalized class, gender, and racial prejudice. The three protagonists—the white Jew, Vinz; the *beur*[6] Muslim, Saïd; and the black Christian, Hubert—encompass the ethno-racial and religious diversity of Paris's suburban *banlieues*, yet they remain united by their common class position, their fast friendship, and ultimately their willingness to stand together against the forces of law and order.

The film's presentation of *banlieue* subjectivities, spaces, and struggles as commensurable thus relies on a representation of masculinized violence as a constituent feature of postcolonial France. Indeed, *La haine* offers little in the way of hope and no room for faith. Kassovitz explicitly sets up the film as a morality tale of a society slowly plunging to its death, its social fabric being eroded by a spiraling dialectic of hate and governed by its own masculine code of street morality.[7] In one scene, Hubert cites a Christian ethic of forgiveness to counter Vinz's Old Testament rhetoric of eye-for-an-eye vengeance against the police who have beaten his friend Abdel into a coma. Vinz retorts, "I'm from the street, and you know what the street taught me: if you turn the other cheek, you end up dead." Religion is reduced to a symbolic diacritic of ethnic difference rather than an integral, embodied, and affective quality of residents' lives or a vector for community making. Whatever their inner beliefs, spiritual practices, or religious upbringing, Hubert, Saïd, and Vinz are portrayed as inherently and inescapably a product of the built environment of the housing projects; their tradition is that of the "ghetto."

In this chapter, I contrast such a representation of hypermasculine "ghetto patrimony" to a different dimension of the *banlieue* audiovisual landscape: an emerging Islamic musical project that emphasizes love and hope over hatred and despair, that seeks to cultivate flowers of peace in the drab concrete of the lower-class *banlieues*. In contradistinction to *La haine*'s erasure of religiosity, pious Muslim hip-hop artists ground their sense of identification not only in the hyperlocalized settings of the *cités* but also in transnational geographies of Islamic humanism. In exploring how these ambivalent identifications are negotiated by gangsta and Sufi rappers with different thematizations of love and hate, peace and violence, I detail how space is sonically racialized and race lyrically spatialized on the French urban peripheries. The result, I argue, is the re-spatialization of the *banlieue* as an embodied Islamic environment mediated by word and sound-image, by poetry and song.

Banlieuescapes

The contemporary constitution of the French *banlieue* as a site for Islamic cultural production has required the appropriation, over several recent decades, of an architectural space explicitly established to "integrate" residents and eliminate cultural practices, social solidarities, and religious publics deemed incompatible with French state secularism (*laïcité*). Arguably an extension of colonial urbanist experiments and the broader "civilizing mission" (*mission civilisatrice*) they enjoined,[8] French state agencies, in alliance with private enterprises, constructed public housing projects in the 1950s and 1960s to absorb excess proletarian populations displaced from the redevelopment of city centers, "repatriated" from the North African colonies fighting wars of independence, or inhabiting the shantytowns (*bidonvilles*) that had been built on the urban fringe by immigrant workers of primarily Algerian origin.[9] The latter, in particular, had become sites for organization, recruitment, provision, and fundraising for the Algerian National Liberation Front (FLN), which had extended its "jihad" against colonialism to France through workers' strikes, demonstrations, political assassinations, and terrorist bombings.[10] As early as 1952, the French state established a National Corporation for the Construction of Housing for Algerian Workers (SONACOTRA) with the explicit purpose of relocating shantytown residents, first to temporary housing (*cités de transit*) and later to rent-subsidized housing projects (*grands ensembles*), financed through the 1958 Priority Urbanization Zone (ZUP) legislation.

Built on the outskirts of Paris, Lyon, and other French cities, with a minimum of 500 units in a combination of high-rise towers and low-rise blocks, the *grands ensembles* balanced imperatives of social mobility and security, circulation, and containment (fig. 10.1). They were constructed as part of a larger moral reform project, as utopian modernist experiments in hygienic social life, centralizing housing, commerce, education, and recreation in immediate proximity to the factories in which many residents were assumed to

Figure 10.1. A housing project (*cité*) in the Parisian suburb (*banlieue*) of Clichy-sous-Bois, 2007. Photograph courtesy of Marianna (Creative Commons Attribution-Share Alike 3.0 Unported license).

work. In the process, they broke up the ethnic communities that had formed in the *bidonvilles,* mixing residents of different backgrounds and incorporating them into formal structures of state control and increasingly bureaucratized police surveillance.[11]

Aspirations of social mobility have proven to be little more than utopian for many of those who have grown up in the housing projects. With the economic downturn of the 1970s and the gradual deindustrialization of the urban peripheries of Paris and Lyon, by the 1990s youth unemployment reached figures above 30 percent and as high as 85 percent for certain housing projects.[12] Young residents often find themselves blocked by a public education system that tracks many of immigrant background to vocational degrees that are increasingly irrelevant, and residence in the *banlieues* itself can have a further stigmatizing effect on young job seekers. Indeed, a number of those I interviewed in the mid-1990s described using relatives' mailing addresses when applying for employment so as to avoid postal-code discrimination. Moreover, the *cités* have been marked by significant physical dilapidation, with many buildings and public facilities suffering from water damage, insulation problems, broken elevators, or worse. The lack of local capital, alongside occasional petty crime and property violence, has brought about the flight of local commerce. This drab built environment creates an aura of audiovisual banality that is repeatedly thematized in fiction and song authored by *banlieue* residents, as well as bemoaned by residents who introduced me to their home environments, the rich lived-space interiors of which contrasted markedly to the external visual monotony of the housing projects. The gray concrete (*béton*) comes to symbolize a life of immobility and repetition, generally contrasted to an imagined elsewhere of bourgeois pleasure or their parents' homelands.[13]

Over the last several decades, the French government has mounted a twofold response to this unfolding socio-spatial crisis. On the one hand, it has initiated a series of urban renewal plans—leading to the creation of a complex network of national commissions, urbanization laws, educational priority zones (ZEPs), and funding programs—designed to reintegrate the *cité* housing projects in question into national and global economies and transform their inhabitants into productive citizens. These included several "Marshall Plans" unleashed following waves of antipolice violence in the early 1990s and most notably in 2005; the plans created a set of tax incentives to attract corporate investment.[14] More recently, the response has involved the demolition of a number of the larger, Le Corbusier–inspired blocks in favor of scattered sites explicitly built to a human scale. On the other hand, successive French governments have responded to the feared growth of "lawless zones" (*zones de non-droit*) with the expansion of *banlieue* security forces.[15] The presence of these forces was further expanded after the 11 September 2001 attacks in New York as part of France's own "war on terror" against Islamist groups believed to use the *cités* as spaces for recruitment and organization. These policing measures have included the criminalization of certain everyday practices (such as assembly in the entryways or basements of public-housing buildings), the detention of countless suspected terrorists, the deportation of hundreds of undocumented immigrants, and the quotidian stops of young *cité* residents in "random" identity checks and searches.[16] Such measures have largely abetted the mounting antagonism between *cité* youth and the police that on occasion translates into violent confrontations labeled by the media "riots" (*émeutes*), if not a more low-intensity "hate" for the French system as a whole.

The challenge for *banlieue* residents is to construct meaningful, flourishing lives under such conditions of economic privation and police harassment. In part this has involved the development of a healthy informal economy—including a series of gray-market institutions revolving around the drug trade or the fencing of stolen consumer items—for the provision of employment as well as goods and services not otherwise locally available or affordable. Daily open-air markets operate in the shadow of boarded-up shopping centers. Residents with vehicles have created an informal taxi service to carry neighbors to and from transportation centers or places of work, commerce, or entertainment that are generally underserved by public transportation, and thus difficult to access from the *cités*. Through after-school tutoring programs, resident associations constitute a parallel, if severely underfunded, education system that attempts to compensate for the depressed conditions in French schools. The same associations also provide day care for working mothers and legal advice for local residents. Indeed, such a parallel structure operates with the tacit knowledge and minimal funding of the French state, which has largely devolved the provision of many such social, educational, and legal services to civic associations.[17]

Moreover, young *banlieue* residents, much like the insurgent architects and planners lauded in Lefebvrean critiques of state-directed "representations of space" embodied in modernist urbanism,[18] have worked to appropriate and domesticate housing projects and transform them into spaces for human freedom and self-expression. They convert the negative spaces of modernist architecture—cellars, garages, concrete courtyards, and so on—into places of both work and leisure. Building entryways become sites for informal commerce; dilapidated playgrounds are repurposed for games and recreation unanticipated by state planners; basement storage rooms are outfitted to serve as clubhouses, association locales, or Islamic prayer rooms. They mark these and other *banlieue* locales with graffiti and tags, creatively destroying them with "bombs" of spray paint. They embellish the discordant *cité* soundscape of traffic, car alarms, construction, and vocal arguments—an acoustic environment faithfully recorded in Jean-Luc Godard's 1967 avant-garde film *Deux ou trois choses que je sais d'elle* (*Two or Three Things I Know about Her*) and likewise captured in *La haine*'s realist soundtrack—with recorded or improvised musical forms of different genres played from portable stereos for small groups of listeners or, on occasion, blasted from apartment windows for all to hear. Even pious Muslims with an ambivalent relation to music find in the apartments, cellars, and corners of the *cités* places for learning and contemplation through the sharing of talk, recorded sermons, and poetry. Indeed, in my experience, these different types of sonic practice coexist in close proximity, with some young men (and occasionally women) moving across them and sharing in their listening conventions. In general, for those lower-class *banlieue* youth often excluded from private nightclubs, such courtyard, entryway, or basement venues become privileged spaces for building social life mediated through sound.

Ghetto Patrimony

Hip-hop in particular has been a salient musical form for young men—as both producers and listeners—to comment on life in the *cités* and respatialize the *banlieue* as a site for collective action and individual fulfillment.[19] Although the French state has contributed to the development of the French hip-hop industry through quotas on radio airplay promoting Francophone musical production, and record labels have commodified images of violence and sentiments of hate for their own profit,[20] hip-hop artists and their listeners have nonetheless constituted a counterpublic for commentary and critique on postcolonial France.[21] Drawing on a "ghettocentric" imaginary of local *cité* belonging, via images largely appropriated from African American popular culture, these artists, allied across putative lines of race, ethnicity, or religion, project both a micro-local identity and a transnational solidarity across "ghetto" spaces.[22] From this ghettocentric subject position, rap artists engage in a vehement denunciation of extant conditions of social and economic exclusion of the *banlieue* housing projects, deploying lyrical, often sexualized, violence as political critique.

By and large, hip-hop artists embrace the entrepreneurialism of their spatializing musical ventures through their adoption of figures of street lore: pimps, drug dealers, and other economic opportunists operating on the margins of legality. In general, the *caillera*[23] (or "gangsta") persona has come to dominate the self-presentation of many male rappers, through their autobiographical boasts, their dress, their gang-style poses and gestures, and the images and sounds of violence in their songs, videos, and cover art. The group 113,[24] for instance, has serially represented itself in song as "marginal" figures "outside the law,"[25] as "fugitives ... presumed to be dangerous,"[26] as "street niggaz [*négros*], *ruff* in spirit and 100 % insubordinate [*insoumis*]."[27]

This situational alliance with the "street" and its boastful claims of thug life are supplemented by rap artists' ghettocentric orientation in their self-organization and symbolic economy, by their emphasis on local identification and action that transcends intervening diacritics of race, ethnicity, or religion. As Lunatic avowed, "If I rap, it's 1 for the street, 2 and 3 for the cash."[28] Rappers thus engage in what Michel de Certeau has termed "spatializing practices,"[29] constructing alternate social totalities and subjectivities on the embers of built and dilapidated *banlieue* forms, endowing them with frameworks of value and hierarchy separate from those projected by the integration projects of the French nation-state.[30] For de Certeau, such forms of appropriation amount to contemporary equivalents of "poaching," with rap artists making a living through the reinvention and re-aestheticization of everyday *cité* life—living, as de Certeau would have it, "on the property of others."[31]

Elsewhere I have discussed the rappers' re-aestheticization of everyday *cité* life in terms of the organization of posses, graffiti tags, and the use of local imagery and identifiable figures in song lyrics, shout-outs, and album cover art.[32] What I am interested in here is the rappers' invocation of a common *banlieue* culture, or "*patrimoine du ghetto*," that supplements (and in some cases replaces) racial, ethnic, or national identification. This transcendent "ghetto heritage" is largely expressed through a gendered kinship idiom in which their age-mates (regardless of cultural or religious commonality) are addressed as classificatory brothers (*frères* or *reufs*) and sisters (*soeurs* or *sistas*), and the larger *cité* community—whether a particular housing project, or the entirety of *banlieue* France—as their family (*famille* or *mi-fa*) or clan. The fraternity they invoke through this idiom is explicitly contrasted with the *fraternité* of the French national triptych, which they depict as racist and hypocritical. As La Clinique rapped in 1998, "That is France: Liberty to shut up and be deported [*fermer sa gueule et prendre son charter*]. Equality for whom? My fraternity starts with my brothers."[33]

In these ways, the invocation of familial belonging and community solidarity proposes local patriotism at various scales of inclusivity in the place of national identity. 113 refers to Vitry-sur-Seine as "my nation" (*ma patrie*),[34] and Assassin famously claimed, "My only nation is my posse.... The flag of unity is planted in the 18th."[35] At the same time, rap artists seek to transcend hyperlocal identifications of race or space and envision a mode of ghettocentricity in which different *banlieue* or *cité* experiences are treated as commensurable and the basis for a unity of struggle. In performed collaborations between artists from different regions, they shout out to their different constituencies, implicitly calling for a transcendence of their differences. As Sniper rapped in their controversial song "La France" (in Sniper 2001):

> In all the *cités*, we stand together
> When we get kicked in the balls, we stand together
> *Négros* and *bougnoules*, we stand together.[36]

Ghetto patrimony thus calls forth a form of pan-*banlieue* solidarity to confront racial discrimination, police harassment, and state violence—themes repeatedly invoked in gangsta rap much as they are in *banlieue* cinema. Hardcore rappers both memorialize the victims of police violence and imagine violent retribution. The language of hate, violence, and revenge continues in the work of many commercially successful *banlieue*-based hardcore groups, including Assassin, Diam's, Ministère AMER, Suprême NTM, and Sniper,[37] among others, who dream of "sacrificing" police officers, exterminating politicians, and setting fire to the government buildings in which they work. Such imagined violence is often sexualized. In a number of hardcore rap tracks, France is feminized as either a fickle lover, a bad mother, or a whore who should be "fucked."[38] In "Est-ce que ça vaut la peine?" (Is it worth it?),[39] Sinistre metaphorizes France through the nationalist imagery of "Marianne," but instead of deploying her as a symbol of radical egalitarianism, he presents her as an icon of hypocrisy and racism.[40] Sinistre wonders, "Does she really love me? . . . Is it worth it that she loves me? . . . Does France love me? In spite of me and my *cité*?" By the end of the track Sinistre decides that the expressed love is only material, good only for sexual gain.

The foreclosure of love and embrace of hate in some ghettocentric rap is often allied with calls for revolution in hip-hop discourse. In tracks produced after the 2005 urban violence, the young men on the street are generally portrayed as "insurgents,"[41] if not "revolutionaries,"[42] even if their "pyromania"[43] is regretted as ultimately self-destructive.[44] Hip-hop visions of an uprising starting on the *banlieue* mean streets are clearly sensationalized for commercial effect, if criminally prosecuted as explicit incitements to violence.[45] Nonetheless, rap artists generally have approached the violence as not the frivolous expression of a generation of youth in revolt but as part of a larger, embedded structure of historical marginalization and resistance. In this regard, evocations of a ghetto patrimony can resonate even with those who do not (or no longer) inhabit the *cité* housing projects themselves but still find themselves—because of age, ethnicity, or religion—on the periphery of the French social, cultural, and political life.

Islamic Spaces, Islamic Sounds

But gangsta rap is not the only genre of hip-hop, and hypermasculine violence is not the only response to the experience of degradation and discrimination in the French *banlieues*. Indeed, "peace, love, unity, and having fun" have been persistent themes in international hip-hop from Afrika Bambaataa's pioneering compositions of the early 1980s through the "conscious rap" of KRS-One and others.[46] While French hardcore rappers generally tend to broach such ideas in nostalgic invocations of earlier, easier times,[47] others view them as a still-salient ethical model of self-cultivation and political action. In particular, since the early 2000s, a vibrant Islamic hip-hop scene has also emerged in the *banlieues* alongside, and sometimes overlapping with, the hardcore rap described above, deploying the broader critique of the French state's racism and hypocrisy toward the imagination of a world of solidarity premised on love rather than hate.

As with other ghettocentric productions, Islamic social worlds in the *banlieues* have historically emerged through a similar process of spatial appropriation and insurgent urbanism. Until recently, the direction of Islamic life in France—including the management of mosques, the organization of communal celebrations, religious education, the certification of halal butchers, and the administration of Islamic cemeteries—has largely been under the control of various immigrant cultural agencies operated by North African and West African states.[48] While there are today over two thousand recognized mosques in France, including over one hundred establishments with dedicated buildings in the Paris region, the creation of independent spaces for public religious practice is still often an uphill battle. Even those mosques that are eventually constructed are subject to strict municipal regulation, limiting their size, their architectural form (with only ten minarets authorized throughout France), and their function. Calls to prayer broadcast outside the mosque are prohibited, as they are in much of the non-Muslim majority world. Although the more popular mosques cannot accommodate the number of worshipers during Friday midday prayers or Ramadan, recent municipal regulations forbid worship spilling over into public streets or squares.

To fill the demand, thousands of prayer rooms in storefronts or in the basements of public housing buildings—both officially recognized and underground—have been established throughout *banlieue* France, the fruits of protracted efforts since the 1980s by local Islamic associations, charitable organizations, and neighborhood groups to provide alternative resources for self-education and spaces for public expressions of piety.[49] They often double as sites for community discussion, private religious education, and collective celebration or simply as spaces for (mostly) men to relax and meditate in the transition from work or school to home. Some of these associations and prayer spaces have become rallying points for a variety of *salāfī* and other reformist Islamist movements, but their ideological orientations depend largely on local communities and the availability of religious scholars to direct them. A number of *banlieue* residents have further joined evangelical groups like the Tablighi Jamaat, an international movement founded in India in the 1920s, which engages in missionary *daʿwa*.

Such developments of Islamic counterpublics[50] have prompted state concerns over a *banlieue* "generation-in-revolt" succumbing to the "temptation of jihad"[51] and of the French *banlieues* becoming a node in an international Islamist network.[52] In response, French security forces have conducted multiple sweeps for suspected terrorists in the *cités*, breaking into prayer rooms and association locales. At the same time, the French government has sought to control Islamic practice in France through the regulation of female dress—officially banning the hijab (headscarf) in public schools and the *niqāb* (face veil) in public altogether[53]—and the 2003 creation of French Councils of the Muslim Faith (CFCM) that would replace (in the words of then interior minister Nicolas Sarkozy, speaking on Radio France 2) an "Islam of garages and cellars" (*Islam des caves et des garages*) with an "Islam of the mosques."[54] As Mayanthi Fernando has emphasized, these efforts at creating an official Islam *of* France (*Islam de France,* as opposed to Islam *in* France) artificially privilege certain masculine institutional structures over private domestic spaces for religious practice.[55] Nonetheless, they have given voice to some *banlieue* groups, particularly a rising number of Sufi orders (*ṭarīqāt*), taken by French observers as less threatening to the state.

Sufism has long been a central site of state interest and knowledge production in France, with early translations, commentaries, and studies of Sufi texts going back to the seventeenth century;[56] colonial officers surveilling North and West African Sufi "lodges" (*zāwāyā*) as potential vectors of resistance while simultaneously promoting rural, popular religious practices as more pliable than urban Islamic institutions and as a counterweight to the Islamic reformism (*salafiyya*) of the nationalist movements;[57] and twentieth-century intellectuals such as René Guenon embracing the esoteric and quietist dimensions of Sufism and assimilating them into a universalist theology, or "sacred science."[58] In general, Sufism has appeared more compatible with French secular models of *laïcité* because of its inward-looking spirituality, its emphasis on the personal and emotional rather than the public and political. Among Muslims in France, Sufism has been historically prominent as a parallel mode of social organization, particularly uniting West African Muslims on both sides of the Mediterranean through material and spiritual exchanges fostered by the Tijaniyya, Muridiyya, and Gnawa orders.[59] Since 1990, France has further become an important node in a transnational Sufi revival, particularly through the Lebanese al-Ahbash, the Turkish Gülen, the Algerian ʿAlawiyya, and the Moroccan Butshishiyya movements, which have taken on expanded political roles in their respective home countries and have increasingly devoted explicit attention to the Muslim diaspora in Europe.[60] These antiextremist groups have a strong educational mission, have published a number of Islamic reference texts in French, and have a widespread online and physical presence across the French urban and suburban landscape.[61] They promote music and the arts as tools of devotion and community building and specifically recruit among artistic and cultural producers in France.

Increasingly, these Sufi groups have allied with the French state to promote an *Islam de France* that is politically moderate and supportive of cohabitation (*le vivre-ensemble*) across ethnic, racial, and religious borders.[62] In 2006, the Paris municipality worked with the Moroccan ethnomusicologist Faouzi Skali of the Butshishiiyya *tarīqa* to create the Institute of Cultures of Islam (ICI), a public center for artistic exhibitions and musical events. Originally located in a temporary facility in the heart of the multicultural and multireligious Goutte-d'Or neighborhood in northern Paris, the ICI sub-

Figure 10.2. The former Masjid El Fath on rue Polonceau, Paris, future site of a branch of the Institut des Cultures d'Islam, 2014. Photograph courtesy of Kambiz GhaneaBassiri.

sequently secured 22 million Euros in funding from the Paris municipality to build a state-of-the-art glass-and-steel facility in the nearby, historically North African Barbès quarter, all in support of the "spread of a modern, secular Islam" (figs. 10.2 and 10.3).[63] Its new location is just blocks away from the French storefront headquarters of the Association of Islamic Charitable Projects (AICP), the international outreach arm of the al-Ahbash movement, which likewise deploys musical education to "preach moderation."[64]

The ICI, then, represents a concrete manifestation of a Sufi revival in the heart of Paris, but the spatial imaginary of French Sufi adepts extends into the *banlieue* as well. On the one hand, Sufi mysticism, as it has been primarily practiced in France as an interiorized, individualized pursuit, is arguably even less dependent on the establishment of a "purified" (halal) physical environment than are some other Islamic traditions or movements and does not call for a transformation of public space. If worshipers do regularly gather for collective meditation (*dhikr*) or in celebration of holidays, they can adapt any number of spaces for the purposes, from municipal community centers to storefront association locales to an adept's private apartment. What sanctifies these spaces are the words and music of devotion, the

Figure 10.3. The future site of the main branch of the Institut des Cultures d'Islam on rue Stéphenson, Paris, 2014. Photographs courtesy of Kambiz GhaneaBassiri.

sounds of divine love expressed in human form. On the other hand, Sufis remain attuned to the socio-spatial worlds adepts inhabit. Indeed, opening one's heart to divine grace involves learning to truly see and listen to one's surroundings, to perceive deeper structures beyond superficial appearances. For the number of hip-hop artists who have begun to follow the Sufi path, this also means taking a step back and reassessing their relationship to the *cité* street. In so doing, they conjoin their invocation of divine "love" (*maḥabba*) with an articulation of a "ghetto patrimony" that is neither sectarian and violent nor deterministic of their identity or future aspirations.

Sufi Rap

Perhaps the most publicly recognized French hip-hop artist to embrace Sufism is the rapper, spoken-word poet, and author Abd al Malik.[65] Born in 1975 as Régis Fayette-Mikano to Catholic Congolese parents, Malik grew up in a rough public-housing project in the Neuhof suburb of Strasbourg. As he explains in his autobiography, *Qu'Allah bénisse la France!* (God bless France!; published in English as *Sufi Rapper: The Spiritual Journey of Abd al Malik*),[66] he lived a double life as a pickpocket and drug dealer, on the one hand, and a brilliant student of philosophy and literature, on the other. Following his brother's lead, he converted to Islam as a teenager and started rapping as part of the group New African Poets (N.A.P.), made up of other Neuhof youth. After an extended period devoted to *daʿwa* with the Tablighi Jamaat, Malik broke with the evangelical movement and flirted with Salafi revivalism, before finally finding his path among the Butshishiyya, devouring Skali's writings and pledging himself in 1999 as a disciple to the order's Morocco-based leader Sidi Hamza (b. 1922). Since then, Malik has embarked on a solo career with four successful albums of spoken-word poetry and three published books by 2015.[67] In addition to winning numerous musical and literary prizes, Malik was decorated as a "knight" (*chevalier*) in arts and letters by the French Ministry of Culture in 2008 and has been named the symbolic head of the ICI.

Malik charts a complicated route between avowals of authenticity and co-optation by state institutions, setting himself up as a liminal figure capable of presenting street aspirations in palatable form to a mainstream French audience while also translating the positive values of *laïcité* and French republicanism to *cité* youth inclined to distrust them. Malik's written and sung texts present a didactic tale of religious conversion from the outside in, from the violent words shouted in the *cités* to a state of inner peace and harmony, from hate to love. Whereas N.A.P.'s first album, *La racaille sort 1 disque* (The gangsta releases an album; 1996), relied on harsh gangsta rap sounds and equally raw themes of life on the streets, their 2000 *À l'intérieur de nous* (Inside us) featured Middle Eastern ornamentations and soft R&B harmonies sung by Malik's wife, the Franco-Algerian recording artist Wallen (Nawel Azzouz). Instead of displaying the scenes of urban decay featured on most hardcore French rap albums, the cover art depicts an interior space, with the three rappers' chest cavities revealed in an X ray, an Islamic star and crescent superimposed over Malik's heart. Malik's first solo album, *La face à face des coeurs* (Heart to heart; 2004) confirms this spatialized thematization of love, borrowing the title from Skali's 1999 treatise on Sufism and featuring a cover photo of Malik revealing his heart behind his jacket and tie. Commenting on this trajectory, Malik later wrote, "In spite of the celebrity that [our first] album brought us, our failure was already certain. . . . We had always tried to prove that we were the purest, the deepest. . . . In music as in life, the point is not to transcribe a mentality or a moment, but to simply translate the language of the heart."[68]

In his autobiography, Malik narrates his upbringing in the *cités* of Neuhof and later the Parisian *banlieue* of Plessis-Robinson as an internalization, but ultimately rejection, of a sense of "desolation" and "internal misery."[69] He describes in stark terms the harsh socio-spatial environment of the *banlieues* characterized by social precarity, unemployment, delinquency, and "real and exaggerated (*fantasmée*) insecurity,"[70] but he also underlines the vibrant family and communal life there, the moments of joy and togetherness across lines of race and ethnicity—a true "multicultural mosaic."[71] In describing the "soundtrack" (*fond sonore*) of Neuhof, he notes both the "roaring motors and squealing brakes of stolen cars mixing with police sirens" and the "funky hymns" of American R&B and soul music.[72] In his 2010 plea for urban peace, *La guerre des banlieues n'aura pas lieu* (The *banlieue* war will not occur), Malik summarizes these reflections with an imagined dictionary entry for "*cité*": "4. A lie. A promise of a better future for the most deprived, but which has turned into a nightmare, into a ghetto. A compost heap [*terreau*] of urban anger. And, although a real joie de vivre can prevail, its inhabitants often suffer from the weight of a destiny that seems insurmountable, as if they were all living in an open-air prison."[73]

Ultimately, for Malik, the true tragedy of the *cités* is that one's ghetto patrimony is taken as spatial predestination, that the drabness of housing-project architecture will determine a featureless life: "The drama of the *cité* is determinism, the belief in an inescapable destiny."[74] Internalized, such a foreboding is transformed into paralyzing anger:

> Fear, rage cloistered me in hate
> Sowed this seed, brought forth misfortune
> So many ups and downs, enabled by rancor
> And hate multiplies, I am its prisoner
> Bit by bit we see that this only leads to pain.[75]

For Malik, the challenge under these conditions is to recognize the poetry of life and find one's solace in an interior space of divine peace.

> One should be careful when one uses words
> the speech of the people, the language of the street
> because from beauty can flow absolute ugliness.
> In trying to be of the street one becomes a sewer.[76]

Malik's own lyrics are explicitly poetic, sung over light melodies from French chanson, jazz, and pop R&B. Malik likewise encourages his listeners to recognize and cultivate the beauty of life in the *cités*, to reject fatalism and hatred and embrace hope and love.

> France is beautiful, you know it's true we love France. . . .
> France is beautiful; look at all those beautiful faces mixed
> together, that's heavy [*ça c'est du lourd*].
> And when you insult this country, you insult your country, in fact
> you insult yourself.
> We need to rise up, we need to fight together.[77]

Jeanette Jouili has interpreted Malik's emphasis on interior spiritual revitalization as an upholding of French secular republican values, though one that reimagines the French nation as an "affective community bound by feelings of love" rather than a rational public sphere of dispassionate citizens and stakeholders.[78] In his volume of poetry and essays *Le dernier français* (The last Frenchman; 2012), Malik does explicitly avow *laïcité* as a fundamental aspect of French life: "Religion should no longer be the potential enemy of the Republic but its major ally. . . . Religion lived in the private sphere, shared, questioned, discovered with others, should become a school for peace. . . . Our Republic must be strong on this count. Intransigent to all attempts to appropriate or deviate from the sacrosanct rules of *laïcité*."[79] But for Malik, this is ultimately a matter not simply of state policy but of self-recognition and personal effort that starts on the *cité* streets. Ultimately Malik sites the spiritual and communal renewal of France in the *banlieues*, consciously maintaining a marked, if cautious, optimism: "The *banlieue* will perhaps tomorrow become the place for the beginning and the end of the quest of all those who seek lost peace. These areas, which are accused of being at the source of all the evils that 'gangrene' our society, will perhaps be the place where all come in search of salvation."[80]

Not all French Muslim hip-hop artists, of course, share Malik's optimism or avowed love for France. Hisham Aidi and Jouili contrast Malik with Médine (Médine Zaouiche),[81] a French-Algerian rapper from Le Havre who mixes the strident sounds of hardcore rap with a vehement and didactic lyrical critique of imperialist violence and global Islamophobia. With a shaved head and prominent beard, and often photographed raising a clenched fist, he lionizes Malcolm X and Black Power militancy, calling himself an "Arabian Panther."[82] Where Malik promulgates nondenominational spirituality and interfaith dialogue, Médine underlines his Islamic specificity in his stage name (French for "Medina"), as well as his albums' themes, imagery, and material forms, producing his music under the Din ("Religion") Records label, with the "i" in "Din" and "Médine" being graphically produced in the form of a minaret. And unlike Malik, he makes no attempt to translate this piety into the terms of *laïcité*: he leaves religious terminology in its original Arabic, dates his albums according to the Islamic hijra calendar, and designs his CD booklets to read from right to left as if they were written in Arabic. He thus ultimately grounds his artistic critique in the broader space-time of Islam.

At the same time, Médine maintains a localized engagement in contemporary *banlieue* France. Nearly every song includes references to current events and French figures his *banlieue* listeners would clearly recognize and to which they might relate. Médine's consistent pedagogical theme is to encourage his audience to understand their ghetto patrimony as part of a broader structure of power and domination. He has conjoined this didactic effort with his work as one of the founding members of the Mouvement des Indigènes de la République, an outspoken, antiracist movement that calls attention to the ongoing, lived effects of France's colonial past and makes forceful claims for reparations and revolutionary political change. Yet, Médine preaches neither hatred nor violence. Although his second album is entitled *Jihad* (2006), the subtitle is "The Greatest Combat Is against Oneself," thus joining Sufi adepts in referencing the "greater" or "spiritual jihad" (*al-jihād al-akbar, al-jihād al-nafsī*), not military force. In the final track, "Jihad," he continues:

> Those who choose the military solution
> Haven't they seen that they use us more than they help us. . . .
> For whites, blacks, and those of immigrant heritage
> My riches are cultural, my combat eternal
> It's the one within me against my evil self.

Thus it is of little wonder that, despite their differences, Médine and Abd al Malik actually have collaborated, notably on Médine's first album (2004), a multiartist reflection on the challenge of the New York 11 September 2001 attacks to Muslims everywhere. Over the years Médine has worked on various collective musical-cum-political projects with a large number of Muslim (and some non-Muslim) hip-hop performers, including many associated with hardcore rap, such as Diam's, Kéry James, Monsieur R, Rim-K (from 113), Salif, Sinik, and Sniper.[83]

Of these, Kéry James has been probably the most prominent in conjoining invocations of ghetto patrimony with Islamic humanism.[84] Like Abd al Malik, this self-proclaimed former street thug and hardcore rapper of Guadeloupean descent from the pioneering hip-hop group Idéal J and later Mafia K'1 Fry subsequently converted to Islam and embarked on a solo career dedicated to inner reflection. In 2002, James organized a mega-concert in the Stade de France soccer stadium in the Parisian *banlieue* of Saint-Denis featuring dozens of hardcore groups, including 113, Fonky Family, and Sniper, under the theme of "Urban Peace," with stark freestyle compositions brought together in explicit invocations of antiracism, solidarity, and inner peace.[85] Two years later he produced a collective album with a similarly diverse group of artists entitled *Savoir et vivre ensemble* (Knowledge and cohabitation), produced by the al-Ahbash association Savoirs et Tolérance and interspersed with Sufi worship songs sung by their Association of Islamic Charitable Projects choral ensemble. The disc had the explicit message of "bringing to light Islam's teachings of peace, fraternity, patience in the face of injustice, generosity, and other human qualities."[86] Its sales proceeds were slated to open a Muslim cultural and artistic center in the Parisian *banlieue* of Gennevilliers.[87]

Conclusion

Overall, in spite of their differences of style and approach, the didactic musical efforts of Abd al Malik, Médine, and Kéry James point to the emergence of new Islamic soundscapes in the French *banlieue* that conjoin architectonic projections of the mean streets with one of an interior space of love and peace. Islam provides a rich semiotic code through which to interpret the trials and tribulations of *cité* life; it provides a framework of belief that allows singers and listeners to contextualize their current struggles within a longer collective history and situate their wanderings along a more consequential personal path toward God; it provides poetry and musical forms that enrich their artistic endeavors and appreciation. In this regard, Islamic sounds and themes supplement African rhythms and Caribbean reggae motifs within French hip-hop that have long called *banlieue* audiences' attention to ongoing issues of slavery and colonialism, to the continuity of what they, drawing on the Jamaican reggae tradition, call "Babylon." They broaden *caillera* personae and ghettocentric perspectives appropriated from US gangsta rap, thus paralleling the adoption of various Islamic perspectives (including Nation of Islam and Five Percent tendencies, but also mainstream Sunni and Sufi varieties) by a number of African American hip-hop artists, including Busta Rhymes, Ice Cube, and Nas. In the cacophonous acoustic environment of the drab *cités*, French Muslim rappers add sounds of love and hope to the clamor of hate and desperation. While it is unclear whether the *banlieues* will truly become a space for salvation, as Malik imagines, he and a few other Islamic rap artists have nonetheless planted a few sprigs of jasmine in their concrete housing projects.

NOTES

1 All translations throughout the chapter are my own unless otherwise noted. I want to thank Olivier Esteves, Michael Frishkopf, Denis Lacorne, Morgan Luker, and Federico Spinetti for comments on various drafts and earlier versions of this

chapter. Field research was sponsored by an initial grant from the US Institute of Peace, and later through generous funding from the Carnegie Corporation of New York.

2 NTM's "Police" (1993) includes a virulent lyrical attack on the French police force. The group's two rappers, Kool Shen and Joey Starr, were arrested and subsequently convicted of disturbing "public order" after performing the song in 1995 (see Prévos 1998; Silverstein 2002; Tshimanga 2009). Cut Killer is the performance name of Anouar Hajoui (b. 1971), a Parisian deejay of Moroccan heritage who was one of the pioneers of France's hip-hop movement in the early 1990s. Piaf (1915–1963) was born poor, abandoned by her birth mother, and raised partially by her maternal grandmother (likewise of Moroccan origin) and partially by the prostitutes employed in the brothel run by her paternal grandmother. "Non, je ne regrette rien," written in 1961 at the end of her career and considered to be one of her most emblematic and autobiographical songs, thematizes moving forward in life beyond past struggles and handicaps.

3 While the film's soundtrack is minimalist, themes of everyday *cité* violence are driven home in a musical collection of hardcore rap and raggamuffin songs "inspired by the film" (as the subtitle to the album goes) and written by well-known hip-hop artists, including Assassin, IAM, Ministère AMER, and MC Solaar (see AAVV 1995). Ministère AMER was subsequently convicted of "provocation to murder" for their contribution to the album *Sacrifice de poulets* (Sacrifice of the cops). *Raggamuffin* (or *ragga*) is a subgenre of reggae that developed in Jamaica in the early 1980s but by the 1990s had been integrated into the French hip-hop scene.

4 Kassovitz loosely based the film on the 1993 death of seventeen-year-old Makomé M'Bowole, shot in the head while in Parisian police custody, reportedly by an accidental firearm discharge.

5 See Vincendeau 2005.

6 "*Beur*" refers to French-born youth of North African origin. The term, a double inversion of the descriptor "*arabe*" in the French slang metathesis known as "*verlan*," likely originated in the *banlieues* during the early 1980s and became popularized by a set of youth activists of that period associated with the Beur Movement (see Aïchoune 1985). While less used by Franco-Maghrebis during the period in which *La haine* was set, it nonetheless had become a widely deployed and recognized ethno-racial marker found in both academic works and the popular press. Indeed, observers commonly referred to the ethno-racial composition of postcolonial France through the triad *black-blanc-beur*, a revision of the colors of the national flag, *bleu-blanc-rouge*, which today has itself become a synonym for "white." For lengthy discussions of racial and ethnic categories in postcolonial France, see Fassin and Fassin 2006; Hargreaves 1995; and Silverstein 2004, among others.

7 On masculine codes of the street, see Lepoutre 1997.

8 See Çelik 1997, 8, 192–193.

9 See Soulignac 1993 for a history of the construction of *banlieue* housing projects. There is a rich ethnographic literature on these lived spaces. See Bouamama 2009; Dubet and Lapeyronnie 1992; Duret 1996; Epstein 2011; Jazouli 1992; Lepoutre 1997; and Wacquant 2008.

10 See House and MacMaster 2006; Sayad and Dupuy 1995.

11 On the *banlieue* housing projects as part of a state social project that prioritizes issues of security and *vivre ensemble*, see Dikeç 2007; Epstein 2011; Fassin 2011; Silverstein and Tetreault 2006; and Wacquant 2008.

12 See Wihtol de Wenden and Daoud 1993, 75.

13 See Charef 1983; Kettane 1985, 36–38. Rap group La Rumeur refers to the housing projects as a "concrete forest" ("Predateur isolé," in La Rumeur 2002), whereas Sinik terms those who live there "prisoners of the concrete" (*condamnés du béton*) ("Si proche des miens," in Sinik 2006). For discussions of the Franco-Maghrebi (*beur*) fiction cited previously, see Hargreaves 1997.

14 Interior Minister Eric Raoult first spoke of a "Marshall Plan for the *banlieues*" in 1995, and almost identical plans of state investment, using the same historical referent, were revived under the Sarkozy presidency in the wake of the 2005 "riots" across the Parisian *banlieues*. But revitalization plans for these areas have been proposed repeatedly since at least 1977. See Damon 2010 (March), and Pinard 2013 (20 February).

15 See Fassin 2011 for an ethnography of the Anti-Criminal Brigade (BAC), the state security force established for patrolling the *cités*. On the discourse of "lawless zones" in France, see Trémolet de Villiers 2002.

16 See Jobard 2006, and specifically his discussion of the racial and spatial profiling during police stop-and-search operations. Male dress or bodily adornments marked as "Islamic" (e.g., *sirwāl* trousers or *ṭāqiyya* prayer caps) notably attract police attention, though they have not been the objects of explicit legislation as female Islamic dress, including the 2004 ban on the hijab in public schools or the 2010 ban on *niqāb* in public spaces.

17 See Kastoryano 2002, 101–102.

18 Lefebvre 1991, 39. See Harvey 2000, 233–255; Miraftab 2009. Insurgent architects work against state or corporate models of urban space that prioritize capital accumulation and governance, and instead seek to build environments that are attuned to the grassroots "representational spaces" of inhabitant ideals.

19 For discussions of the history and politics of hip-hop/rap in France, see Bazin 1995; Cannon 1997; Durand 2002; Gross et al. 1994; Molinero 2011; Mucchielli 1999; Prévos 1998. This section draws from my longer discussion of "ghetto patrimony" in Silverstein 2012a. Rap is certainly not the only musical form produced or consumed in the *cités*, with thriving Algerian *raï*, Moroccan *gnawa*, Berber

kabyle, Antillean *zouk*, Congolese *soukous*, Jamaican reggae, Punjabi *bhangra*, and various other musical scenes connecting *banlieue* youth transnationally with listening publics in North Africa, sub-Saharan Africa, the Caribbean, the Indian Ocean, and beyond. But, since the late 1980s, it has been the one musical form that consistently unites *banlieue* youth across ethnic and racial lines, that is accessible to monolingual French speakers, that has minimal financial barriers to entry, and that is malleable to multiple, alternative musical styles. Indeed rap/*raï*, rap/reggae, rap/*soukous* fusions have become increasingly common across the past two decades.

20 See Silverstein 2002.

21 On the notion of a counterpublic, see Warner 2002. Charles Hirschkind (2009) has expanded this idea to discuss the emergence of mass-mediated Islamic counterpublics that defy Habermasian presumptions of a secular public sphere. For an application of this approach to France, see Jouili 2014.

22 See Kelley 1996. In borrowing the term "ghettocentricity" I am echoing rap artists' own deployment of the term "ghetto," which they explicitly appropriated from the African American hip-hop lexicon. As Wacquant (2008) argues, French *banlieues* should not be conflated with the relative ethno-racial homogeneity of American inner cities.

23 "*Caillera*" is a *verlan* rendition of "*racaille*," or "scum," a term of insult that has been ambivalently appropriated by some young *cité* men and particularly gangsta rap artists. See note 6.

24 The name "113" refers to the building number in which the group's founding members grew up. As I discuss later in this chapter, the names of rap groups, albums, and songs often reference the microspatial environments that animate their lives and musical sensibilities. See Silverstein 2002.

25 "Marginal," in 113 2005.

26 "Les evades," in 113 1998.

27 "C'est ici que la vie commence," in 113 1998.

28 "HLM3," in Lunatic 2000.

29 de Certeau 1984, 96.

30 See Castells 1983, 73–96.

31 de Certeau 1984, xii.

32 See Silverstein 2002.

33 "Est-ce aç la France?," in AAVV 1998.

34 "Les evades," in 113 1998.

35 "Kique ta merde," in Assassin 1993. See Cannon 1997, 162–163. "The 18th" is the arrondissement of Paris from where the group hails.

36 "*Bougnoules*" is a derogatory term for North Africans, dating from the colonial era, that has been ambivalently appropriated by some rap artists.

37 See "L'état assassin," in Assassin 1995; "Extrême miné," in AAVV 1998; "Sacrifice de poulets," in AAVV 1995; "Qu'est-ce qu'on attend," in Suprême NTM 1995; "Hommes de loi," in Sniper 2006.

38 For example, Monsieur R, "La FranSSe," in Monsieur R 2004; Sniper, "La France," in Sniper 2001. The general verb used for such sexualized violence is *"niquer,"* a slang term with Arabic etymology formed from a French word.

39 In AAVV 1998.

40 See also Expression Direkt, "Fin de lutte," in AAVV 1998.

41 Kazkami, "Insurgé," in Mac Kregor 2006.

42 Monsieur R, "Revolutionaire," in Monsieur R 2006.

43 Sinik, "Un monde meilleur," in Sinik 2006.

44 See Sniper, "Brûle," in Sniper 2006.

45 In addition to prosecutions of Suprême NTM and Ministère AMER, already discussed, other lawsuits have been brought against La Rumeur, Sniper, and Monsieur R for public abuse, defamation, or incitement to violence against the national police. See Silverstein 2012a; Tshimanga 2009.

46 Afrika Bambaataa (b. 1957), a deejay from the South Bronx, is credited as the "godfather" of hip-hop, having christened the artistic movement with its current name. He and his Zulu Nation crew of MCs, deejays, breakdancers, and grafitti artists spread hip-hop internationally on overseas tours, including to France. KRS-One (Lawrence Parker, b. 1965), an MC likewise from the South Bronx, was a member of the hardcore rap group Boogie Down Productions before embarking on a solo career and founding the Temple of Hip-Hop political movement.

47 See Suprême NTM, "Tout n'est pas si facile," in Suprême NTM 1995. See Aidi 2014 for a brilliant discussion of the ongoing and complex relations between French and American hip-hop scenes and the ongoing importance of African American musical cultures for French Muslim youth.

48 See Bowen 2010; Laurence 2012.

49 See Kepel 1991, 229–242.

50 See Hirschkind 2009.

51 Pujadas and Salam 1995.

52 This was highlighted with the March 2012 killing spree of Toulouse-Algerian Mohamed Merah who claimed ties to al-Qaeda; the January 2015 murder of workers for the *Charlie Hebdo* satirical weekly by Chérif and Saïd Kouachi who claimed affiliation with al-Qaeda in the Arabian Peninsula; and the November 2015 attacks in Paris by a group of gunmen and suicide bombers affiliated with ISIS. For an expanded discussion of the French state securitization of Islam and its discriminatory effects, see Geisser 2003.

53 See Bowen 2006; Scott 2007; Silverstein 2004.

54 Delattre 2003 (April 14). See Laurence 2012.

55 See Fernando 2010, 2014.

56 These include key Orientalist works by Barthélemy d'Herbelot (1625–1695) and François Pétis de la Croix (1653–1713).

57 The nineteenth-century anticolonial revolts were indeed occasionally organized by Sufi leaders using the translocal organizational structures of the orders, the notable example being the fifteen-year uprising led by the Algerian Qadiriyya leader ʿAbd al-Qadir (1808–1883). On the complex relations between French colonialism and African Sufism, see Clancy-Smith 1994; Laremont 2000; Seeseman and Soares 2009; Silverstein 2012b; Soares 2005; Trimingham 1998, 255; and Umar 2006.

58 See Sedgwick 2004 for a comprehensive intellectual biography of Guénon.

59 See Kane 2008; Kapchan 2007; Salzbrunn 2002.

60 See Skali 1999, 18. The al-Ahbash, with Ethiopian roots, are not a Sufi *ṭarīqa* per se, but their connections to and influences from the Naqshbandiyya, Qadiriyya, and Rifaʿiyya orders have been well documented (see Donahue 2008 and Hamzeh and Dekmejian 1996). On the Gülen movement, see Ebaugh 2010 and Yavuz and Esposito 2003. On the ʿAlawiyya, see Lings 1971. On the Butshishiyya, see Ben Driss 2002; Bouasria 2012; Haenni and Voix 2007; Kapchan 2011; Nabti 2007; and Zeghal 2008.

61 See the official websites: http://www.saveurs-soufies.com (Butshishiyya), http://fr.fgulen.com/ (Gülen), http://www.apbif.org/ (al-Ahbash), and http://aisa-net.com/ (ʿAlawiyya).

62 See Aidi 2011.

63 http://www.institut-cultures-islam.org/ici/d-ici-2014/. On the ICI project and its relationship to the history of the French state management of Islam, see Davidson 2012, 205–219.

64 http://www.apbif.org.

65 On the life, politics, and musical production of Abd al Malik, see Aidi 2011; Bourderionnet 2011; and Jouili 2013.

66 Abd al Malik 2004b.

67 Malik's iconic albums—*Gibraltar* (2006), *Dante* (2008), and *Château rouge* (2010a)—each won first prize in the "urban music" category of the French Victoire de la Musique Awards. A film version of his autobiography, *Qu'Allah bénisse la France*, directed by Abd al Malik, was released in 2014.

68 Abd al Malik 2004b, 175.

69 Ibid.

70 Ibid., 14–15.

71 Ibid., 14.

72 Ibid., 15.

73 Ibid., 41–42.

74 Ibid., 81.

75 "Noir et blanc," in Abd al Malik 2004a.

76 "Céline," in Abd al Malik 2006.
77 "C'est du lourd," in Abd al Malik 2006.
78 Jouili 2013, 72.
79 Abd al Malik 2012, 223–224.
80 Abd al Malik 2010b, 167.
81 Aidi 2011; Jouili 2014.
82 Médine 2008.
83 Several of these were converts or reverts to Islam, notably Diam's (Mélanie Georgiades) who converted to Islam in 2008, but also Akhenaton (Philippe Fragione) of IAM and Kool Shen (Bruno Lopes) of NTM. As discussed earlier, rap collaborations often cross religious lines, with some groups, such as 113 and Sniper, including both Christian and Muslim artists. Religiosity, when invoked in lyrics, tends to be framed as a nonsectarian submission to God, and particularly Islamic themes are presented inclusively and in explicit opposition to France's official discourse of *laïcité*. See Molinero 2011 and Silverstein 2012a.
84 For a discussion of Kéry James and his Islamic project, see Molinero 2011, 112–114.
85 The concert was later released as a CD/DVD collection (AAVV 2002).
86 James 2002.
87 See Médioni 2004 (7 June).

PART FIVE

Central and South Asia

CHAPTER ELEVEN

Ideal Form and Meaning in Sufi Shrines of Pakistan

A Return to the Spirit

KAMIL KHAN MUMTAZ

In the practical aspects of production and sensory perception, sound is as relevant to music as bricks are to architecture. In the context of Islam, what is relevant is the meanings of forms in these arts within the Islamic system of belief and praxis. However, the internalization of religious concepts varies according to the temperament and capacity of individuals, and within Islam these different approaches are characterized by three major currents or tendencies: shariʿa (Islamic law), *kalām* (theological discourse), and *ṭarīqa* (the spiritual path).

There is little support for the arts in either the legal prescriptions of shariʿa or the intellectual debates of *kalām*. But the artist, and all those whose hearts are full of love for their Creator, find a resonance with their temperaments in *ṭarīqa*, also known as *ʿirfān* (gnosis), *ḥaqīqa* (Truth), *taṣawwuf* (Sufism), or *ʿishq* (love; here, the path of love), with its practice of *dhikr* (remembrance; i.e., the remembrance and verbal invocation of the Beloved), its intoxication with *jamāl* (beauty; i.e., the beauty of the Beloved), and the lover's desire for *ḥuḍūr* (presence; i.e., the presence of the Beloved).

Love

Among the names of Allah are *al-Rahmān*, "the Exceedingly Compassionate," *al-Rahīm*, "the Exceedingly Merciful," and *al-Wadūd*, "the Loving." As the Qurʾan declares, "Say, [O Prophet]: 'if you love God, follow me, [and] God will love you and forgive you your sins; for God is much-forgiving, a dispenser of grace'" (3:31).[1]

Not surprisingly, the most consistent theme in the arts of Islam is love. In the *Mathnawi* quatrains of Rumi; in the poetic *Divan* of Hafiz; in popular ballads, romances, and epic tales known across the Muslim world, such as *Laila and Majnun*—in all these, the metaphors and symbols used to describe the states and stations of the human soul filled with the love of the Divine are similar to those used in miniature paintings of the South Asian tradition to illustrate not only these legendary stories but also the *rāgas* (melodic systems of South Asia) of classical Indian music, which carry extramusical meanings.[2] Similarly, in the Turkish-Anatolian tradition, the *nāy* (an end-blown flute made of reed or cane) is a metaphor for the human soul that, like the reed, longs to return to its home by the river's edge. The *nāy* provides the musical accompaniment for the *samāʿ* (spiritual audition) of the Turkish Mevlevi order, while the *samāʿ* as practiced within the South Asian Chishtiya order entails performances in the *qawwāli* genre, in which mystical verses are sung to the accompaniment of music.

In music, the emotional states evoked by the *rāgas* are well known and sometimes indicated by their very names, and reinforced by the seasons and times of the day prescribed for their performance. Again, love is a constant theme. *Rāgamālā* paintings (*see plates 6, 7, and 8*) include *rāgas* depicting love in union and *rāginīs* depicting love in separation.[3] Often evoking the affective beauty of music and musicians within a stunning built environment, including exquisite buildings, gardens, or idealized nature scenes, and usually linked to poetic texts, such paintings express the deep connections among multiple artistic manifestations of spiritual love while affirming the importance of such connections as pointing to a unified source in the Divine.

In architecture, the intended spiritual message may be explicitly stated through inscribed texts or symbolically expressed in the forms of mural decorations. Thus, for example, the theme of the Prophet as God's mercy and the beloved of God can be gleaned from the texts, frescos, and glazed tile mosaics adorning the walls and ceilings of the Wazir Khan Mosque in Lahore (figs. 11.1 and 11.2). The Qur'anic text Sūrat al-Fatiha framing the central arch to the prayer hall, with a fresco panel on an adjacent pillar to the north of the central arch (fig. 11.3a), can be read as a metaphor for the Prophet, the hair-like aerial roots of the banyan tree in the fresco recalling the events that took place at Hudaybiyya, where the Prophet's head was shaved in accor-

Figure 11.1. (a, *top*) Wazir Khan Mosque, Lahore. Parapets with *mudakhil* and eight-pointed star. (b, *bottom*) Wazir Khan Mosque, Lahore. Photographs: K. K. Mumtaz.

Figure 11.2. (a, *top*) Dome medallions invoking blessings upon the Prophet. Wazir Khan Mosque, Lahore. (b, *bottom*) Quotations from Sufi masters on the attributes of servanthood. Wazir Khan Mosque, Lahore. Photographs: K. K. Mumtaz.

Figure 11.3. (a, *top*) Banyan tree and clouds. Wazir Khan Mosque, Lahore. (b, *bottom*) A pair of cypresses in a garden signifying the Lovers in Paradise. Wazir Khan Mosque, Lahore. Photographs: K. K. Mumtaz.

Figure 11.4. (a, *left*) Cypress with intertwined vine, signifying the Lover and the Beloved. Wazir Khan Mosque, Lahore. (b, *right*) *Muqarnas* inside the Wazir Khan Mosque, Lahore. Photographs: K. K. Mumtaz.

dance with the hajj rites, and his hair was tossed on a mimosa tree.[4] The allusion is reinforced by the clouds appearing in the fresco panel—harbingers of rain and a metaphor for Allah's Mercy.[5] In fact in recognizing the Prophet as the symbol of God's Mercy, we have the key to the meanings of the decorations on the mosque. We read the cypress, with its symmetric form, as the *al-insān al-kāmil*, the perfect human being. With its top bent, it symbolizes the submission (*islām*) of the perfect Muslim. Entwined with the branches of the fruit tree or vine, it represents the embrace of the "Lover and Beloved" (fig. 11.4a). Two cypresses in a garden, facing the panel described above, are "lovers in Paradise" (fig. 11.3b), while the bold calligraphy above the *miḥrāb* identifies them as Allah and Muhammad (fig. 11.5a). And, after having walked through its gates, traversed its court, and feasted on the delights of its *īwān* (vaulted hall, walled on three sides), if you still do not recognise the import of its message, then read, as you must when you leave the mosque, the Persian inscription above the exit: "The prophet Muhammad [literally, Muhammad the Arab] is the honor of this world and the hereafter [literally, of both worlds] / Shame on anyone who does not respect him [literally, dust upon the head which is not the dust of his threshold]!" (fig. 11.5b).

Figure 11.5. (a, *top*) Calligraphy with "Allah" and "Muhammad," the Beloved and the Lover. Wazir Khan Mosque, Lahore. (b, *bottom*) Persian inscription above the exit of the Wazir Khan Mosque, Lahore. Photographs: K. K. Mumtaz.

Dhikr

Outside, above the central arch of the main entrance of the Wazir Khan Mosque, in bold *nastalīq* letters is the formula "the best of remembrances [*dhikr*]," followed by the principal testimony of remembrance: "There is no god but Allah" (*lā ilāha illā Allāh*), and the date 1045 AH, that is, 1635 CE, when the mosque was completed.

Dhikr (the term means "remembrance" or "invocation") is recognized as a way of worship, as a form of prayer and a means of drawing closer to Allah. The Qur'an enjoins the worshiper to remember Allah constantly and intensely, because "remembrance of God is indeed the greatest [good]" (29: 45). Architecturally inscribed in mosques such as Wazir Khan, *dhikr* also constitutes a central ritual practice in all Sufi *ṭarīqas* (orders), each of which prescribes invocation of one of the names of Allah or formulae including one or more names. Such *dhikr* may also be accompanied by music as in the Mevlevi and Chishtiya *samāʿ*. Rituals incorporating prayer, *dhikr*, Qur'anic recitation, poetic chant, and sometimes music are often known as *ḥaḍra* (presence).

The invocation of the names of Allah are not necessarily verbalized. The *ḥaḍra* or *dhikr al-ṣadr*, "invocation of the heart/breast," may take the form of rhythmic movements of the body, with or without a prescribed method of breathing, or may be practiced without any outward signs. Certain apparently nonsensical phrases, woven into *qawwāli* performance in South Asia,[6] are cryptic versions of the name, understood by those initiated into the mysteries of the spiritual path. Other forms may employ instruments alone without any vocalizing. In South Asia, the rhythms played on the large *dhol* drums associated with Sufi shrine festivals have their own coded language of *dhikr* phrases, and it is not uncommon to see some listeners go into *hāl* (a spiritual state) on hearing the beat of the drum or to see groups of devotees encircling the drummer, swaying to the movement of the *dhammāl* dance, arms thrust heavenward with the forefingers pointing to the sky in a gesture invoking Allah, the One above.

Muqarnas, a series of tiny niches (fig. 11.4b), provide another example of the interface between architecture and *dhikr*. Placed in the upper corners of a square chamber, at the junction with the circular dome above, in the corners of arched entrances, or as cornices and column capitals, this element is found in an amazing variety of forms, from Spain and Morocco to the Middle East, Central Asia, and India. The basis is always a complex three-dimensional geometry of half arches and segmented domes forming a honeycomb of niches corbelling one above the other. But each geographic region has its distinct system, and each system allows for an infinite variety of permutations and combinations.

A Sufi lodge, or place reserved for meditation, is also called a *zāvia* (Arabic, *zāwiya*), meaning an angle or corner. The prayer niche, *miḥrāb*, is a symbol of the heart,[7] and its concave form (Urdu, *tas*) in the *muqarnas* suggests an enclosure or constriction of space. But the intervening spaces (*shaparak*) between each pair of niches suggest an opening or expansion of space. This alternation between constriction and expansion mirrors the rhythmic breathing in and breathing out that accompanies the invocation, or *dhikr*. It also recalls the alternation of the states (*aḥwāl*) of the seeker (*sālik*), which are divided into two categories: *qabḍ* and *basṭ*, constriction and expansion. Just as the *dhikr* carries the seeker through successive stages on the spiritual journey, so the succession of niches expands upward and outward from each corner to meet the circular base of the dome in an all-encompassing unity. Among other references to the *dhikr* are the geometric patterns of alternating inward and outward pointing eight-pointed stars, the one being the negative image of the other, and the *mudakhil* designs, usually on parapets, in which an acanthus-like motif alternates with a negative inverted image of itself.[8]

Ḥaḍra

While love is the motivating force, and *dhikr* is the ritual method, the goal is *ḥuḍūr*, or *ḥaḍra*, the actual "presence" of the Beloved. In a *ḥadith qudsi*, God, speaking on the tongue of the Prophet, says, "Nothing brings men near to Me like the performance of that which I made obligatory upon them, and through supererogatory acts My servant [i.e., man] comes even nearer to Me until I love him. When I have bestowed My love on him, I am his hearing with which he hears, his sight with which he sees, his tongue with which he speaks, his hand with which he grasps, and his feet with which he walks."[9]

On this journey to God, the seeker passes through stages, or stations (*maqāmāt*), including *makhāfa* (fear), *maḥabba* (love), and *maʿrifa* (knowledge or gnosis), and experiences many spiritual states (*aḥwāl*; plural of *ḥāl*). From *makhāfa*, a fear of losing favor with the Beloved, the seeker submits to the observance of obligatory prayer and then proceeds to *maḥabba* and the performance of supererogatory acts of devotion, such as *dhikr*, till he reaches his goal, *maʿrifa*, the stage of "knowledge"—not exoteric knowledge but inner, "heart knowledge," *ʿirfān*, the knowledge of the Real (*ḥaqīqa*).

The *aḥwāl* or *wajd* (finding) are states of heightened awareness, states of spiritual intoxication, including the pain and ecstasy of love. In South Asia, it is in these states, during extraordinary performances of *qawwāli*, that listeners and performers report having "seen" the *rāga* personified.[10] Something akin to such a state is experienced in the presence of breathtaking landscapes or sublime works of art and architecture, particularly sacred art, when one is conscious of being in the presence of a power infinitely greater than oneself and experiences an overwhelming sense of majesty, grandeur, and even infinity. This is the stage at which all distinctions between subject and object are dissolved, where the music is not "seen" in a visible form and architecture is not "heard" as frozen music; rather, hearing and seeing are transcended in the presence of absolute beauty itself. This is the state of *wiṣāl* (union), the stage at which God says, "I am his hearing with which he hears, his sight with which he sees, his tongue with which he speaks, his hand with which he grasps, and his feet with which he walks."

Beauty and *Iḥsān*

The emphasis on beauty among the foundational principles of Islam is illustrated by the famous hadith Jibril (a "saying" concerning the Prophet and the angel Jibril [Gabriel]): "A stranger came into the presence of the Prophet and his companions and, after asking the Prophet to tell him about *islām* [submission] and *imān* [faith], said: 'Tell me about *iḥsān*,' to which the Prophet replied, 'That you worship Allah as if you see Him, for if you don't see Him then truly He sees you.' After the stranger left, the Prophet informed the companions, 'He was Jibril, who came to you to teach you your *dīn* [religion].'"[11]

We note that two of the three defining principles or concepts of the Islamic religion are *islām*, or submission to the will of Allah, and *imān*, the articles of faith and belief that are Islam's basic tenets. The third principle is that of *iḥsān*. The root of the word *iḥsān* is *ḥusn*, which means "beauty." The connection between worship and beauty is amply established in the Qur'an, which tells us that "God's [alone] are the most beautiful Names [*al-asmā' al-ḥusna*]; invoke Him, then, by these" (7:180) and that "He is God, the

Creator, the Maker who shapes all forms and appearances! His [alone] are the attributes of perfection" (59:24). In other words, Allah, who is without form, can be known through His beautiful attributes or qualities, foremost of which is beauty.

Each of the ninety-nine names of Allah, the *al-asmāʾ al-ḥusna* in the Qurʾan, is an attribute or quality. While His qualities are infinite, they are sometimes categorized into those of His majesty, *Jalāl*, and those of His beauty, *Jamāl*.[12] Indeed, one of His names is al-Jamīl, "the Beautiful," and according to a hadith, "Allah is Beautiful and He loves beauty" (Sahih Muslim, Book 001, Hadith no. 164). So we can worship Him not only by invoking His beautiful names but also by doing what is beautiful, by reflecting the quality of beauty in everything we do and everything we make. Thus the making or doing of art—including music and architecture—itself becomes an act of worship and a mode of invocation.

Form and Meaning

The Islamic philosopher Seyyed Hossein Nasr notes, "According to [the traditional doctrine], everything in the macrocosmic world consists of both an external form (*ṣūra*) and an inner meaning (*maʿna*) . . . the inner reality of the cosmos . . . is based upon a harmony which imposes itself even upon the corporeal domain . . . [and is expressed] in Islamic sources in the distinction between form (*ṣūra*) and meaning (*maʿna*)." "[T]his harmony lies at the heart of the traditional plastic arts and is the foundation of traditional architecture and other arts dealing with material forms." Thus "poetry is the result of the imposition of the Spiritual and Intellectual Principle upon the matter or substance of language. This Principle is also inextricably related to Universal Harmony [*tanāsub*] and its concomitant rhythm, which is to be found throughout cosmic manifestation." Moreover, "there is an element in poetry which corresponds to the feminine rather than the masculine aspect of the Divine Reality. If the Intellect can be said to correspond symbolically to the masculine principle, the Logos itself being usually symbolized in such a way, poetry then corresponds to the feminine pole which is at once an extrusion of the masculine and its passive and substantial complement."[13]

To the qualities of "Majesty," *Jalāl*, and "Beauty," *Jamāl*, we should add "Perfection," *Kamāl*, which, in the words of Frithjof Schuon, "is realized on the one hand in terms of absoluteness and on the other hand in terms of infinity: in reflecting the Absolute, beauty realizes a mode of regularity, and in reflecting the Infinite, it realizes a mode of mystery. Beauty, being perfection, is regularity and mystery."[14]

Jamāl

As I have said, "*Jamāl*" literally means "Beauty," but more particularly the supposedly feminine qualities of mystery, such as melody in music; lyricism in poetry; and elegance, grace, and refinement of form in both the visual and the performing arts. It also includes subtlety and nuance, as well as the style and manner of expression or presentation, as in the quality of voice, or *adaigi*, in vocal renditions.[15] In architecture, these qualities are reflected in the curvilinear forms of arches; in surface embellishments, such as arabesques; in the qualities of the materials, such as their purity, textures, and colors; and in details of juxtaposition and transition between materials, levels, structural and architectonic elements.

Jalāl

Again, "*Jalāl*" literally means "Majesty," particularly the supposedly masculine qualities of regularity, as in the rhythmic order of South Asian *tāl* cycles; the ascending and descending (*arohi* and *awrohi*) structure in the modal system of *rāgas*; or the mathematical and geometrical relations of symmetry, balance, and proportions in the visual arts and *qāfiya* and *radīf*, or rhythmic meters and rhyming sequences in poetry.

In architecture, these qualities are reflected in the logic and clarity of structure, spatial organization, and the governing discipline of planning modules, grids, and axes. The presence of *Jalāl* is most strongly experienced through size, scale, and proportion of built forms in space and of spaces contained and defined by the built forms. For example, in the Badshahi Mosque in Lahore (fig. 11.6), the entire complex is composed within a perfect square. The size and placing of every element on plan, section, and elevation is derived from a system of proportionate subdivision of the whole.

Figure 11.6. (a, *top*) *Jalāl*, *Jamāl*, and *Kamāl*. Badshahi Mosque, Lahore. (b, *bottom*) Badshahi Mosque, Lahore, interior. Photographs: K. K. Mumtaz.

Jamāl and *Jalāl* in Architecture and Music

Thus, while mathematical rigor governs rhythms and symmetries and provides the basis for the *Jalāli* aspect, or Majesty, balance, harmony, and proportions govern the lyrical arabesques and traceries of surface decorations and reflect the *Jamāli* aspect, Beauty. Moreover, the elements are orchestrated into a hierarchy in which the scale is modulated to match the experience of the Badshahi Mosque by observers as they approach it from a distance and move in and through its spaces.

Likewise, a typical performance of South Asian classical music begins with an introduction, the *alap*, which uses the *rāga*'s melodic form and structure but dwells on subtle nuances and emotional qualities. The more structured middle sections unfold within the framework of *theka* and *qaida* rhythm cycles. The final sections are indeed a playful, joyful, ecstatic interplay between melody and rhythm, bringing together both *Jalāl* and *Jamāl*.

Kamāl and Ideal Forms

Kamāl (Perfection) can be gauged only in relation to some normative standard, a desired objective, goal, or ideal form.[16] Every traditional building type, and every classical *rāga*, has a predetermined essential typology, a prototype, a generic or "ideal" form. Needless to say, no two buildings of the same type or genre, or renditions of the same *rāga*, are in fact identical. A single form, such as the *hasht bihisht* building plan (fig. 11.7) or the *darbari* musical *rāga*, may be manifested in an infinite variety of constructions/compositions while still being essentially a *hasht bihisht* or *darbari*.[17] This diversity is due to specific construction materials, site topology, user requirements, and climate in the case of a building or the medium and format of the lyrics, performers, audience, built environment, and occasion in the case of music. Nevertheless, the work of the musician and the architect, whether master or apprentice, begins with copying from a preexisting model.

To understand the importance of copying, it is necessary to understand the central place of ideal forms (*mithāl*) in the Islamic—especially Sufi—theory of aesthetics and the creative process within Islam's traditional worldview and cosmology.

Figure 11.7. Taj Mahal, Agra, elevation and plan. © Ebba Koch. Courtesy of Ebba Koch.

Traditionally, the term "art" is applied to making or doing anything that meets the dual criteria of utility and beauty. Utility—appropriateness to function and purpose—relates to quantity and the more obvious practical and physical aspects of material and form. But beauty relates to a quality of the Divine. In the cosmic creative process, these qualities are reflected as natural and artificial objects and acts on the earthly plane. However, some objects and acts are more "transparent"; that is, the ideal forms are more readily recognized in them than in others, which are more "opaque." Thus every earthly object or act takes on a symbolic meaning to the extent that it reflects its heavenly archetype.[18]

The "perfect Man" (*al-insān al-kāmil*),[19] the fully realized human being, is a mirror that reflects all of the Divine qualities, that is, absolute Being. This is his essential nature, his true self, and it is a potential within every human. To realize his potential, man must recover his primordial nature, made in the image of God, which he supposedly lost at Adam and Eve's fall from grace. It is when his human nature recovers its original wholeness that access to the Spirit, the Eye of the Heart (*ʿayn al-qalb*), becomes possible.[20] He must undertake an inward journey from the body, through the soul (*nafs*), and to the heart, for it is the "heart" that is the seat of the Spirit (*rūḥ*). Only when the "eye of the heart" is opened can it contemplate the Real (*al-ḥaqīqa*) and "gain sight of the light of God."[21]

In societies rooted in the idealist metaphysical worldview, human development is measured in terms of the progress made on this journey toward enlightenment. In these societies, the role of art, including music and architecture, has been to support this spiritual quest or journey by reminding us of our role and function in this life, by pointing to our true goal and illuminating the way toward it.

Within this framework the artist—musician or architect—cannot presume to be original or to create beauty. Beauty already exists, out there, as an objective reality. One can aspire only to reflect it in one's work. However, copying or working from prescribed models is in practice never simply a mechanical process of reproduction. It involves intelligent interpretation, adaptation, and application of critical judgment and discernment at every step of the way.

Figure 11.8. Tomb of Hazrat Dawood Bandagi, Shergarh, Pakistan. Photograph: K. K. Mumtaz.

Maʿna

The content or *maʿna* (inner reality, purpose, or meaning) of an artwork is inseparable from the nuanced layers and shared values of its cultural context, as embedded in the complex language of symbolic forms. But to understand its *maʿna* for builders and users, performers and listeners, we need to turn to source documents, such as inscriptions or other writings.

Sometimes such accounts of *maʿna* combine architectural and sonic features. In his account of the design and construction of the tomb of a Sufi saint (fig. 11.8), the sixteenth-century Lahore architect Ustad Bazid tells us this:[22]

> Before every brick that we put in place I would invoke God's blessings upon the holy Prophet, may Allah's blessings and peace be upon him. Virtuous men, devotees, and seekers of the spiritual path would recite the chapter *Ikhlās* [Qurʾan, 112] twice over as they passed on each load of bricks or mortar. There were so many people and such a crowd that each turn to hand over the bricks would take rather a long while and

with great difficulty. In this manner the construction of the radiant tomb was accomplished in four years. The following chronogram was written on its completion:

> This pure tomb of Hazrat Dawood
> May God forever spread its shadow wide
> By the radiant beauty of its appearance
> The eyes gain sight of the light of God
> He who looks upon it with the eye of meditation
> Cannot take his gaze away from it
> To the chant of *lā ilāha illā hu* [there is no God but He]
> When recited beneath this dome
> From this which has no parallel
> comes forth the sound of *waḥdahu lā sharīk* [He is one and has no associate]
> To determine the year of its completion
> it has been said *muddi ẓillahu abda* [extend its shadow to eternity].[23]

We see that the tomb is conceived and built as an act of devotion. It embodies *ḥaḍra,* both as the spiritual "presence" of the saint and as the sounded ritual anticipated to occur within his tomb. The intention or purpose (*maʿna*) of both construction and ritual is to "spread its shadow wide," that is, to propagate the guidance and teachings of the saint. We are told that the "radiant beauty of its appearance" is designed to enable the seeker to "gain sight of the light of God," and for the adept on the Sufi path, "who looks upon it with the eye of meditation," it is a support, a vehicle that brings the adept into communion with the Divine. To the chant of "*lā ilāha illā hu*" comes the standard response of "*waḥdahu lā sharīka lahu.*"

The basic form of the Sufi tomb is often a cubic chamber with a hemispherical dome. The cube symbolizes the earthly, material body, while the dome represents the spiritual realm, the heavenly sphere above.[24] In this metaphor, the body of the Lover rises upward toward the Beloved, and the Spirit descends halfway to meet it. This meeting of the lover and the Beloved is *wiṣāl,* "union," the ultimate goal of the Sufi.

While ritual incantations in the form of *qawwāli, samāʿ, dhikr,* and devotional poetry sung in *kāfi* and other musical modes can be witnessed at numerous Sufi shrines across the Indian subcontinent, these performances invariably take place outside the tomb chamber. As a result, there is no physical correspondence between the architecture and the sonic quality of the music.

Geometry plays an integral part in the design of Sufi shrines, not only in determining the proportions of the building in plan, section, and elevation, but also in decorative details, such as curvilinear arabesques and polygonal *girah* (knot) patterns. These are not merely mechanical tools for setting out buildings and decorating surfaces; rather, they are profoundly connected with the metaphysics of the sacred sciences of number and geometry.[25]

The Ikhwan al-Safaʾ (Brethren of Purity), an anonymous group of scholars of the fourth century AH (tenth century CE), placed the science of numbers at the root of all the sciences, "the foundation of wisdom, the source of knowledge and pillar of meaning."[26]

> Know, brother, that the Creator, most exalted, created as the first thing from His light of unity the simple substance [*al-jawhar al-basīṭ*] called the Active Intellect [*ʿaql*]—as 2 is generated from 1 by repetition. Then the Universal Soul was generated from the light of the Intellect as 3 is generated by adding unity to 2. Then the *hyle* was generated by the motion of the Soul as 4 is generated by adding unity to 3.[27]

> Know, oh brother . . . that the study of sensible geometry leads to skill in all the practical arts, while the study of intelligible geometry leads to skill in the intellectual arts because this science is one of the gates through which we move to the knowledge of the essence of the soul, and that is the root of all knowledge.[28]

While the "sensible geometry" (related to sensory perception) of form, proportion, and the permutations of number "leads to skill in all the practical arts," such as the production of melody, harmony, and rhythm in the audible music of the chant of "*lā ilāha illā hu*," "intelligible geometry" (related to the intellect, soul, and spirit) leads to knowledge of the essence of the soul, the root of all knowledge, including the inner reality (*ḥaqīqa*), the meaning (*maʿna*) of the "sound of *waḥdahu lā sharīk*" (He is one and has no associate) that comes forth "from this [dome]."

Thus every form, proportion, and decorative scheme becomes a ground for contemplation of higher realities. Each composition is contained by a frame that establishes a finite universe, reflecting a cosmos created in perfect balance, in perfect harmony, made up of a diversity of elements governed by symmetry and proportion, with a unique center, the origin, to which everything must return. On closer examination, each element turns out to be a microcosmic representation of the larger scheme, with its own frame containing a symmetrical arrangement of elements and a unique center.

Decorative geometric patterns called *girah* (knots) are made up of lines interwoven into nets or webs that constantly appear to change as the eye traces them across the stone surface. The spaces between the lines appear now as pattern and now as ground, adding a layer of ambiguity and paradox to the relationship between the apparent, *ẓāhir*, and the hidden, *bāṭin*, between simplicity and complexity. This unveiling or unfolding of the same truth at each level is experienced as one moves toward and through the tomb structure.

The center of a Sufi shrine's *qibla* wall (facing toward the Kaʿba in Mecca) typically contains an elaborately decorated *miḥrāb* (prayer niche), which allows the individual to perform the ritual prayer in relative seclusion, undisturbed by the movement of other devotees circulating around the grave of the saint. Qurʾanic references to this niche make clear its symbolism as the innermost sanctuary, the heart, where one is in the presence of God. The niche is where the Virgin Mary spent her confinement in prayer (3:37). A similar niche appears in the Qurʾanic chapter entitled al-Nur (The Light):

> God is the light of the heavens and the earth. The parable of His light is, as it were, that of a niche [*mishkāh*] containing a lamp: the lamp is enclosed in glass, the glass shining like a radiant star: a lamp lit from a blessed tree—an olive-tree that is neither of the east nor of the west—the oil whereof [is so bright that it] would well nigh give light [of itself] even though fire had not touched it: light upon light! (24:35)

The equivalency of the *mishkāh* of the *Sūrat al-Nūr* and the *miḥrāb* as a niche for prayer is affirmed on every other prayer mat, depicting a lamp hanging from an arch. Indeed it is here, in this innermost sanctuary, that "the eyes gain sight of the light of God."[29]

Yet another symbol associated with both light and sound is the minaret, or *manāra*—literally, a beacon of light that guides the traveler to his goal. The *muʾadhdhin* (muezzin) traditionally ascends the *manāra*, also known as *miʾdhana* (place of *adhān*), to call the faithful to prayer by reciting the *adhān* prior to each of the daily prayers. In a Sufi tomb, a pair of minarets often flank the entrance to mark the way for the pilgrim; alternatively, miniature forms of them mark the corners of the main chamber.

Figure 11.9. Pak Wigah Mosque, Gujrat, Pakistan. Photograph: K. K. Mumtaz.

The *mithāl*—ideal forms—can be read as a language of symbols whose meanings may be implicit or made explicit through the word. The import of the spoken word is enhanced and magnified when it is rendered melodically, and the written word, as rendered in calligraphy and mural inscriptions, reinforces the abstract symbolisms of ideal musical or architectonic forms.

The recitation of the Qurʾan (*qirāʾa*) and the Muslim call to prayer (*adhān*) are without doubt among the most powerful and moving forms of sound production in Islamic praxis. So also are the numerous musical genres of Sufi gnostic poetry (*ʿarifana kalām*), for instance in the Mevlevi audition (*samāʿ*), the Chistiya *qawwāli*, chants of the Shadhili *ḥaḍra*, Punjabi and Sindhi *kāfis*, *ḥamd* glorifications of God, and *naʿt* homages to the Prophet, not only sung in architectural settings, but even forming part of community activities during the construction of these buildings, as the case of Hazrat Dawood's tomb illustrated earlier.

A remarkable contemporary example of such a community project is the story of the Pak Wigah mosque (fig. 11.9),[30] some thirty kilometers south of

Figure 11.10. Volunteers working at the Pak Wigah Mosque. Photograph: K. K. Mumtaz.

the city of Gujrat. The client for the mosque is an eye surgeon, Dr. Sahibzada Mohammad Farakh Hafeez , and a shaykh of a Sufi *ṭarīqa* (the Naushahi order) who traces his spiritual and family ancestry back to the saint who presided over a gathering of Sufis at this site in 1739 CE.

The designs call for extensive marble carving, but the combined output of two teams of professional masons is too slow, and finally both teams are sent packing. And then a miracle happens. A hundred stone carvers materialize out of nowhere to take up the work. Twice a week, they appear after dark and work through the night (fig. 11.10). The site is ablaze with powerful lights. The music of hymns and chants playing over the loudspeakers all but drowns the din of more than forty power tools. The air is filled with marble dust that turns everything chalky white: white hair, white faces with liquid eyes and tracks of joyful tears running down the cheeks. At the break of dawn, the work stops, the stone carvers say their morning prayers in congregation, and disperse. Washed and changed, they step into the day as ordinary teachers, lawyers, paramedics, and shopkeepers, and go about their daily routines.

Not one of them has held a mason's tool before. The venerable doctor himself has become not only an accomplished draftsman but a remarkable calligrapher as well. With no previous training in the art of calligraphy, he one day starts to compose the required texts in an entirely new script,[31] perfectly balanced and proportionate, clearly the result of pure inspiration. He draws directly on the stone. One team cuts out the stencils; another does the rough shaping; a third, the fine chiseling; a fourth, the polishing and finishing. Among the new workforce are several teenagers who were sent to work on the project by their parents to keep them out of trouble. These good-for-nothing dropouts have blossomed into fine and utterly devoted artisans.

The transformative nature of such projects is something we have experienced not only in our own work as designers but equally in the lives and attitudes of clients, builders, artisans, and ordinary visitors. Whether these transformations are due to some quality of the architecture, the association of these places with pious persons, the presence of their holy relics, or the performance of sounded rituals, there is no doubt that these spaces and their associated sounds can lead us to feel the presence of the Divine.

Trying to link sound and vision is an alluring prospect, but it is typically carried out on the horizontal, sensory plane. The intention and purpose of music and architecture in Islam is to realign us to the vertical axis, to link and integrate all sensory phenomena on the plane of the Spirit. Any link between sound and vision at the sensory level is incidental and far removed from the intention and purpose of Islamic building and sonic practices. The link is realized at a metasensory level, precisely in a return to the Spirit.

NOTES

1 All quotations from the Qur'an are from Asad 1980.

2 North Indian classical music includes elements from both the Hindu and Islamic traditions, and is identified with and owned by each community without reservation.

3 *Rāgas* are masculine and depicted by male figures; *Rāginīs* are feminine and depicted by female figures; while *Ragputra*, literally meaning "son of a *rāga*," are lesser or derived variations. For illustrations and details of the symbolism used in *rāgamālā* paintings of the Kangra school, see Randhawa 1971.

4 For a detailed account see Lings 1985, 247–256.

5 *Bārān-e rahmat*, a Persian phrase in common local usage, meaning "rain of Mercy." The Prophet is referred to as *Raḥmatan li-l-ʿālamīn*, "God's Mercy toward all the worlds," in the Qur'an (21: 107).

6 For example, *nadrey deem, tanadeereyna*; or *yalali, noomtana-nana*.

7 See Burckhardt 2007, 52.
8 See for example Bakhtiar 1976, 15–16, for concepts of "The Reflective Mirror" and "The Breadth of the Compassionate," and p. 100 for geometric expressions of complementary pairs of spiritual stations, *maqāmāt*, including contraction/expansion (*qabḍ/basṭ*).
9 *Sahih al-Bukhari, al-Riqaq*, 38, reproduced in *al-Khatib al-Tabrizi* 2006, book 9, chapter 2.
10 A vivid illustration of the power of devotional music and poetry in the spiritual quest is the account of a Hindu seeker of his own experience on visiting Hazrat Nizamuddin Awliya (d. 1325 CE), "In his tears I could see my country, my parents, the statue of Krishna Ji playing the flute. The notes of the flute were in harmony with Khwaja Muhammad's song. It felt as if Krishna Ji was playing his flute and dancing with me at the same time, and I also seemed to be dancing within *Hazrat's* tears with Krishna Ji, constantly repeating *juz ishq namī gunjad*. Krishna Ji also seemed to be repeating the same refrain." For the full account see chapter 13 of Nizami Dehlvi, n.d., which is an Urdu translation of extracts from the Persian book *Chihil Ruzeh*, an account of the lives of all the notable Chishtiya saints and a biography of Hazrat Nizamuddin Awliya, by a Hindu prince, Raj Kumar Hardev Dehlevi.
11 al-Khatib al-Tabrizi 2006, book 1, chapter 1.
12 See Hughes 2001, 220.
13 Nasr 1987, 89–92. See also al-Ghazali's (1058-1111 CE) *Kimiya-yi Saʿadat* ("Alchemy of Happiness"), chapter 5, "Concerning Music and Dancing as Aids to the Religious Life," in al-Ghazali 2007, 55–66. See also Abu al-Fazal (1551–1602 CE) on the subject of painting and calligraphy in Abu al-Fazal 1988, 182–184.
14 Schuon 1990, 177.
15 "*Adaigi*" is an Urdu word meaning "style and manner of expression or presentation" in the performing arts.
16 In the Platonic sense, connected with the ideal plane (*ʿalam al-khayāl* or *ʿalam al-mithāl*). For a detailed description of this term, see Chittick 1994.
17 The *hasht bihisht* is a three-by-three "magic square" with eight squares around the central one. The term literally means "eight paradises," and the arrangement forms the basis of the plans for many Islamic buildings, including tombs. See Koch 2006, 26–27, 154. Numerous popular film songs and musical settings of *ghazal* poems are composed in the *rāga darbari*, which is said to have been created by Taansen in the court (*darbar*) of the Mughal Emperor Akbar.
18 See introduction to Lings 2001, where he maintains that true artistic creativity requires an action of the Spirit and that in the Greek tradition, this function was embodied by Apollo, the god of light; the muses were then further aspects of the same function. In this context, Lings maintains that it is truer to say that Apollo is not the god of light but the light of God.

19 Here, the term "man" refers to the masculine principle (and implies the feminine principle) in all humans, men and women.

20 See Lings 1986.

21 As in the inscription on the tomb of the Sufi saint Dawood described below.

22 This account, given in an extract from the book *Muqamaat e Dawoodi*, by Abdul Baqi, is included in appendix 2, at the end of the monograph *Ahwal al Sheikh Dawood Jhunniwal*, an Urdu translation of a thesis by Mohammad Haidar, written in March 1931 and privately published by Sayyid Mohammed Mohsin, in Lahore (the latter not dated).

23 According to the *abjad* system, the sum of the numeric value of the letters in the formula at the end of the inscription ("extend its shadow to eternity") gives the date of completion. We can presume that this poem was originally inscribed on the structure, though we have not found it at the site. But there are numerous similar examples from other buildings, such as the inscription at the entrance to Data Durbar, the shrine of Hazrat Ali Hujveri: *Ganj bakhsh-e faiz-e ʿalam mazhār-e nūr-e Khuda / naqisān-rā pir-e kamil kamilan-ra rahnamā* (The bestower of treasures of the bounty of the world, the manifestation of the Light of God/ The perfect mentor for the imperfect ones, a guide for the perfected ones).

24 Ardalan and Bakhtiar 1973, 74, 75.

25 See Critchlow 1976.

26 Ibid., 42.

27 Nasr 1978, 46n12. "*Hyle*" (literally, "wood") is Aristotle's term for "prime matter." Aristotle contrasted *hyle* with *morphe* (form).

28 Critchlow 1976, 7.

29 Abdul Baqi 1990.

30 Design started circa 2001; main structure largely completed by 2014.

31 Mainly Qur'anic verses that refer to the Prophet, selected by the shaykh according to the location of each inscription.

CHAPTER TWELVE

The Social and Sacred Microcosm of the *Kiiz Üi*

Space and Sound in Rituals for the Dead among the Kazakhs of Mongolia

SAIDA DAUKEYEVA

In western Mongolia, the Turkic-Muslim Kazakhs commemorate the dead in rituals involving Qur'anic recitation and mourning laments (*joqtau*) that are held in the round felt-covered dwelling, yurt (*kiiz üi*; literally, "felt house").[1] This custom, largely discontinued in contemporary Kazakhstan, has persisted among the local Kazakh community since their arrival in Mongolia in the late nineteenth century, through the socialist to the postsocialist period, sustained by their mobile pastoral way of life, cohesive kinship and lineage bonds, and syncretic worldview that blends Islam with indigenous shamanic beliefs. Among the life-cycle rituals practiced by the community, these are the most unvarying and strictly observed in their temporal, spatial, and sonic arrangement. When a person dies, ceremonies before and after the funeral are conducted in the deceased's *kiiz üi*, regardless of the time of year and location. The *kiiz üi* then serves as the main site of subsequent memorial feasts up to the seventh (*jetisi*) or fortieth (*qyrqy*) day. Religious chant by a mullah and lamentation by female relatives of the deceased are the only forms of sound expression permitted in the ceremonies, music being forbidden in this context. The spatial arrangement of the rituals inside the *kiiz üi* follows an established pattern that maps the social division of the yurt in terms of gender, age, seniority, and status and reflects the Kazakhs' sacred beliefs.

This chapter presents an ethnographic and analytical account of these rituals for the dead, exploring the social and sacred meanings of the *kiiz üi* and *joqtau*. It derives from my fieldwork in the western Mongolian province (*aimag*) of Bayan-Ölgii and in Kazakhstan between 2004 and 2015, drawing in particular on my observation of a memorial feast in the provincial center, the city of Ölgii, in August 2004; on interviews with women-mourners; and on communication with Mongolian Kazakh repatriates (*oralmandar*) in Kazakhstan.[2] As I examine how the *kiiz üi*—a seasonal nomadic dwelling among Mongolia's Kazakhs—provides a venue for the death rituals and how performance of the lament is enacted in it, I seek to explain why the rituals are held there and what role *joqtau* plays in the ritual context. I thus investigate the interplay of space and sound—vernacular architecture and mourning lament—in order to cast light on the social and spiritual connotations of the ritual practice.

Contemporary academic discourse in Kazakhstan has interpreted the *kiiz üi* as a model of the Kazakhs' social and sacred universe, a symbolic cultural space that, within shamanic and death rituals, aided the shaman and the dead soul in their transition to the other world.[3] Cross-cultural studies in ethnomusicology have furthermore indicated the significance of laments and funeral music in facilitating the deceased's passage to the afterlife and the role of the lamenter as a mediator between the living and the dead.[4] The chapter juxtaposes these academic interpretations with the testimonies of insiders and my own observations in order to form a culturally contextualized understanding of the rituals and offer an insight into the combined spatial-visual and auditory experience of their participants.

Community

The western region of Mongolia, which borders China, Russia, and Kazakhstan, is home to some 100,000 Kazakhs, mainly inhabiting the provinces of Khovd and Bayan-Ölgii. The Kazakhs of Mongolia derive originally from nomadic clans in northeastern and central Kazakhstan, notably the Kerei, Naiman, and Uaq of the *Orta jüz* (Middle Horde) clan confederation. Ancestors of present-day Mongolian Kazakhs migrated to China's northwestern region of Xinjiang in the course of the eighteenth and nineteenth centuries, seeking refuge from the Jungar attacks and Russian expansion over their territories. Subsequent political upheavals in Manchu-Qing China and Soviet Kazakhstan caused many of them from the 1860s onward to migrate over the Altai Mountains and resettle in western, or Outer, Mongolia. In 1940, the local Kazakh community gained semiautonomy in the newly created province (*aimag*) of the Mongolian People's Republic, Bayan-Ölgii. The dissolution of the Soviet Union generated a process of emigration from western Mongolia to Kazakhstan. Although many community members have since migrated to their historical homeland, the Kazakhs continue to form the majority (about 90 percent) of the province's population and occupy a prominent political status in the *aimag*.[5]

Mongolian Kazakhs share their language and aspects of their social organization and cultural practice with Kazakhs more broadly. But unlike their kin in Kazakhstan, who were sedentarized in the early twentieth century, they have retained pastoralism as an important livelihood strategy during the socialist period and after the collapse of the Soviet-backed economic system.[6] Much like the rest of Mongolia's population, many current Kazakh residents of Bayan-Ölgii engage in mobile pastoralism either themselves or through networks of relatives, migrating across the province during the year. Their residence patterns vary by season and location. In autumn, winter, and spring, people live in sheltered seasonal dwellings (*ystyq üi*; literally, "warm house"), such as log cabins and mud-and-brick houses in districts (*sum*) or cottages and multistory buildings in the *aimag* center. In early summer, rural and some urban dwellers set out on province-wide migration to highlands, spending midsummer in alpine camps (*jailau*). As they move to various locations and settle in small communities (*auyl*), their dwelling is the transportable nomadic yurt, *kiiz üi*. Those who do not participate in the seasonal migration set up yurts on the outskirts of *sum* and *aimag* centers or in the courtyards of their private houses for use as an extra living or reception space. Constructed from domestically produced material and practical in use, the *kiiz üi* is thus a prominent form of vernacular architecture in western Mongolia, integral to the Kazakhs' way of life and annual migratory cycle (fig. 12.1).

The Felt House

The round, felt-covered yurt found today among Mongolia's Kazakhs belongs to the Turkic type of tent, with a dome-shaped roof, used by the nomads of Eurasia for millennia.[7] It is composed of a wooden lattice framework (*kerege*) serving as the wall, a separate door (*esik*), bent poles (*uyq*) forming the yurt's

Figure 12.1. Yurts (*kiiz üi*). Tsengel *sum*, Bayan-Ölgii, August 2015. Photograph: S. Daukeyeva.

roof, and a wooden ring (*shangyraq*) at the top that holds the poles together and provides a ventilation hole for the smoke coming from the stove (*oshaq*, *ottyng basy*) situated in the center below. The yurt's self-supporting wooden structure is covered with layers of reed mats, felt, and canvas sheets tied to the *kerege* with hair ropes (*arqan* or *basqūr*). The size of the yurt varies according to the number of holes (*köz*; literally, "eye"; or *bas*, "head") in the rim of the *shangyraq* and the number of lattice sections (*qanat*; literally, "wing") of the *kerege*. Kazakh yurts in western Mongolia are usually quite spacious, comprising up to a hundred *köz* and six *qanat*. Regardless of its size, a yurt is easy to transport and takes about two hours to set up (fig. 12.2).

The spatial orientation of the *kiiz üi* and internal arrangement of people and objects follow a long-established pattern that reflects the Kazakhs' sacred beliefs and social hierarchy according to gender, age, seniority, and status.[8] The door of the *kiiz üi* is oriented to the east, toward the sunrise, and its back wall to the west, toward the sunset and in the general direction of Mecca. The area in the western part of the *kiiz üi* directly opposite the door is the place of honor (*tör*) designed for the master of the household and

Figure 12.2. The wooden structure of a yurt (*kiiz üi*). Ulaankhus *sum*, Bayan-Ölgii, August 2015. Photograph: S. Daukeyeva.

senior people, as well as for praying and keeping precious household objects and attributes of worship, such as the Qur'an and a prayer mat (*jainamaz*). A notional line from the entrance to the *tör* divides the yurt's space into gendered areas. The southern section of the *kiiz üi*, located to the right (*ong jaq*) as seen from the place of honor, is the male area (*erler jaghy*), which represents a public guest side and a site for conducting most life-cycle rituals. The northern section, to the left (*sol jaq*) of the *tör*, is the female area (*äielder jaghy*), which serves as a private domestic side for routine everyday activities. Women may also occupy the right section (*ong jaq*) of the *kiiz üi*, particularly in cases when their position there is considered temporary. This provision applies to guests and household members who are thought to be in a state of transition from one status to another, such as young, unmarried girls, brides, and deceased women before burial.[9] The internal space of the *kiiz üi* is further divided into upper and lower sections (*joghary jaq, tömen jaq*) to differentiate the age and status of its occupants. The upper section, west of the stove, is reserved for senior family members and respected visitors. The opposite, lower section, east of the stove, is occupied by junior family members and others of inferior status. A descending order of seniority and status thus pertains in the allocation of people and objects from west to east, or from the upper to the lower section of the *kiiz üi*.[10]

Beyond this general hierarchy, the disposition of persons and things in individual households reflects notions of lineage and inheritance. In people's discursive practice, these notions are expressed with reference to the *shangyraq*, the ring at the top of the *kiiz üi*, which serves as a symbol of home and a line of descent, being traditionally inherited and passed down the generations by the youngest son of the family (fig. 12.3). A household in which the *shangyraq* has been passed down through several generations of the family, and where the youngest son lives with his parents, is known as *qara shangyraq* (literally, "black *shangyraq*," or ancestral home), and one in which the *shangyraq* has been started anew is called *otau* (home of a young family). The spatial distribution of family members differs in these two types of household.[11]

In everyday life, then, people position themselves inside the *kiiz üi* in ways that encode various aspects of their identity and social relations within a par-

Figure 12.3. The ring at the top of a yurt (*shangyraq*). Ulaankhus *sum*, Bayan-Ölgii, August 2015. Photograph: S. Daukeyeva.

ticular household. In this sense, the domestic space of the *kiiz üi* is both flexible and formalized in that it articulates notions of gender, seniority, status, and lineage in complex and dynamic, though culturally recognizable, ways.

In the past, when the *kiiz üi* was the primary type of dwelling among the Kazakh nomads, it was the scene of many a social gathering, ritual, and music performance. In the late nineteenth century, the Russian ethnographer Petr Makovetskii observed: "The yurt is the center of all contemporary life of the Kazakh. Here he is born and grows up; here is all his domestic and social life, his crafts, poetry, and art, and here, too, his worldview is formed. In the yurt the entire life of the Kazakh with its steppe joy and grief passes."[12] Following the introduction of permanent winter dwellings in the mid-nineteenth to early twentieth century and the social transformations of the socialist era, some practices historically held in the *kiiz üi* have lapsed, while others have been transferred to a variety of venues. For example, the wedding ritual of "unveiling the bride's face" (*betashar*), traditionally performed near the threshold of the groom's yurt as a token of the bride's initiation into married life, can nowadays equally take place in a private house in a district center or at a restaurant in Ölgii city, and its spatial enactment varies in these different venues. As the architectural landscape of western Mongolia has diversified, ritual performance has adapted to the varying environment of the people's lives.

One ritual practice among the local Kazakh community, however, continues to take place primarily in the *kiiz üi*. This is the series of ceremonies conducted after a person's death.

Death Rituals

When someone dies, the deceased's body is placed in a *kiiz üi*, where it is prepared for burial and from which it is carried to the grave.[13] This is done irrespective of the time of year and location, whether in summer or winter quarters, in the country, a district or *aimag* center, or during seasonal migration. In winter, when people normally relocate to warmer, sheltered dwellings (*ystyq üi*), a yurt is specially set up to conduct the funeral ceremonies. In the city, a yurt may be placed next to an urban house (fig. 12.4). If a person dies during seasonal migration, people stop and erect a yurt to observe the custom. The deceased, irrespective of gender, age, and status, is laid in

Figure 12.4. A mourning *kiiz üi* (to the right) next to a mud-and-brick house. Ölgii, Bayan-Ölgii, August 2004. Photograph: S. Daukeyeva.

the right section (*ong jaq*) of the mourning yurt (*qaraly kiiz üi*). There, a ritual washing (*arulau*) is performed and preparations for burial (*jerleu*) are made according to the Muslim custom, which includes recitation of the *janaza* prayer by a mullah.

Before the funeral the deceased spends a night (*tünetu*) in his or her *kiiz üi*.[14] In keeping with the Muslim tradition of prompt burial, funerals are usually held on the day after death or as soon as possible. But if a person dies away from home, irrespective of time, he or she is brought home for an overnight stay or a "stop" (*eru bolu*)[15] and is buried on the following morning. During that night the family gathers in the *kiiz üi* and stays awake, guarding (*küzetu*) the deceased. Relatives, friends, and others wishing to offer their condolences to the bereaved family arrive throughout the night and in the morning and share in a ritual meal called the "guest feast" (*qonaq asy*).[16]

As the visitors enter the mourning yurt, the women of the family start to wail and lament. Conventionally, the main lamenter (*joqtaushy*), such as the mother, wife, or sister of the deceased, is joined by a group of female relatives who weep (*jylau*) or perform poetically and musically coherent laments (*joq-*

tau) to the same or different melodies ad libitum, expressing their grief in a free, arbitrary way. Female visitors may respond to their lamentation with songs of comfort or condolence (*basu aitu, uatu, jūbatu*), musically similar to or different from the *joqtau*. Such an interchange of laments occurs only when the bereaved woman and visitor first see each other after the death and is therefore known as *köris* (from "*körisu*"; literally, "to see each other"; or "*bet köru*," "to see one's face").

On the day of the funeral, as the deceased is carried away, the women wail and lament again. Their sorrowful lamentation then resumes when the funeral procession returns to the yurt. Subsequent memorial feasts are held in the same *kiiz üi* up to the seventh (*jetisi*) or fortieth (*qyrqy*) day.[17] During the feasts, animals are slaughtered, a meal is served in memory of the deceased, his or her clothes are distributed to relatives, and new clothes are given to three people who washed the body before burial. In the place where the ritual washing took place, forty candles (*shyraq*) are burnt, and after the feasts, the *kiiz üi* is moved away or dismantled, and stones are placed around that area to prevent people from stepping in.

The memorial feasts are punctuated by women's lamentation, sung upon the arrival of new visitors and when people are gathered around for the meal. Performance of the lament alternates with recitation of the Qur'an (*Qūran oqu*), prayers (*dūgha*), admonitions (*uaghyz*), and blessings (*bata*) given by the mullah,[18] which open and close individual sittings of the meal and tea. Female lamentation and male religious chant are the only forms of sound expression permitted during the ceremonies. Singing and instrumental playing, such as performance on the two-stringed lute, *dombyra*, associated with joyful occasions, are excluded from this context. During the period of mourning (*aza*),[19] which lasts for up to one year, the bereaved family is accordingly forbidden to hold or attend celebrations (*toi*) or to marry.[20]

The spatial enactment of the memorial feasts inside the *kiiz üi*, from the positioning of their participants to the placement of ritually significant objects, follows an established pattern that maps onto the general hierarchical division of the yurt in terms of gender, age, seniority, and status. While the lamenters sit on the left, female side of the *kiiz üi*, ranked from west to east in descending order of status and seniority, the mullah is seated on the other side, locating himself according to his age in relation to other men present (fig. 12.5; *see plate 9*).[21] If the deceased was the master of the household, the *tör* where he would be seated in life is left empty; above it, his photograph is

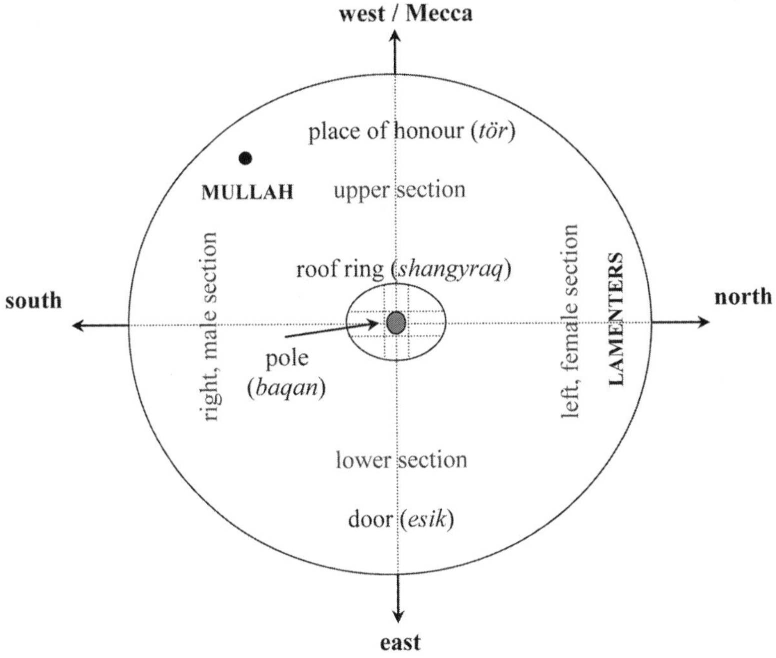

Figure 12.5. Layout of the *kiiz üi* during memorial feasts in Bayan-Ölgii. Diagram: S. Daukeyeva.

displayed, and to the left, his clothes and trappings of his horse's harness are hung along the wall (fig. 12.6).[22]

Between the main feasts, lamentation may occur in any dwelling or outdoors, where visitors meet with bereaved women. Laments may also be performed beyond the one-year mourning period, on occasions of belated condolences. This, however, happens rarely, as relatives are expected to visit the bereaved family promptly after the death.[23]

The first and successive anniversaries of the deceased (*as, jyldyq*) do not commonly feature laments and are not necessarily held in a *kiiz üi*. In the past, they took place at summer camps, in yurts and outdoors, and a favorite form of entertainment, along with horse races, wrestling, and games, was singing and instrumental contests (*aitys, dombyra saiys*).[24] Nowadays time and place vary, and *as* includes words of commemoration and recitation of the Qur'an. The meaning of *as*, though, remains the same: it marks the end of the mourning period and the resumption of normal life. Animal sacrifice,

Figure 12.6. The photograph of the deceased and his clothes hung along the wall. Ölgii, Bayan-Ölgii, August 2004. Photograph: S. Daukeyeva.

distribution of clothes, and performance of *joqtau* before *as* signify the last tribute to the deceased, and *as* itself is considered a celebration (*toi*) rather than an occasion for mourning.[25] Members of the bereaved family can now engage in entertainment and marry. Thus, the easing of the prescription as to the feast's venue coincides with the termination of the period of lamenting and relaxation of the restriction on music-making.

Kazakh Worldview and Beliefs about Death

Rituals for the dead as practiced today offer a distinctive insight into the Kazakhs' worldview and religious beliefs. Although they follow the Sunni branch of Islam, the Kazakhs have historically observed a syncretic form of religiosity that absorbed indigenous, heterogeneous beliefs (*senim-nanymdar*), such as shamanism, animism, the cult of ancestor spirits (*äruaq-tar*), and the worship of the sky deity Tengri (*Tängir*).[26] Among the Kazakh pastoralists in western Mongolia situated at the northeastern frontier of the Muslim world, where Islam has been in contact with shamanism and Buddhism, veneration of nature and animistic beliefs continue to inform everyday social life. Decades of socialism, when public worship was targeted and its practitioners persecuted, did not profoundly affect private domestic spiritual practice. Despite the resurgence of Islam among the community in the postsocialist period, stimulated by the religious training of Mongolian Kazakh students in the Middle East and the building of a few mosques in the *aimag* funded by foreign investors, there is no active institutional worship centered on mosques. People attend the mosque on rare special occasions, such as betrothal (*neke qiu*),[27] which can also be performed by a mullah elsewhere. Only a minority of local inhabitants—mainly elderly—pray, and even fewer fast during the month of Ramadan. Rather than representing a distinct social realm, observance of Islam is integrated into everyday life in the form of customs and devotional practices (*dini salt-dästurler, ädet-ghūryptar*) centered on family and communal occasions. These include recitation of the Qur'an, prayers, and blessings, as well as specific ceremonies linked to the annual and life cycles. Apart from engaging in these Islamic devotional practices, Mongolian Kazakhs observe ritualistic customs and taboos, known as *yrym* (popular belief or an omen or sign) and *tyiym* (prohibition, taboo), which are rooted in shamanism. These are believed to guard against misfortune, while their violation may entail adversity.[28]

The intertwining of Muslim and indigenous beliefs in local Islam manifests itself distinctly in the people's notions of death (*qaza, ölim*) and mourning (*aza*). Kazakhs have traditionally understood death as a return to a primordial state, a phase within the perpetual cycle of life and death.[29] Upon death, as the deceased's body ends its earthly existence, the soul (*jan*) undergoes a transition to the world of spirits (*äruaqtar*).[30] In this world, before burial, the deceased assumes the status of a guest (*qonaq*). Hence the name of the ritual meal served during this time, *qonaq asy* (literally, "guest feast").[31] The deceased's passage to the other world—or the "last journey" (*songghy sapar*)—is thought to occur within one year and comprise several stages represented by the third, seventh, and fortieth days, marked by corresponding memorial feasts.[32] Insiders variously interpret the meaning of these dates. But it is generally believed that the fortieth day has a particular significance, marking the final transition of the deceased's soul to the spirit world.[33]

The commemorative practice rests on the belief in a mutual relation between the living and the dead, which is captured in a popular saying: "If the dead are not content, the living will not prosper" (*Öli riza bolmai, tiri baiymaidy*).[34] While closely connected to their living relatives, the spirits of ancestors (*ata-baba äruaghy*) are perceived as "a threatening mysterious force."[35] The rituals performed at the feasts—animal sacrifice, the offering of food, and distribution of the deceased's clothes among relatives—are intended to honor (*qūrmetteu*) the deceased, appease the departing spirit, and provide it with everything necessary in the afterlife.[36] By appeasing the spirit and aiding its transition to that world, the feasts thereby also serve to secure the well-being of the living.

Ultimately, performance of the rituals is intended to avert the potential danger associated with death, a critical, liminal phase in the cycle of human existence, and maintain the social and universal order. Funerals and commemorative feasts are communal events attended by large numbers of people. Soon after an individual dies, relatives from near and far gather in his or her home to pay tribute to the deceased and render their support to the bereaved family. According to custom, all relatives should come and see (*körisu, bet köru*) the deceased's family within the one-year period. Collective remembrance of the dead is consistent with the community's everyday existence as pastoralists in a peripheral region of Mongolia that relies on mutual assistance and solidarity within family and clan networks. But the coming together of relatives also serves to reaffirm social bonds and re-create a sense of cohesion and unity disturbed by death.

In what follows, I consider the implications of the meanings outlined for the custom of holding the feasts in the *kiiz üi* and the tradition of women's wailing and lamentation.

The Mourning House

The significance of the *kiiz üi* in the cycle of human life is highlighted in a popular maxim: "A Kazakh comes into this world in the yurt and should leave it for eternity from the yurt."[37] For present-day inhabitants of western Mongolia, where this transportable nomadic dwelling is part and parcel of everyday life, its use within death rituals is, in part, a matter of convenience: it provides a suitable space for laying the body of the deceased and preparing it for burial, as well as a spacious area for accommodating large numbers of visitors during memorial feasts. But, quite apart from its practical purpose, holding the ceremonies in the *kiiz üi* has a ritual significance and is considered an obligatory custom (*yrym*). Like other aspects of the rituals previously outlined, it is an expression of respect (*qūrmet*) toward the dead to carry them to the grave from the *kiiz üi* and honor their memory there. Failure to observe this custom, as my informants explained, is not only disrespectful toward the deceased but a disgrace (*ūyat*) for the family. Moreover, it is believed to be a bad omen (*jaman yrym*), for it may lead to further deaths among close relatives.[38]

What lies behind these beliefs and taboos? Why is the *kiiz üi* considered a ritually significant place for seeing off and remembering the dead?

In contemporary academic literature on dwellings of the Turkic-Mongol nomads, the yurt has been interpreted as a symbolic cultural space—a model of the universe for its inhabitants, reflective of their cosmological and social views.[39] According to such interpretations, the *kiiz üi* embodies the three-layered structure of the universe in Kazakh cosmology, its floor representing the earth; its *shangyraq*, the sky; and its internal space, the human world, with the central pole (*baqan*) symbolizing the tree of life.[40] Abdesh Toleubaev in his article "The Yurt in the Kazakhs' Worldviews, Beliefs, and Rituals" draws an analogy between "the small house" of the yurt and "the great house" of the space between the earth and sky, worshiped by ancient Turks. He refers to Kazakh riddles, in which earth and sky are likened to the nomadic dwelling, and the inscription on the monument to the Turkic khan Kultegin, which depicts the rise of humankind between the Heaven and Earth.[41]

Further to the cosmological connections, researchers point to anthropomorphic and zoomorphic associations present in the morphology of the *kiiz üi*, as can be seen in the application of the names "skeleton/bone" (*süiek*), "navel" (*kindik*), "front" (*aldy*), "back" (*arqa*), "head" (*bas*), "eye" (*köz*), "ear" (*qūlaq*), and "feet" (*ayaq*) to its various structural elements. For example, the wooden frame of the yurt can be referred to as its "skeleton," and the center, as its "navel," while elements of the lattice framework (*kerege*) are called the "head," "eye," "ear," and "feet."[42]

The internal space of the *kiiz üi* is discussed in terms of the symbolism of its circular shape; its vertical division into *kerege*, *uyq*, and *shangyraq*; its horizontal division into gendered areas and four sections corresponding to the cardinal points; and the social and sacred significance of its specific areas, such as the place of honor (*tör*), the door (*esik*) or threshold (*bosagha*), the hearth (*oshaq*), and the roof ring (*shangyraq*). *Shangyraq*, symbolically standing for the whole yurt, is in particular viewed as a representation of the heavenly world of ancestor spirits. As oral tradition and early ethnographic accounts have it, during healing and divination rituals, the shaman (*baqsy*) would ascend to the *shangyraq* along the central pole (*baqan*) to seek protection and guidance of the *äruaqs*.[43] Similarly, it is said that at commemorative ceremonies, the soul of the deceased would travel along the *baqan* or a funerary lance set up in the middle of the yurt to leave this world for the next through the *shangyraq*.[44]

This symbolic strand of interpretation has been criticized by Anna Portisch in an anthropological study of a Kazakh craft tradition in Mongolia as irrelevant to the contemporary social uses and meanings of the *kiiz üi* among the local Kazakh community. The author argues that there is an interpretive disjuncture between the meanings of the *kiiz üi* in the context of economic and social livelihood in western Mongolia and its treatment in academic studies in Kazakhstan, where the *kiiz üi* no longer serves as an everyday dwelling but has gained a distinct cultural significance as an attribute of ancient nomadic ways of life and spiritual worldviews. Such treatment, she maintains, departs from the reality of social practice in western Mongolia, reflecting instead the cultural and intellectual discourse in present-day Kazakhstan, where discussion of Kazakh identity, culture, and spirituality has gained currency since independence as part of the nation-building project.[45]

Is the notion of the *kiiz üi* as a symbolic representation of Kazakh cosmological views relevant to the present-day practice of death rituals among Mongolian Kazakhs, or should the critique regarding interpretations of their craft tradition be held true in the case of this practice too?

Responses of my informants—residents of Bayan-Ölgii and repatriates in Kazakhstan, ordinary ritual practitioners and scholars—indicate that, while its meanings are differently articulated in local discourse and academic literature, the *kiiz üi* is certainly invested with a sacred quality (*kie*) by virtue of signifying the center of family and communal life, happiness and prosperity, and a space in which the living are constantly connected with their ancestor spirits. Thus, as I was told, the rituals are held in the *kiiz üi* because it is the deceased's home (*shangyraq*), hearth (*oshaq*), and threshold (*bosagha*).[46] As the Mongolian Kazakh historian and ethnographer Babaqūmar Qinayat explained to me, a person leaving this world is akin to a guest or a traveler setting off on a long journey. When going away, one should spend a night in one's *shangyraq* or *qara shangyraq* (ancestral home). Hence, the custom of laying the deceased for an overnight stay or a stop in the person's *kiiz üi* before burial. Similarly, when returning home from a journey, one should first go and greet (*sälem beru*) one's *shangyraq*. Even if there is nobody in the *kiiz üi*, upon entering, it is customary to say, "*Assalaumaghaleiküm*."[47] This is believed to be a good omen (*jaqsy yrym*) because the *kiiz üi*, the *shangyraq*, has a special quality (*qasiet*): it is a receptacle of spirits. As Babaqūmar said, "On the *shangyraq* ancestor spirits sit, all happiness sits." Other dwellings among the Kazakhs are not considered *shangyraq*.

In the *kiiz üi*, the body of the deceased is laid out in the right section (*ong jaq*) to signify the person's transition to the status of a guest or a temporary member of the household. Studies have suggested a connection between the *ong jaq* and the idea of ritualized transition in general. It is the area where childbirth once took place, where a bride is conventionally seated, where a young couple is betrothed, and where the body of a dead person is laid. As the anthropologist Nurila Shakhanova points out, "The life of an individual would begin in the right, male section of the yurt, and would also end there; its life cycle would have come full circle."[48] Positioning a body with the head turned toward Mecca and the feet toward the door aligns the deceased propitiously for passage to the other world. The tradition of carrying the dead feet first from the *kiiz üi*—nowadays through the door and formerly from below the framework (*kerege*) of the yurt[49]—relates to the belief that, while a child comes into this world head first, the deceased should leave this world for eternity feet first. The burning of candles after the funeral in the place where the washing (*arulau*) took place has a dual purpose and significance: to purify it and expel evil spirits and to betoken continuity of succession in the household. The *kiiz üi* thus provides an appropriate place for holding the rituals before the funeral by virtue of its spatially encoded and materially expressed sacred connotations.

Another, practical reason for performing the ceremonies before the funeral in the *kiiz üi* concerns the taboo against stepping into the area of *arulau*, considered to be ritually impure. About this taboo, Babaqūmar remarked that, while the movable yurt is fumigated and taken down or lifted and moved to another place, in a permanent dwelling, the floor splashed with water during the washing would have to be removed.

The ways my informants explained why memorial feasts up to the seventh or fortieth day are also held in the *kiiz üi* were broadly consistent with the interpretations suggested in the studies cited earlier.[50] Although none of them spoke of the dead soul's transition into the spirit world in terms of its ascent up the *baqan*, they nevertheless did link this transition to the physical space of the *kiiz üi*. According to Babaqūmar, until the third day, the soul is sitting on the *kerege*; up to the seventh day, on the *shangyraq*; and after the fortieth day, it leaves its home. The Mongolian Kazakh ethnographer Biqūmar Kämalashūly writes that after the third day, the *äruaq* flies away from its *shangyraq*; after the seventh day, it returns; and following the fortieth day, its material form decays.[51] The memorial feasts are thereby held in a physical environment that is associated with, and believed to be auspicious toward, the deceased's transition to the afterlife.

Another implication of holding the death rituals in the *kiiz üi*, not verbalized by the insiders, relates to the social organization of its space. As noted previously, funerals and memorial feasts are communal affairs, and their efficacy rests on collective performance of the ceremonies. Holding the rituals in the *kiiz üi* imparts a sense of communal involvement and cohesion. Here, the community of relatives appears in a formally organized spatial order that articulates relations among them and with the deceased. Associated with the idea of transition in the life cycle, the socially arranged circular space of the yurt can similarly be understood as representing a communal circle. The *kiiz üi* thus serves as an important setting for the death rituals because it embodies the Kazakhs' worldview and social universe in the way that no other kind of architecture does.

Lament

Performance of the lament (*joqtau*) enters into the complex of obligatory ceremonies (*yrym*) that are seen as an expression of respect toward the deceased. My informants stressed the compulsory nature of *joqtau*. Women in the deceased's family ought to wail and lament, even if their mourning song consists of only a few quatrains. There are no professional dirge singers in western Mongolia. If none of the women in the family is capable of performing a lament, they are taught before the memorial feasts by other female relatives or, in some cases, by a male *aqyn*, a person adept at versifying and singing impromptu. Inability of close female relatives to lament is generally disapproved of as being disrespectful and even harmful to the dead. A popular saying among Mongolian Kazakhs goes, "A woman who is unable to lament does not let the deceased rest his head in peace" (*Joqtau aita almaghan äiel ölikting basyn shiritedi*).[52] Conversely, to sing the lament outside the rituals is considered to be a bad omen, for it is capable of causing death. The beliefs and taboos attached to *joqtau* are thus similar to those associated with the *kiiz üi*. The role and meanings of the lament are equally manifold.

Joqtau communicates the state of mind (*köngil*) of the bereaved following the loss of a close person. It is a personal expression of grief intended to be shared with and responded to by the community of relatives. But it is also a ritualized performance that follows established conventions as to ritual behavior as well as poetic and sonic form. These are not learned through special training but are absorbed from childhood through observation and practice.

Despite its profoundly emotional manner, performance of *joqtau* is not entirely spontaneous and uncontrolled. When a lamenter sings, far from pouring out her feelings, she should be alert to what is happening around her and who is coming in and should respond accordingly. If she is unable to control her sung grief, a close relative calms her down, or another woman takes on the lamentation. The lamenter's ritualized behavior relies on an awareness of customs and an ability to apply it in a dynamic and interactive social context. Knowledge of how *joqtau* should be enacted in the space of the *kiiz üi* and how a lamenter should be positioned in relation to other mourners, religious reciter(s), and visitors, whose number and composition are likely to vary as the feast evolves, is also part of correct performance of the ritual. Women sit from west to east according to seniority and degree of relatedness to the deceased. This seating order (though not necessarily the geographic orientation), maintained during fortieth-day feasts in the *ystyq üi*, is also observed by Mongolian Kazakh repatriates (*oralmandar*) in Kazakhstan when holding the feast in an urban apartment. My informant Esengül Käpqyzy, originally from Bayan-Ölgii but now living in Almaty, told me that at the feast in memory of her mother-in-law in the winter of 2012, visitors approached the lamenters in order of their seating, from inner wall to entrance, according to age and status. As they greeted and hugged them, the women began wailing and lamenting, and some of the female visitors responded to them with *basu aitu*.

Esengül explained to me that, from her experience of lamenting, *joqtau* should be sung with varying words at different points in the ceremonies and to different visitors. When meeting new visitors, the lamenter should make some reference to them (e.g., "From afar, longing have you come?") and express emotions appropriate to their relationship. Specific phrases are used before and after the funeral. When the body is taken to the grave, the lamenter may sing: "To the soil is he going? To the black earth is he going down?" When meeting the relatives returning from the funeral, they sing: "Has soil covered his face? Has he been entrusted to the black earth? Will he not come back now?" When clothes are given to three people who performed the washing, the lamenter may say: "Have his clothes been given out? Have the piles [of clothes] been distributed?" The visitors, too, should know how to pay their respects to the lamenters and how to respond to their *joqtau* at the moment of "seeing each other" (*körisu*). As the visitor attempts to comfort the lamenter and stop her lamentation, the lamenter should not immediately yield, as this is considered ill-mannered, but should continue wailing for some time.

Lament and religious chant are never performed simultaneously: whereas *joqtau* is sung immediately after death, as relatives are arriving, the Qur'an is recited only after the funeral. When a mullah starts reciting the Qur'an, women stop their lamentation out of respect for the Holy Word. Esengül recollected that during the feast for her mother-in-law, new visitors came in to express their condolences while the mullah was reading a passage from the Qur'an on behalf of the deceased.[53] Therefore the lamenters and visitors waited until he had finished and only then started to sing *köris*. Sometimes, I was told, the mullah may start reciting the Qur'an to give women respite or calm down an overemotional lamentation.

Thus, performance of *joqtau* follows an established code of ritual behavior and interaction among lamenters, the religious reciter, and those coming to express condolences to the bereaved family. The interchange of laments between mourners and visitors and the alternation of mourning lament and religious chant lend themselves to dramatic enactment, as they take place at a communal, publicly attended event and are appraised by relatives.

Poetic and musical expression in the lament are similarly ritualized. *Joqtau* is based on the *jyr* verse form, with a seven- to an eight-syllable quantitative meter. The first couplet of the quatrain is usually of abstract or figurative content, while the other two lines allude to the specific instance of death.[54] The deceased is referred to in the third person or with generic names or

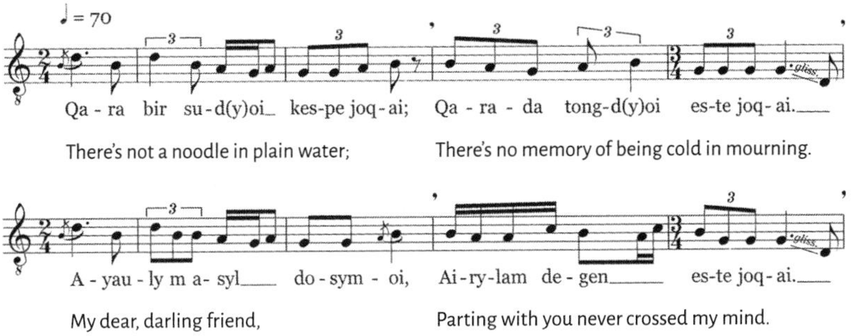

Music example 12.1. Typical *joqtau* melody: *joqtau* on the death of a friend (first strophe), performed by Tärtipkhan Uatkhan. Tsengel *sum*, Bayan-Ölgii, June 2005. Transcription: Saida Daukeyeva.

terms of affection—there is a taboo on pronouncing the names of the dead (*at tergeu*). *Joqtau* lyrics may be more or less personalized and elaborate, depending on the lamenter's versifying skill, but in composing or improvising the lyrics, she often employs poetic clichés and conventional phrases for particular cases of bereavement.

JOQTAU CLICHÉ PHRASES

Joqtau on the death of a father

High into the air the white falcon has flown, Stroking the earth with his wings.
When I come from afar, longing, Who will stroke my forehead?

Joqtau on the death of a mother

If you say "stop," I shall stop, And then I shall be quiet.
Oh, my mother, may I encircle you, Who can replace you?

Musically, *joqtau* represents an arrangement of couplets in question-response form repeated throughout the song. Typical of the local song repertoire in general, *joqtau* melodies in western Mongolia are in diatonic major modes, though, by contrast to other songs, they have the narrower range of a fifth—or, rarely, a sixth—and often descending patterns. *Joqtau*s are rhythmically unstable and irregular, being sung in a recitative-like manner with syllabic rendering of the words (see music examples 12.1 and 12.2).[55]

My informants described *joqtau* melodies as *mūngly* (sad) and *zarly* (sorrowful). Such melodies, I was told, are considered inauspicious and potentially dangerous for the living outside the ritual context, even if sung with-

Music example 12.2. Typical *joqtau* melody: *joqtau* on the death of a mother (first strophe), performed by Shäpei Shäukebai. Sagsai *sum*, Bayan-Ölgii, June 2005. Transcription: Saida Daukeyeva.

out words. In actual performance, the melody is interspersed with wailing, weeping, sobs, and exclamations.[56]

JOQTAU AND *BASU AITU* LYRICS

Joqtau on the death of a friend

There's not a noodle in plain water; There's no memory of being cold in mourning.
My dear, darling friend, Parting with you never crossed my mind.

I put on a dress With sparkling hems.
She respected me so much, She couldn't look me in the face.

On the mountaintop A *saiga* antelope is playing.
Now my friend is gone, I burn inside with molten fire.

Basu aitu (song of comfort)

Be well, my age-mate, be sound; In these times it's hard to thrive.
Life, once over, will never come back; May well-being be given to those left behind.

There's no life that does not fade; There's no iron that does not break.
Come what may, be strong; Life passed cannot return.

As several lamenters greet newcomers with their mourning songs, sometimes sung to different tunes simultaneously, and the visitors respond to them with songs of condolence and consolation, their collective lamentation gives rise to a complex polyphony of voices and sounds.

Laments and funeral music in cross-cultural traditions have been described as a means of facilitating the dead's transition to the other world, whereby the performer acts as a mediator between the living and the dead.[57] In her article about the Finnish-Karelian lament *itkuvirsi*, Elizabeth Tolbert points to elements of the ancestor cult and Eurasian shamanism inherent in the lament tradition and to the shared role of lamenter and shaman in "healing, divination, and direct communication with the spirit world through trance."[58] As she analyses the metaphorical texts of laments, their unusual musical means, and their ecstatic performance style, she interprets the lament as a "secret language of the ritual" that has a "magico-religious power," protecting the deceased during the dangerous liminal period of the rite of passage and aiding him on his way to Tuonela, the mythical land of the dead.[59]

Performance of *joqtau* could similarly be compared with the former shamanic rituals among the Kazakhs in which the shaman's singing and instrumental playing served to transport him to the other world, where he sought the aid of ancestor spirits. Both kinds of ritual practice have historically taken place in the *kiiz üi*. My interviews, though, suggest that *joqtau* is not explicitly referred to as a medium between this world and the next and that its performance is not specifically linked to the dead spirit's transition within the space of the yurt. Unlike the Finnish-Karelian and Sibe laments or Hmong funeral music, the lyrics of the Kazakh *joqtau* do not make reference to traveling to the other world or give instructions to the dead on how to reach it. Nevertheless, the insiders' statements imply that the lament is understood to have a mediatory power.

Joqtau is sung for the dead. It is a form of direct communication with the dead spirit who is believed to hear (*estiu*) it. Along with other ritual ceremonies, such as animal sacrifice, feasting, the distribution of clothes, and holding of the rituals in the *kiiz üi*, it serves to appease the *äruaq* and ensure its well-being in the other world. In a more general sense, performance of *joqtau* can be understood to be conducive to a gradual dissociation of the spirit from the living, a means by which the newly deceased relinquishes this world.[60] The obligation to sing *joqtau* and the taboo on singing it in inappropriate situations attest to a belief in the power of the lament to transport to the other world. In this respect it is not incidental that performance of *joqtau* should mark stages within the ritual conveying the idea of transition: when visitor greets lamenter, when the deceased's body is taken to the grave, when relatives return from the funeral, and when clothes are given to the people who washed the deceased.[61] It is as if, through the medium of *joqtau* sung by a close female relative, the deceased's ties to the living are loosened. And when the lament is performed in the *kiiz üi*, its meanings chime with the sacred purpose of the dwelling.

But just as *joqtau* is performed for the dead, so it is also intended for the living. By paying tribute to the deceased and helping the soul to pass into the other world, performance of *joqtau* protects the family from the danger threatening it after the person's death and secures their future well-being. The exchange of the lament and the reciprocal condolence song at the moment of *körisu* is a social act by which the family and community come together through the sharing of grief. At this moment all wrongs and discords should be forgotten, and people become reconciled. Ritual performance thus enables people to reaffirm their mutual allegiances and social bonds, and its efficacy is enhanced by its setting in the *kiiz üi*, where social relations are spatially mapped out.

Performance of *joqtau* within the death rituals also allows for a display of the family's honor and gendered responsibilities. The ability of a family to conduct the funeral and commemorative ceremonies in accordance with socially established customs, including performance of the lament, validates its right to esteem in the eyes of the community. Funerals and memorial feasts are not devoid of an element of representation, and their performance is widely discussed and judged. The role of women as mourners is dual. It is both their prerogative and their duty toward a dead relative and the family. While endorsing their power as mediators with the spirit world, comparable to men's power over communal affairs, it also serves to uphold the honor of the family, which resides primarily with its men. The obligatory nature of the female *joqtau*, appraised by relatives, thus arises in part from the fact that it enables men to assert the family's honor and propriety.

It is significant, therefore, that men exert a degree of control over women's performance of the lament. Instructive in this respect was a scene that I observed when I attended the seventh-day memorial in Ölgii in 2004. During the feast, in an interval between sittings of the meal, women, tired from their prolonged wailing, stopped for a while. Then the elder brother of the deceased, who was overseeing the feast, as he saw new visitors coming into the *kiiz üi*, prompted the women quietly: "*Jyla, jyla*" (Weep, weep). Similarly, Esengül told me that during the feast for her mother-in-law, to spare the mourners from exhaustion, her husband advised them to lament only at the coming of respected senior persons. But when they did not lament for a visitor who arrived unacknowledged and turned out to be a Qurʾan reciter for the deceased, her husband reproached them saying: "Why didn't you lament?" The interplay of gender roles underlying *joqtau* performance is one of the factors that have sustained the ritual practice.

Conclusion

Mongolian Kazakh death rituals in their spatial, literary, sonic, and performative aspects thus construct an intricate web of meanings relevant to the living and the dead. They hold a sacred significance, reflecting the people's notions of the universal order of things and their deeply rooted beliefs and taboos concerning life and death. Although insiders may not be vocal about the spiritual dimension of the rituals or may offer varying interpretations of the *kiiz üi* and *joqtau,* their ritual practice bears witness to a unifying spirituality that is integral to the people's everyday lives and is informed by a nomadic cultural knowledge passed down through the generations. The rituals also provide a context for articulating and validating social relations and reaffirming concepts and values relating to kinship, lineage, seniority, gender, honor, and propriety. An individual's expression and experience of mourning within the rituals is thus profoundly social. As the relationship with protecting spirits of the other world is understood to be in essence an extension of relations in this world, the sacred and social aspects of the rituals for the dead are closely intertwined.

Above all, performance of the rituals serves as a strategy for passing through the critical, transitional stage associated with death. Reflecting on the importance of this rite of passage, Babaqūmar Qinayat said: "Death is a chaotic state. It's the end of one process and the beginning of a new life." Imbued with dual spiritual-social significance, both architectural environment and sonic performance assume a mediatory role, and their integration in the ceremonies has an important ritual purpose. Through their enactment in the space of the *kiiz üi* and the sound of *joqtau,* the rituals create a protective microcosm for the dead and the living and thus facilitate a transition from death to the afterlife.

NOTES

1 The common rendering of *kiiz üi* in European languages as "yurt" is a misnomer derived from the Turkic word for a campsite, *jūrt* in Kazakh (see Bloom and Blair 2009, 279). For transliteration of Kazakh words and names I use the following symbols to represent specific phonemes of the Kazakh language currently written in Cyrillic: ä (for ә), gh (for ғ), q (for қ), ng (for ң), ö (for ө), ū (for ұ), and ü (for ү).

2 In particular, Özila Mūsakhan (Ölgii, Bayan-Ölgii, August 2004), Tärtipkhan Uatkhan (Tsengel, Bayan-Ölgii, June 2005), Shäpei Shäukebai (Sagsai, Bayan-Ölgii, June 2005), Aqedil Toishan (Almaty, June, October 2011), Babaqūmar Qinayat (Almaty, March–June 2012), Esengül Käpqyzy (Almaty, March 2012), Erlan Töleutai (Almaty, April 2012), Mamyrkhan Qojakhmet (Sagsai, Bayan-Ölgii, August 2015), and Baqytgül Altai (Ölgii, Bayan-Ölgii, August 2015).

3 See Ibraev 1980; Toleubaev 2000; Shakhanova 1998, 2004; Toishan 2007.

4 See Tolbert 1990; Harris 2004; Falk 2004.

5 See Qinayatūly 2007; Diener 2009.

6 See Finke 1999, 2004.

7 On the history of the yurt, see Kharuzin 1896; Marghulan 2007. On the Kazakh *kiiz üi* in western Mongolia and its differences from the Mongolian *ger* see Potanin 1881; Róna-Tas 1961.

8 See Toleubaev 2000; Shakhanova 2004, 32–62; Toishan 2007; Portisch 2007, 82–85.

9 In the past, women would also occupy the right side during childbirth.

10 On a similar social division of the Mongolian *ger* and its connections with shamanism and Buddhism see Humphrey 1974, 273–275; Pegg 2001, 171–172.

11 See Portisch 2007, 80–85.

12 Makovetskii 1893, 14, my translation. The author refers to Kazakhs as "Kyrghyz," using the ethnonym adopted in Russian and European official documents and ethnographic literature between the mid-eighteenth century and the beginning of the twentieth.

13 The following account of death rituals among Mongolian Kazakhs is based on my fieldwork observations, information elicited from ritual participants and ethnographers (particularly Aqedil Toishan, Babaqūmar Qinayat, and Esengül Käpqyzy), and studies on Kazakh funeral and commemorative practices in western Mongolia (Musakhan 1997, 61–78; Kämalashūly 1995, 61–69; 2004, 1–44).

14 The *kiiz üi* should belong to the deceased's family. In the absence of a family yurt, a *kiiz üi* of close paternal relatives is used or, in rare cases, a new yurt is acquired.

15 This word otherwise refers to halting during a nomadic migration.

16 In Kazakhstan, the custom of guarding the dead before a funeral and the meal served during this time are also known as *shildekhana*; the term is also applied to a night's watching over a newly born child and a feast on the fortieth day after birth

(see Toleubaev 1991, 112, 129). Another term for the "guest feast" is *qūdai tamaq* (God's meal).

17 Formerly, all memorial feasts up to the fortieth day among the community took place in the *kiiz üi* throughout the year. Nowadays, in winter, when weather conditions are cold and gusty, it is usually taken down after the seventh day, and the fortieth-day memorial is held in the family's "warm house" (*ystyq üi*). My fieldwork suggests that the practice of holding fortieth-day memorials in the *ystyq üi* has been adopted recently because of the increasing use of permanent seasonal dwellings among Mongolia's Kazakhs.

18 The word "*dūgha*" comes from the Arabic "*duʿāʾ*," "*uaghyz*" comes from "*waʿẓ*," and "*bata*" derives from *Al-Fatiha* (The Opening), the name of the first sura of the Qurʾan.

19 From the Arabic "*ʿazāʾ*" (consolation).

20 This prohibition is relaxed after the forty-day period if the deceased was a senior person who left behind offspring and whose passing is therefore considered more a cause to celebrate a life than to grieve a death.

21 When the fortieth-day memorial is held in an *ystyq üi* in winter, the disposition of ritual participants replicates that in the *kiiz üi* as far as practically possible.

22 The display of a photograph and clothes of the deceased during memorial feasts represents a modern adaptation of the former custom of displaying an effigy of the deceased (*tūl*) and mourning over it, which was discontinued in the late nineteenth century. Like the *tūl*, the dead person's belongings are believed to serve as a receptacle of his soul and, thus, as his substitutes (see Toleubaev 1991, 106–111).

23 Traditionally laments were sung on the seventh or fortieth day before the ritual of *at tūldau* at which the horse of a deceased man, perceived as his substitute (*tūl at*) and a receptacle of his spirit, had its mane and tail cut; and finally after one year, when the horse was sent for sacrificial slaughter. This tradition is not current nowadays.

24 For early accounts of *as* in Kazakhstan and the Altai region see Altynsarin 1870; Plotnikov 1870; Radlov [Radloff] 1989, 315–319; Qarsyūly 1991, 55, 65–66, 116–117.

25 The emotional tone of *as* may vary in individual cases. If the departed is a young person, people continue to grieve and the mood of the feast is mournful.

26 Islam was introduced in the cities of southern Central Asia during the Arab conquest in the eighth century CE and over the following centuries spread among Turkic nomads of the steppes, partly through traveling Sufi holy men. Because of their isolation from the mosques and madrasas, the pastoral communities acquired only a basic knowledge of the Muslim tenets and practices, and retained elements of shamanism, animism, and ancestor worship even after nominally embracing Islam. By the time the Kazakh Khanate was formed in the fifteenth century, Islam had been accepted as the predominant religion among the Kazakhs. Under Russian colonization in the eighteenth to the nineteenth cen-

turies, Tatar mullahs were sent to Kazakhstan to proselytize Islam as part of the policy to strengthen the influence of Tsarist administration. But the number of mullahs was later reduced and their authority restricted. This and the Kazakhs' pastoral nomadic ways of life contributed to the survival of pre-Islamic beliefs in a Muslim identity. See Valikhanov 1984, 1985a, 1985b; Olcott 1987, 18–20, 79; Akiner 1995, 17–18, 28; Aryn et al. 2007.

27 From the Arabic *nikāḥ*.

28 The nineteenth-century Kazakh ethnographer Shoqan Valikhanov, describing *yrym* in his essay, "Traces of Shamanism among the Kyrghyz [Kazakhs]," wrote: "They are those popular customs which Europeans call amongst themselves superstitions and prejudices, and which in shamanism make up the ceremonial part of their worship. [Y]rym is also the name of customs performed as omens" (Valikhanov 1985b, 62, my translation). Violation of an *yrym*, he noted, causes harm (*kesir*), such as misfortune, mass loss of animals, and disease (1985b, 51).

29 See Valikhanov 1985b, 62. The interplay of shamanic and Islamic elements in the Kazakh concept of death is reflected in the etymology of the words denoting "dead." In addition to using the original Kazakh words "*ölgen*" (dead) and "*qaitys bolghan*" (literally, "the one who has returned"), the Kazakhs also refer to the deceased as "*marqūm*," an Arab loan-word (*marḥūm*) meaning, "the one who has been shown mercy," which connotes the Islamic notion of death as mercy from Allah (see Racy 1986, 28–30).

30 The Kazakh word "*äruaq*" (pl., *äruaqtar*) derives from the Arabic "*arwāḥ*," the plural form of "*rūḥ*" (spirit).

31 Aqedil Toishan, Babaqūmar Qinayat, personal communications; Toleubaev 1991, 88–90, 112–113; Ernazarov 2003, 127–128.

32 The dates of the feasts have pre-Islamic origins (see Toleubaev 1991, 119–137). The Kazakhs' observance of these dates, especially the fortieth-day memorial, links them to other Muslim societies, where commemorative practice on these dates is similarly thought to originate in local ancient beliefs and have localized meanings.

33 A similar belief pertains to the fortieth day after birth: it is thought that on this day the newly born child is given a human soul by Tengri, and this is celebrated by the ritual of *shildekhana* (Aqedil Toishan, personal communication). Accordingly, before the fortieth day a baby may be called *qūdaidyng balasy* (God's child) and after it *adamnyng balasy* (man's child) (Babaqūmar Qinayat, personal communication).

34 Aqedil Toishan, Babaqūmar Qinayat, personal communications; Musakhan 1997, 61; Kämalashūly 2004, 7.

35 Toleubaev 1991, 112.

36 Aqedil Toishan, Babaqūmar Qinayat, personal communications; Toleubaev 1991, 112–114; Kämalashūly 1995, 61–69, Kämalashūly 2004; Musakhan 1997, 68–71.

37 See Kämalashūly 2004, 35; cf. Kochumkulova 2011.

38 Aqedil Toishan, Babaqūmar Qinayat, Esengül Käpqyzy, personal communications; Kämalashūly 1995, 66; Kämalashūly 2004, 35–36.

39 See Feagre 1979; Jukovskaya 1988; Humphrey and Vitebsky 1997; Bloom and Blair 2009.

40 An early account of the three-layered structure of the world in Kazakh shamanism and worship of Tengri is found in Valikhanov 1985b, 58. Recent treatments of the *kiiz üi* in the context of the Kazakh worldview include Ibraev 1980; Toleubaev 2000; Shakhanova 1998, 2004; Toishan 2007.

41 Toleubaev 2000, 165–166. The monument to Kultegin is located in the valley of the Orkhon River in central Mongolia and dates back to the eighth century. A line of the inscription reads: "When the blue Heaven above and the brown Earth beneath arose, between the twain Mankind arose" (Büchner and Doerfer 2012).

42 Toleubaev 2000, 166–167; Shakhanova 2004, 32–33.

43 Toleubaev 2000, 166.

44 Ibraev 1980, 44.

45 Portisch 2007, 151–187.

46 Tärtipkhan Uatkhan, Shäpei Shäukebai, Aqedil Toishan, Babaqūmar Qinayat, Esengül Käpqyzy, Mamyrkhan Qojakhmet, personal communications.

47 From the Arabic "*As-salāmu ʿalaykum*" (Peace be upon you).

48 Shakhanova 2004, 62, my translation.

49 The base (*irge*) of the *kerege* adjacent to the door in the right section (*ong jaq*) of the *kiiz üi* is thought to represent a boundary between this world and the next (Kämalashūly 2004: 35–36; Babaqūmar Qinayat, personal communication).

50 In particular, Ibraev 1980; Toleubaev 2000.

51 Kämalashūly 2004, 5.

52 Aqedil Toishan, Babaqūmar Qinayat, personal communications; Kämalashūly 1995, 66.

53 The deceased's family commonly asks a mullah or several mullahs to read the entire Qur'an for the deceased (*Qūran qatym tüsiru*) within seven or forty days after the death. Individual excerpts (suras and *āyas*) from the Qur'an are recited during memorial feasts and the rest of it is read by the mullah(s) independently elsewhere. This custom has developed relatively recently in both Kazakhstan and Mongolia.

54 Such an alternation of couplets, abstract and specific in content, is not unique to *joqtau* but is also found in other song genres, notably *qara öleng* (simple song) based on an eleven-syllable verse form.

55 See also Musakhan 1997; Sipos 2001.

56 These are often emulated even when, disregarding the prohibition, a lament is sung outside the ritual, as was the case with my informant Tärtipkhan Uatkhan recorded in audio examples 12.1 and 12.2.

57 See Tolbert on Finnish-Karelian laments (1990), Harris on laments among the Sibe of Xinjiang (2004, 113–115), and Falk on Hmong funeral music (2004).

58 Tolbert 1990, 47.

59 Tolbert 1990, 50–52.

60 Rituals for the dead are thus the converse of the rituals for the newly born, particularly the feast on the fortieth day after birth (*shildekhana*), whose purpose is to bring the child into the society of the living (Aqedil Toishan, personal communication; Toleubaev 1991, 129–130).

61 Lamentation that once accompanied the ritual of *at tūldau* (see note 23) carried a similar meaning.

PART SIX

Iran

CHAPTER THIRTEEN

Listening to Pictures in Iran

ANTHONY WELCH

This chapter will examine references to musicians and musical instruments in several key Persian texts, notably during the Timurid (1370–1501 CE) and Safavid (1501–1722 CE) periods, with a view toward elucidating the relationship between music and architecture in Iranian visual arts. To this end, I specifically consider both representations of music that form part of built environments and literary or pictorial representations of music making that take place within the built environment.

Images of Music before Islam

Written during four decades, from 980 to 1020 CE, the *Shahnameh* (Book of Kings) is Iran's great epic and the towering achievement of the poet Ferdowsi. Presenting the poetical history of Iran's monarchs before the seventh-century advent of Islam, it is a major source of information about ancient Iranian literary, visual, and musical culture. The poet speaks to us about *rūd* (resplendent music) and *sarwad* (song) and describes various instruments, including the harp (*chang*), lute (*ʿūd*), and end-blown reed flute (*nāy*). Ferdowsi notes that processions were marked by the sounds of trumpets, tambourines, and many kinds of drums: the importance of a person was often indicated by the number of instruments and accompanying performers, and music was an integral part of political meaning and display.

Among the earliest representations of musical instruments and musi-

Figure 13.1. Great Iwan, Taq-i Bustan, Kermanshah, Iran. Photo: Mehdi Khonsari.

cians are the celebrated relief sculptures at the grotto of Taq-i Bustan (literally, "Arch of the Garden") near Kermanshah in northwestern Iran. Large recessed and carved panels, dating between 590 and 628 CE, are filled with details of royal hunts. In the first of them, the shah, significantly larger than any of his companions, hunts wild boars, while singers, harpists, and flutists provide suitable musical accompaniment from the safety of royal barges (fig. 13.1). The second panel shows us an orchestra of harpists on the left side and a military band on the right. This is a huge array of musicians forming part of an imperial *kamargāh* (hunt), though they are not hunting. The repertoire of music that went with it must have been carefully planned and rehearsed long before the actual hunt took place. *Kamargāh* music was certainly different in kind and composition from a court reception, where there would have been a *nawbat* (announcement) of a few instruments, such as drums, cymbals, and horns. The hunt that took place at Taq-i Bustan was surely more extravagant and symbolic than later hunts, for it looks as if the shah was accompanied by a veritable orchestra.

To the preceding example of outdoor musical activity *represented* in a built environment (i.e., the grotto) can be added literary depictions of music *taking place* in a structure. In one of the episodes of the *Shahnameh,* the blustering and overconfident Iranian hero Bizhan has agreed to rid a wilderness region of wild boars that have been threatening its people. After his inevitable success against the beasts, he stretches out in a flowery meadow near which Manizheh, the beautiful daughter of the hostile Turanian king Afrasiyab, is relaxing with her retinue of lovely women. "The whole plain echoed with the sound of music and singing, as if welcoming his soul." Anxious to impress, Bizhan puts on every bit of his finery: his golden diadem, armbands covered in jewels, a jeweled belt, and Rumi (that is, Byzantine) cloak. He and Manizheh instantly fall in love, and she sequesters him in her royal tent, though they are hardly alone:

> She washed his feet in rosewater and musk and had an elaborate meal set before the two of them; wine was brought and the tent was cleared of everyone except Manizheh's musicians, who stood before them with lutes and harps. The ground was spread with brocade sewn with gold coins and embroidered like a peacock, and the tent was filled with the scents of ambergris and musk. Old wine in crystal goblets overcame the warrior's defenses. . . . Manizheh called for musicians; each of the young women was dressed in Chinese brocades and to the sound of their lutes, Bizhan and Manizheh passed the day in pleasure.[1]

Bizhan is happily subjected to this assault on all of his senses, and the text specifically identifies lutes and harps as the musical instruments of choice in the seduction. To them are added precious "old wine in crystal goblets," the splendid cuisine, and the sheer beauty of textiles, in the architectural framework of the royal tent. Swept away by this potent mixture of passions, neither Manizheh nor Bizhan gives a thought to the consequences.

Music in Iran and the Middle East in the Early Islamic Era

The connection between music and the built environment maintained significance into the Islamic era. The performance of appropriate music in formal aristocratic spaces demonstrated power, prestige, and aesthetic sensibilities, all attributes of kingship that extended far beyond the stories from the *Shahnameh*. Already in the reign of the Umayyad caliph Yazid (680–683 CE), rulers were eager to enhance their reputation by bringing to their courts the best contemporary musicians, and their enthusiasm for a life of luxury and display was in good part expressed in their patronage of music.

Early in the Umayyad period, music, consumption of wine, and games of chance came to be identified with a specific house, a club in Medina operated by one of the Quraysh:

> The new Caliph Yazid was passionately addicted to music; a lover of hawks and hounds, of apes and leopards; and fond of merry feasting. His appetite for revelry was shared by his courtiers and the men he set in power. It was in his reign that music appeared at Mecca and Madina. One of the fashionables of Quraysh took a house for the use of his friends as a club, and provided it with chess and dice and other means of pastime. People began to learn to play musical instruments, and to drink wine openly.[2]

In the context of the Qurʾan and the Prophet's Hadith (Traditions), the activities of these Umayyad notables, including wine drinking, gambling, idol worship, and music making, as well as their associated specific architectural spaces in Mecca and Medina, are subject to moral condemnation.[3]

In a painting from the Umayyad desert palace of Qasr al-Hayr al-Gharbi in Syria, dating from 724 to 727 CE, a middle panel is occupied by a mounted archer pursuing two deer, while an upper panel shows a lute player and a *nāy* player standing under two arches, presumably an explicit reference to the costly architectural space in which court musicians would typically be performing. Images of musicians are one of the principal motifs on later ceramics, metalwork, textiles, and manuscript illustrations: musical performance was one of the great pleasures of court life, and it seems to have been crucial in defining the aristocratic class. Music making was shown in a variety of venues and architectural contexts: in gardens and garden pavilions, on rooftops, in tombs, and at aristocratic or royal entrances and exits, like the *nawbat*. Musicians could become famous and wealthy like the master Ziryab in ninth-century Córdoba who transformed not only music but also taste, manners, aesthetics, and social graces in Islamic Spain.

In a blue-glazed twelfth- to thirteenth-century bowl from Iran (fig. 13.2), a solitary lutenist sits in the center of a circle of listeners who are sharing fruit from two bowls, a representation of music making and of musician-audience proxemic relations that suggests the built environment of a convivial party. An ornamental Kufic inscription circles the interior, while the exterior is decorated with a love poem. Seljuq Turkish emirs of the eleventh,

Figure 13.2. Ceramic bowl with musician and verse of Persian lyric poetry, Iran, late twelfth to early thirteenth century. Metropolitan Museum of Art, 57.61.16; Henry G. Leberthon Collection, gift of Mr. and Mrs. A. Wallace Chauncey, 1957, OASC.

twelfth, and early thirteenth centuries supported courts throughout their domains in the Middle East and Iran, each court vying with all the others to attract the best talents. Singers in these venues entertained convivial parties of the sort described in the *Kitab al-Aghani*, the tenth-century encyclopedia of music and musical performance by Abu al-Faraj al-Isbahani, which constitutes one of the most important documents of Abbasid cultural life in Baghdad.[4] That culture collapsed under the onslaught of the Mongols when they besieged and captured Baghdad in 1258 CE.

Il-Khan Dynasty

The Mongols brought with them an instrumental tradition that was also closely linked to alcohol consumption and parties and that defined drinking spaces. Leading an embassy from Louis IX to the Great Khan Möngke between 1253 and 1255 CE, the Flemish monk Willem van Ruysbroeck (ca. 1210–ca.1279 CE) wrote a vivid and credible report that contains tantalizing hints about Mongol musical practices in the thirteenth century:

> There is always *cosmos* [*kumiss*, or fermented mare's milk] near the [Mongol] house, before the entry door, and beside it stands a guitar-player with his guitar. Lutes and vielles such as we have I did not see there, but many other instruments which are unknown among us. And when the master begins to drink, then one of the attendants cries with a loud voice, "Ha!" and the guitarist strikes his guitar, and when they have a great feast they all clap their hands, and also dance about to the sound of the guitar, the men before the master, the women before the mistress. And when the master has drunken, then the attendant cries as before, and the guitarist stops.[5]

Willem does not seem to have been impressed by the music, though he did note that consumption of *kumiss* "greatly provokes urine."

In addition to performing on string instruments (lutes, vielles, zithers, and guitars), the Mongols used reed pipes, drums, and flutes. Despite the attention to ritual music, representations of musicians, musical performance, and their related built environments are rare under Mongol patronage. In one painting from a *Shahnameh* manuscript produced in Shiraz (rather than Tabriz, which was the capital of the Mongol Il-Khanate in Iran) about 1330 CE, Bahram Gur sits under a tree and strums a large lute, while he nonchalantly prepares to deal with an approaching witch. However, technically and artistically impressive illustrations from Il-Khan manuscripts, such as the 1306–1314 CE *World History of Rashid al-Din*, the circa 1335 CE Great Mongol *Shahnameh*, or the *Kalila and Dimna* animal fables of similar date and provenance, are devoid of depictions of musical instruments, identifiable musicians, or their performance spaces: instruments and musicians were presumably considered insignificant.

Timur and Timurid Princes

Timur's (Tamerlane's) invasion of the Middle East and Iran in the late fourteenth century brought major changes to the patronage of music and depictions of performance. His sons, grandsons, and other princes of Timurid lineage were installed as governors in Herat, Shiraz, Tabriz, Isfahan, and other Persian cities, and they lavished attention on artists and provided sumptuous support for the arts. Rival princes sought recognition and reputation, and through their competition in this so-called Century of Princes (from the late fourteenth to early sixteenth centuries), Iranian cities experienced remarkable cultural activity, especially revolving around palaces and aristocratic residencies. Royal and aristocratic patrons vied with each other for exceptional talent, whether in sports, crafts, music, manuscript painting, or calligraphy, and they were proud to announce their successes and loath to let it be known when they failed. Two of the most active and well-trained princes were Giat al-din Baysongor (Baysunghur, 1397–1433 CE) and his brother Ibrahim (r. 1415–1435 CE), sons of Timur's son and successor, Shahrokh Mirza (1377–1447 CE). The contemporary chronicler Dawlatshah recounts Baysunghur's formidable achievements as a patron and practitioner of many arts, including music:

> He possessed both beauty and perfection, good fortune and propitious luck; in patronage of the arts and artistic ability he was renowned throughout the world. During his time calligraphy and poetry gained currency, and artisans and literati, hearing of his reputation, entered his service from all regions and areas. . . . He strove to create opulence and rewarded his comrades and companions with exquisite objects.
>
> It is related that during Baysunghur's time Khwaja Yusuf Andigani had no equal in all the world in recitation and singing. Khwaja Yusuf's Davidic voice pierced the heart, and his Chosroic melody augmented the agony of passion. Sultan Ibrahim b. Shahrukh in Shiraz several times asked [his brother] Baysunghur for Khwaja Yusuf, but he refused. Finally he sent 100,000 dinars in cash to Prince Baysunghur [in Herat] to send him Khwaja Yusuf. In reply Sultan Baysunghur sent this line:
>
> "We do not sell our Joseph. You keep your black silver."[6]

Although the brothers exchanged manuscripts, verbal niceties, and precious objects, the worth of Khwaja Yusuf was beyond price.

Under the patronage of the Timurid princes, manuscript illustration flourished, and some paintings contained musical images. In 1429 CE, Prince Baysunghur commissioned a sumptuous copy of the animal fables of *Kalila and Dimna*. The first folio shows Baysunghur enjoying an elaborate garden party as carefully laid out as a formal reception indoors. He wears a golden crown, sits on elaborate carpets, and holds a gold cup with wine drawn from one of five bottles and a large basin of wine under the portable golden table. He is regally entertained by a harpist at the bottom of the page, a *kamāncheh* (bowed fiddle) player at the left, and a lutenist in the lower right, beside whom is a singer with his right hand raised to guide his singing. Instruments and their players are precisely rendered, and the prince is watching over the event with the knowledgeable air of a connoisseur of music as well as of wine and good parties. Although we do not know what was being performed, we know that it must have been of the highest quality. From the evidence of other paintings we can be all but certain that this is a portrait of the prince himself who is intently listening to the singing of the gifted Yusuf, whom Baysunghur had refused to relinquish.

Musical performances often took place in buildings as well as in gardens, where sunshine, blossoming trees, and rippling streams added to the ambience of a perfect afternoon. Another mid-fifteenth-century Timurid painting, unusual for being on silk rather than on paper, is a large and lavish depiction of luxurious youth. It is not part of a manuscript but rather a single page, originally mounted in a large album of pictures and calligraphies. An aristocratic couple reclines under a flowering tree in a garden. A male servant pulls off the prince's boot; a female musician plays the *kamāncheh*, and we can infer that the brilliantly colored parrot joins in the song. As in the previous painting, we can suggest that the prince is Baysunghur. The painter would have been keen to represent his patron favorably, and the portrait here resembles Baysunghur's features in the 1429 *Kalila and Dimna* manuscript: a round face, almond-shaped eyes, small mouth, and sometimes, though not always, the hint of a delicate moustache. It is a limited and often-repeated iconography of lovely companions, pitchers of wine, blossoming trees, sweets and fruit to eat, and bird song and music in the lavish frame of a sumptuous garden: their senses must have been delighted. The princely image in this painting is a carefully constructed ideal bringing together youthful features, flowing outlines, sumptuous clothing, erotic associations, and the soul's longing for

God. It is in large measure a language of love, whether in melody or words. Sinuous beauty is a much worked ideal in early Timurid painting, and the image of ideal loving couples remains one of its fixed emblems until the last decades of the fifteenth century. Its melodic implications would have been obvious to those who were portrayed: we do not know what music was performed here, but we can be sure that it was intended to convey "the agony of passion" to which Dawlatshah refers.

Behzad

Given less to spiritual imaging and more to the representation of an identifiable, solid, and interconnected world was Master Kamal ud-Din Behzad of Herat, who flourished from around 1480 to 1535 CE. His gifts of precise representation and measured composition transformed the canons of Iranian painting. He also provided some of the most careful and accurate depictions of musical instruments and performance in formal and well-defined architectural spaces. Most celebrated is the frequently reproduced double-page frontispiece to one of the classics of Iranian literature, the *Bustan* of Saʿdi. In a 1488 CE copy of this text housed in the Egyptian National Museum in Cairo, Behzad depicts a celebration at the royal court of Sultan Husayn Bayqara (r. 1470–1506 CE), a direct descendant of Timur and the last of the great Timurid rulers of eastern Iran. In the upper-right corner of the double page an elderly woman listens to a flute played by an itinerant musician hoping for a meal. Both she and the musician are appropriately located in a humble outbuilding. Elsewhere, servants are preparing food and drink for the assembled worthies. Behzad presents us with compelling images of working people who are not the idealized aristocrats of early Timurid art; instead, Behzad portrays cooks, peasants, servers, drunks, and bouncers, among others. The party is presided over by Sultan Husayn, shown in the middle of the left-hand page; the sultan extends a white rose to a young man in dressed in blue. In the lower right, another youth in blue sings from a book, and he is joined by a seated, singing man in white. An inebriated youth in green has collapsed in a stupor, and his cap rolls on the ground. Everyone is well past the point of polite behavior except for the sultan, the singers, and a musician who is concentrating on playing an enormous lute that almost completely conceals him. The gifted patron presides over a complex palace architecture of intersecting planes and brilliant colors that reverberates with sound and with rollicking humor. And among the working class, eager to please and earn their keep, are the musicians. More than any other Persian painter, Behzad brought the imagery of musical instruments and the concentrated labor of performance into the repertoire of Iranian painting. His work is therefore a turning point, and it parallels the attention that chroniclers of the early seventeenth century, such as Eskandar Monshi and Qadi Ahmad, give to poets, painters, and musicians in their histories of the Safavid monarchs.[7] Musicians are members of the entertainment world; they are a valued and even essential part of court life, and their music helps define royal space. Indeed, with Timurid and especially Safavid patrons, they become appreciated as part of what defines their princes' worlds.

Music and Art under the Safavids (1501–1722 CE)

In a painting from the *Shahnameh* (ca. 1522–1544 CE) compiled for Shah Tahmasp (r. 1524–1576 CE), the great hero of the *Shahnameh,* Rustam, rescues his king Kai Kabud from the demons of Mazandaran. There is a rush of loyal followers around the huge, ornate throne. Amid all the jubilation, a tambourine player, a *nāy* player, and a lutenist try to make themselves heard. The ubiquity of these figures suggests that kings and champions regularly traveled with a basic complement of attendant musicians, just in case they might be needed to provide background music for memorable events such as this one. Under the patronage of Safavid kings and princes, calligraphers and painters enjoyed particular status, so much so that their lives and individual proclivities became suitable for commentary. For instance, the painter of a picture from the *Shahnameh* for Shah Tahmasp was Aqa Mirak (1520–1576 CE), about whom we learn some tantalizing details from the Safavid chronicler Eskandar Monshi, writing in the early seventeenth century:

> Aqa Mirak Esfahani, an eminent *seyyed* and an outstanding artist, became the shah's personal friend and intimate companion. [The shah was] an excellent artist, presumptuous though it is of me to include his name in the list of the artists of the period. The shah was [also] the pupil of the celebrated artist Sultan Mohammad. From his youth, the

> [shah] had shown great interest in painting, and artists like Behzad and Sultan Mohammad, who were at the top of their profession, used to work in the royal library.[8]

Eskandar Monshi also turns his attention to Shah Tahmasp's nephew Ibrahim, a multitalented and gifted patron and practitioner not only of visual arts but also of music:

> Sultan Ibrahim Mirza [was] a most talented and cultured man, who wrote a fine *nastaʿlīq* hand, was a skilled miniaturist, an outstanding musician, proficient in the art of composing rounds, the pupil of Mowlana Qasem Qanuni in the art of composing ballads, an accomplished player of string instruments, and proficient in the crafts of carpentry, and the manufacture of musical instruments.[9]

So while Eskandar Monshi devotes a number of pages to describing the lives and achievements of painters, including the shah, he only briefly mentions musicians other than Prince Ibrahim, whose virtues are too many to be ignored. Nevertheless, Shah Tahmasp seems to have evinced a certain wariness or even an outright hostility toward music and musicians, and the shah's real feelings revealed themselves sometimes with brutal clarity. The reasons for his anger seem to come from distrust and from a skewed recognition of the power of music:

> Since Shah Tahmasp always eschewed all practices forbidden by religious law, musicians found little favor with him. He fired most of those who already had employment at court. . . . The shah had the idea that perhaps the royal princes, by associating with them, might begin to pay too much attention to music, and that they might corrupt the emirs who were their moral tutors and guardians and thus generate a general demand at court for such forbidden pleasures.[10]

The precarious nature of music composition and performance at the shah's court is underscored in another nearly contemporary source, the treatise of 1606 CE by Qadi Ahmad, a respected official at the Safavid court, in his brief biography of the unfortunate Mawlana Qasim Qanuni:

> [The Mawlana] was equally famous as a performer on the *sāz* and as a theorist. . . . In those days, for fear of the shah, none dared listen to music or keep a singer. . . . [Prince Ibrahim] built for him an excellent

> house in the Panj-bagh of the Chahar-bagh. The musician performed for him every morning and evening, and his fame spread far and wide. . . . He was an excellent player on the *ṭanbūr,* and his disgrace was followed by the order of the shah that all players and singers, and in particular Qasim Qanuni, should be put to death.[11]

A few musicians managed to retain positions, but they were evidently less valued than painters and calligraphers, about whom there is more precise information. The disfavor in which their profession fell under Shah Tahmasp also affected the art of manuscript painting, so that the representation of musical instruments and performers is scarcer than it might otherwise have been. Plagued by nightmares and infused with guilt, the shah regularly issued proclamations of personal and moral regeneration as a means of defending Iran from its external enemies and its internal weaknesses. He rejected the consumption of drugs and alcohol and publicly renounced the visual and musical arts as distractions from important affairs of state. His hostility became most pronounced in 1556 CE when he issued an *Edict of Sincere Repentance* rejecting uncontrolled passions and lumping together music, dancing, and singing with the consumption of alcohol: they were subject to the strictest interpretations of Shiʿi orthodoxy. He fired most of those who already had employment at court, and only a very few musicians managed to retain positions of any sort after 1556. But even if the role of musicians in court circles became much more circumscribed after the promulgation of the *Edict,* they could still be represented in illustrations of classic Iranian texts. Ironically, some of the finest pictorial renderings of musicians and instruments appear in the mid-sixteenth century when the profession is suffering the most, both in how it is practiced and in how it is represented. Here, doctrinal critical attitudes toward music are at least partly responsible for music's visual celebration, whereby the music-architecture nexus becomes transformed to a purely visual frame. To some extent, they are also conducive to the prominence given to music in interior spaces, where music becomes invisible and inaudible to the general public.

One example keenly makes this point. King Zahak is the personification of evil in the *Shahnameh*. The devil has caused two snakes to grow from his shoulders, and they hiss and torment him and demand daily meals of human brains. When Zahak is finally captured by the hero Faridun, he and his snakes are chained for all eternity deep in the interior of the massive Mount Damavand (*see plate 10*). The illustration by the great painter Sultan Muhammad from the Shah Tahmasp *Shahnameh* (ca. 1522–1544) shows Zahak in a mountain cave; dragon-shaped clouds sweep above him; his feet and arms are chained. But despite the horror of this event, elegant youths parade through the mountain; most of them take time out from this primeval drama to hunt with falcons or to wander through the twisting crags of rock. Their graceful horses wait patiently at the lower right, and opposite them a musician plays an elegant long-necked *ṭanbūr*. Faridun has just saved Iran from an utter evil, but this musician calmly sings an appropriate lyric (perhaps the very passage from the *Shahnameh* itself) that seems to give no hint of the near catastrophe. It is as if there are two episodes in a divided space: Faridun, his immediate followers, and Zahak fill the upper half of the page, while the lower half is occupied by the grandees of the court, who are not aware that anything significant has transpired.

In a painting by Sultan Muhammad's son Mirza ʿAli from a 1539–1543 manuscript of the *Khamsah* of the poet Nizami, Shah Khusraw's court singer, Barbad, rehearses a song to be performed for the shah's beloved, Shirin. The musician sits next to a polygonal pool near the center of the court and practices on his elegantly decorated *chārtar*, a four-string lute. He is accompanied only by a tambourine player. The courtyard space is convivial, filled with conversation and activity and certainly not quiet. This may be one of the most accurate depictions of Shah Tahmasp's entourage—when the king was not yet thirty years old and still fond of elaborate architecture, garden parties, and complex manuscript paintings. Though we do not know his name, this contemporary personification of Barbad is obviously intended to represent a distinguished Safavid master of this art and the best available lutenist at the royal court.

In another painting in the style of Mirza ʿAli, an exaggeratedly skinny, sinuous youth is portrayed sitting beside a stream in a simple landscape with gold sky. He is playing on the *kamāncheh* and is likely a known musician, though he is not identified by name. He is no longer a member of a group, nor is this portrait part of a manuscript illustration. Instead, it is a single page, separate from a text, that may have been included in an album of paintings devoted to music. The youth may be an aspiring soloist whose portrait is being painted as a gift for an admiring patron (*see plate 11*).

Music and the *Divan* of Hafiz

For the first twenty years of his long reign, the Safavid monarch Shah Tahmasp (r. 1524–1576 CE) was a passionate patron of the visual and musical arts. The chronicler Eskandar Monshi reports that the arts were his chief joy in life: "Whenever the shah could relax from the affairs of state, he spent his time painting."[12] Of the painters who worked at his court in Tabriz, the most notable was Sultan Muhammad, who contributed three illustrations to a copy of the *Divan* of Hafiz made for Tahmasp's younger brother Sam Mirza between 1526 and 1527 CE. These include two of the most impressive and informative paintings of the practice and performance of music in an architectural setting at the Safavid court. Folio 86v (*see plate 12*) shows a prince, presumably Shah Tahmasp, presiding over the *ʿĪd al-Fiṭr,* the feast ending Ramadan, the annual month of fasting. It begins as soon as the *hilāl* (crescent moon) is sighted, and on the roof of the ornate garden pavilion we see three men in ostentatious prayer, gazing piously at the crescent moon just barely visible in the upper left. Protected by two bodyguards, the princely patron is enthroned under an *īwān,* a golden arched vault, and below his feet is inscribed the name of the painter, Sultan Muhammad. All but one of the participants is male, while a solitary woman surreptitiously peers from a curtained second-story window at the right. Seated men are opulently dressed and welcome the food and drink being conveyed to them by servants at the left and in the lower right. The feast takes place at dusk in a garden replete with roses in full bloom. Inscribed on the octagonal frieze at the top of the polygonal pavilion is a verse from the *Divan* of Hafiz:

> Roses and friends eagerly await, for it is the time of ʿId.
> Wine bearer, behold the refulgent moon in the king's respondent
> face and bring wine!
> He is fortunate, a noble ruler, O God, spare him from the evil eye.[13]

The verses identify event and participants, and the garden setting defines the royal architecture. A fence separates the inner circle of celebrants from a wider curve of guests, most of them talking and eagerly awaiting food and drink. It is a deceptive garden, not earth or grass, but rather carpet, the middle ground revealing a green carpet and the lower part of the scene covered by a black floral carpet filled with flowers. To the far left is a quintet of musicians, two playing lutes, one playing the *nāy*, and two playing the tambourine. As with musicians performing at social functions, their music is presumably barely heard despite their best efforts. Their placement seems to reflect seniority: concealed by their instruments, the tambourine players are the youngest and are barely visible; somewhat more visible, the *nāy* player is vigorously striving to be heard, but he is largely concealed by one of the lutenists, keenly aware of his seniority and reputation, who is concentrating on being heard by the king. It is a complex event, mixing architecture, music, and convivial party. Perhaps Sultan Muhammad has produced actual portraits of the individual musicians and guests so that this representation of the lutenist shows us Shah Tahmasp's most highly regarded classical musician in the early days of the shah's reign.

Less complex is folio 67 from the same 1526–1527 *Divan* of Hafiz. A young man and young woman in a verdant garden are entertained by two dancing women with castanets. In the lower right a middle-aged performer on the *nāy* and a very youthful tambourine player provide rhythm and melody for the dancers, while movement and song are matched by swooping birds turning in the air (*see plate 13*). A third page from the 1526–1527 *Divan* of Hafiz is the richest and most diverse of these paintings of music making (*see plate 14*) in an elaborate architectural space. It is also signed by Sultan Muhammad and bears a single inscription at the top of the picture: "The angel of mercy took the reveling cup and tossed it down, as rose-water, on the cheeks of houris and angels."[14] On a mundane level, the polygonal building is an upscale tavern, but on an elevated higher level it is a vision of spiritual transcendence. Contained within an ornamental band, five angels cavort on the roof and exchange food and wine. Directly below them in a window niche is a white-bearded man reading a book; this may well be a humorous representation of Hafiz, the mystical poet himself, who is astonished by the activities going on around him that have been stirred to life by his poetry. Leaning over from the balcony, a server hauls up a jug of wine, and beside him, an experienced drinker initiates an anxious innocent into bibulous joys. On the ground floor, a tough-looking server in a red jacket dips a jug into a huge vat of wine to give to the man in blue who comes forward with a jug and a tally sheet. Outside the tavern, a white-bearded elder gives wine to a new drinker, beside whom is an outraged customer so drunk and so angry (at the poor quality of this vintage?) that his turban is falling off. The grassy space outside the tavern wall is filled with frenzied musical activity. An enthusiastic *nāy* player responds to a tambourine accompaniment. At the far left is a staggering white-bearded dancer dressed in orange and green. Above him is a classical Iranian musician, calm and concentrated on playing his *kamāncheh*, but beside him is a worried tambourine-player who is face-to-face with three *qalandārs* ("itinerant pilgrims"), one banging a tambourine, the other two vigorously clapping, and all of them wildly singing.[15] This early sixteenth-century unrestrained, furious trio is directly and deliberately competing with the more conventional and sedate musicians for attention and reward. From the angels on the roof to the wild men on the ground, this is a raucously funny but profound painting that captures the ambiguity in Hafiz's mystical poetry. A straightforward legalistic approach to this event might have focused on the painter's indulgence in ornate architecture, which is otherwise inveighed against in various hadith. Likewise, it could have condemned the prince's party and the tavern keeper's apparent lack of official approval as breaking all the rules about alcohol, dancing, and music. But to Hafiz, nothing is broken, for these are all metaphors, reflections of mystical verities, and the painting is really about different ways to approach the divine. Sultan Muhammad's picture is perhaps the richest source in all Iranian art for the contemplation of architecture amid the varieties of music, musicians, and musical performance, and it evokes the power of music to lead a viewer toward profound transcendence.

NOTES

1 Ferdowsi 2007, 311–313.
2 Schroeder 1955, 212.
3 These remarks may, however, have been effective Abbasid (650–1258 CE) propaganda against the Umayyads.
4 See al-Isbahani 1952.
5 Van Ruysbroeck 1900, 62–63.
6 Quoted and translated in Thackston 1989, 22–23.
7 See Monshi 1978; Qadi Ahmad 1959.
8 Monshi 1978, 270.
9 Ibid., 311.
10 Ibid., 281–282.
11 Qadi Ahmad 1959, 163–164.

12 Monshi 1978, 280–281.
13 Translation from Welch 1976, 67.
14 Translation from ibid., 63.
15 Depictions of *qalandārs* are chiefly preserved in albums (notably Hazine 2153) compiled for Bahram Mirza, the brother of Shah Tahmasp, in the Topkapı Saray Museum, Istanbul. Many of them bear attributions to one Muhammad Siyah Qalam and challenge the norms of fifteenth-century Timurid painting. They show outlandish, even frightening, figures from the distant steppes of Central Asia.

CHAPTER FOURTEEN

Of Mirrors and Frames

Music, Sound, and Architecture at the Iranian Zūrkhāneh

FEDERICO SPINETTI

An enduring and yet continually evolving historical institution in urban Iran, *zūrkhānehhā* (plural of *zūrkhāneh*) are the gymnasia that provide the locale for training in and practice of the "sport of the ancients" (*varzish-i bāstānī*), an indigenous Iranian athletic discipline that entails a combination of martial arts and strength training exercises and that is performed to the accompaniment of drumming and sung poetry in conjunction with forms of Shiʿi worship.[1] The popularity of *zūrkhāneh* practice in contemporary Iran remains comparatively marginal vis-à-vis sports of mass appeal, such as soccer or freestyle wrestling, and is not spread equally in all sectors of society. Nevertheless, active *zūrkhānehhā* are present in most Iranian cities and towns and continue to attract a lively community of practitioners. Such ongoing relevance has come under the scrutiny of current scholarship in Iranian and Islamic studies emphasizing the social, historical, ideological, and religious significance of *zūrkhāneh* sports.[2] In this chapter, I consider sound environment and music, aspects that, despite their centrality to the performance of the "sport of the ancients," have received scarce attention in existing scholarship.[3] I approach this topic from the specific angle of the relationship of music and sonic performance with the built environment. I argue that such a relationship is vital to an understanding of the lived experience of both space and sound at the Iranian *zūrkhāneh*. In particular, I identify two distinct yet intertwined levels of signification on which music and architecture operate and converge: that of "mirroring" and that of "framing." I deploy these two metaphors as a theoretical model to examine, respectively, symbolic-referential and performative-pragmatic processes of meaning production in architecture and music. While this interpretive grid is here specifically applied to the Iranian *zūrkhāneh*, this study aims to highlight on a more general level the significance of lived architectural space for an understanding of musical performativity and meaning and, more broadly, of auditory culture and experience. The materials and reflections presented in this chapter are based on fieldwork comprising a number of trips to the area I made between 2006 and 2008. As part of my ethnographic research, I visited several gymnasiums across Iran, including those in major cities, such as Tehran, Mashhad, and Isfahan, as well as smaller centers, such as Kashan, Yazd, Sanandaj, Sabzevar, and Quchan.

Zūrkhāneh affiliates include male amateur athletes of all ages who attend the gymnasium both for their routine workouts and for social activity. Gymnasiums have one resident singer-musician, called a *murshid*, who not only provides music performance but also holds a leadership role within the community of athletes.[4] The schedule of workout sessions may vary, with the most active *zūrkhānehhā* opening twice a day (early morning and evening) several days a week, allowing athletes to attend at their desired time. Typically a single session is held on Fridays, holidays, and commemorative days and attracts numerous guests and visitors.[5]

While it appears that *zūrkhānehhā* are historically linked to bazaar professions and the lower strata of society—a feature that partly continues to this day—their social makeup now includes individuals from a variety of backgrounds, including educated professionals and members of the religious establishment. Within the *zūrkhāneh* community (*jamʿiyyat*), affiliates organize themselves according to a hierarchical structure that in many respects resembles that of Sufi brotherhoods and that disregards the everyday social or economic status of members, instead configuring ranks on the basis of seniority and experience, as well as ethical and spiritual authority.[6] Members ideally cultivate an ethos of self-discipline and moral rectitude molded on the Islamic chivalric code known as *javānmardī* (Arabic, *futūwa*), thus promoting a combination of bodily strength with values such as humility, self-abnegation, and commitment to social and moral justice. This ideal is in the first place embodied by a code of etiquette that includes the respect and obedience paid to elderly athletes and the *murshid*, as well as the ritual of *rukhsat*—the request for permission that athletes seek from veterans and the *murshid* before they address the attendees with a speech or perform an individual exercise.[7] Mystical and Sufi overtones are also present, with an emphasis on taming the appetites of the mundane self (*nafs*) in favor of the spiritual reawakening of the "soul" (*rūh*). This understanding of bodily discipline as a vehicle of moral and spiritual perfecting is epitomized in the figure of the *pahlavān*, the noble wrestling "champion" who, despite the decline of wrestling in *zūrkhāneh* practice since the 1930s, continues to provide a powerful role model in *zūrkhāneh* discourse and imagination. Quite predictably, the *javānmardī* ideal fits the actual lives of some *zūrkhāneh* practitioners better than it does those of others. It can also be at odds with perceptions among the Iranian public, where the reputation of the *zūrkhāneh* often oscillates between contrasting representations, that is, as a hub of moral qualities or as a lair of thugs and troublemakers. Nevertheless, *javānmardī* certainly remains a vital notion not only in the hierarchical organization of *zūrkhāneh* communities but also in their self-representation.[8]

While there is little doubt that the association with the *javānmardī* ethos goes back to the premodern history of the *zūrkhāneh*, contemporary readings of its relevance for *zūrkhāneh* identity tend to gravitate toward discursive constructions and historical narratives that have coalesced in the course of the twentieth century. Such narratives have been elaborated and sustained within both the *zūrkhāneh* community and Iranian scholarly and state official discourse. In particular, with the advent of the modernizing and nationalistic thrust of the Pahlavi dynasty, the *zūrkhāneh* and its cultivation of *javānmardī* values have become inextricably linked to cultural nationalism. In part, the *zūrkhāneh* was regarded with suspicion because of its association with Qajar patronage and its perceived potential for political subversion, and it was targeted as an old-fashioned institution that required modernization. This was achieved primarily by eradicating traditional Iranian wrestling (*kushti-yi pahlavānī*) from the gymnasia and promoting freestyle wrestling regulated by modern bureaucratic sport institutions; these developments helped transform the *zūrkhāneh* from a breeding ground for professional wrestlers in premodern times into a gymnasium devoted almost uniquely to what became known since the 1930s as the "sport of the ancients." As part of the same modernizing process, however, the *zūrkhāneh* was reimagined as a testimony of cultural heritage, with associated historical narratives centering on its role in Iranian national history, particularly as a bulwark of heroic resistance against foreign invasions since pre-Islamic times.[9] This reading of the *zūrkhāneh* as a shrine of Iranian heroic values has become pervasive in contemporary identity perceptions. It has intersected with the time-honored ideological universes both of Sufism and Islamic mysticism—often linked to the veneration and memorialization of the *zūrkhāneh* patron saint, the fourteenth-century poet, mystic, and wrestler Purya-yi Vali—and of Shiʿism and its associated worship of the imams.[10] Shiʿi identity, while by no means novel, has certainly gained momentum since the establishment of the Islamic Republic and is accompanied by narratives viewing the *zūrkhāneh* as historically linked to the defenders of Shiʿism against persecution, with their associated celebration of martyrdom.[11] To these ideological formations there must be added modern sport's agonistic attitudes, particularly among younger gymnasts. Emphasis on athletic skills and competitiveness is sustained by a network of nationwide tournaments that, though already initiated in the Pahlavi period, has significantly expanded in post-revolutionary Iran thanks to the efforts of the Federation of Ancient Sport and Pahlavani Wrestling, which has codified point-based competition regulations and, more generally, organized *zūrkhāneh* practice through modern sports-related bureaucratic structures. As a corollary, *javānmardī* tends to be understood here as the local equivalent of Olympic values and fair play. The International Zurkhaneh Sports Federation, founded in 2004, has been instrumental to this process. It has promoted the internationalization of the "sport of the ancients" by establishing branches in several countries around the world, financing the construction of *zūrkhāneh* buildings abroad, and organizing international team competitions.[12]

All these facets of ideology and identity coexist in contemporary *zūrkhānehhā*, and interpretations of their relationship on the part of individual practitioners or different *zūrkhāneh* enclaves may range—depending on subject position or circumstance—from integration and combination to tension and contradiction.[13] They are of central significance for the architectural and musical universes to be explored in this chapter. In my discussion, I focus on everyday athletic sessions in neighborhood *zūrkhāneh* buildings that are by and large designed along traditional lines. An analysis of competition performances and tournaments deserves separate treatment because of some dissimilarities in musico-athletic dynamics, in the hierarchical ordering of participating athletes, and often in architectural context—particularly for competitions taking place in modern sports stadiums.

Music, Sound, and Athletics

Contemporary *zūrkhāneh* practice consists of a series of gymnastic exercises performed collectively by a variable number of athletes and arranged in an ordered sequence that may take from about one to three hours to be completed. Some numbers require team synchronization, whereas others are executed in turn by individual gymnasts. Although the order of exercises has local variants and allows a modicum of flexibility, it is fairly standardized. It includes the following: *davidan* (literally, "running"), that is, warmup jogging; *shinā* (literally, "swimming"), synchronized pushups performed with legs wide apart and pressing against a wooden bar (*takhteh-yi shinā*) placed on the floor; *narmish* (literally, "suppleness"), which comprises a variety of synchronized stretching and calisthenic exercises performed without apparatus; *mil* (literally, "clubs"), a synchronized weightlifting exercise where each athlete holds two Indian clubs and rolls them above and behind his shoulders;[14] *pā* (literally, "legs"), which comprises various synchronized movements centered on the use of legs, such as running in place, stamping, and kicking; *charkh* (literally, "whirl"), an individual exercise where athletes take turns spinning swiftly on their body axis while moving in concentric circles; and *kabbādeh*, the concluding individual exercise named after a bow-shaped iron rod with chain and rattling disks that gymnasts swing left and right over their heads.[15] One additional individual exercise, called *sang* (literally, "stone, weight"), is usually performed outside the standard gymnastic sequence: lying faceup on the floor, the athlete performs crunches and uses two large, shield-shaped wooden boards as weights for strength training (figs. 14.1 and 14.2).

The *zūrkhāneh* exercises stand in a symbiotic relationship with music performance. The music is provided by the *murshid*, who plays a large, clay goblet drum (*żarb*) and a bronze bell (*zang*) (*see plate 15*).[16] At times, a senior *murshid* may be accompanied by a younger one or by a pupil (*shāgird*), who is thus given the opportunity to practice performing in an athletic session.[17] The *murshid*'s drumming comprises a range of binary and ternary rhythmic cycles that are structurally related to the timing and patterning of kinetic movements, with each exercise possessing its own specific rhythm or rhythms. Most exercises display internal articulation with varying degrees of complexity and a varying number of sections with their distinctive designations. Such kinetic articulation is reflected by corresponding rhythmic varia-

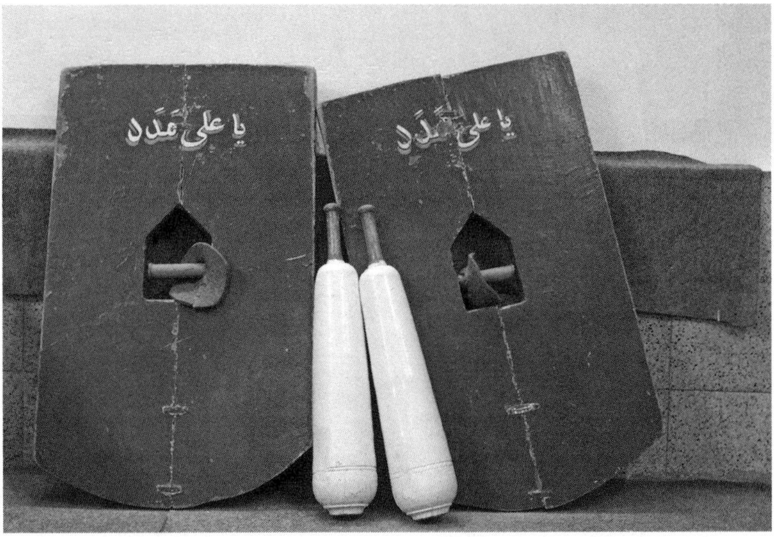

Figure 14.1. *Zūrkhāneh* shields (*sang*) and clubs (*mil*). Zurkhaneh Nirumand, Kashan, 2006. Photograph courtesy of Stefano Triulzi.

tions, including pattern and speed changes.[18] The *zang* is used to signal the beginning, the end, and internal changes of each exercise. *Murshidhā* (plural of *murshid*) complement their drumming by singing poetic passages employing melodic materials often modeled on the *dastgāh* system of Iranian classical music, including both improvisatory, *radīf*-based sequences and composed *taṣnīfs*. *Murshidhā* who are familiar with the terminology and subdivisions of the *dastgāh* system commonly consider the mode *humāyun*, conventionally associated with the attributes of heroism and virility, as the most genuine and ancient mode of the *zūrkhāneh*.[19] Evidence gathered on a large number of workout sessions indicates that the use of *humāyun* is as widespread as that of other modes, such as *bayāt-i turk*, *shūr*, or *dashtī*. Popular and film music, however, as well as Shiʿi religious chanting—including responsorial forms, such as the *nūḥeh*—are equally frequent sources. A similar situation obtains in matters of poetic repertoire. The view that Ferdowsi's *Shahnameh*, the eleventh-century "Iranian national epic," is the primary and original poetic repository for *zūrkhāneh* performances is almost ubiquitous among practitioners and commentators alike, despite the apparently limited role that the *Shahnameh* plays in contemporary practice vis-à-vis other sources, including mystical classical verses as well as contemporary, vernacular, and

Figure 14.2. Athlete performing the *kabbādeh* exercise. Zurkhaneh Shahid Doktor Chamran, Mashhad, 2006. Photograph courtesy of Stefano Triulzi.

devotional poetry.[20] Many view this composite musical and poetic repertoire as the result of historical stratification and innovation, while some deplore it as a contamination and loss of authenticity. It remains uncertain whether the prominence assigned to *humāyun* and the *Shahnameh*—on a theoretical, if not practical, level—reflects premodern practices or, on the contrary, a composite musical and poetic repertoire has long been familiar to *zūrkhāneh* circles. In either case, the important symbolic position that *humāyun* and the *Shahnameh* maintain in *zūrkhāneh* discourse—and the identity issues that are thereby perceived to be at stake—can hardly be disjoined from the institution's increasing association with cultural nationalism since the 1930s and the related pursuit and assertion of a legitimate pedigree in terms of historical heritage, national heroism, and musical and poetic classicism.[21]

The *murshid*'s performance is integral to a broader sound environment comprising many communicative and sonic enunciations. These include blessings and salutations (*salavāt*) typically addressed to distinguished guests or athletes, *rukhsat* courtesy formulas, and prayers (*duʿā*) uttered chorally by all attendees. Speeches of various lengths given by prominent athletes or the *murshid*—for commemoration, ethical guidance, or commentary on a variety of current issues—are also a distinctive feature of *zūrkhāneh* sessions, particularly in the pauses between exercises,[22] and so is the *ghazalkhānī*, the unaccompanied singing of lyrical verses performed by an athlete or a guest before the onset of the *shinā* exercise.[23]

Mirrors: Refractions in Architectural and Musico-Athletic Symbolism

The *zūrkhāneh*'s musical, sonic, and kinetic nexus has deep relationships with the built environment where it takes place. *Zūrkhānehhā* are constructed purposefully to suit music and athletic performance, as well as to visually and spatially embody concepts that are central to the social organization and the ethical-religious values of *zūrkhāneh* practitioners. I wish to illustrate this considering architecture as "built environment" in the broadest sense, including structural elements of construction and interior design and layout, as well as visual trappings, furniture, and objects (fig. 14.3).

Zūrkhānehhā display a number of fundamental structural features. Typically, they consist of one main, open room of various sizes and plans: square,

Figure 14.3. Exterior of the Zurkhaneh Astan-i Quds, Mashhad, 2006. Photograph courtesy of Stefano Triulzi.

rectangular, cruciform, or, more rarely, circular. This room may or may not be complemented by niches or ancillary open-space chambers. The main room features a sunken pit, called *gowd,* which serves as the arena for most athletic exercises. The *gowd* sits below ground level by about one meter and is generally octagonal. Its size depends on the size of *zūrkhāneh* buildings. The space surrounding the *gowd* at ground level is generally occupied by seats for guests and the audience and is also used for individual stationary athletic exercises, such as *sang*; for individual prayers (*ṣalāt*); or as a resting area. A hemispherical or polygonal dome (*gunbad*) covers the main room and usually features a skylight at its summit, whether an open oculus or a lantern. The spatial relationship between the *gunbad* and the *gowd* is such that the cusp of the dome corresponds axially to the center of the sunken pit, directly overlooking it (fig. 14.4). Another important element of the *zūrkhāneh* built environment is the rostrum where the *murshid* sits, which is called the *sardam*. Made of wood or brickwork, the *sardam* is built above ground level along one side of the *gowd* and overlooks it (fig. 14.5).[24]

The referential and symbolic relationship between architecture, music, and athletic exercises can be addressed through the metaphor of the mirror—a particularly useful tool for considering how music and architecture can communicate and shape a universe of values and ideological constructs.

Figure 14.4. *Gowd-gunbad* axial relationship. Zurkhaneh Abi Talib, Sabzevar, 2006. Photograph courtesy of Stefano Triulzi.

Figure 14.5. *Sardam* (rostrum). Zurkhaneh Sahib-i Zaman, Yazd, 2006. Photograph courtesy of Stefano Triulzi.

The advantage of this notion with respect to the cognate notion of text lies in its emphasis on the dialogue between different media and codes, pointing to the intertextual resonances between architecture and music as well as between these and ideological discourse. The architectural features of the *zūrkhāneh* are replete with symbolic meanings that are interlaced with and mirrored by those encoded in musico-athletic practice, the refraction between them being central to the production of meaning in the experience of *zūrkhāneh* affiliates. Particularly apt in this context is the proposition—entertained in various branches of architectural and environmental studies—that designed physical environments are socially meaningful in that they encode values and concepts that play key roles in the construction of selves, both individual and collective.[25] The relationship between built environments and selves is dynamic, entailing both the agency and influence of the former and the active interpretive ability of the latter, and thus offers a significant parallel with the variability and intersubjectivity of signification processes in music. Although I will categorize and systematize these symbolic associations on the basis of my ethnographic findings, such associations, while ensconced in fields of discourse known to the majority of *zūrkhāneh* affiliates, are subject to variable emphases.

The *zūrkhāneh* dome is often associated with the idea of the "zenith" (*quṭb*), an architectural metaphor for proximity to the divine and spiritual height. The *gunbad* may also be likened to the dome of a mosque or a Sufi shrine and, as such, understood to encode in material form the sacredness of the *zūrkhāneh* environment. Likewise, the *gowd* is a most symbolically meaningful site: by corresponding axially to the dome, it represents a mirror image of the divine world on earth—a receptacle of sacredness and a primary ritual space. The octagonal shape of the *gowd* may occasionally be associated with that of Jerusalem's Dome of the Rock. On entering the *gowd*, athletes routinely revere its sacredness by kneeling and kissing the floor. The low level of the pit's floor, requiring athletes to stand "at the feet" of anyone else, is customarily understood to encode the ideals of humility and self-sacrifice that are central to the chivalric ethos of the *zūrkhāneh*. The same ideal is built into the traditional low doorway of *zūrkhānehhā*, which requires one to bow as a sign of modesty and reverence (fig. 14.6).[26]

Zūrkhānehhā typically display also a variety of visual trimmings that relate to aspects of the *javānmardī* ethos and may variously be configured depending on the ideological proclivities of specific *zūrkhānehhā*—along the lines,

Figure 14.6. Traditional *zūrkhāneh* low doorway. Zurkhaneh Sahib-i Zaman, Yazd, 2006. Photograph courtesy of Stefano Triulzi.

say, of Iranian national history and nationalism, Shiʿism, Sufism, modern sports imagery, or a combination of all these. *Zūrkhāneh* walls are adorned with images of a martial kind, especially the legendary fights of Rustam, the hero of Ferdowsi's *Shahnameh*; images of a religious kind, particularly those of the imams ʿAli or Hussein, often represented as warriors; the ubiquitous images of the ayatollahs Ruhollah Khomeini and Ali Khamenei, as well as photographs of *zūrkhāneh* martyrs (*shahīd*) fallen during the Iran-Iraq War; images that memorialize the *zūrkhāneh* lineage of masters and authoritative figures, ranging from the patron saint of the *zūrkhāneh*, Purya-yi Vali, to contemporary athletes and *murshidhā*, whether of national or local significance; images and objects that have clear links with the symbolic universe of Sufism, including the dervishes' alms bowl, ax, and deerskin; and images of sports icons, whether directly related to the *zūrkhāneh* world (e.g., the wrestling champion Ghulamreza Takhti) or not (e.g., the African American boxer Mohammad Ali) (fig. 14.7).[27]

These features of architectural and interior design symbolism relate to musico-athletic practice at various levels, including the objects and designed spaces most directly relevant to such practice. Musical instruments are assigned symbolic meanings. The large hourglass drum, or *żarb*, is most often thought of as the descendant of ancient war drums, a quintessential martial instrument related to Iranian national heroism, and so is the bell, or *zang*, whose hemispherical shape may be additionally likened to the dome of a mosque. All athletic tools and exercises are interpreted as symbols, whether religious or martial, or a combination of both. For example, *zūrkhāneh* clubs (*mil*) represent ancient war maces; wooden planks (*takhteh*) for pushups are likened to swords (typically, reference is made to Imam ʿAli's double-bladed sword, *zulfiqār*); the two heavy weights called *sang* are most commonly deemed to represent war shields or, more specifically, the door of the Khaybar fortress, torn off and used as a shield by Imam ʿAli; the *kabbādeh* is considered to be a replica of a war bow; and both the *pā* and *charkh* exercises may be associated with techniques of martial training aimed at strengthening balance and agility, with whirling being sometimes alternatively linked to the spinning of Sufi adepts during rituals.[28]

Spatially locating the source of musical sound, the *sardam*, where the *murshid* sits and performs, is built and understood as a replica of a pulpit (particularly that of Shiʿi preachers) or, alternatively, as a stylized and meta-architectural representation of a mosque (fig. 14.8).

Figure 14.7. (a, *top*) Painting depicting the legendary fight between the *Shahnameh*'s hero, Rustam, and his son, Suhrab. Zurkhaneh Astan-i Quds, Mashhad, 2006. Photograph: F. Spinetti. (b, *bottom*) Portraits of Ghulamreza Takhti (*left*) and Imams ʿAli (*center*) and Hussein (*right*). Zurkhaneh Sahib-i Zaman, Yazd, 2006. Photograph courtesy of Stefano Triulzi.

Figure 14.8. *Sardam* built as a meta-architectural representation of a mosque. Zurkhaneh Takhti, Sabzevar, 2006. Photograph courtesy of Stefano Triulzi.

These associations, together with the elevated location of the *sardam*, meaningfully situate musical sound in the *zūrkhāneh* ideological universe: they not only encode the preeminence of the *murshid* in the *zūrkhāneh* social hierarchy but also underline the ethical-religious valence of the sound delivered from the *sardam*. Indeed, the poetic and song repertoire performed in *zūrkhānehhā*, although variable and largely dependent on the choices of individual *murshidhā*, often made in response to the inclinations of their communities of athletes, is central to sustaining and conveying the *zūrkhāneh* value system, with a clear prevalence of epic poetry, classical poetry on mystical and moral themes, and songs in praise of the imams ʿAli and Hussein.

Poetic content, the perceived aesthetic quality of vocal delivery, and the drive and pace of drumming, together with the visually apprehended vigorous bodily gestures of the *murshid*, were often pointed out to me as crucial factors in heightening the athletes' kinetic engagement and psychophysical experiences. Some *zūrkhāneh* affiliates described a process of deeply internalizing the images of Imam ʿAli or the hero Rustam in the course of performance, a process verging on identification. It is worth remarking here that mirrors are fairly widespread furnishings on *zūrkhāneh* walls. Besides helping athletes to monitor their gymnastic execution, mirrors both symbolically reference the notion of purity of the self and visually embody the process of doubling and reflection. In consonance with the mystical interpretation of the *gowd-gunbad* axial relationship as a conduit between the divine and human worlds, the *zūrkhāneh* musico-athletic nexus can be viewed as activating the process of purification of the self to which at least some athletes aspire in performance. In some interpretations, and much like those athletic exercises that repeat, the cyclic and repetitive rhythmic patterns become embodied metaphors for, and vehicles for the visualization of, a vortex moving upward, like a spiral, from the pit to the summit of the dome, itself a visual metaphor of mystical ascent across architectural space.[29]

We can apply Kevin Lynch's concept of "imageability" to this net of symbolic refractions. In *The Image of the City*, a work in urban studies, Lynch defines imageability as "that quality in a physical object which gives it a high probability of evoking a strong image in any given observer" and uses it to explore how designed urban environments are made intelligible by their inhabitants thanks to mental pictures and mappings. These "environmental images" are central not only to practical orientation but also to our symbolic, social, affective, and existential understanding of built environments.[30] I contend that imageability is likewise a significant component of the experience of musico-athletic performance. While I do not mean to sideline the specifically aural level of semiotic reference in music,[31] music in the *zūrkhāneh*, along with athletic performance, acts as both a sonic experience and a visual utterance and possibility, effecting a synesthetic integration of aural perception and vision.[32] Music is for listening, and it is for seeing. The imageability of the musico-athletic whole lies in its ability, on the one hand, to evoke visual narratives in consonance and dialogue with architectural and decorative morphology and, on the other hand, to help an individual to visualize, as well as embody and feel, a symbolically transfigured dimension of the self. Music here not only comprises bodily action that is visually apprehended—for example, in the rhythmic motor activity of athletes as well as in the performance gestures of the *murshid*—but also serves a catalyst for visual imagination. It is through its imageability that musico-athletic performance most intensely relates to architecture on a symbolic-referential level, such that the religious, ethical, and martial symbols sounded and embodied in musico-athletic practice intersect with those built into architecture, reinforcing one another in a web of communicative cross-references, a web of mirrors.

Frames: Social Interaction in Sound and Space

Moving beyond the symbolic and referential level of signification, the music-architecture or sound-space nexus can be profitably examined in terms of the social relations and performative interactions it activates. This dimension is aptly encapsulated by the metaphor of the "frame," a notion that I derive primarily, albeit rather loosely, from symbolic interactionism, where it has provided a means to theorize about the conditions, conventions, and assumptions that shape definitions and possibilities of interpretation of a given interaction or event.[33] While I share a concern with interpretation, here I wish to foreground specifically sensory—visuospatial and auditory—patterned contexts and their proxemic implications. I am interested in looking at architectural and musico-athletic frames as processes of emplacement, whereby spatial and auditory configurations at once enable and constrain possibilities for meaningful social and performative interactions.

Key to my consideration of the framing power of sonic and kinetic events at the Iranian *zūrkhāneh* is their performative dimension, where the production of meaning resides primarily in processes and possibilities of embodiment and action. Central here is the role of sound and bodily movement, and their interrelation through synchronization and gestural patterns, in contributing to the social articulation of space. As the ethnomusicologist Sara Cohen remarks, "Music . . . plays a unique and often hidden role in the social and cultural production of place and, through its peculiar nature, it foregrounds the dynamic, sensual aspects of this process emphasizing, for example, the creation and performance of place through human bodies in action and motion."[34] In a similar vein, albeit without laying emphasis on sound, anthropological approaches to architecture have emphasized the notion of space as a lived environment that at once shapes and is shaped by the communicative and bodily interactions of people inhabiting and using it. For example, in her examination of Southeast Asian indigenous vernacular architecture, Roxana Waterson states,

> Rules about the uses of space provide one of the most important ways by which the built environment can be imbued with meaning; reflexively, that environment itself helps to mould and reproduce a particular pattern of social relationships. This production of meaning may take place, firstly, through the positioning and manipulation of objects in space, and secondly, through the human body itself—its placement in, movement through, or exclusion from a particular space, or in people's spatial interactions with each other.[35]

This understanding of the built environment as an interactive process informs my examination of the synergies and dynamics between *zūrkhāneh* architectural and musico-athletic frames. Here, both music and architecture emerge as proxemic, kinesic, and relational phenomena, affording coordinates for intersubjective auditory, behavioral, and performative interactions.[36] Music is not only an auditory and temporal phenomenon but also a spatial one that engenders patterns of orientation and movement within, as well as access to, architectural spaces.[37] Likewise, architecture is not only a visual and spatial object but also an auditory and temporal process. One might posit, in parallel to the "imageability" of music, the notion of "hearability" of architecture to refer, on the one hand, to architecture's role in channeling and structuring aural attention and events so as to generate specific sonic experiences and, on the other hand, to highlight that the architectural artifact as a lived environment is experienced, known, and engaged with by social actors in time and through the crucial contribution of aural—and musical—means. As a corollary, the experiential and cognitive significance of designed environments comes to be defined as much by their aural identity as by their visual and spatial qualities.[38]

Zūrkhāneh architecture and music operate as frames in the first place by demarcating the gymnasium as a social enclosure. The walled *zūrkhāneh* buildings entrench in tangible, material form the specific social structure that characterizes *zūrkhāneh* communities, which dismantles everyday social and power relations and reassembles them according to hierarchical patterns related to the *javānmardī* ethics. Entering the *zūrkhāneh* built environment is equivalent to crossing a ritual threshold to a reconfigured social space. Here, spatial design directly affects social interactions by fostering communal participation. The open space in the main *zūrkhāneh* room, with the substantial absence of secluded areas, is an important element in engendering constant collective interaction, as well as behavioral surveillance. The *zūrkhāneh* soundscape defines enclosure along similar lines. During athletic performance, the *murshid*'s music permeates architectural space and envelops the community of affiliates and participants through sonic intensity. This totalizing aural experience is reinforced by the widespread use of loudspeakers in contemporary *zūrkhānehhā*, so that the source of sound, while spatially and visually identifiable, cannot be aurally pinpointed. This overall saturation of the sound environment in physical space results in a tangible demarcation and structuring of social space. Sound channels the focus of intersubjective interaction into collective participation, minimizing the possibility of secluded verbal exchanges among athletes or guests. Moreover, in most *zūrkhānehhā*, the music pours out beyond architectural borders into the surroundings, providing a recognizable index of the *zūrkhāneh* socio-architectural enclosure in the geography of the outside urban landscape.[39]

A second framing aspect that I will explore is "the spatial production of sound"—that is, the ways in which the social organization of space plays a vital role in the unfolding of musico-athletic performance. Particularly illustrative in this respect is the manner in which athletes inhabit the octagonal pit. Their arrangement and distribution embody and articulate the *zūrkhāneh* social hierarchy in spatial terms. Athletes line up in a circle or, if the pit is large enough, in concentric circles within the pit, all of them facing the center. Their position in the circle is defined by its relationship to the *murshid*'s rostrum, which is placed above one of the sides of the octagon. Novices (*nawcheh*)—located at the lower end of the social hierarchy—occupy the arc of the circle that is most removed from the rostrum, facing the *murshid*. Moving along to the right and the left of the pit toward the *sardam*, athletes are positioned in ascending order of seniority, covering all intermediary stages in the *zūrkhāneh* social ladder. At the top of the hierarchy are the "veterans" (*pishkesvat*) and—by virtue of hereditary authority—the descendants of Prophet Mohammad (*sayyid*). These stand at the opposite side of the circle to the novices, right beneath the *sardam*, with their backs to the *murshid*. At the very center of the pit there is only one position available, that of the *myāndār*, "the owner of the center," who is turned so as to face the *murshid*. The *murshid* assigns someone to this position at every change of exercise and, following the ritual of *rukhsat*, it is taken up in turns by the most authoritative athletes of the *zūrkhāneh*. The *myāndār* occupies the highest rank in the social relations mobilized in performance as he alone directs athletic exercises and is followed and obeyed by all other athletes (*see plate 16*).

This distribution of spatial ownerships in the pit constitutes in fact a human architecture, which provides the fundamental configuration of the *zūrkhāneh*'s proxemic relations and can be ultimately transferred outside the perimeters of *zūrkhāneh* buildings.[40] Such patterned configuration is crucial to the fabric and dynamics of musical performance. Central here is the role of the *myāndār*, who sets the pace and the duration of athletic exercises by communicating with the *murshid* using conventional gestural or verbal cues. The spatial alignment between *myāndār* and *murshid*, who are positioned so as to face each other, enables the interactive communication between the two, which provides the backbone of both musical performance and kinetic activity. In effect, the *myāndār* participates actively in musical delivery. Through the cadence of his athletic movements, he suggests the tempo of rhythmic cycles to the *murshid*; through verbal and gestural signs, he signals changes of speed or pattern within exercises that require changes in the articulation or tempo of drumming and dictates the overall duration of rhythmic sequences, calling the end of each exercise.[41] The *myāndār* negotiates such decisions in the course of performance, both in response to the prowess and endurance of the specific group of athletes he is leading and in dialogue with the *murshid*. In fact, the interaction between *murshid* and *myāndār* largely shapes the articulation of singing, especially with regard to the length of poetic or melodic sequences. While athletic considerations by and large take precedence here (indeed, poems may not be performed in their entirety), the *myāndār* must be able to prompt the *murshid* to conclude his vocal delivery at an appropriate moment by taking into account and accommodating melodic elements (such as phrase length or melodic cadences) as well as poetic units (such as couplets). The *myāndār* is thus required to have sensibility to musical and poetic structures. He is both director of exercises and, ultimately, musical codirector. His position within the social organization of space in the *gowd* makes him an intermediary both in athletic terms, as he is the visual point of reference for the athletes and the *murshid* as to kinetic performance, and in musical terms, as he is the vehicle through which the musical utterances of the *murshid* intertwine with athletic performance. In this sense, the *myāndār* owns the center both spatially and sonically.[42] He mediates and ties together space and sound, highlighting how spatial frames—the geometry of positioning in the *gowd* and alignment between *gowd* and *sardam*—are key to the articulation and the aesthetics of musico-athletic performance.

Finally, a third "framing" process could be best defined as "the sonic production of space,"[43] that is, the ways in which sonic events activate and regulate interactions with architectural space. In the *zūrkhāneh*, not only is the ownership of spatial positions significant on a symbolic and performative level; of equal importance is the temporality of the access to and movement within architectural space. A priority right, based on the athletes' seniority and authority, often regulates this temporality. For example, athletes enter the *gowd* according to a hierarchically ordered temporal sequence, with veterans entering first and all others following. Entering the *zūrkhāneh* itself—whether on the part of athletes or guests—is likewise an event to which particular attention is paid. Rules of precedence, and more generally the attention paid to access to and movement within space, actualize the *zūrkhāneh* social structure in time, in effect temporalizing architecture and infusing the interactions with it with meaning.

If ownership of and access to space are equally central in the *zūrkhāneh*—that is, if architecture acquires meaning as it is lived socially and performatively (and not only apprehended symbolically) as well as temporally (and not only as a durable, static object)—it is not surprising to observe that interactions with space acquire a sonic dimension in the *zūrkhāneh*. An instructive example here is the practice known as *vārid kardan*, literally, "letting in." This term indicates the enunciations that the *murshid* dedicates as a tribute to authoritative guests or athletes as they enter the *zūrkhāneh* building or the *gowd*. Depending on the rank or recognized authority of those who enter, the *murshid* marks their entrance by dedicating them a blessing (*ṣalavāt*) or accompanying the blessing with one or more bell tolls or one or more drum rolls. These sonic markers must be performed regardless of whether the entrance occurs before or during an athletic performance. In many instances the *murshid* weaves the *vārid kardan* into the flow of his musical delivery, while on other occasions—usually as a tribute to very illustrious guests or athletes—the *vārid kardan* temporarily interrupts musico-poetic and athletic execution. In fact, from a phenomenological perspective, the *vārid kardan* ought to be considered as integral to music performance inasmuch as, together with the highly variable interactions between *myāndār* and *murshid*, it shapes the malleable fabric of musical delivery in real time. Indeed, music is here part of a composite acoustic ecological system. The same flexibility that concerns sonic events applies to interactions with architectural space, particularly as to their occurrence in time. While the rules of access to and positioning within space are structured and their associated sonic events are patterned, the *vārid kardan* further exemplifies how lived interactions with architectural space are to some degree flexible, situational, and unpredictable. As the sociologist of architecture Thomas Gieryn states, "Buildings stabilize social life. They give structure to social institutions, durability to social networks, persistence to behavior patterns. . . . And yet, buildings stabilize *imperfectly*. . . . We deconstruct buildings materially and semiotically, all the time. . . . Buildings . . . sit somewhere between agency and structure."[44] In his original discussion, Gieryn emphasizes agency primarily in terms of material and discursive manipulation and deconstruction of buildings, but I find that his propositions similarly apply when we consider the temporal dimension of architecture as lending variability and agency to human engagement with space.

The *vārid kardan*, as well as the distinctive rhythmic cycles associated with each exercise of the "sport of the ancients," provides auditory markers of events that occur in space and thus can be cognitively apprehended through aural means even when they might be concealed to visual perception. As many athletes have pointed out to me, recognizing rhythmic cycles by their sound allows one to know what happens in the pit. Similarly, when they hear the *vārid kardan*, the athletes know that someone has entered the *zūrkhāneh* or the pit, even if they may not see the newcomer; the ritual enunciation also directs their attention to the location in the built environment where the event is taking place. Here, the imageability of music, the ability of sound to produce images and to be experienced/known/perceived visually, intersects with the hearability of space, that which allows space to be known and explored aurally. This illustrates how the temporal and interactive dimension of lived architecture is one with sonic and musical events, quintessentially temporal phenomena that acquire here a central role in activating and articulating spatial and proxemic phenomena. Architectural space is here lived in time and in sound and apprehended, known, and acted upon by means of auditory experience.[45]

Both the temporality of interactions with space and their sonic catalysts play an important role in sustaining the ethics of social relations in the *zūrkhāneh*. It is significant in this respect that, depending on their rank and thus on the resulting forms of salutations they receive from the *murshid* upon entering the *zūrkhāneh* or the *gowd*, veterans are conferred titles such as *ṣalavātī* (deserving of blessing), *ṣāhib-i zang* (owner of the bell), or *ṣāhib-i żarb* (owner of the drum). This stresses that their status is recognized and asserted not only by their ownership of specific locations within the built environment but also by the sonic enunciations linked to their interaction with space in specific moments of high symbolic valence. Given the temporal and auditory dimensions of socially lived architecture, ownership of space is equivalent to ownership of sound in the context of the *zūrkhāneh*.

Concluding Remarks

Through an investigation of the symbolic-referential intersections of musical and architectural features (a dimension I have labeled "mirroring") and the pragmatic processes unfolding in music and architecture as patterned settings for communicative interactions (a dimension I have called "framing"), I have proposed a way of understanding how sound, built environment, and bodily movement are conjointly experienced at the Iranian *zūrkhāneh*. This represents an attempt at a multisensory approach to both architecture and music, beyond the confines of putatively discrete auditory and visual or spatial domains. While vision and spatial coordinates come to be central to interrogating aural experience, sound and movement come to gain center stage in decoding how architecture is lived. Ultimately, the consideration of a further enlarged sensory complex, including olfactory as well as muscular and tactile perceptions, would be a profitable and quite natural continuation of this line of inquiry into the experiential nature of the space-sound nexus.

NOTES

1 The term "*zūrkhāneh*" (literally, "house of strength") refers in the first place to the designed built environment of the gymnasium. By extension, it may also refer to the athletic activities undertaken therein (more commonly called "sport of the ancients" or "sport of the *zūrkhāneh*," *varzish-i zūrkhānehī*), as well as to the group of people who share affiliation to a gymnasium. In this chapter, all these meanings of the term will be employed.

2 Most recent contributions include Ridgeon 2007 (republished in a modified version in Ridgeon 2010, 166–209) and Rochard 2000, 2002. See also Spinetti 2010b.

3 References to the *zūrkhāneh* in ethnomusicological studies in European languages are few and cursory. See for example Barkechli 1961; Zonis 1973, 11, 12. In Persian, a detailed classification and notation of *zūrkhāneh* rhythms was published under the guidance of one of the most respected and authoritative contemporary *murshedhā*, Faramarz Najafi Tehrani (Najafi Tehrani and Hijazi 1992). On *zūrkhāneh* drum rhythms and playing techniques see also Darvishi 2005, 373–385.

4 Some *zūrkhānehhā* have more than one resident *murshid*. This may be particularly the case in *zūrkhānehhā* that are part of well-subsidized sport centers, such as the Zurkhaneh Astan-i Quds in Mashhad, and that attract a great number of practitioners. Partaw Beza'i Kashani (2003, 36–40) argues that, in premodern Iran, *murshid*—as leader of the assembly—and drummer (*żarbgir*) were distinct figures.

5 The *zūrkhāneh* is traditionally a strictly male environment. While the presence of female spectators is generally allowed, it remains quite rare and is mostly confined to occasional attendances by tourists, whether Iranian or foreign. There are, however, several women active within *zūrkhāneh*-related sport institutions. Currently efforts are being undertaken to extend the performance of the "sport of the ancients" to female teams in the context of sport centers rather than in more traditional, neighborhood *zūrkhānehhā*. See Spinetti 2010b.

6 For an interpretation of the *zūrkhāneh* social structure informed by Victor Turner's notion of *communitas*, see Ridgeon 2010, 170–172.

7 *Javānmardī* includes also lending support to people in need within or outside the *zūrkhāneh* community. For example, in the ceremony known as *gulrizān* funds are collected among members to this end.

8 On the historic ties between *zūrkhāneh*, Sufism, and the Islamic code of chivalry—

as well as premodern professional guilds organized along this code—see Partaw Beza'i Kashani 2003, 25–34; Piemontese 1964; Ridgeon 2010; Rochard 2002. The latter offers also a compelling interpretation of the ambiguous reputation of the *zūrkhāneh* based on historical inquiry.

9 For a comprehensive bibliography and illuminating discussion on these topics, see Rochard 2002, 322–323 and passim. See also Chehabi 1995, 50–51, and, in relation to the broader topic of sport and modernization in Iran, Chehabi 2002, 279–280.

10 On Purya-yi Vali, see Piemontese 1965 and Partaw Beza'i Kashani 2003, 131–139.

11 Chehabi (2012) mentions the existence of Zoroastrian and Jewish *zūrkhānehhā* in Iran in the mid-twentieth century. There are currently several active *zūrkhānehhā* in Iranian Kurdistan, where the majority of the population is Sunni. Discussion of these contexts is beyond the scope of this chapter. Suffice it to note that on a prolonged visit to Sanandaj I could observe how prayers and invocations of Imam ʿAli featured regularly in *zūrkhāneh* sessions among Sunni Kurds.

12 On these developments in postrevolutionary Iran, see Chehabi 2002, 282–283 and Ridgeon 2010, 180–190. See also Spinetti 2010b.

13 While the integration of different narratives and levels of identity affiliation can be considered as the norm, some *zūrkhāneh* members assert that the genuine roots of the *zūrkhāneh* reside in (pre-Islamic) Iranian national heroism and that current emphases on Shiʿism are spurious. This may be complemented by contrasting the notions of Iranian mysticism (*irfān-i īrānī*) and Islamic mysticism (*irfān-i islāmī*). Also, competition-oriented members may display a certain discomfort with *zūrkhānehhā*, where agonistic performance is not the focus and ample room is instead devoted to socialization and speeches by elderly athletes. For a discussion of the complex ideological universe outlined in this chapter in terms of "multivocality" see Ridgeon 2010, 169, 190–204.

14 A shorter round of *mil* is often inserted between *davidan* and *shinā* and called *mil-i avval* (literally, "first clubs"). Following the *mil* team exercise, individual athletes may engage in juggling and acrobatics with clubs (*mil-bāzī* or *shirinkārī*).

15 Besides being an athletic tool, the *kabbādeh* can be reasonably considered a percussion instrument given the clatter it is made to produce in synch with the drumbeat during athletic performance. Indeed Darvishi (2005, 602–605) includes it in his encyclopedia of Iranian musical instruments.

16 See Darvishi 2005, 373–385, 584–587.

17 Some of the *murshidhā* I met belong to hereditary families, while the majority do not. The *murshid*'s art (*hunar-i murshidī*) is still largely handed down through the traditional master-pupil apprenticeship system, which, however, has been complemented in recent years by formal instruction methods through collective courses and master classes. As part of the current sport-oriented modernization process, juried competitions of *murshidhā* have also been introduced.

18 For instance, the *mil* exercise is usually divided into a slow-paced part, called *mil-i sangin* or *sarnavāzī*, and a faster one, called *mil-i tund* or *shallāqī*. Similarly, *charkh* may be performed at different speeds and with different step patterns, and accordingly named *chamanī, khurāsānī, tīz*, etc. See Najafi Tehrani and Hijazi 1992, 103–107, 112–115, 118–119, and Darvishi 2005, 373–385.

19 See Spinetti 2010b.

20 While poetry singing is central to the *murshid*'s performance, some exercises, notably *kabbādeh*, are instead accompanied by the *murshid* by counting the athlete's lifts. The *charkh* exercise is normally not accompanied by singing.

21 On this issue, with specific reference to the *Shahnameh*, see also Ridgeon 2010, 197, 208, and Chehabi 2012. To my knowledge, the performance of another poetic text traditionally linked to the *zūrkhāneh*, Mir Najat Isfahani's eighteenth-century *masnavī* titled *Gul-i kushtī* (The flower of wrestling), has almost disappeared from contemporary practice. On this text see Partaw Beza'i Kashani 2003, 111–114, 393–427.

22 Speeches are particularly dear to traditionalist and elderly members, while their usefulness is debated among competition-oriented athletes. Quite predictably, they have been expunged from competition sessions.

23 *Ghazalkhānī* may entail the performance of a variety of poetry genres, such as *ghazal* and quatrains (*rubāʿī*). A most characteristic topos here is that of the repented former jailbird or ruffian who imparts the values of ethical behavior and group solidarity to his fellow *zūrkhāneh* affiliates. I am thankful to Dr. Sasan Fatemi for bringing this point to my attention in an interview of July 2008.

24 On *zūrkhāneh* architectural features and the *sardam* see Partaw Beza'i Kashani 2003, 35–36, 40–46.

25 Most significant to my present purposes are contributions from symbolic interaction theory applied to architectural sociology (for example Smith and Bugni 2006) and environment-behavior studies (for example Rapoport 1982). For a semiotic perspective see Eco 1980.

26 This architectural feature is increasingly rare, as newly constructed or renovated *zūrkhānehhā* tend to display larger, if not grandiose, entrances.

27 On Ghulamreza Takhti's life and role in Iranian sports and politics see Chehabi 1995, where the association of not only Takhti, but also the hero Rustam, Imam ʿAli, and Purya-yi Vali with *javānmardī* values and the *pahlavān* ideal is discussed (pp. 48–49).

28 For further discussion of the symbolic associations of *zūrkhāneh* interior decoration, objects, and gymnastic tools see Ridgeon 2010, 190–199.

29 I am grateful to Dr. Hamidreza Ardalan for first pointing me toward this reading in an interview conducted in July 2008 (see Spinetti 2010b).

30 Lynch 1960, 4, 9. See also Eco 1980, in particular his discussion of the connota-

tive functions of architecture (23–27), and Rapoport 1982 (particularly 11–34, 137–176) for a relevant perspective on meaning-generating and mnemonic cues in the built environment from the vantage point of nonverbal communication and pragmatics.

31 See, for instance, Turino 1999.

32 See the discussion in Erlmann 2004a, particularly 3–6, 16–17.

33 See in particular Goffman 1974, 7–11, 21–82, and passim, and also Bateson 1972, 177–193. Rapoport's discussion of environmental meaning and its relationship to behavioral and communicative patterns is in many respects congruent with Bateson's and Goffman's notion of frames (1982, 55–86, 177–195).

34 Cohen 1995, 445.

35 Waterson 1990, 167.

36 For an approach to musical meaning and sound experience that significantly resonates with the one adopted here see Clayton 2001 and 2008 (with their ample bibliographic references), particularly Clayton's application of psychologist James Gibson's ecological theory of perception (and its related notion of affordance) as well as of the concept of entrainment. See also Gibson 1977. For a discussion of proxemics as part of an analysis of meaning production in architecture in relation to "anthropological systems," see Eco 1980, 49–56.

37 For a discussion of the spatial and relational qualities of sound from the angle of mediated sound consumption in Western urban cultures, see Bull 2004. Spatialization and temporalization of acoustic phenomena are discussed in Feld 1996, 97–98.

38 See Sheridan and van Lengen 2003 for an interestingly related and more in-depth discussion of "buildings as sounding forms" (37) from the perspective of architectural practice and education. Germane to my discussion is the notion of "aural architecture" elaborated in Blesser and Salter 2007.

39 The *zūrkhāneh* may thus be fittingly defined as an "acoustic community," to use a term originally coined by Raymond Murray Schafer (1977, 214–217). Note that Schafer's discussion emphasizes the distinction—quite relevant in the *zūrkhāneh* context—between acoustic and visual spaces. However, in contrast to Schafer's original formulation, acoustic space as the "volume of space in which the sound can be heard" (214) does not per se define participation in the *zūrkhāneh* community. Acoustic space *either* forms *or* indexes the community depending on whether one is inside or outside architectural space. Rather than speak of an acoustic community, we might find the notion of "auditory subculture" (Blesser and Salter 2007, 7) to prove more appropriate here: a group of people who are drawn together not by a somewhat undifferentiated inclusion within a generic sonic space but rather by their active engagement in decoding, understanding, and manipulating specific spaces by aural means.

40 This occurs, for example, when *zūrkhāneh* performances take place in sports stadiums or on occasion of staged displays, such as those that have involved a number of *zūrkhāneh* groups on tour abroad.

41 The *myāndār*'s code of cues includes verbal utterances (typically shouting "*ʿAli!*" or "*ʿAlī-yi Pahlavān!*") and gestures such as hand-signals (to count down rhythmic cycles for example) or making the *shinā* wooden plank clack against the floor.

42 It is not insignificant here that, acoustically, the *myāndār* is located at the focal point where sound waves converge within the domed architecture of the *zūrkhāneh*.

43 Here I evidently echo Lefebvre 1991.

44 Gieryn 2002, 35.

45 Particularly in this regard, the notion of aural architecture explored by Blesser and Salter (2007, especially pp. 2–8) is most significant for my discussion. My interpretive line here has numerous points of contact also with the concept of acoustemology elaborated by Steven Feld (1996), particularly in its emphasis on "sounding as a condition of and for knowing" with the corollary that "the experience of place potentially can always be grounded in an acoustic dimension" (97). See also Sheridan and van Lengen 2003: "the aural perception of space contributes to the experiential identity of an environment" (37).

REFERENCES

113. 1998. *Ni barreaux, Ni barrières, Ni frontières*. CD. Invasion Records.

———. 2005. *113 Degrés*. CD. Sony/BMG.

AAVV. 1995. *La haine. Musiques inspirées du film*. CD. Delabel.

———. 1998. *Sachons dire non*. CD. Untouchable/EMI.

———. 2002. *Urban Peace*. CD. Universal/Sony/EMI.

ʿAbbadi, Mojtar. 1965–1966. "Las fiestas profanas y religiosas en el reino de Granada." *Miscelánea de Estudio Árabes y Hebráicos* 14–15:89–96.

Abd al Malik. 2004a. *La face à face des coeurs*. CD. Atmosphériques/Universal.

———. 2004b. *Qu'Allah bénisse la France!* Paris: Albin Michel.

———. 2006. *Gibraltar*. CD. Gibraltar/Atmosphériques.

———. 2008. *Dante*. CD. Polydor/Universal.

———. 2010a. *Château rouge*. CD. Barclay/Universal.

———. 2010b. *La guerre des banlieues n'aura pas lieu*. Paris: Le Cherche Midi.

———. 2012. *Le dernier français*. Paris: Le Cherche Midi.

Abdelkafi, Jellal. 2012. "Evolving Medinas." In *The Medina: The Restoration and Conservation of Historic Islamic Cities*, edited by Marcello Balbo, 55–97. London: I. B. Tauris.

Abdul Baqi bin Jan Muhammad. 1990. *Muqamaat e Dawoodi*. Translated from Persian to Urdu by Dr. Khawaja Hameed Yazdani. In *Ahwahl al Sheikh Dawood Jhunniwal*, by Mohammad Haidar, appendix 2. Renala Khurd, Pakistan: Sayyid Muhammad Mohsin.

ʿAbdun, ʿAbd al-Hakim. 2001. *al-Musiqa al-Shafiya li-l-Buhur al-Safiya*. Cairo: al-ʿArabi.

Abu al-Fazal. 1988. *Ain-e akbari (Urdu Translation)*. Translated by Maulvi Muhammad Fida Ali. Lahore: Sang-e-Meel Publications.

Abu-Zahra, Nadia. 1997. *The Pure and the Powerful: Studies in Contemporary Muslim Society*. Reading, UK: Ithaca.

Aïchoune, Farid, ed. 1985. *La beur génération*. Paris: Sans Frontière/Arcantère.

Aidi, Hisham. 2011. "The Grand (Hip-Hop) Chessboard: Race, Rap and Raison d'Etat." *Middle East Report* 41 (260): 25–39.

———. 2014. *Rebel Music: Race, Empire, and the New Muslim Youth Culture*. New York: Pantheon.

Akın, Günkut. 1995. "The 'Müezzin Mahfili' and Pool of the Selimiye Mosque in Edirne." *Muqarnas* 12:63–83.

Akiner, Shirin. 1995. *The Formation of the Kazakh Identity: From Tribe to Nation-State*. London: The Royal Institute of International Affairs.

Akkach, Samer. 2005. *Cosmology and Architecture in Premodern Islam: An Architectural Reading of Mystical Ideas*. Albany: SUNY Press.

Aksoy, Bülent. 1985. "Tanzimat'tan Cumhuriyet'e Musiki ve Batılılaşma." In *Tanzimat'tan Cumhuriyet'e Türkiye Ansiklopedisi*, 1212–1248. Istanbul: İletişim Yayınları.

Alberti, Leon Battista. (1485) 1989. *On the Art of Building in Ten Books*. Translated by J. Rykwert, N. Leach, and R. Tavernor. 2nd ed. Cambridge, MA: MIT Press.

al-Farabi, Abu Nasr. n.d. *Kitab al-Musiqa al-Kabir*. Cairo: Dar al-Katib al-ʿArabi.

al-Farahidi, al-Khalil bin Ahmad. 1984. *Kitab al-ʿAyn*. 7 vols. Qum, Iran: Dar al-Hijra.

Al Faruqī, Lois Ibsen. 1978. "Ornamentation in Arabian Improvisational Music: A Study of Interrelatedness in the Arts." *The World of Music* 20 (1): 17–32.

al-Ghazali, Abu Hamid Muhammad ibn Muhammad. 2007. *Alchemy of Happiness (Kimiya-yi Sa'adat)*. Translated by Claud Field. Petaling Jaya, Selangor, Malaysia: Islamic Book Trust.

al-Hanbali. 1998. *Shadhrat al-Dhahab fi Akhbar man Dhahab*. 9 vols. Beirut: Dar al-Kutub al-ʿIlmiyya.

al-Isbahani, Abu al-Faraj. 1952. *Kitab al-Aghani*. Cairo: Dar al-Kutub al-Misriyya.

al-Isbahani, Abu al-Faraj, and ʿAbd al-Salam Muhammad Harun. 1927. *Kitab al-Aghani*. Cairo: Matbaʿat Dar al-Kutub al-ʿArabiyya.

al-Jabaqji, ʿAbd al-Rahman. n.d. *al-Fulklur wa-l-Qudud al-Halabiyya*. Aleppo: Dar al-Turath.

al-Khatib al-Baghdadi. 1931. *Ta'rikh Baghdad*. Vol. 1. Cairo: Maktabat al-Khanji.

al-Khatib al-Tabrizi. 2006. *Mishkat al-Masabih*. Translated by James Robson. 2 vols. Lahore: Shaikh Muhammad Ashraf.

al-Ladhiqi, Muhammad bin ʿAbd al-Hamid. 1986. *al-Risala al-Fathiyya fi al-Musiqa*. Kuwait: The National Council for Culture, Arts and Letters.

Almagro, Antonio. 2007. "The Dwellings of Madīnat al-Zahrā': A Methodological Approach." In *Revisiting al-Andalus: Perspectives on the Material Culture of Islamic Iberia and Beyond*, edited by Glaire D. Anderson and Mariam Rosser-Owen, 27–52. Medieval and Early Modern Iberian World. Leiden, the Netherlands: Brill.

al-Mahalli, Muhammad bin ʿAli. 1991. *Shifa' al-Ghalil fi ʿIlm al-Khalil*. Beirut: Dar al-Jil.

al-Malla, Bassam. 1993. *Ayyam Shamiyya*. TV serial. Damascus: Syrian Arab Television.

al-Maqqari. 1967. *Analectes sur l'histoire et la littérature des arabes d'Espagne*. Edited by R. Dozy et al. 2 vols. London: Oriental Press.

al-Munajjid, Salahaddin, and Stefan Wild, eds. 1979. *Rihlatan ila Lubnan*. Beirut: Orient Institute.

al-Nahawi, Ibn Jinni. 1989. *Kitab al-ʿArud*. 2nd ed. al-Safaʾ, Kuwait: Dar al-Qalam.

al-Qalaa, Saadallah Agha. 1997. *Nahj al-Aghani*. TV program. Damascus: al-Awj Productions.

al-Qashani, ʿAbd al Razzaq. n.d. *Tafsir al-Qashani. Part I, Surahs 1–18*. ʿAmman: Fons vitae: Royal Aal al-Bayt Institute for Islamic Thought.

AlSayyad, Nezar. 2011. *Cairo: Histories of a City*. Cambridge, MA: Belknap.

Altynsarin, Ybyrai. 1870. "Ocherk obychaev pri pohoronah i pominkah u kirgizov Orenburgskogo vedomstva." *Zapiski Orenburgskogo otdela Imperatorskogo Russkogo geographicheskogo obshchestva* 1:101–122.

al-Urmawi al-Baghdadi, Safi al-Din. 1986. *Kitab al-Adwar fi al-Musiqa*. Cairo: al-Hayʾa al-Misriyya al-ʿAmma li-l-Kitab.

Amor, Cherif. 2004. "Semantics of the Built Environment: Arab American Muslims' Home Interiors." In *Design with Spirit: EDRA35—Proceedings of the 35th Annual Conference of Environmental Design Research Association*, edited by Dwight Miller and James A. Wise, 8–15. Edmund, OK: EDRA.

ʿAmri, Nelly. 2009. "Le Samāʿ dans les milieux soufis du Magreb (VIIe–Xe/XIIe–XVIe siècles): Pratiques, Tensions et Codifications." *al-Qantara* 30 (2): 491–528.

And, Metin. 1971a. *Meşrutiyet Döneminde Türk Tiyatrosu: 1908–1923*. Ankara: Türkiye İş Bankası.

———. 1971b. "Eski İstanbul'da Fransız Sahnesi." *Tiyatro Araştırmaları Dergisi* 2:77–102.

———. 1983. *Türk Tiyatrosu: Cumhuriyet Dönemi*. Ankara: Türkiye İş Bankası Kültür Yayınları.

Anderson, Angela. 2014. "Muslims Viewed as 'Non-Muslims': The Alevi Precincts of Anatolia." In *The Religious Architecture of Non-Muslim Communities across the Islamic World*, edited by Mohammad Gharipour, 57–75. Leiden, the Netherlands: Brill.

Anderson, Glaire D. 2007. "Villa (munya) Architecture in Umayyad Córdoba: Preliminary Considerations." In *Revisiting al-Andalus: Perspectives on the Material Culture of Islamic Iberia and Beyond*, edited by Glaire D. Anderson and Mariam Rosser-Owen, 53–79. Medieval and Early Modern Iberian World. Leiden, the Netherlands: Brill.

———. 2012. "Concubines, Eunuchs and Patronage in Early Islamic Córdoba." In *Reassessing the Roles of Women as "Makers" of Medieval Art and Architecture*, edited by Therese Martin, 633–669. Leiden, the Netherlands: Brill.

———. 2013. *The Islamic Villa in Early Medieval Iberia: Aristocratic Estates and Court Culture in Umayyad Córdoba*. Aldershot, UK: Ashgate.

Andrews, Walter, and Irene Markoff. 1987. "Poetry, the Arts, and Group Ethos in the Ideology of the Ottoman Empire." *Edebiyat* 1 (1): 28–70.

Ankerl, Guy. 1981. *Experimental Sociology of Architecture: A Guide to Theory, Research, and Literature*. The Hague: Mouton.

Aracı, Emre. 2006. *Donizetti Paşa: Osmanlı Sarayının İtalyan Maestrosu*. Istanbul: Yapı Kredi Yayınları.

———. 2010. *Naum Tiyatrosu: 19. Yüzyıl İstanbulu'nun İtalyan Operası*. Istanbul: Yapı Kredi Yayınları.

Arcas Campoy, María. 2006. "El criterio de los juristas malikíes sobre ciertas prácticas rituales en el ribât: Al-Andalus y norte de África." *Miscelánea de Estudio Árabes Y Hebráicos (Sección árabe-Islam)* 55:37–48.

Ardalan, Nader, and Laleh Bakhtiar. 1973. *The Sense of Unity: The Sufi Tradition in Persian Architecture*. Chicago: University of Chicago Press.

Arjona Castro, Antonio. 1982. *Anales de Córdoba musulmana, 711–1008*. Colección Estudios y Documentos (Monte de Piedad y Caja de Ahorros de Córdoba) 4. Córdoba: Monte de Piedad y Caja de Ahorros de Córdoba.

Arkoun, Mohammed. 2003. "Rethinking Islam Today." *Annals of the American Academy of Political and Social Science* 588:18–39.

Artan, Tülay. 2000. "Aspects of the Ottoman Elite's Food Consumption: Looking for 'Staples,' 'Luxuries,' and 'Delicacies,' in a Changing Century." In *Consumption Studies and the History of the Ottoman Empire, 1550–1922: An Introduction*, edited by Donald Quataert, 107–200. Albany, NY: SUNY Press.

Aryn, Erlan, Orazaq Ismagulov, and Serik Ajigali, eds. 2007. *Religioznye verovaniya i obryady kazakhov (Qazaq khalqynyng dini nanym-senimderi)*. Biblioteka Kazakhskoi Etnographii 46. Astana, Kazakhstan: Altyn kitap.

Asad, Muhammad. 1980. *The Message of the Quran*. Gibraltar: Dar al-Andalus. Distributed by Brill.

Asani, Ali S. 2011. "Enhancing Religious Literacy in a Liberal Arts Education through the Study of Islam and Muslim Societies." In *The Harvard Sampler: Liberal Education for the Twenty-First Century*, edited by J. Shephard, S. Kosslyn, and E. Hammonds, 1–31. Cambridge, MA: Harvard University Press.

Assassin. 1993. *Le futur que nous réserve-t-il?* CD. Delabel.

———. 1995. *L'homocide volontaire*. CD. Delabel.

ʿAtiq, ʿAbd al-ʿAziz. 1987. *ʿIlm al-ʿarud wa-l-qafiya*. Beirut: Dar al-Nahda.

Avcioğlu, Nebahat. 2008. "Istanbul: The Palimpsest City in Search of Its Architext." *RES: Anthropology and Aesthetics* 53/54:190–210.

Avery, Kenneth S. 2004. *A Psychology of Early Sufi Samāʿ: Listening and Altered States*. London: Routledge.

Ayad, Hani M. 2011. "Community Area Based Development in the Northern Region of Syria: Case Study of Urban Aleppo." *Alexandria Engineering Journal* 50 (4): 407–419.

Babaie, Sussan. 1994. "Shah ʿAbbas II, the Conquest of Qandahar, the Chihil Sutun, and Its Wall Paintings." *Muqarnas* 11:125–142.

Bakhtiar, Laleh. 1976. *Sufi: Expressions of the Mystical Quest*. London: Thames and Hudson.

Balbo, Marcello. 2012. "Rethinking Medinas in a Changing Mediterranean." In *The Medina: The Restoration and Conservation of Historic Islamic Cities*, edited by Marcello Balbo, 3–11. London: I. B. Tauris.

Barceló, Miguel. 1998. "The Manifest Caliph: Umayyad Ceremony in Córdoba, or the Staging of Power." In *The Formation of al-Andalus, Part 1: History and Society*, edited by Manuela Marín, 425–455. Aldershot, UK: Ashgate.

Bardakçı, Murat. 1986. *Maragalı Abdülkadir.* Istanbul: Pan Yayıncılık.

Barkechli, M. 1961. "La Musique des 'zour-khaneh' et ses rythmes caractéristiques." *Journal of the International Folk Music Council* 13:73.

Barletta, Vincent. 2005. *Gestos clandestinos: La literatura aljamiado-morisca como práctica cultural.* Zaragoza: Instituto de Estudios Islámicos de Oriente Próximo.

Başgöz, Ilhan. 1967. "Dream Motif in Turkish Folk Stories and Shamanistic Initiation." *Asian Folklore Studies* 26 (1): 1–18.

Bateson, Gregory. 1972. *Steps to an Ecology of Mind: Collected Essays in Anthropology, Psychiatry, Evolution, and Epistemology.* Chicago: University of Chicago Press.

Baydar, Evren K. 2010. *Osmanlı'nın Avrupalı Müzisyenleri.* Istanbul: Kapı Yayınları.

Bazin, Hugues. 1995. *La culture hip-hop.* Paris: Desclée De Brouwer.

Becker, Judith. 2004. *Deep Listeners: Music, Emotion, and Trancing.* Bloomington: Indiana University Press.

Behrens-Abouseif, Doris. 1989. *Islamic Architecture in Cairo: An Introduction.* Leiden, the Netherlands: Brill.

———. 1999. *Beauty in Arabic Culture.* Princeton, NJ: Markus Wiener Publishers.

Behrens-Abouseif, Doris, and Leonor E. Fernandes. 1985. "An Unlisted Monument of the Fifteenth Century: The Dome of Zawiyat al-Damirdash." *Annales Islamogiques* 21:105–121.

Bell, Catherine M. 1992. *Ritual Theory, Ritual Practice.* New York: Oxford University Press.

Ben Driss, Karim. 2002. *Sidi Hamza al Qaâdiri Bouchich. Le renouveau du Soufisme au Maroc.* Milan: Arché.

Bennigsen, Alexandre, and S. Enders Wimbush. 1986. *Muslims of the Soviet Empire.* Bloomington: Indiana University Press.

Beranek, Leo L. 1979. *Music, Acoustics and Architecture.* New York: R. E. Krieger.

———. 1992. "Music, Acoustics, and Architecture." *Bulletin of the American Academy of Arts and Sciences* 45 (8): 25–46.

Berthomé, François, and Michael Houseman. 2010. "Ritual and Emotions: Moving Relations, Patterned Effusions." *Religion and Society: Advances in Research* 1 (1): 57–75.

Bianca, Stefano. 2007. *Medieval Citadels between East and West.* Turin: Umberto Allemandi; The Aga Khan Trust for Culture.

Bijsterveld, Karin, ed. 2013. *Soundscapes of the Urban Past: Staged Sound as Mediated Cultural Heritage.* Bielefeld, Germany: Transcript.

Bilici, Faruk. 1998. "The Function of Alevi-Bektashi Theology in Modern Turkey." In *Alevi Identity: Cultural, Religious, and Social Perspectives*, edited by Tord Olsson, Elisabeth Özdalga, and Catherine Raudvere, 51–26. Istanbul: Swedish Institute in Istanbul.

Birdwhistell, Ray L. 1970. *Kinesics and Context: Essays on Body Motion Communication.* Philadelphia: University of Pennsylvania Press.

Birge, John Kingsley. 1937. *The Bektashi Order of Dervishes.* London: Luzac.

Blesser, Barry, and Linda-Ruth Salter. 2007. *Spaces Speak, Are You Listening? Experiencing Aural Architecture.* Cambridge, MA: MIT Press.

Bloom, Jonathan, and Sheila Blair, eds. 2009. "Tent." *The Grove Encyclopedia of Islamic Art and Architecture.* Oxford: Oxford University Press.

Boloix Gallardo, Bárbara. 2006. *De la taifa de Arjona al reino Nazarí de Granada (1232–1246): En torno a los orígenes de un estado y de una dinastía.* Jaén, Spain: Instituto de Estudios Giennenses.

———. 2011. "Las primeras celebraciones del mawlid en al-Andalus y Ceuta, según la Tuhfat al-Mugtarib de al-Qashtālī y el Maqsad al-Sharīf de al-Bādisī." *Anaquel de Estudios Árabes* 22:79–96.

———. Forthcoming. "Commercial Trade in the Nasrid Kingdom." *Medievalia.*

Born, Georgina, ed. 2013. *Music, Sound and Space: Transformations of Public and Private Experience.* Cambridge: Cambridge University Press.

Borneman, John. 2007. *Syrian Episodes: Sons, Fathers, and an Anthropologist in Aleppo.* Princeton, NJ: Princeton University Press.

Bouamama, Saïd. 2009. *Les classes et quartiers populaires: Paupérisation, ethnicisation, et discrimination.* Paris: Éditions du Cygne.

Bouasria, Abdelilah. 2012. "La Tariqa Qadiria Boutchichi au Maroc: La genèse d'un Soufisme de marché?" *Mamfakinch, February 22.* https://www.mamfakinch.com/la-tariqa-qadiria-boutchichi-au-maroc-la-genese-dun-soufisme-de-marche/.

Bourderionnet, Olivier. 2011. "A 'Picture-Perfect' Banlieue Artist: Abd Al Malik or the Perils of a Conciliatory Rap Discourse." *French Cultural Studies* 22 (2): 151–161.

Bourdieu, Pierre. 1977. *Outline of a Theory of Practice.* Cambridge: Cambridge University Press.

———. 1979. "The Kabyle House or the World Reversed." In *Algeria 1960: The Disenchantment of the World; The Sense of Honour; The Kabyle House or the World Reversed. Essays by Pierre Bourdieu,* 133–153. New York: Cambridge University Press.

———. 1993. *Sociology in Question.* London: Sage.

Bowen, John Richard. 2006. *Why the French Hate Headscarves.* Princeton, NJ: Princeton University Press.

———. 2010. *Can Islam Be French? Pluralism and Pragmatism in a Secularist State.* Princeton, NJ: Princeton University Press.

Brosius, Christiane, and Ute Hüsken. 2010. "Change and Stability of Rituals: An Introduction." In *Ritual Matters: Dynamic Dimensions in Practice,* edited by Christiane Brosius and Ute Hüsken, 1–28. New Delhi: Routledge.

Büchner, Victor F., and Gerhard Doerfer. 2012. "Tañri." In *Encyclopaedia of Islam.* 2nd ed., edited by P. Bearman, Th. Bianquis, C. E. Bosworth, E. van Donzel, and

W. P. Heinrichs. Brill Online. http://referenceworks.brillonline.com/browse/encyclopaedia-of-islam-2.

Bull, Michael. 2004. "Thinking about Sound, Proximity, and Distance in Western Experience: The Case of Odysseus's Walkman." In *Hearing Cultures: Essays on Sound, Listening, and Modernity*, edited by Veit Erlmann, 173–190. Oxford: Berg.

Bull, Michael, and Les Back. 2003. *The Auditory Culture Reader*. Oxford: Berg.

Burckhardt, Titus. 1976. *Art of Islam: Language and Meaning*. London: World of Islam Festival.

———. 2007. "Art and Liturgy." In *Voices of Islam*, edited by Vincent J. Cornell, 4:49–58. Westport, CT: Praeger.

Bush, Olga. 2006. "Architecture, Poetic Texts and Textiles in the Alhambra." Unpublished PhD diss., New York University, Institute of Fine Arts.

Busquets, Joan, ed. 2005. *Aleppo: Rehabilitation of the Old City*. Cambridge, MA: Harvard University Graduate School of Design.

Cabanelas, Darío. 1988. *El techo del Salón de Comarese en la Alhambra: Decoración, policromía, simbolismo y etimología*. Granada: Patronato de la Alhambra y Generalife.

Çağatay, Alii Rıfat. 1895. "Fenn-i Musiki Nazariyatı." *Malumat* 1–7, 9–14, 16, 20, 23, 28.

Calero Secall, María Isabel. 1987. "Los Banū Sīd Būna." *Sharq al-Andalus* 4:35–44.

Calvo Capilla, Susanna. 2011. "Mujeres mecenas: De al-Andalus al Oriente." In *al-Andalus paradigma y continuidad*, edited by Emilio González Ferrín, 129–54. Seville: Tres Culturas, Fundación.

Cannon, Steven. 1997. "Paname City Rapping: B-Boys in the Banlieues and Beyond." In *Post-Colonial Cultures in France*, edited by Alec G. Hargreaves and Mark McKinney, 150–166. London: Routledge.

Carlson, Marvin. 1989. *Places of Performance: The Semiotics of Theatre Architecture*. Ithaca, NY: Cornell University Press.

Castells, Manuel. 1983. *The City and the Grassroots: A Cross-Cultural Theory of Urban Social Movements*. Berkeley: University of California Press.

Caswell, Fuad Matthew. 2011. *The Slave Girls of Baghdad: The Qiyan in the Early Abbasid Era*. London: I. B. Tauris.

Çelebi, Evliya. 1834–1850. *Narrative of Travels in Europe, Asia and Africa, in the Seventeenth Century*. Translated by Joseph von Hammer. London: Oriental Translation Fund.

Çelebi, Evliya, Robert Dankoff, and Sooyong Kim. 2011. *An Ottoman Traveller: Selections from the Book of Travels by Evliya Çelebi*. New York: Eland Publishing.

Çelik, Zeynep. 1997. *Urban Forms and Colonial Confrontations: Algiers under French Rule*. Berkeley: University of California Press.

Chabrol, Claude, and Louis Marin. 1974. *Le récit évangélique*. Paris: Aubier Montaigne.

Charef, Mehdi. 1983. *Le thé au harem d'Archi Ahmed*. Paris: Mercure de France.

Chehabi, Houchang E. 1995. "Sport and Politics in Iran: The Legend of Gholamreza Takhti." *International Journal of the History of Sport* 12 (3): 48–60.

———. 2002. "The Juggernaut of Globalization: Sport and Modernization in Iran." *International Journal of the History of Sport* 19 (2–3): 275–294.

———. 2012. "Zūrkhāna." In *Encyclopaedia of Islam*, 2nd ed., edited by P. Bearman, Th. Bianquis, C. E. Bosworth, E. van Donzel, and W. P. Heinrichs. Brill Online. http://referenceworks.brillonline.com/browse/encyclopaedia-of-islam-2.

Chih, Rachida. 2007. "What Is a Sufi Order? Revisiting the Concept through a Case Study of the Khalwatiyya in Contemporary Egypt." In *Sufism and the "Modern" in Islam*, edited by Martin van Bruinessen and Julia Day Howell, 21–38. London: I. B. Tauris.

Chittick, William C. 1994. *Imaginal Worlds: Ibn al-ʿArabi and the Problem of Religious Diversity*. Albany, NY: SUNY Press.

Clancy-Smith, Julia. 1994. *Rebel and Saint: Muslim Notables, Populist Protest, Colonial Encounters (Algeria and Tunisia, 1800–1904)*. Berkeley: University of California Press.

Classen, Constance, David Howes, and Anthony Synnott. 1994. *Aroma: The Cultural History of Smell*. London: Routledge.

Clayton, Martin. 2001. "Introduction: Towards a Theory of Musical Meaning (in India and Elsewhere)." *British Journal of Ethnomusicology* 10 (1): 1–17.

———. 2008. "Toward an Ethnomusicology of Sound Experience." In *The New (Ethno)musicologies*, edited by Henry Stobart and Martin Stokes, 135–169. Lanham, MD: Scarecrow.

Cohen, Sara. 1995. "Sounding out the City: Music and the Sensuous Production of Place." *Transactions of the Institute of British Geographers* 20 (4): 434–446.

———. 2012. "Bubbles, Tracks, Borders and Lines: Mapping Music and Urban Landscape." *Journal of the Royal Musical Association* 137 (1): 135–170.

Colla, Elliott. 2012. "The Poetry of Revolt." In *Dawn of the Arab Uprisings: End of an Old Order?*, edited by Bassam Haddad, Rosie Bsheer, and Ziad Abu-Rish, 77–82. London: Pluto.

Connell, John, and Chris Gibson. 2003. *Sound Tracks: Popular Music, Identity, and Place*. London: Routledge.

Corbin, Alain. 1998. *Village Bells: Sound and Meaning in the 19th-Century French Countryside*. New York: Columbia University Press.

Critchlow, Keith. 1976. *Islamic Patterns: An Analytical and Cosmological Approach*. New York: Schocken Books.

Damon, Julien. 2010. "Les mots qui comptent: Plan Marshall pour les banlieues." *Sciences Humaines*, March.

Danielson, Virginia. 1997. *The Voice of Egypt: Umm Kulthum, Arabic Song, and Egyptian Society in the Twentieth Century*. Chicago: University of Chicago Press.

Darvishi, Mohammad Reza. 2005. *Dayereh-yi Alma'aref-i Sazha-yi Iran. Jild-i Duvum: Pust Sedaha va Khudsedaha-yi Navahi-yi Iran / Encyclopaedia of the Musical Instruments of Iran*. Volume II: *Membranophones and Idiophones in Regional Music*. Tehran: Mahoor Institute of Culture and Art.

Davidson, Naomi. 2012. *Only Muslim: Embodying Islam in Twentieth Century France.* Ithaca, NY: Cornell University Press.

Davila, Carl. 2004. "Between the Spoken and the Written." In *The Muwashshah: Origins, History and Present Practice.* Proceedings of the 2004 SOAS Conference, 99–113. London: SOAS, University of London.

———. 2009. "Fixing a Misbegotten Biography: Ziryab in the Mediterranean World." *al-Masaq: Islam and the Medieval Mediterranean* 21 (2): 121–136.

de Certeau, Michel. 1984. *The Practice of Everyday Life.* Translated by Steven Rendall. Berkeley: University of California Press.

De Jong, Frederick. 1976. "Cairene Ziyâra-Days: A Contribution to the Study of Saint Veneration in Islam." *Die Welt Des Islams* 17 (1/4): 26–43.

———. 1989. "The Iconography of Bektashiism: A Survey of Themes and Symbolism in Clerical Costume, Liturgical Objects and Pictorial Art." *Manuscripts of the Middle East* 4:7–29.

de la Granja, Fernando. 1969. "Festivales cristianas en al-Andalus (materiales para su estudio)." *al-Andalus* 34:1–53.

Delattre, Bernard. 2003. "L'islam sorti 'des caves et des garages.'" *La Libre Belgique,* April 14.

del Moral, Celia. 1997. "La literatura en el periodo nazarí." In *Estudios Nazaríes,* edited by Concepción Castillo Castillo, 29–83. Granada: Universidad de Granada.

del Moral, Celia, and Fernando N. Velásquez Basanta. 1994. "La casida mawlidiyya de Abu l-Qasim al-Barji." *al-Andalus Maghreb* 2:83–120.

Denny, Walter. 1985. "Music and Musicians in Islamic Art." *Asian Music* 17 (1): 37–68.

Diener, Alexander C. 2009. *One Homeland or Two? The Nationalization and Transnationalization of Mongolia's Kazakhs.* Stanford, CA: Stanford University Press.

Dikeç, Mustafa. 2007. *Badlands of the Republic: Space, Politics, and Urban Policy.* Oxford: Wiley-Blackwell.

Dinç, Ayhan, Özden Çankaya, and Nail Ekici, eds. 2000. *İstanbul Radyosu: Anılar, Yaşantılar.* Istanbul: Yapı Kredi Kültür Yayıncılık.

Dinçer, Fahriye. 2004. "Formulation of Semahs in Relation to the Question of Alevi Identity in Turkey." Unpublished PhD diss., Boğaziçi University.

Divaev, Abubekir. 1889. "Drevnekirgizskie pohoronnye obychai." *Izvestiya Obshchestva izucheniya archeologii, istorii i etnographii pri Imperatorskom Kazanskom universitete* 14 (1–6): 181–187.

Dodds, Jerrilynn Denise. 1992. *al-Andalus: The Art of Islamic Spain.* New York: Metropolitan Museum of Art.

Donahue, Katherine. 2008. "The Religious Trajectories of the Moussaoui Family." *ISIM Review* 21:18–19.

D'Ottone, Arianna. 2010. "Il manoscrito vaticano arabo 368, Haditīt Bayāḍ wa Riyāḍ. Il codice, il testo, le immagini." *Rivista di Storia della Miniatura* 14:55–70.

———. 2013. *La storia di Bayāḍ e Riyāḍ (Vat. Ar. 368): Una nuova edizione e traduzione.*

Studi e Testi (Biblioteca Apostolica Vaticana), 479. Vatican City: Biblioteca Apostolica Vaticana.

Dressler, Markus. 2013. *Writing Religion: The Making of Turkish Alevi Islam.* New York: Oxford University Press.

Dubet, François, and Didier Lapeyronnie. 1992. *Les quartiers d'exil.* Paris: Seuil.

Du Bois, William D. 2001. "Design and Human Behavior: Sociology of Architecture." In *Applying Sociology: Making a Better World,* edited by William D. Du Bois and R. Dean Wright, 30–45. Boston: Allyn and Bacon.

Duindam, Jeroen Frans Jozef, Tülay Artan, and I. Metin Kunt, eds. 2011. *Royal Courts in Dynastic States and Empires: A Global Perspective.* Leiden, the Netherlands: Brill.

Durand, Alain-Philippe, ed. 2002. *Black, Blanc, Beur: Rap Music and Hip-Hop Culture in the Francophone World.* Lanham, MD: Scarecrow.

Duret, Pascal. 1996. *Anthropologie de la fraternité dans les cités.* Paris: Presses Universitaires de France.

During, Jean. 1998. "A Critical Survey on Ahl-e Haqq Studies in Europe and Islam." In *Alevi Identity: Cultural, Religious and Social Perspectives,* edited by Tord Olsson, Elizabeth Özclalga, and Catharina Raudvere, 105–126. Istanbul: Swedish Institute in Istanbul; distributed by RoutledgeCurzon.

Ebaugh, Helen. 2010. *The Gülen Movement: A Sociological Analysis of a Civic Movement Rooted in Moderate Islam.* Dordrecht, Germany: Springer.

Eco, Umberto. 1972. "A Componential Analysis of the Architectural Sign/Column." *Semiotica* 5 (2): 97–117.

———. 1980. "Function and Sign: The Semiotics of Architecture." In *Signs, Symbols, and Architecture,* edited by Geoffrey Broadbent, Richard Bunt, and Charles Jencks, 11–70. Chichester, UK: Wiley.

Edwards, Brian, Magda Sibley, Mohamed Hakmi, and Peter Land, eds. 2006. *Courtyard Housing: Past, Present, and Future.* New York: Taylor and Francis.

Elias, Norbert. 1983. *The Court Society.* New York: Pantheon Books.

El-Said, Issam, and Ayse Parman. 1976. *Geometric Concepts in Islamic Art.* London: World of Islam Festival.

El Sandouby, Aliaa Ezzeldin Ismail. 2008. "The Ahl al-Bayt in Cairo and Damascus: The Dynamics of Making Shrines for the Family of the Prophet." Unpublished PhD diss., UCLA.

Epstein, Beth. 2011. *Collective Terms: Race, Culture, and Community in a State-Planned City in France.* New York: Berghahn Books.

Ergin, Nina. 2008. "The Soundscape of Sixteenth-Century Istanbul Mosques: Architecture and Qur'an Recital." *Journal of the Society of Architectural Historians* 67 (2): 204–221.

———. 2013. "A Multi-Sensorial Message of the Divine and the Personal: Qur'anic Inscriptions and Recitation in Sixteenth-Century Ottoman Mosques." In *Callig-*

raphy and Architecture in the Muslim World, edited by Mohammad Gharipour and Irvin C. Schick, 105–118. Edinburgh: Edinburgh University Press.

[Ergin] Cichocki, Nina. 2005. "The Life Story of the Çemberlitaş Hamam: From Bath to Tourist Attraction." Unpublished PhD diss., University of Minnesota.

Erlmann, Veit. 2004a. "But What of the Ethnographic Ear? Anthropology, Sound, and the Senses." In *Hearing Cultures: Essays on Sound, Listening and Modernity*, edited by Veit Erlmann, 1–20. Oxford: Berg.

———. 2004b. *Hearing Cultures: Essays on Sound, Listening and Modernity*. Oxford: Berg.

Ernazarov, Jasqairat. 2003. *Semeinaya obryadnost kazakhov: Simvol i ritual*. Almaty: Zapadno-Kazakhstanskii oblastnoi tsentr istorii i archeologii.

Es, Murat. 2013. "Alevis in Cemevis: Religion and Secularism in Turkey." In *Topographies of Faith: Religion in Urban Spaces*, edited by Irene Becci, Marian Burchardt, and José Casanova, 25–44. Leiden, the Netherlands: Brill.

Eyuboğlu, İsmet Zeki. 1980. *Bütün yönleriyle Bektaşilik (Alevilik)*. Istanbul: Yeni Çıgır Kitabevi.

Falk, Catherine. 2004. "Hmong Instructions to the Dead: What the Qeej Says in the Qeej Tu Siav." *Asian Folklore Studies* 63 (1–2): 1–29, 167–220.

Faroqhi, Suraiya, and Christoph K. Neumann, eds. 2004. *Ottoman Costumes: From Textile to Identity*. Istanbul: Eren.

Fassin, Didier. 2011. *La force de l'ordre: Une anthropologie de la police des quartiers*. Paris: Seuil.

Fassin, Didier, and Eric Fassin, eds. 2006. *De la question sociale à la question raciale. Représenter la société française*. Paris: La Découverte.

Feagre, Torvald. 1979. *Tents: Architecture of the Nomads*. London: John Murray.

Feld, Steven. 1990. *Sound and Sentiment: Birds, Weeping, Poetics, and Song in Kaluli Expression*. 2nd ed. Philadelphia: University of Pennsylvania Press.

———. 1996. "Waterfalls of Song: An Acoustemology of Place Resounding in Bosavi, Papua New Guinea." In *Senses of Place*, edited by Steven Feld and Keith H. Basso, 91–135. Santa Fe, NM: School of American Research Press.

———. 2004. *The Time of Bells: Soundscapes of Italy, Finland, Greece and France*. CD. VoxLox.

———. 2012. *Jazz Cosmopolitanism in Accra. Five Musical Years in Ghana*. Durham, NC: Duke University Press.

Feld, Steven, and Keith H. Basso, eds. 1996. *Senses of Place*. Santa Fe, NM: School of American Research Press.

Feldman, Walter. 1996. *Music of the Ottoman Court: Makam, Composition and the Early Ottoman Instrumental Repertoire*. Intercultural Music Studies 10. Berlin: Verlag für Wissenschaft und Bildung.

Ferdowsi, Abdolqasem. 2007. *Shahnameh: The Persian Book of Kings*. Translated by Dick Davis. London: Penguin.

Fernandes, Leonor. 1980. "The Evolution of the Khanqah Institution in Mamluk Egypt." Unpublished PhD diss., Princeton University.

———. 1983. "Some Aspects of the Zawiya in Egypt at the Eve of the Ottoman Conquest." *Annales Islamogiques* 19:9–17.

Fernández Manzano, Reynaldo. 1995. "Iconografía y otros aspectos de los instrumentos musicales en al-Andalus." In *Música y Poesía del Sur de al-Andalus: Granada-Sevilla*, 79–89. Barcelona: Lunwerg.

———. 1997. "Instrumentos musicales en al-Andalus." In *El Saber en al-Andalus: Textos y Estudios*, vol. 1, edited by Pedro Cano Ávila and Ildefonso Garijo Galán, 101–136. Seville: Universidad de Sevilla, Secretariado de Publicaciones.

Fernando, Mayanthi. 2010. "Reconfiguring Freedom: Muslim Piety and the Limits of Secular Law and Public Discourse in France." *American Ethnologist* 37 (1): 19–35.

———. 2014. *The Republic Unsettled: Muslim French and the Contradictions of Secularism*. Durham, NC: Duke University Press.

Fierro, Maribel. 1992. "The Treatises against Innovations (*kutub al-bidaʿ*)." *Islam* 69: 204–246.

———. 1996. "On al-Fāṭimī and al-Fāṭimiyyūn." *Jerusalem Studies in Arabic and Islam* 20:130–161.

Finke, Peter. 1999. "The Kazakhs of Western Mongolia." In *Contemporary Kazakhs: Cultural and Social Perspectives*, edited by Ingvar Svanberg, 103–139. Richmond, UK: Curzon.

———. 2004. *Nomaden im Transformationsprozess: Kasachen in der post-sozialistischen Mongolei*. Münster: Lit.

Fleischer, Cornell H. 1986. *Bureaucrat and Intellectual in the Ottoman Empire: The Historian Mustafa Ali (1541–1600)*. Princeton, NJ: Princeton University Press.

Folsach, Kjeld, and Joachim Meyer, eds. 2005. *The Ivories of Muslim Spain: Papers from a Symposium Held in Copenhagen from the 18th to the 20th of November 2003*. Journal of the David Collection, vol. 2.2. Copenhagen: David Collection.

Forsyth, Michael. 1985. *Buildings for Music: The Architect, the Musician, and the Listener from the Seventeenth Century to the Present Day*. Cambridge, MA: MIT Press.

Foster, Robert. 2002. "Bargains with Modernity in Papua New Guinea and Elsewhere." In *Critical Modern: Alternatives, Alterities, Anthropologies*, edited by Bruce Knauft, 57–81. Bloomington: Indiana University Press.

Frishkopf, Michael. 1999. "Sufism, Ritual, and Modernity in Egypt: Language Performance as an Adaptive Strategy." Unpublished PhD dissertation, UCLA.

———. 2000. "Inshad Dini and Aghani Diniyya in Twentieth-Century Egypt: A Review of Styles, Genres, and Available Recordings." *Middle East Studies Association Bulletin* 34 (2): 167–183.

———. 2001. "Tarab in the Mystic Sufi Chant of Egypt." In *Colors of Enchantment: Visual and Performing Arts of the Middle East*, edited by Sherifa Zuhur, 233–269. Cairo: American University in Cairo Press.

———. 2011. "Ritual as Strategic Action: The Social Logic of Musical Silence in Canadian Islam. In *Muslim Rap, Halal Soaps, and Revolutionary Theater: Artistic Developments in the Muslim World,* edited by Karin van Nieuwkerk, 115–148. Austin: University of Texas Press.

———. 2013. "Against Ethnomusicology: Language Performance and the Social Impact of Ritual Performance in Islam." *Performing Islam* 2 (1): 11–43.

Gallagher, Sally K. 2012. *Making Do: Navigating a Generation of Change in Family and Work*. Syracuse, NY: Syracuse University Press.

Gaonkar, Dilip Parameshwar, ed. 2001. *Alternative Modernities*. Durham, NC: Duke University Press.

García Arenal, Mercedes. 2012. "Shurafa' in the Last Years of al-Andalus and in the Morisco Period: Laylat al-Mawlid and Genealogies of the Prophet Muhammad." In *Sayyids and Sharifs in Muslim Societies: The Living Links to the Prophet,* edited by Kazuo Morimoto, 161–185. London: Palgrave Macmillan.

García Gómez, Emilio. 1988. *Foco de Antigua Luz sobre la Alhambra: Desde un texto de Ibn el-Jatıb en 1362*. Madrid: Instituto Egipcio de Estudios Islámicos en Madrid.

———. 1996. *Poemas árabes en los muros y fuentes de la Alhambra*. 2nd ed. Madrid: Instituto Egipcio de Estudios Islámicos en Madrid.

Gazimihal, Mahmut R. 1975. *Ülkelerde kopuz ve tezeneli sazlarımız*. Ankara: Ankara Üniversitesi Basımevi.

Geisser, Vincent. 2003. *La nouvelle islamophobie*. Paris: La Découverte.

Genette, Gérard. 1997. *Palimpsests: Literature in the Second Degree*. Lincoln: University of Nebraska Press.

Gharipour, Mohammad, and Irvin Cemil Schick, eds. 2013. *Calligraphy and Architecture in the Muslim World*. Edinburgh: Edinburgh University Press.

Gibson, James. 1977. "The Theory of Affordances." In *Perceiving, Acting and Knowing: Toward an Ecological Psychology,* edited by Robert Shaw and John Bransford, 67–82. Hillsdale, NJ: Lawrence Erlbaum Associates.

Gieryn, Thomas F. 2000. "A Place for Space in Sociology." *Annual Review of Sociology* 26:263–296.

———. 2002. "What Buildings Do." *Theory and Society* 31 (1): 35–74.

Gilsenan, Michael. 1973. *Saint and Sufi in Modern Egypt: An Essay in the Sociology of Religion*. Oxford: Clarendon.

Godard, Jean-Luc. 1967. *Deux ou trois choses que je sais d'elle*. Film. UGC, Films Sirius, CFDC, Tamasa Distribution.

Goffman, Erving. 1974. *Frame Analysis: An Essay on the Organization of Experience*. London: Harper and Row.

Goitein, Shelomo Dov. 1967. *A Mediterranean Society: The Jewish Communities of the Arab World as Portrayed in the Documents of the Cairo Geniza*. Berkeley: University of California Press.

Gökmen, Mustafa. 1991. *Eski İstanbul Sinemaları*. Istanbul: İstanbul Kitaplığı Yayınları.

Goldziher, Ignaz. 1971. *Muslim Studies (Muhammedanische Studien)* 2. London: Allen and Unwin.

Golombek, Lisa. 2007. "The Draped Universe of Islam." In *Late Antique and Medieval Art of the Mediterranean World*, edited by Eva Rose F. Hoffman, 97–114. Malden, MA: Blackwell.

Gölpınarlı, Abdülbāki. 1963. *Alevī-Bektāşī Nefesleri*. Istanbul: Remzi Kitabevi.

González Costa, Amina. 2009. "Un ejemplo de la hermenéutica sufí del Corán en al-Andalus: El comentario coránico Idāh al-Hikma de Ibn Barrajān (m. 536/1141) de Sevilla." In *Historia del Sufismo en al-Andalus: Maestros Sufíes de al-Andalus y el Magreb*, edited by Amina González Costa and Gracia Lopez Anguita, 41–66. Madrid: Almuzara.

González Costa, Amina, and Gracia Lopez Anguita, eds. 2009. *Historia del Sufismo en al-Andalus: Maestros Sufíes de al-Andalus y el Magreb*. Madrid: Almuzara.

Gordon, Matthew. 2004. "ʿArib al-Maʾmuniya: A Third/Ninth Century-ʿAbbasid Courtesan." In *Views from the Edge: Essays in Honor of Richard W. Bulliet*, edited by Neguin Yavari, Lawrence G. Potter, and Jean-Marc Ran Oppenheim, 86–100. New York: Columbia University Press.

Grabar, Oleg. 1978. *The Alhambra*. Cambridge, MA: Harvard University Press.

Gramatikova, Nevena. 2011. *Neortodoksalniyat Isylam v Bŭlgarskite Zemi*. Sofia: Gutenburg Publishing.

Greve, Martin. 1995. *Die Europäisierung orientalischer Kunstmusik in der Türkei*. Berlin: Peter Lang.

Gronow, Pekka. 1981. "The Record Industry Comes to the Orient." *Ethnomusicology* 25 (2): 251–285.

Gross, Joan, David McMurray, and Ted Swedenburg. 1994. "Arab Noise and Ramadan Nights: Rai, Rap, and Franco-Maghrebi Identity." *Diaspora* 3 (1): 3–39.

Grueneisen, Peter. 2003. *Soundspace: Architecture for Sound and Vision*. Basel, Switzerland: Birkhäuser.

Habermas, Jürgen. 1984. *The Theory of Communicative Action*. Vol. 1: *Reason and the Rationalization of Society*. Translated by Thomas McCarthy. Boston: Beacon.

———. 1987. *The Theory of Communicative Action*. Vol. 2: *Lifeworld and System: A Critique of Functionalist Reason*. Translated by Thomas McCarthy. Boston: Beacon.

Haenni, Patrick, and Raphaël Voix. 2007. "God by All Means: Eclectic Faith and Sufi Resurgence among the Moroccan Bourgeoisie." In *Sufism and the "Modern" in Islam*, edited by Martin van Bruinessen and Julia Day Howell, 241–256. London: I. B. Tauris.

Haider, Gulzar. 1988. "Islam, Cosmology, and Architecture." In *Theories and Principles of Design in the Architecture of Islamic Societies: A Symposium Held by the Aga Khan Program for Islamic Architecture at Harvard University and the Massachusetts Institute of Technology, Cambridge, Massachusetts, November 6–8, 1987*, edited by Margaret

Bentley Ševčenko, 73–85. Cambridge, MA: Aga Khan Program for Islamic Architecture, 1988.

———. 1996. "Muslim Space and the Practice of Architecture." In *Making Muslim Space in North America and Europe*, edited by Barbara Daly Metcalf, 31–45. Berkeley: University of California Press.

Hall, Edward T. 1966. *The Hidden Dimension*. Garden City, NY: Doubleday.

Hamori, Andras. 1974. *On the Art of Medieval Arabic Literature*. Princeton, NJ: Princeton University Press.

Hamzeh, A. Nizar, and Hrair R. Dekmejian. 1996. "A Sufi Response to Political Islamism: al-Ahbash of Lebanon." *International Journal of Middle East Studies* 28:217–229.

Hanna, Nelly. 2003. *In Praise of Books: A Cultural History of Cairo's Middle Class, Sixteenth to the Eighteenth Century*. Syracuse, NY: Syracuse University Press.

Haqqi, Haytham. 1996. *Khan al-Harir*. TV serial. Aleppo, Syria: Sharikat Halab al-Duwaliyya.

Hargreaves, Alec G. 1995. *Immigration, "Race," and Ethnicity in Contemporary France*. New York: Routledge.

———. 1997. *Immigration and Identity in Beur Fiction: Voices from the North African Immigrant Community in France*. 2nd ed. Oxford: Berg.

Harris, Dianne Suzette, and D. Fairchild Ruggles. 2007. "Landscape and Vision." In *Sites Unseen: Landscape and Vision*, edited by Dianne Suzette Harris and D. Fairchild Ruggles, 5–30. Pittsburgh, PA: University of Pittsburgh Press.

Harris, Rachel. 2004. *Singing the Village: Music, Memory and Ritual among the Sibe of Xinjiang*. Oxford: Oxford University Press.

Harvey, David. 2000. *Spaces of Hope*. Berkeley: University of California Press.

Haşim Bey. 1864. *Şarkı Mecmuası*. 2nd ed. Istanbul: n.p.

Hinz, W. 2012. "Dhirāʿ." In *Encyclopaedia of Islam*. 2nd ed., edited by P. Bearman, Th. Bianquis, C. E. Bosworth, E. van Donzel, and W. P. Heinrichs. Brill Online. http://referenceworks.brillonline.com/browse/encyclopaedia-of-islam-2.

Hirsch, Eric. 1996. *The Anthropology of Landscape*. Oxford: Clarendon.

Hirschkind, Charles. 2009. *The Ethical Soundscape: Cassette Sermons and Islamic Counterpublics*. New York: Columbia University Press.

Hoffman, Valerie J. 1995. *Sufism, Mystics, and Saints in Modern Egypt*. Columbia: University of South Carolina Press.

Hoffman-Ladd, Valerie J. 1992. "Devotion to the Prophet and His Family in Egyptian Sufism." *International Journal of Middle East Studies* 24 (4): 615–637.

Holl, Steven, Juhani Pallasmaa, and Alberto Perez-Gomez. 2006. *Questions of Perception: Phenomenology of Architecture*. San Francisco: William Stout.

Homerin, Th. 2001. *From Arab Poet to Muslim Saint: Ibn al-Farid, His Verse, and His Shrine*. 2nd ed. Cairo: American University in Cairo Press.

House, Jim, and Neil MacMaster. 2006. *Paris 1961: Algerians, State Terror, and Memory*. Oxford: Oxford University Press.

Howard, Deborah, and Laura Moretti. 2009. *Sound and Space in Renaissance Venice. Architecture, Music, Acoustics*. New Haven, CT: Yale University Press.

Howes, David. 2005. *Empire of the Senses: The Sensual Culture Reader.* Oxford: Berg.

Hughes, Thomas Patrick. 2001. *A Dictionary of Islam*. New Delhi: Asian Educational Services.

Humphrey, Caroline. 1974. "Inside a Mongolian Tent." *New Society*, October 31.

Humphrey, Caroline, and Piers Vitebsky. 1997. *Sacred Architecture*. Boston: Little, Brown and Company.

Ibn ʿAbd Allah Shushtari, ʿAli. 1988. *Poesía estrófica (cejeles y/o muwaššaḥāt) atribuida al místico granadino aš-Šuštarī (siglo XIII d.C.)*. Edited by Federico Corriente. Madrid: Consejo Superior de Investigaciones Científicas, Instituto de Filología, Departamento de Estudios Arabes.

Ibn ʿAbd Rabbih. 1983. *al-ʿIqd al-Farid*. 7 vols. Beirut: Dar al-Kitab al-ʿArabi.

Ibn ʿAbd Rabbih and Issa J. Boullata. 2006. *The Unique Necklace: al-ʿIqd al-Farid*. Vol. 2. Great Books of Islamic Civilisation. Reading, UK: Garnet.

Ibn al-ʿArabi, Muhyi al-Din. 1998a. *Shajarat al-Kawn = L'arbre du monde*. Translated by Maurice Gloton. Paris: Les Deux Océans.

———. 1998b. *Tarjuman al-Ashwaq*. Beirut: Dar Sader.

Ibn al-Haytham. 1983. *Kitab al-Manazir.* Edited by Abdelhamid Sabra. Kuwait: The National Council for Culture, Arts and Letters.

Ibn al-Khatib, Lisan al-Din. 1956. *Kitab Aʿmal al-Aʿlam*. Edited by E. Lévi-Provencal. Beirut: Dar al-Makshuf.

———. 1968. *Nufadat al-Jirab fi ʿUlalat al-Ightirab*. Edited by Ahmad Mukhtār ʿAbd al-Fattah ʿAbbādi. Cairo: Dar al-Katib al-ʿArabi.

———. 1970. *Rawdat al-Ta ʿrif bi'l-Hubb al-Sharif.* Edited by Muhammad Kattani. 2 vols. Casablanca: Dar al-Thaqafa.

———. 1973. *al-Ihata fi Akhbar Gharnata*. Edited by Muhammad ʿAbd Allah ʿInan. Cairo: Maktabat al-Khanji.

Ibn al-Qutiya, Muhammad Ibn ʿUmar. 2009. *Early Islamic Spain: The History of Ibn al-Qūṭīya: A Study of the Unique Arabic Manuscript in the Bibliothèque Nationale de France, Paris, with a Translation, Notes and Comments*. Translated by David James. London: Routledge.

Ibn al-Saʿi, ʿAli ibn Anjab, Shawkat M. Toorawa, and Julia Bray. 2015. *Consorts of the Caliphs: Women and the Court of Baghdad*. Library of Arabic Literature. New York: New York University Press.

Ibn ʿArabi. n.d. *al-Futuhat al-Makkiyya*. 4 vols. Beirut: Dar Ihyaʾ al-Turath al-ʿArabi.

Ibn Hayyan, Abu Marwan Hayyan ibn Khalaf. 1937. *al-Muktabis: Tome troisième, chronique du règné du Calife Umayade ʿAbd Allāh à Cordoue*. Textes arabes relatifs à l'histoire de l'occident musliman 3. Paris: P. Geuthner.

———. 2001. *Crónica de los emires Alḥakam I y ʿAbdarraḥmān II entre los años 796 y 847 (Almuqtabis II-1)*. Edited by Maḥmūd ʿAlī Makkī. Translated by F. Corriente. Serie

Estudios Islámicos. Zaragoza, Spain: Instituto de Estudios Islámicos y del Oriente Próximo.

———. 2003. *al-Sifr al-Thani Min Kitab al-Muqtabas*. Edited by Mahmud ʿAli Makki. al-Tabʿah 1. al-Riyad: Markaz al-Malik Faysal lil-Buhuth wa-al-Dirasat al-Islamiyah.

Ibn Hayyan, Abu Marwan Hayyan ibn Khalaf, Real Academia de la Historia, and Joaquín Vallvé. 1999. *Muqtabis II: Anales de Los Emires de Córdoba Alhaquém I (180–206 H./796–822 J.C.) y Abderramán II (206–232/822–847)*. 1st ed. Madrid: Real Academia de la Historia.

Ibn Khaldun. n.d. *Muqaddima*. Beirut: Dar Ihyaʾ al-Turath al-ʿArabi.

———. 1958. *The Muqaddimah: An Introduction to History*. Translated by Franz Rosenthal. 3 vols. Bollingen Series 43. New York: Pantheon Books.

Ibn Manzur. n.d. *Lisan al-ʿArab al-Muhit*. 3 vols. Beirut: Dar Lisan al-ʿArab.

Ibn Muhammad Qartajanni, Hazim. 1986. *Minhaj al-Bulaghaʾ wa Siraj al-Udabaʾ*. Edited by Muhammad al-Habib ibn al-Khuja. Beirut: Dar al-Gharb al-Islamı.

Ibn Rushd. 1986. *Talkhis Kitab al-Shiʿr*. Edited by Charles Butterworth and Ahmad Abd al-Magid Haridi. Cairo: The General Egyptian Book Organization.

Ibn Sina, Abu Ali. 1984. *Kitab al-Shifaʾ*. 10 vols. Qum, Iran: Maktabat al-Najafi.

Ibn Zamrak, Muhammad ibn Yusuf. 1997. *Diwan Ibn Zamrak al-Andalusi*. Edited by Muhammad Tawfiq Nayfar. Beirut: Dar al-Gharb al-Islami.

Ibn Zaydun. 1951. *Diwan*. Edited by Karam al-Bustani. Beirut: Maktabat Sadir.

Ibraev, Bek. 1980. "Kosmogonicheskie predstavleniya nashih predkov." *Dekorativnoe iskusstvo SSSR* 8:40–45.

Ibrashy, May. 2005. "The Cemeteries of Cairo and the Comite de Conservation." In *Making Cairo Medieval*, edited by Nezar Al Sayyad, Irene A. Bierman, and Nasser O. Rabbat, 235–256. Lanham, MD: Lexington Books.

Ikhwan al-Safaʾ. n.d. *Rasaʾil Ikhwan al-Safaʾ wa Khillan al-Wafaʾ*. 4 vols. Beirut: Dar Sadir.

İnalcık, Halil. 1954. "Ottoman Methods of Conquest." *Studia Islamica* (2): 103–129.

Ingold, Tim. 2000. *The Perception of the Environment: Essays on Livelihood, Dwelling and Skill*. New York: Routledge.

Ingold, Tim, and Ray Lucas. 2007. "The 4 A's (Anthropology, Archeology, Art and Architecture): Reflections on a Teaching and Learning Experience." In *Ways of Knowing: New Approaches in the Anthropology of Experience and Learning*, edited by Mark Harris, 287–305. Oxford: Berghahn Books.

Iskander, John. 2001. "Saints or Charlatans: The Social Construction of Sanctity in Contemporary Egypt." Unpublished PhD diss., University of California Santa Barbara.

Jäger, Ralf. 1996. *Türkische Kunstmusik und ihre handschriftlichen Quellen aus dem 19. Jahrhundert* 8. Münster: Schriften zur Musikwissenschaft aus Münster.

James, Kéry. 2002. *Savoir et vivre ensemble*. CD. Naïve.

Jameson, Frederic. 2003. *Postmodernism, or the Cultural Logic of Late Capitalism*. Durham, NC: Duke University Press.

Jayyusi, Salma Khadra. 1992a. "Andalusī Poetry: The Golden Period." In *The Legacy of Muslim Spain*, edited by Salma Khadra Jayyusi, 317–366. Leiden, the Netherlands: Brill.

———. 1992b. "Nature Poetry in al-Andalus and the Rise of Ibn K̲h̲afāja." In *The Legacy of Muslim Spain*, edited by Salma Khadra Jayyusi, 367–397. Leiden, the Netherlands: Brill.

Jazouli, Adil. 1992. *Les années banlieues*. Paris: Seuil.

Jobard, Fabien. 2006. "Police, justice et discriminations raciales." In *De la question sociale à la question raciale. Représenter la société française*, edited by Didier Fassin and Eric Fassin, 211–229. Paris: La Découverte.

Johnson, Kathryn V. 1996. "Sanctity and the Shariʿah: An Egyptian Mystic's Analysis of the Role of the Saints (Awliyaʾ) as Guardians of the Revelation." *Islamic Studies* 35 (3): 307–331.

Jouili, Jeanette. 2013. "Rapping the Republic: Utopia, Critique and Muslim Role Models in Secular France." *French Politics, Culture and Society* 31 (2): 58–80.

———. 2014. "Refining the Umma in the Shadow of the Republic: Performing Arts and New Islamic Audio-Visual Landscapes in France." *Anthropological Quarterly* 87 (4): 1079–1104.

Jukovskaya, Nataliya. 1988. *Kategorii i simvolika traditsionnoi kultury mongolov*. Moscow: Glavnaya redaktsiya vostochnoi literatury izdatelstva Nauka.

Kafadar, Cemal. 1993. "The Myth of the Golden Age: Ottoman Historical Consciousness in the Post-Süleymanic Era." In *Süleymān the Second and His Time*, edited by Halil İnalcık and Cemal Kafadar, 37–48. Istanbul: Isis.

———. 1997. "The Question of Ottoman Decline." *Harvard Middle East and Islamic Review* 4 (9): 30–75.

Kämalashūly, Biqūmar. 1995. *Mongholiyadaghy qazaqtardyng salt-dästurleri*. Ölgii, Mongolia: Bayan-Ölgii aimaq baspakhanasy.

———. 2004. *Qazagha qatysty dini salt-dästurler jäne dini ūghymdar*. Ölgii, Mongolia: Bayan-Ölgii aimaq baspakhanasy.

Kane, Abdoulaye. 2008. "Senegalese Sufi Orders in the Transnational Space: Moving Religious Activities from Home to Host Countries and Creating Diasporic Identities." In *Migration and Creative Expressions in Africa and the African Diasporas*, edited by Toyin Falola, Niyi Afolabi, and Aderonke Adesanya, 471–81. Durham, NC: Carolina Academic Press.

Kapchan, Deborah. 2007. *Traveling Spirit Masters: Gnawa Trance and Music in the Global Marketplace*. Middletown, CT: Wesleyan University Press.

———. 2011. "Learning to Listen: The Sound of Sufism in France." *The World of Music* 51 (2): 65–89.

Karabey, Lâika. 1966. "'Münir'in Cesaret.'" In *Üstad Münir Nurettin Selçuk'un 50. San'at Yılı Jübilesi*, 14. Istanbul: Nebioğlu Yayınevi.

Karakaya-Stump, Ayfer. 2010. "Documents and *Buyruk* Manuscripts in the Private Archives of Alevi *Dede* Families: An Overview." *British Journal of Middle Eastern Studies* 37 (3): 273–286.

Karamustafa, Ahmet T. 2006. *God's Unruly Friends: Dervish Groups in the Islamic Later Middle Period, 1200–1550*. Oxford: Oneworld.

Karaosmanoğlu, Kerem. 2013. "Beyond Essentialism: Negotiating Alevi Identity in Urban Turkey." *Identities: Global Studies in Culture and Power* 20 (5): 580–597.

Kastoryano, Riva. 2002. *Negotiating Identities: States and Immigrants in France and Germany*. Princeton, NJ: Princeton University Press.

Kelley, Robin D. G. 1996. "Kickin' Reality, Kickin' Ballistics: Gangsta Rap and Postindustrial Los Angeles." In *Droppin' Science: Critical Essays on Rap Music and Hip Hop Culture*, edited by William Eric Perkins, 117–158. Philadelphia: Temple University Press.

Kepel, Gilles. 1991. *Les banlieues de l'Islam: Naissance d'une religion en France*. Paris: Seuil.

Kettane, Nacer. 1985. *Le sourire de Brahim*. Paris: Denoël.

Kharuzin, Nikolai. 1896. *Istoriya razvitiya jilishcha u kochevyh i polukochevyh turkskih i mongolskih narodnostei Rossii*. Moscow: Tovarishchestvo skoropechatni A. A. Levinson.

Kinross, Lord Patrick. 1964. *Atatürk: The Rebirth of a Nation*. London: Weidenfeld and Nicolson.

Knott, Kim. 2005. "Spatial Theory and Method for the Study of Religion." *Temenos* 41 (2): 153–184.

Knysh, Alexander. 2000. "Ibn al-Khatīb." In *The Literature of al-Andalus: The Cambridge History of Arabic Literature*, edited by María R. Menocal, Raymond P. Scheindlin, and Michael Sells, 358–371. Cambridge: Cambridge University Press.

Koch, Ebba. 2006. *The Complete Taj Mahal*. London: Thames and Hudson.

Kochumkulova, Elmira. 2011. "A Kyrgyz Was Born in the Yurt and Will Die in the Yurt: Kyrgyz Funeral Customs." *The Times of Central Asia*, May 12.

Kohlberg, Etan. 2012. "Zayn al-ʿĀbidīn, ʿAli B. Husayn." In *Encyclopaedia of Islam*, 2nd ed., edited by P. Bearman, Th. Bianquis, C. E. Bosworth, E. van Donzel, and W. P. Heinrichs. Brill Online. http://referenceworks.brillonline.com/browse/encyclopaedia-of-islam-2.

Kompridis, Nikolas. 1993. "Learning from Architecture: Music in the Aftermath to Postmodernism." *Perspectives of New Music* 31 (2): 6–23.

Köprülü, Mehmet Fuat. 2006. *Early Mystics in Turkish Literature*. Translated by Gary Leiser and Robert Dankoff. London: Routledge.

Kosal, Vedat. 1999. *Western Classical Music in the Ottoman Empire*. Istanbul: Istanbul Stock Exchange.

Krims, Adam. 2007. *Music and Urban Geography*. New York: Routledge.

Kronenburg, Robert. 2012. *Live Architecture: Venues, Stages and Arenas for Popular Music*. London: Routledge.

Kulin, Ayşe. 1996. *Bit Tatlı Huzur: Fotoğraflarla Münir Nureddin Selçuk'un Yaşam Öykusü*. Istanbul: Sel Yayıncılık.

Kürkçüoğlu, Kemal. 1962. *Süleymaniye Vakfiyesi*. Ankara: Vakıflar Umum Müdürlüğü.

Kütükoğlu, Mübahat. 1983. *Osmanlılarda Narh Müessesesi ve 1640 Tarihli Narh Defteri*. Istanbul: Enderun Kitabevi.

Lacan, Jacques. 1977. *The Four Fundamental Concepts of Psycho-Analysis*. Translated by Alan Sheridan. London: Hogarth.

Lane, Edward William. 1842. *An Account of the Manners and Customs of the Modern Egyptians*. London: Ward, Lock.

Langer, Robert. 2010. "'Marginalised Islam': The Transfer of Rural Rituals into Pluralist Contexts and the Emergence of Transnational 'Communities of Practice.'" In *Ritual Matters: Dynamic Dimensions in Practice*, edited by Christiane Brosius and Ute Hüsken, 1–28. New Delhi: Routledge.

Laoust, Henri. 1962. "Le Reformisme d'Ibn Taymiya." *Islamic Studies* 1 (3): 27–47.

Lapidus, Ira M. 1988. *A History of Islamic Societies*. Cambridge: Cambridge University Press.

Laremont, Ricardo René. 2000. *Islam and the Politics of Resistance in Algeria, 1783–1992*. Trenton, NJ: Africa World Press.

La Rumeur. 2002. *L'ombre sur la mesure*. CD. Emi Music.

Laurence, Jonathan. 2012. *The Emancipation of Europe's Muslims: The State's Role in Minority Integration*. Princeton, NJ: Princeton University Press.

Lavan, Luke, Ellen Swift, and Toon Putzeys. 2007. "Material Spatiality in Late Antiquity: Sources, Approaches and Field Methods." In *Objects in Context, Objects in Use: Material Spatiality in Late Antiquity*, edited by Luke Lavan, Ellen Swift, and Toon Putzeys, 1–44. Late Antique Archeology 5. Leiden, the Netherlands: Brill.

Lawlor, Robert. 1982. *Sacred Geometry: Philosophy and Practice*. London: Thames and Hudson.

Lawrence, Denise L., and Setha M. Low. 1990. "The Built Environment and Spatial Form." *Annual Review of Anthropology* 19:453–505.

Leaman, Oliver. 2004. *Islamic Aesthetics: An Introduction*. Edinburgh: Edinburgh University Press.

Lefebvre, Henri. 1991. *The Production of Space*. Translated by Donald Nicholson-Smith. Malden, MA: Blackwell.

Lepoutre, David. 1997. *Coeur de banlieue: Codes, rites et langages*. Paris: O. Jacob.

Levin, Theodore Craig, and Valentina Süzükei. 2006. *Where Rivers and Mountains Sing: Sound, Music, and Nomadism in Tuva and Beyond*. Bloomington: Indiana University Press.

Lévi-Provençal, Evariste. 1950. "La visite d'Ibn Battuta à Grenade." In *Mélanges offerts à William Marçais par l'Institut d'Études Islamiques de l'Université de Paris*, 214–225. Paris: G. P. Maisonneuve.

Lévi-Provençal, Évariste, et al. 1990. *Historia de España Menéndez Pidal. [Suivi de] Arte Califal Tomo V.* Madrid: Espasa-Calpe.

Leyshon, Andrew, David Matless, and George Revill, eds. 1998. *The Place of Music.* New York: Guilford.

Lifchez, Raymond, ed. 1992. *The Dervish Lodge: Architecture, Art, and Sufism in Ottoman Turkey.* Berkeley: University of California Press.

Lings, Martin. 1971. *A Sufi Saint in the Twentieth Century: Shaikh Ahmad Al-ʿAlawi: His Spiritual Heritage and Legacy.* Berkeley: University of California Press.

———. 1985. *Muhammad: His Life Based on the Earliest Sources.* Lahore: Suhail Academy.

———. 1986. "The Seven Deadly Sins in the Light of the Symbolism of Number." In *The Sword of Gnosis: Metaphysics, Cosmology, Tradition, Symbolism*, edited by Jacob Needleman, 218–229. London; Boston: Arkana.

———. 2001. *Collected Poems.* New York: Midpoint Trade Books.

Lirola Delgado, Jorge. 2002. "Ibn al-Jatīb." In *Diccionario de autores y obras andalusíes*, edited by Jorge Lirola Delgado and José Miguel Puerta Vílchez, 643–698. Seville: Junta de Andalucía.

López-Morillas, Consuelo. 1994. *Textos aljamiados sobre la vida de Mahoma: El Profeta de los Moriscos.* Salamanca: Consejo Superior de Investigaciones Científicas: Agencia Española de Cooperación Internacional.

Low, Setha M., and Denise Lawrence-Zúñiga, eds. 2003. *The Anthropology of Space and Place: Locating Culture.* Malden, MA: Blackwell.

Lugo Acevedo, María Luisa. 2008. *El Libro de Las Luces: Leyenda aljamiada sobre la geneología de Mahoma.* Madrid: SIAL Ediciones.

Lunatic. 2000. *Mauvais oeil.* CD. Warner.

Lynch, Kevin. 1960. *The Image of the City.* Cambridge, MA: MIT Press.

MacDonald, Duncan B., and Abu Hamid al-Ghazzali. 1902. "Emotional Religion in Islām as Affected by Music and Singing (Concluded from P. 748, October, 1901)." *Journal of the Royal Asiatic Society of Great Britain and Ireland*, January: 1–28.

Mac Kregor. 2006. *Insurrection.* CD. Hematom Concept.

Madelung, Wilferd. 2012. "Zayd B. Ali B. Husayn." In *Encyclopaedia of Islam*, 2nd ed., edited by P. Bearman, Th. Bianquis, C. E. Bosworth, E. van Donzel, and W. P. Heinrichs. Brill Online. http://referenceworks.brillonline.com/browse/encyclopaedia-of-islam-2.

Makariou, Sophie. 2010. "The al-Mughīra Pyxis and Spanish Umayyad Ivories: Aims and Tools of Power." In *Umayyad Legacies: Medieval Memories from Syria to Spain*, edited by Antoine Borrut and Paul M. Cobb, 313–336. Leiden, the Netherlands: Brill.

Makki, Mahmud ʿAli. 1991. *al-Mada'ih al-Nabawiyah.* Beirut: Maktabat Lubnan; al-Duqqi, al-Jizah: al-Sharikah al-Misriyah al-ʿAlamiyah li-l-Nashr, Lunjman.

Makovetskii, Petr. 1893. "Yurta (letneee jilishche kirgiz)." *Zapiski Zapadno-Sibirskogo otdela Imperatorskogo Russkogo geographicheskogo obshchestva* 15 (3): 1–15.

Mango, Andrew. 1999. *Atatürk*. London: John Murray.

Maqrizi, Ahmad ibn ʿAli. n.d. *al-Mawaʿiz wa-l-Iʿtibar bi-Dhikr al-Khitat wa-l-Athar*. http://www.alwaraq.net.

Marcus, Abraham. 1989. *The Middle East on the Eve of Modernity: Aleppo in the Eighteenth Century*. New York: Columbia University Press.

Marcus, Scott Lloyd. 2007. *Music in Egypt: Experiencing Music, Expressing Culture*. New York: Oxford University Press.

Marfil Ruiz, Pedro. 2000. "Córdoba de Teodosio a Abd al-Rahmán III." In *Visigodos y Omeyas: Un debate entre la antigüedad tardía y la alta edad media (Mérida, abril de 1999)*, edited by L. Caballero Zoreda and P. Mateos Cruz, 117–141. Madrid: Archivo Español de Arqueología.

Marghulan, Alkei. 2007. "Kazakhskaya yurta i ee ubranstvo." In *Trudy po kulture pismennosti kazakhskogo naroda*, 2nd ed., edited by Danel Marghulan and Erlan Arynov, 51–67. Astana, Kazakhstan: Altyn kitap.

Marín, Manuela. 2000. *Mujeres en al-Andalus*. Madrid: Consejo Superior de Investigaciones Científicas.

Markoff, Irene. 1986. "The Role of Expressive Culture in the Demystification of a Secret Sect of Islam: The Case of the Alevis of Turkey." *The World of Music* 28 (3): 42–56.

———. 1993. "Music, Saints, and Ritual: Samāʿ and the Alevis of Turkey." In *Manifestations of Sainthood in Islam*, edited by Grace Martin Smith and Carl W. Ernst, 95–110. Istanbul: Isis.

———. 2002a. "Arif Sağ–Alevi Bağlama Teacher and Performer Par Excellence." In *The Garland Encyclopedia of World Music*, edited by Virginia Danielson, Scott Lloyd Marcus, and Dwight Reynolds, 6:789–792. New York: Garland.

———. 2002b. "Alevi Identity and Expressive Culture." In *The Garland Encyclopedia of World Music*, edited by Virginia Danielson, Scott Lloyd Marcus, and Dwight Reynolds, 6:793–800. New York: Garland.

———. 2009. "Gelin Canlar Bir Olalım: Türkiye'de Alevî-Bektasî Ortak Bilincinde Bağlayıcı Güc Olarak Müzik ve Şiir." In *Geçmişten Günümüze Alevî-Bektaşî Kültürü*, edited by Ahmet Yaşar Ocak, 416–429. Ankara: T. C. Kültür ve Turizm Bakanlığı Yayınları.

Markussen, Hege Irene. 2012. *Teaching History, Learning Piety: An Alevi Foundation in Contemporary Turkey*. Lund, Sweden: Sekel Förlag.

Martin, Elizabeth. 1994. *Architecture as a Translation of Music*. Pamphlet Architecture 16. New York: Princeton Architectural Press.

McPherson, J. W. 1941. *The Moulids of Egypt (Egyptian Saints-Days)*. Cairo: Ptd. N.M. Press.

Médine. 2004. *11 séptembre (récit du 11ème jour)*. CD. Din.

———. 2006. *Jihad: Le plus grand combat est contre soi-même*. CD. Din.

———. 2008. *Arabian Panther*. CD. Din.

Médioni, Gilles. 2004. "Les rappeurs d'Allah." *L'Express*, June 7.

Melchert, Christopher. 2008. "The Relations of the Ten Readings to One Another." *Journal of Qur'anic Studies* 10:73–87.

Mélikoff, Irène. 1974. "Le problème kızılbaş." *Turcica* 6:49–67.

Mestyan, Adam. 2011. "A Garden with Mellow Fruits of Refinement: Music Theatres and Cultural Politics in Cairo and Istanbul, 1867–1892." Unpublished PhD diss., Central European University.

———. 2013. "Music and Power in Cairo: Azbakkiya." *Urban History* 40 (4): 1–22.

Metcalf, Barbara Daly, ed. 1996. *Making Muslim Space in North America and Europe*. Berkeley: University of California Press.

Mikov, Lyubomir. 2005. *Izkustvoto na Heterodksnite Myusyulmani v Bŭlgariya (xvi–xx vek): Bektashii i Kizilbashi/Alevii*. Sofia: Marin Drinov.

Milligan, Melinda J. 1998. "Interactional Past and Potential: The Social Construction of Place Attachment." *Symbolic Interaction* 21 (1): 1–33.

Mimar Sinan. 2006. *Sinan's Autobiographies: Five Sixteenth-Century Texts*. Edited by Howard Crane, Esra Akın, and Gülru Necipoğlu. Leiden, the Netherlands: Brill.

Miraftab, Faranak. 2009. "Insurgent Planning: Situating Radical Planning in the Global South." *Planning Theory* 8 (1): 32–50.

Misr Lagnat Hifz al-Athar al-ʿArabiyya al-Qadima. 1887. "Comité Bulletins 1887–1888." *Comité Bulletins/Comité de Conservation Des Monuments de l'Art Arabe*.

———. 1933. "Comité Bulletins 1933–1935." *Comité Bulletins/Comité de Conservation Des Monuments de l'Art Arabe*.

Molinero, Stéphanie. 2011. "The Meanings of Religious Talk in French Rap Music." In *Religion and Popular Music in Europe*, edited by Thomas Bossius, Andreas Häger, and Keith Kahn-Harris, 105–123. London: I. B. Tauris.

Monroe, James T. 1971. "The Historical Arjūza of Ibn ʿAbd Rabbihi, a Tenth Century Hispano Arabic Epic Poem." *Journal of the American Oriental Society* 91:67–95.

Monshi, Eskandar Beg. 1978. *History of Shah ʾAbbas the Great*. Translated by Roger M. Savory. 2 vols. Persian Heritage Series 28. Boulder, CO: Westview.

Monsieur R. 2004. *Politikment Incorrekt*. CD. Diamond.

———. 2006. *Black Album*. CD. Diamond/Nocturne.

Moore, Diane. 2007. *Overcoming Religious Illiteracy*. New York: Palgrave Macmillan.

Mortada, Hisham. 2003. *Traditional Islamic Principles of Built Environment*. London: RoutledgeCurzon.

Mubarak, ʿAli. 1886. *al-Khitat al-Tawfiqiyah al-Jadidah li-Misr al-Qahirah wa-Muduniha wa-Biladiha al-Qadimah wa-al-Shahirah*. Bulaq, Egypt: al-Matbaʿah al-Kubrá al-Amiriyah.

Mucchielli, Laurent. 1999. "Le rap, tentative d'expression politique et de mobilisation collective des jeunes des quartiers relégués." *Mouvements, Sociétés, Politique et Culture* 3 (Mar.–Apr.): 60–63.

Muecke, Mikesch W., and Miriam S. Zach, eds. 2007. *Resonance: Essays on the Intersection of Music and Architecture*. Ames, IA: Culicidae Architectural Press.

Muhammad, Suʿad Mahir. 1971. *Masajid Misr wa-Awliyaʾuha al-Salihun*. Cairo: al-Majlis al-Aʿla li-l-shuʾun al-Islamiyya.

Münzer, Jerónimo. 1991. *Viaje por España y Portugal (1494–1495)*. Madrid: Ediciones Polifemo.

Musakhan, Ozila. 1997. "Traditsionnaya pesennaya kultura kazakhov Mongolii." Unpublished Candidate of Science diss., Auezov Institute of Literature and Art, Academy of Sciences of the Republic of Kazakhstan.

Mustafa ʿAli. 2003. *The Ottaman Gentleman of the Sixteenth Century: Mustafa ʿAli's Mevaidü'n-nefais fi kevaidi'l-mecalis—"Tables of Delicacies Concerning the Rules of Social Gatherings."* Translated by Douglas S. Brookes. Cambridge, MA: Department of Near Eastern Languages and Civilizations, Harvard University.

Nabti, Mehdi. 2007. "Des soufis en banlieue parisienne: Mise en scène d'une spiritualité musulmane." *Archives de Sciences Sociales des Religions* 140:49–68.

Najafi Tehrani, Faramarz, and Asadallah Hijazi. 1992. *Ritmha-yi Varzishi (Ritmha-yi Zarb-e Zurkhanehʾi)*. Tehran: Intisharat-i Part.

N.A.P. 1996. *La racaille sort 1 disque*. CD. Arista/BMG.

———. 2000. *À l'intérieur de nous*. CD. Arista/BMG.

Nas, Peter J. M., and Chantal G. Brakus. 2004. "The Dancing House: Instances of the Human Body in City and Architecture." In *Body as Medium of Meaning*, edited by Suhayla Shahshahani, 27–56. Münster: Lit; distributed, Piscataway, NJ: Transaction.

Nasir-i Khusraw. 2001. *Nasir-i Khusraw's Book of Travels (Safarnama): A Parallel Persian-English Text*. Edited and translated by Wheeler Thackston. Costa Mesa, CA: Mazda.

Nasr, Seyyed Hossein. 1978. *An Introduction to Islamic Cosmological Doctrines*. London: Thames and Hudson.

———. 1987. *Islamic Art and Spirituality*. Ipswich, UK: Golgonooza.

Navagero, Andrea. 1563. *Il viaggio fatto in Spagna et in Francia dal magnifico M. Andrea Navagiero*. Venice: Domenico Farri.

Necipoğlu, Gülru. 1995. *The Topkapı Scroll—Geometry and Ornament in Islamic Architecture*. Santa Monica, CA: Getty Center for the History of Art and the Humanities.

———. 2005. *The Age of Sinan: Architectural Culture in the Ottoman Empire*. Princeton, NJ: Princeton University Press.

Nizami Dehlvi, Khowaja Hasan. n.d. *Nizami Bansari*. Lahore: Nigarishat Publishers.

Nwiya, Paul. 1970. *Exégèse coranique et langage mystique: Nouvel essai sur le lexique technique des mystiques musulman*. Beirut: Dar El-Machreq Éditeurs.

Nykl, A. R. 1941. *Historia de los amores de Bayad wa Riyad*. New York: Hispanic Society of America.

Ocak, Ahmet Yaşar. 1994. "Kalenderi Dervishes and Ottoman Administration from the Fourteenth to the Sixteenth Centuries." In *Manifestations of Sainthood in Islam*, edited by Grace Martin Smith and Carl W. Ernst, 239–255. Istanbul: Isis.

———. 1996. *Türk Sûfîliğine Bakışlar.* Istanbul: İletişim.

O'Connell, John M. 2000. "Fine Art, Fine Music: Controlling Turkish Taste at the Fine Arts Academy." *Yearbook for Traditional Music* 33:117–142.

———. 2003. "Song Cycle: The Life and Death of the Turkish Gazel: Review Essay." *Ethnomusicology* 47 (3): 399–414.

———. 2005. "In the Time of Alaturka: Identifying Difference in Musical Discourse." *Ethnomusicology* 49 (2): 177–205.

———. 2010. "Alabanda: Brass Bands and Musical Methods in Turkey." In *Giuseppe Donizetti Pascià: Traiettorie musicali e storiche tra Italia e Turchia / Musical and Historical Trajectories between Italy and Turkey*, edited by Federico Spinetti, 19–37. Saggi e Monografie 7. Bergamo: Fondazione Donizetti.

———. 2011. "A Staged Fright: Musical Hybridity and Religious Intolerance in Turkey (1923–1938)." *Twentieth-Century Music* 7 (1): 1–26.

———. 2013. *Alaturka: Style in Turkish Music. (1923–1938).* SOAS Musicology Series. Aldershot, UK: Ashgate.

Ohtoshi, Tetsuya. 1995. "The Egyptian Book of the Visit as Historical Material." *Bulletin of the Society for Near Eastern Studies in Japan* 38 (2): 143–161.

———. 2006. "Cairene Cemeteries as Public Loci in Mamluk Egypt." *Mamluk Studies Review* 10 (1): 83–116.

Olcott, Martha Brill. 1987. *The Kazakhs.* Stanford, CA: Hoover Institution Press, Stanford University.

Orihuela, Antonio, and Ángel C. López López. 1990. "Una nueva interpretación del texto de Ibn al-Jatīb sobre la Alhambra." *Cuadernos de la Alhambra* 26:121–144.

Özdamar, Ali. 1991. *Beyoğlu in the 1930's: Through the Lens of Selahattin Giz.* Istanbul: Çağdaş Yayıncılık, Galeri Alfa.

Pallasmaa, Juhani. 1996. *The Eyes of the Skin: Architecture and the Senses.* New York: Wiley.

Pamuk, Şevket. 2000. *İstanbul ve Diğer Kentlerde 500 Yıllık Fiyatlar ve Ücretler (1469–1998).* Ankara: T. C. Başbakanlık Devlet İstatistik Enstitüsü.

Panofsky, Erwin. 1997 [1927]. *Perspective as Symbolic Form.* New York: Zone Books.

Parlak, Erol. 2000. *Türkiye'de El İle (Şelpe) Bağlama Çalma Geleneği ve Çalış Teknikleri.* Ankara: T. C. Kültür Bakanlığı.

Partaw Beza'i Kashani, Husayn. 2003. *Tarikh-i Varzish-i Bastani-yi Iran (zurkhaneh).* Tehran: Intisharat-i Zavvar.

Pegg, Carole. 2001. *Mongolian Music, Dance, and Oral Narrative: Performing Diverse Identities.* Seattle: University of Washington Press.

Pérès, Henri. 1983. *Esplendor de al-Andalus: La poesía andaluza en árabe clásico en el siglo xi: Sus aspectos generales, sus principales temas y su valor documental*. Translated by Mercedes García-Arenal. Madrid: Hiperión.

Picken, Laurence Ernest Rowland. 1975. *Folk Musical Instruments of Turkey*. New York: Oxford University Press.

Piemontese, Angelo. 1964. "L'organizzazione della 'zurxāne' e la 'futuwwa.'" *Annali dell'Istituto Universitario Orientale di Napoli*, special issue in honor of Laura Veccia Vaglieri, n.s., 14, pt. 2:453–473.

———.1965. "La leggenda del santo-lottatore Pahlavān Mahmud Xvāresmi Puryā-ye Vali." *Annali dell'Istituto Universitario Orientale di Napoli*, n.s., 15:167–213.

Pinard, Sarah. 2013. "40 ans de 'Plan Banlieue.'" *Le Figaro*, February 20.

Pinch, Trevor, and Karin Bijsterveld, eds. 2011. *The Oxford Handbook of Sound Studies*. Oxford: Oxford University Press.

Pinckney Stetkevych, Suzanne. 1996. "Abbasid Panegyric and the Poetics of Political Allegiance: Two Poems of al-Mutanabbi on Kāfr." In *Qasida Poetry in Islamic Asia and Africa*, vol. 1 of *Classical Traditions and Modern Meanings*, edited by Stefan Sperl and Christopher Shackle, 35–63. Leiden, the Netherlands: Brill.

Plato. 1955. *The Republic*. Translated by Desmond Lee. Middlesex, UK: Penguin.

Plotnikov, Vladimir. 1870. "Pominki (As): Etnographicheskii ocherk iz byta zauralskih kirgizov." *Zapiski Orenburgskogo otdela Imperatorskogo Russkogo geographicheskogo obshchestva* 1:137–151.

Portisch, Anna. 2007. "Kazakh Syrmaq-Production in Western Mongolia: Learning and Skill in a Domestic Craft Tradition." Unpublished PhD diss., School of Oriental and African Studies, University of London.

Potanin, Grigorii. 1881. *Ocherki Severo-Zapadnoi Mongolii*. 2 vols. Saint Petersburg: V. Kirshbaum.

Prado-Vilar, Francisco. 1997. "Circular Visions of Fertility and Punishment: Caliphal Ivory Caskets from al-Andalus." *Muqarnas* 14:19–41.

———. 2005. "Enclosed in Ivory: The Miseducation of al-Mughira." *Journal of the David Collection* 2 (1): 138–163.

Prévos, André. 1998. "Hip Hop, Rap, and Repression in France and the U.S." *Popular Music and Society* 22 (2): 67–84.

Prokopovych, Markian, ed. 2013. "Music and the City: The Modern Times." Thematic Issue of *Urban History* 40 (3).

Puerta Vílchez, José Miguel. 1990. *Los Códigos de Utopía de la Alhambra de Granada*. Granada: Diputación Provincial de Granada.

———. 2001. "El vocabulario estético de los poemas de la Alhambra." In *Pensar la Alhambra*, edited by José Antonio González Alcantud and Antonio Malpica Cuello, 69–88. Rubí, Barcelona: Anthropos; Granada: Diputación Provincial de Granada, Centro de Investigaciones Etnológicas Angel Ganivet.

———. 2002. "La cultura y la creación artística." In *Historia Del Reino de Granada*, edited by Rafael Gerardo Peinado Santaella, Manuel Barrios Aguilera, and Francisco Andújar Castillo, 1:349–413. Granada: Universidad de Granada.

———. 2007. "La Alhambra de Granada, o la caligrafía elevada al rango de arquitectura." In *7 Paseos por la Alhambra*, edited by María Angustias Cabrera, 301–386. Granada: Proyecto Sur de Ediciones.

Puerta Vílchez, José Miguel, and Juan Agustín Nuñez Guarde. 2010. *Leer la Alhambra: Guía visual del monumento a través de sus inscripciones*. Granada: Patronato de la Alhambra y Generalife/Edilux.

Pujadas, David, and Ahmed Salam. 1995. *La tentation du Jihad: L'Islam radical en France*. Paris: J.-C. Lattès.

Qabbani, Nizar. 2000 [1983]. *Qissati maʿa al-Shiʿr*. Beirut: Manshurat Nizar Qabbani.

Qadi Ahmad. 1959. *Calligraphers and Painters: A Treatise by Qāḍī Aḥmad, Son of Mīr-Munshī (circa A.H. 1015/A.D. 1606)*. Translated by Vladimir Minorsky and T. Minorsky. Washington, DC: Smithsonian Institution.

Qalahji, ʿAbd al-Fattah Rawwash Rawwas. 1988. *Min Shiʿr Amin al-Jundi*. Damascus: Syrian Ministry of Culture.

Qarsyūly, Saqai. 1991. *Küi kerueni: Kümbirli küiler kerueni; Küi jäne küishiler khaqyndaghy angyzdar men aqikhattar.* Edited by Rysbek Zūrghanbaiūly. Ölgii, Mongolia: Bayan-Ölgii aimaq baspakhanasy.

Qassab Hassan, Najat. 1995. *Hadith Dimashqi 1884–1983*. Damascus: Alif Baʾ-al-Adeeb Publishers.

Qinayatūly, Zardykhan. 2007. *Mongholiadaghy qazaqtar.* Almaty: Düniejüzi qazaqtarynyng qauymdastyghy.

Qureshi, Regula. 1996. "Transcending Space: Recitation and Community among South Asian Muslims in Canada." In *Making Muslim Space in North America and Europe*, edited by Barbara Daly Metcalf, 46–64. Berkeley: University of California Press.

Rabo, Annika. 2005. *A Shop of One's Own: Independence and Reputation among Traders in Aleppo*. New York: I. B. Tauris.

Racy, Ali Jihad. 1986. "Lebanese Laments: Grief, Music, and Cultural Values." *The World of Music* 28 (2): 27–40.

———. 1991. "Creativity and Ambience: An Ecstatic Feedback Model from Arab Music." *The World of Music* 33 (3): 7–28.

———. 2003. *Making Music in the Arab World: The Culture and Artistry of Tarab*. Cambridge: Cambridge University Press.

Radlov, Vasily [Radloff, Wilhelm]. 1989. "Turkskie Stepnye Kochevniki." In *Iz Sibiri: Stranitsy Dnevnika*, edited by S. I. Vainshtein, translated by K. D. Tsivina and B. E. Chistova, 247–347. Moscow: Glavnaya redaktsiya vostochnoi literatury izdatelstva Nauka. Originally published in German as *Aus Sibirien: Lose Blätter aus meinem Tagebuche*. Leipzig: T. O. Weigel, 1893.

Raghib, Yusuf. 1970. "Les Premieres Monuments Funeraires de l'Islam." *Annales Islamogiques* 9:21–36.

Randhawa, Mohindar Singh. 1971. *Kangra Ragamala Paintings*. New Delhi: National Museum.

Rapoport, Amos. 1982. *The Meaning of the Built Environment: A Nonverbal Communication Approach*. Beverly Hills, CA: Sage.

Rasmussen, Steen Eiler. 1962. *Experiencing Architecture*. Cambridge, MA: MIT Press.

Reeves, Edward B. 1995. "Power, Resistance, and the Cult of Muslim Saints in a Northern Egyptian Town." *American Ethnologist* 22 (2): 306–323.

Reindl-Kiel, Hedda. 2010. "The Vakf of Moralı Beşir Ağa in Argos." In *Monuments, Patrons, Contexts: Papers on Ottoman Europe Presented to Machiel Kiel*, edited by Maximilian Hartmuth and Ayşe Dilsiz, 107–128. Leiden, the Netherlands: Nederlands Instituut voor het Nabije Oosten.

Reynolds, Dwight F. 2008. "al-Maqqarī's Ziryab: The Making of a Myth." *Middle Eastern Literatures* 11 (2): 155–168.

———. 2009. "Music in Medieval Iberia: Contact, Influence and Hybridization." *Medieval Encounters* 15 (2/4): 236–255.

———. 2017a. "Song and Punishment." In *Arabic Humanities, Islamic Thought: a Festschrift for Everett K. Rowson*, edited by Joseph E. Lowry and Shawkat M. Toorawa, 211–232. Leiden, the Netherlands: Brill.

———. 2017b. "The Qiyan of al-Andalus." In *Concubines and Courtesans: Women and Slavery in Islamic History*, edited by Matthew S. Gordon and Kathryn A. Hain, 100–123. Oxford: Oxford University Press.

Ridgeon, Lloyd. 2007. "The Zūrkhāna between Tradition and Change." *Iran: Journal of the British Institute of Persian Studies* 45:243–265.

———. 2010. *Morals and Mysticism in Persian Sufism: A History of Sufi-Futuwwat in Iran*. London: Routledge.

Ripley, Colin, Marco Polo, and Arthur Wrigglesworth, eds. 2007. *In the Place of Sound: Architecture | Music | Acoustics*. Newcastle, UK: Cambridge Scholars Publishing.

Rippin, Andrew, ed. 2006. *The Blackwell Companion to the Qur'an*. Boston: Blackwell.

Robinson, Cynthia. 2002. *In Praise of Song: The Making of Courtly Culture in al-Andalus and Provence, 1005–1134 A.D.* Leiden, the Netherlands: Brill.

———. 2006. "Trees of Love, Trees of Knowledge: Toward the Definition of a Cross-Confessional Current in Late-Medieval Iberian Spirituality." In "Interrogating Iberian Frontiers: A Cross-Disciplinary Approach to Mudéjar History, Religion, Art, and Literature," edited by María Feliciano, Cynthia Robinson, and Leyla Rouhi, special issue, *Medieval Encounters* 12 (3): 388–435.

———. 2007a. *Medieval Andalusian Courtly Culture in the Mediterranean Ḥadīth Bayāḍ Wa-Riyāḍ*. London: Routledge.

———. 2007b. "Love in the Time of Fitna: 'Courtliness' and the 'Pamplona' Casket." In *Revisiting al-Andalus: Perspectives on the Material Culture of Islamic Iberia and Be-*

yond, edited by Glaire D. Anderson and Mariam Rosser-Owen, 99–114. Medieval and Early Modern Iberian World. Leiden, the Netherlands: Brill.

———. 2008. "Toward a Poetics of Ornament in Granada's Alhambra: Allegorizing Metaphor." *Muqarnas* 25 (special issue in honor of Oleg Grabar's eightieth birthday): 185–214.

———. 2009. "Lisān al-Dīn Ibn al-Khatīb." In *Essays in Arabic Literary Biography*, edited by Roger Allen, Terry De Young, Joseph E. Lowry, and Devin E. Stewart, 159–174. Wiesbaden, Germany: Harrassowitz.

———. 2013. "Where Have All the Boys Gone?: The Lady of the 'Sala de Justicia' Ceilings and Nasrid Poetics of Sacred and Profane Love." In *Eros and Sexuality in Islamic Art*, edited by Francesca Leoni and Mika Natif, 65–98. London: Ashgate.

Rochard, Philippe. 2000. "Le 'sport Antique' des Zurkhāne de Téhéran: Formes et significations d'une pratique contemporaine." Unpublished PhD diss., Université Aix-Marseille.

———. 2002. "The Identities of the Iranian Zūrkhānah." *Iranian Studies* 35 (4): 313–340.

Roeder, George Jr. 1994. "Coming to Our Senses." *Journal of American History* 81 (3): 1112–1122.

Roemer, Hans R. 1990. "The Qizilbash Turcomans: Founders and Victims of the Safavid Theocracy." In *Intellectual Studies on Islam: Essays Written in Honor of Martin B. Dickson*, edited by Michel M. Mazzaoui, and Vera B. Moreen, 27–40. Salt Lake City: University of Utah Press.

Rogers, J. M. 2012. "al-Ḳāhira." In *Encyclopaedia of Islam*. 2nd ed., edited by P. Bearman, Th. Bianquis, C. E. Bosworth, E. van Donzel, and W. P. Heinrichs. Brill Online. http://referenceworks.brillonline.com/browse/encyclopaedia-of-islam-2.

Róna-Tas, András. 1961. "Notes on the Kazak Yurt of Western Mongolia." *Acta Orientalia Academiae Scientiarum Hungaricae* 12:79–102.

Rosselló Bordoy, Guillermo. 1995. "Música y arqueología: Organología musical y hallazgos arqueológicos." *Música y Poesía del Sur de al-Andalus*, 69–75.

Rosser-Owen, Mariam. 2007. "Poems in Stone: The Iconography of ʿāmirid Poetry, and Its 'Petrification' on ʿāmirid Marbles." In *Revisiting al-Andalus: Perspectives on the Material Culture of Islamic Iberia and Beyond*, edited by Glaire D. Anderson and Mariam Rosser-Owen, 83–98. Medieval and Early Modern Iberian World. Leiden, the Netherlands: Brill.

Rubiera Mata, María Jesús. 1970. "Los poemas epigráficos en Ibn Yayyāb en la Alhambra." *al-Andalus* 25:453–473.

———. 1976. "De nuevo sobre los poemas epigráficos de la Alhambra." *al-Andalus* 41:207–211.

———. 1984. *Ibn al-Jayyāb, el otro poeta de la Alhambra*. Granada: Junta de Andalucía, Consejería de cultura y medio ambiente: Patronato de la Alhambra y Generalife.

———. 2008. "El Califato Nazarí." *al-Qantara* 29 (2): 293–305.

Ruggles, D. Fairchild. 1993. "Arabic Poetry and Architectural Memory in al-Andalus." *Ars Orientalis* 23:171–178.

———. 1997a. "Humayun's Tomb and Garden: Typologies and Visual Order." In *Gardens in the Time of the Great Muslim Empires*, edited by Attilio Petruccioli, 173–186. Muqarnas Supplements 7. Leiden, the Netherlands: Brill.

———. 1997b. "The Eye of Sovereignty: Poetry and Vision in the Alhambra's Lindaraja Mirador." *Gesta: International Center of Medieval Art* 36 (2): 180–189.

———. 2000. *Gardens, Landscape, and Vision in the Palaces of Islamic Spain*. University Park: Pennsylvania State University Press.

———. 2007. "Making Vision Manifest: The Frame, View, and Screen in Islamic Culture." In *Sites Unseen: Landscape and Vision*, edited by Dianne Suzette Harris and D. Fairchild Ruggles, 131–156. Pittsburgh, PA: University of Pittsburgh Press.

———. 2008. *Islamic Gardens and Landscapes*. Philadelphia: University of Pennsylvania Press.

———. 2011. *Islamic Art and Visual Culture: An Anthology of Sources*. Malden, MA: Wiley-Blackwell.

Ruiz Souza, Juan Carlos. 2004. "El Palacio de Comares de la Alhambra de Granada: Tipologías y funciones; Nuevas propuestas." *Cuadernos de la Alhambra* 40:77–102.

Saait, Mekki. 1933. "Münir Nurettinin Yuvasında." *Yedigün* 30:10–12.

Safran, Janina M. 2000. *The Second Umayyad Caliphate: The Articulation of Caliphal Legitimacy in al-Andalus*. Cambridge, MA: Center for Middle Eastern Studies of Harvard University. Distributed by Harvard University Press.

Sahibinin Sesi. 1928. "Türkçe Plak Kataloğu: Catalogue des disques Turcs." Catalogue. Istanbul.

———. 1929. "Türkçe Plakların Esamisi: En Maruf Sanatkârlar En Hassas Plaklar." Catalogue. Istanbul.

———. 1930. "Sahibinin Sesi, His Master's Voice: Münir Nureddin Beyin Plarkarı Listesi." Catalogue. Istanbul.

———. 1934. "Marconi Radyoları: 'Sahibinin Sesi' [']ne Mensuptur." Catalogue. Istanbul.

Şahin, Şehriban. 2005. "The Rise of Alevism as a Public Religion." *Current Sociology* 53 (3): 465–485.

Salamandra, Christa. 1998. "Moustache Hairs Lost: Ramadan Television Serials and the Construction of Identity in Damascus, Syria." *Visual Anthropology* 10 (2–4): 226–246.

———. 2004. *A New Old Damascus: Authenticity and Distinction in Urban Syria*. Bloomington: Indiana University Press.

Salmi, Ahmed. 1956. "Le genre des Poèmes de Nativité (maulūdiyya-S), dans le Royaume de Grenade et au Maroc au XIIIe et XIVe siècle." *Hespéris* 43:335–435.

Salzbrunn, Monika. 2002. "Transnational Senegalese Politics in France." *ISIM Newsletter* 10:29.

Samuels, David W., Louise Meintjes, Ana Maria Ochoa, and Thomas Porcello. 2010. "Soundscapes: Toward a Sounded Anthropology." *Annual Review of Anthropology* 39:329–345.

Samwini, Nathan Iddrisu. 2003. *The Muslim Resurgence in Ghana since 1950 and Its Effects upon Muslims and Muslim-Christian Relations*. Birmingham, UK: University of Birmingham.

Sánchez, Francisco Franco. 1992. "Andalusíes y Magrebíes en torno a los Banū Sīd Bono/a de Guadalest y Granada." In *Actas Del II Coloquio Hispano-Magrebí de Ciencias Históricas «Historia, Ciencia y Sociedad,» Granada 6–10 Noviembre de 1989*, 217–232. Madrid: Agencia Española de Cooperación Internacional; Institución de Cooperación con el Mundo Árabe.

Sawa, George D. 1985. "The Status and Roles of the Secular Musicians in the Kitāb al-Aghānī (Book of Songs) of Abu al-Faraj al-Iṣbahānī (d. 356 A.H. / 967 A.D.)." *Asian Music* 17 (1): 69–82.

Sayad, Abelmalek, and Eliane Dupuy. 1995. *Un Nanterre algérien, terre de bidonvilles*. Paris: Autrement.

Schafer, Raymond Murray. 1977. *The Tuning of the World*. New York: Knopf.

Schechner, Richard. 1988. *Performance Theory*. New York: Routledge.

Schechner, Richard, and Victor W. Turner. 1985. *Between Theater and Anthropology*. Philadelphia: University of Pennsylvania Press.

Schielke, Samuli. 2008. "Policing Ambiguity: Muslim Saints-Day Festivals and the Moral Geography of Public Space in Egypt." *American Ethnologist* 35 (4): 539–552.

Schimmel, Annemarie. 1965. "Some Glimpses of the Religious Life in Egypt during the Later Mamlūk Period." *Islamic Studies* 4 (4): 353–392.

———. 1982. *As through a Veil: Mystical Poetry in Islam*. New York: Columbia University Press.

———. 1985. *And Muhammad Is His Messenger: The Veneration of the Prophet in Islamic Piety*. Chapel Hill: University of North Carolina Press.

———. 1996. "A Good Word Is like a Good Tree." http://www.amaana.org/articles/schimtree.htm.

———. 2007. *Occident and Orient: My Life in East and West*. Translated by Karin Mittmann. Lahore: Iqbal Academy.

Schroeder, Eric. 1955. *Muhammad's People*. Portland, ME: Bond Wheelwright.

Schulze, Holger, ed. 2008. *Sound Studies: Traditionen—Methoden—Desiderate. Eine Einführung*. Bielefeld, Germany: Transcript.

Schuon, Frithjof. 1990. *Esoterism as Principle and as Way*. Bedfont, UK: Perennial Books.

Schutz, Alfred, and Thomas Luckmann. 1989. *The Structures of the Life-World*. Evanston, IL: Northwestern University Press.

Scognamillo, Giovanni. 1990. *Türk Sinema Tarihi (1896–1986)*. Istanbul: Metis Yayınları.

Scott, Joan. 2007. *The Politics of the Veil*. Princeton, NJ: Princeton University Press.

Scott, John. 2000. *Social Network Analysis: A Handbook*. Thousands Oaks, CA: Sage Publications.

Sedgwick, Mark J. 2004. *Against the Modern World: Traditionalism and the Secret Intellectual History of the Twentieth Century*. Oxford: Oxford University Press.

Seeseman, Rüdiger, and Benjamin Soares. 2009. "'Being as Good Muslims as Frenchmen': On Islam and Colonial Modernity in West Africa." *Journal of Religion in Africa* 39 (1): 91–120.

Sells, Michael. 1989. *Desert Tracings: Six Classical Arabian Odes*. Middletown, CT: Wesleyan University Press.

Shakhanova, Nurila. 1998. *Mir traditsionnoi kultury kazakhov: Etnographicheskie ocherki*. Almaty, Kazakhstan: Qazaqstan.

———. 2004. *Simvolika traditsionnoi kazakhskoi kultury: Uchebnoe posobie*. Almaty, Kazakhstan: Qazaq universiteti.

Shannon, Jonathan H. 2003a. "al-Muwashshahāt and al-Qudūd al-Halabiyya: Two Genres in the Aleppine Wasla." *MESA Bulletin* 37 (1): 82–101.

———. 2003b. "Emotion, Performance, and Temporality in Arab Music: Reflections on Tarab." *Cultural Anthropology* 18 (1): 72–98.

———. 2004. "The Aesthetics of Spiritual Practice and the Creation of Moral and Musical Subjectivities in Aleppo, Syria." *Ethnology* 43 (4): 381–391.

———. 2005. "Metonyms of Modernity in Contemporary Syrian Music and Painting." *Ethnos* 70 (3): 361–386.

———. 2006. *Among the Jasmine Trees: Music and Modernity in Contemporary Syria*. Middletown, CT: Wesleyan University Press.

Shefer-Mossensohn, Miri. 2010. *Ottoman Medicine: Healing and Medical Institutions, 1500–1700*. Albany, NY: SUNY Press.

Sheridan, Ted, and Karen van Lengen. 2003. "Hearing Architecture: Exploring and Designing the Aural Environment." *Journal of Architectural Education* 52:37–44.

Shiloah, Amnon. 1979. *The Theory of Music in Arabic Writings (c. 900–1900): Descriptive Catalogue of Manuscripts in Libraries of Europe and the U.S.A.* Munich: G. Henle Verlag.

———. 1992. "The Dimension of Sound." In *The World of Islam: Faith, People, Culture*, edited by Bernard Lewis, 2nd ed., 161–180. London: Thames and Hudson.

———. 1995. *Music in the World of Islam: A Socio-Cultural Study*. Detroit, MI: Wayne State University Press.

Silverstein, Paul A. 2002. "'Why Are We Waiting to Start the Fire?': French Gangsta Rap and the Critique of State Capitalism." In *Black, Blanc, Beur: Rap Music and Hip-Hop Culture in the Francophone World*, edited by Alain-Philippe Durand, 45–67. Lanham, MD: Scarecrow.

———. 2004. *Algeria in France: Transpolitics, Race, and Nation*. Bloomington: Indiana University Press.

———. 2012a. "Le patrimoine du ghetto: Rap et racialisation de la violence dans les banlieues françaises." In *L'Atlantique Multiracial: Discours, Politiques, Dénis*, edited by James Cohen, Andrew J. Diamond, and Philippe Vervaecke, 95–118. Paris: Karthala.

———. 2012b. "In the Name of Culture: Berber Activism and the Material Politics of 'Popular Islam' in Southeastern Morocco." *Material Religion* 8 (3): 330–353.

Silverstein, Paul A., and Chantal Tetreault. 2006. "Postcolonial Urban Apartheid." *Items and Issues* 5 (4): 8–15.

Sims, Eleanor. 2002. *Peerless Images: Persian Painting and Its Sources*. New Haven, CT: Yale University Press.

Singer, Amy. 2002. *Constructing Ottoman Beneficence: An Imperial Soup Kitchen in Jerusalem*. Albany, NY: SUNY Press.

———. 2008. *Charity in Islamic Societies*. Cambridge: Cambridge University Press.

Sinik. 2006. *Sang froid*. CD. Six-O-Nine/Warner Music France.

Sipos, János. 2001. *Kazakh Folksongs from the Two Ends of the Steppe*. Budapest: Akadémiai Kiadó.

Skali, Faouzi. 1999. *La face à face des coeurs. Le Soufisme aujourd'hui*. Gordes, France: Editions du Relié.

Small, Christopher. 1998. *Musicking: The Meanings of Performing and Listening*. Hanover, NH: University Press of New England.

Smith, Ronald W., and Valerie Bugni. 2002. "Designed Physical Environment as Related to Selves, Symbols, and Social Reality: A Proposal for a Paradigm Shift for Architecture." *Humanity and Society* 26 (4): 293–311.

———. 2006. "Symbolic Interaction Theory and Architecture." *Symbolic Interaction* 29 (2): 123–155.

Sniper. 2001. *Du rire aux larmes*. CD. Desh/Warner.

———. 2006. *Trait pour trait*. CD. Desh/Warner.

Soares, Benjamin. 2005. *Islam and the Prayer Economy: History and Authority in a Malian Town*. Ann Arbor: University of Michigan Press.

Soulignac, Françoise. 1993. *La banlieue parisienne: Cent cinquante ans de transformations*. Paris: La Documentation Française.

Sözer, Hande. 2014. *Managing Invisibility: Dissimulation and Identity Maintenance among Alevi Turks*. Leiden, the Netherlands: Brill.

Spinetti, Federico, ed. 2010a. *Giuseppe Donizetti Pascià: Traiettorie musicali e storiche tra Italia e Turchia / Musical and Historical Trajectories between Italy and Turkey*. Saggi e Monografie 7. Bergamo: Fondazione Donizetti.

———, dir. 2010b. *Zurkhaneh: The House of Strength—Music and Martial Arts of Iran*. Documentary film, 105 min. University of Alberta, Lab 80 film.

Sterne, Jonathan. 1997. "Sounds like the Mall of America: Programmed Music and the Architectonics of Commercial Space." *Ethnomusicology* 41 (1): 22–50.

———, ed. 2012. *The Sound Studies Reader*. London: Routledge.

Stetkevych, Jaroslav. 1993. *The Zephyrs of Najd: The Poetics of Nostalgia in the Classical Arabic Nasīb*. Chicago: University of Chicago Press.

Stewart, Kathleen. 1996. "An Occupied Place." In *Senses of Place*, edited by Steven Feld and Keith H. Basso, 137–166. Santa Fe, NM: School of American Research Press.

Stokes, Martin, ed. 1994a. *Ethnicity, Identity, and Music: The Musical Construction of Place*. Oxford: Berg.

———. 1994b. "Introduction: Ethnicity, Identity and Music." In *Ethnicity, Identity and Music: The Musical Construction of Place*, edited by Martin Stokes, 1–28. Oxford: Berg.

Subtelny, Maria Eva. 1989. "The Cult of Holy Places: Religious Practices among Soviet Muslims." *Middle East Journal* 43 (4): 593–604.

Suprême NTM. 1995. *Paris sous les bombes*. CD. Sony/Epic.

Tambar, Kabir. 2010. "The Aesthetics of Public Visibility: Alevi *Semah* and the Paradoxes of Pluralism in Turkey." *Comparative Studies in Society and History* 52 (3): 652–679.

Task Force on the Arts. 2008. *Report on the Task Force on the Arts*. Harvard University. http://www.harvard.edu/sites/default/files/content/arts_report.pdf.

Taylor, Charles. 1999. "Two Theories of Modernity." *Public Culture* 11 (1): 153–174.

Taylor, Christopher Schurman. 1990. "The Cult of the Saints in Late Medieval Egypt." Unpublished PhD diss., Princeton University.

———. 1998. *In the Vicinity of the Righteous Ziyara and the Veneration of Muslim Saints in Late Medieval Egypt*. Islamic History and Civilization. Studies and Texts, vol. 22. Boston: Brill.

Terjeman, Siham. 1993. *Daughter of Damascus: A Memoir*. Austin: University of Texas Press.

Thackston, Wheeler M. 1989. *A Century of Princes: Sources on Timurid History and Art*. Cambridge, MA.: The Aga Khan Program for Islamic Architecture.

Thibaud, Jean-Paul. 2003. "The Sonic Composition of the City." In *The Auditory Culture Reader*, edited by Michael Bull and Les Back, 329–341. Oxford: Berg.

Thompson, Emily. 2002. *The Soundscape of Modernity: Architectural Acoustics and the Culture of Listening in America*. Cambridge, MA: MIT Press.

Tietze, Andreas. 1982. "Mustafa ʿĀli on Luxury and the Status Symbols of Ottoman Gentlemen." In *Studia Turcologica Memoriae Alexii Bombaci Dicata*, edited by Aldo Gallotta and Ugo Marazzi, 584–590. Naples: Herder.

Toishan, Aqedil. 2007. "Kiiz üi: Qūrylymy, mythologiyalyq tüpki mäni." *Qazaq Respublikasy Ūlttyq Ghylymi academiyasynyng Khabarlary: Til, ädebiet seriyasy* 6 (166): 11–18.

Tolbert, Elizabeth. 1990. "Magico-Religious Power and Gender in the Karelian Lament." In *Music, Gender and Culture*, edited by Marcia Herndon and Susanne Ziegler, 41–56. ICTM Study Group on Music and Gender. Wilhelmshaven, Germany: Florian Noetzel Verlag.

Toleubaev, Abdesh. 1991. *Relikty doislamskih verovanii v semeinoi obryadnosti kazakhov (XIX–nachalo XX vekov)*. Alma-Ata, Kazakhstan: Ghylym.

———. 2000. "Yurta v predstavleniyah, verovaniyah i obryadah kazakhov." In *Kochevoe jilishche narodov Sredneii Azii i Kazakhstana*, edited by G. P. Vasiliev, 165–178. Moscow: Nauka.

Tonna, Jo. 1990. "The Poetics of Arab-Islamic Architecture." *Muqarnas* 7:182–197.

Totah, Faedah. 2006. "Historic Preservation, Discourses of Modernity, and Lived Experience in the Old City of Damascus, Syria." Unpublished PhD diss., Department of Anthropology, University of Texas at Austin.

Touma, Habib. 2003. *The Music of the Arabs*. 2nd ed. Portland, OR: Amadeus.

Trachtenberg, Marvin. 2001. "Architecture and Music Reunited: A New Reading of Dufay's 'Nuper Rosarum Flores' and the Cathedral of Florence." *Renaissance Quarterly* 54 (3): 740–775.

Trémolet de Villiers, Vincent. 2002. "'Les zones de non-droit' dans la République Française, mythe ou réalité." Thèse de 3ème cycle, Université de Paris II.

Trimingham, John Spencer. 1998. *The Sufi Orders in Islam*. 2nd ed. New York: Oxford University Press.

Tshimanga, Charles. 2009. "Let the Music Play: The African Diaspora, Popular Culture, and National Identity in Contemporary France." In *Frenchness and the African Diaspora: Identity and Uprising in Contemporary France*, edited by Charles Tshimanga, Didier Gondola, and Peter J. Bloom, 248–276. Bloomington: Indiana University Press.

Turino, Thomas. 1999. "Signs of Imagination, Identity, and Experience: A Peircian Semiotic Theory for Music." *Ethnomusicology* 43 (2): 221–255.

Turner, Victor W. 1977. *The Ritual Process: Structure and Anti-Structure*. Ithaca, NY: Cornell University Press.

Uluç, Hincal. 2010. "Melek Sineması Nasıl Kurtarılıyor?" *Sabah*, April 23.

Umar, Muhammad S. 2006. *Islam and Colonialism: Intellectual Responses of Muslims of Northern Nigeria to British Colonial Rule*. Leiden, the Netherlands: Brill.

Ünlü, Cemal. 2004. *Git Zaman, Gel Zaman: Fonograf—Gramofon—Taş Plak*. Istanbul: Pan Yayıncılık.

Valikhanov, Shoqan. 1984. "Tenkri (Bog)." In *Sobranie sochinenii*, 1:208–215. Alma-Ata, Kazakhstan: Glavnaya redaktsiya Kazakhskoi Sovetskoi Entsiklopedii.

———. 1985a. "O musulmanstve v stepi." In *Sobranie sochinenii*, 2:71–75. Alma-Ata, Kazakhstan: Glavnaya redaktsiya Kazakhskoi Sovetskoi Entsiklopedii.

———. 1985b. "Sledy shamanstva u kirgizov." In *Sobranie sochinenii*, 4:48–70. Alma-Ata, Kazakhstan: Glavnaya redaktsiya Kazakhskoi Sovetskoi Entsiklopedii.

Vallejo Triano, Antonio. 1995. *Madīnat al-Zahrā': El salón de 'Abd al-Raḥmān III*. Córdoba: Junta de Andalucía, Consejería de Cultura.

———. 2006. *Madinat al-Zahra': Official Guide to the Archeological Complex*. [Andalusia, Spain]: Junta de Andalucía, Consejería de Cultura.

———. 2010. *La ciudad califal de Madinat al-Zahra': Arqueología de su excavación*. 1st ed. Colección Naturaleza y Medio Ambiente. Córdoba: Editorial Almuzara.

Van Deusen, Kira. 2004. *Singing Story, Healing Drum: Shamans and Storytellers of Turkic Siberia*. Montreal: McGill-Queen's University Press.

Van Ruysbroeck, Willem. 1900. *The Journey of William of Rubruck to the Eastern Parts of the World, 1253–55, as Narrated by Himself, with Two Accounts of the Earlier Journey of John of Pian de Carpine*. Edited and translated by William Woodville Rockhill. London: Hakluyt Society.

Velásquez Basanta, Fernando N. 1995. "Abū Jaʿfar Ahmad Ibn Safwān: Otro poeta místico malagueño del siglo XIV a la luz de la Ihāta de Ibn al-Jatīb." In *Homenaje al Profesor José María Fórneas Besteiro*, edited by Concepción Castillo Castillo, 1:627–644. Granada: Universidad de Granada.

Viguera, María Jesús, and Concepción Castillo Castillo. 2001. *El esplendor de los Omeyas cordobeses: La civilización musulmana de Europa occidental*. Granada: Junta de Andalucía, Consejería de Cultura a través de la Fundación El Legado Andalusí.

Vincendeau, Ginette. 2005. *La Haine*. Urbana: University of Illinois Press.

Vitruvius. 1960. *The Ten Books on Architecture*. Translated by Morris Hicky Morgan. New York: Dover.

Vryonis, Speros. 1971. *The Decline of Medieval Hellenism in Asia Minor and the Process of Islamization from the Eleventh through the Fifteenth Century*. Berkeley: University of California Press.

Wacquant, Loïc J. D. 2008. *Urban Outcasts: A Comparative Sociology of Advanced Marginality*. Cambridge, MA: Polity.

Warner, Michael. 2002. *Publics and Counterpublics*. New York: Zone Books.

Waterhouse, Paul. 1921. "Music and Architecture." *Music and Letters* 2 (4): 323–331.

Waterson, Roxana. 1990. *The Living House: An Anthropology of Architecture in South-East Asia*. Singapore: Oxford University Press.

Waugh, Earle H. 1989. *The Munshidin of Egypt: Their World and Their Song*. Studies in Comparative Religion. Columbia: University of South Carolina Press.

Welch, Stuart Cary. 1976. *Persian Painting: Five Royal Safavid Manuscripts of the Sixteenth Century*. New York: G. Braziller.

———. 1979. *Wonders of the Age: Masterpieces of Early Safavid Painting, 1501–1576*. Cambridge, MA: Fogg Art Museum, Harvard University.

Wensinck, Arent Jan, and Bazmee Ansari. 2012. "Baḳīʿ al-G͟harḳad." In *Encyclopaedia of Islam*. 2nd ed., edited by P. Bearman, Th. Bianquis, C. E. Bosworth, E. van Donzel, and W. P. Heinrichs. Brill Online. http://referenceworks.brillonline.com/browse/encyclopaedia-of-islam-2.

Whiteley, Sheila, Andy Bennett, and Stan Hawkins. 2004. *Music, Space and Place: Popular Music and Cultural Identity*. Aldershot, UK: Ashgate.

Wihtol de Wenden, Catherine, and Zakya Daoud. 1993. *Banlieues . . . intégration ou explosion?* Panoramiques 12. Condé-sur-Noireau, France: Corlet; Paris: Arléa.

Williams, Caroline. 1985. "The Cult of Alid Saints in the Fatimid Monuments of Cairo Part II: The Mausolea." *Muqarnas* 3:39–60.

Winter, Michael. 1982. *Society and Religion in Early Ottoman Egypt: Studies in the Writings of ʿAbd al-Wahhab al-Shaʿrani*. New Brunswick, NJ: Transaction Books.

———. 2004. *Egyptian Society under Ottoman Rule, 1517–1798*. London: Routledge.

Wittkower, Rudolf. 1988. *Architectural Principles in the Age of Humanism*. London: Academy Editions.

Wright, Owen. 1993. "Mūsīḳī." In *Encyclopædia of Islam*, edited by C. E. Bosworth, E. van Donzel, W. P. Heinrichs, and Ch. Pellat, 2nd ed., 7:681–689. Leiden, the Netherlands: Brill.

———. 2004. "The Sight of Sound." In *Muqarnas* 21:359–371.

———. 2010. *Epistles of the Brethren of Purity: On Music. An Arabic Critical Edition and English Translation of Epistle 5*. Oxford: Oxford University Press.

Xenakis, Iannis. 2008. *Music and Architecture: Architectural Projects, Texts and Realizations*. Edited by Sharon Kanach. Iannis Xenakis Series, vol. 1. Hillsdale, NY: Pendragon.

Yaltkaya, Şerefeddin. 1942. "Kara Ahmet Paşa Vakfiyesi." *Vakıflar Dergisi* 2:83–97.

Yavuz, M. Hakan, and John L. Esposito. 2003. *Turkish Islam and the Secular State: The Gülen Movement*. Syracuse, NY: Syracuse University Press.

Yazıcı, Ezgi. 2010. "Theatre in Nineteenth-Century Istanbul: Cases for the Translation of an Architectural Typology." MA thesis, Middle East Technical University, Ankara.

Yönetken, Halil Bedi. 1963. *Derleme Notaları I*. Istanbul: Orkestra.

Young, Gregory, Jerry Bancroft, and Mark Sanderson. 1993. "Musi-Tecture: Seeking Useful Correlations between Music and Architecture." *Leonardo Music Journal* 3:39–43.

Yürekli, Zeynep. 2012. *Architecture and Hagiography in the Ottoman Empire: The Politics of Bektashi Shrines in the Classical Age*. Farnham, Surrey, UK: Ashgate.

Zeghal, Malika. 2008. *Islamism in Morocco: Religion, Authoritarianism and Electoral Politics*. Princeton, NJ: Markus Wiener.

Zenlund, Darrow Gary. 1991. "Post-Colonial Aleppo, Syria: Struggles in Representation and Identity." Unpublished PhD diss., University of Texas at Austin.

Zeranska-Kominek, Slawomira. 1990. "The Classification of Repertoire in Turkmen Traditional Music." *Asian Music* 21 (2): 90–109.

Zhelyazkova, Antonina. 1998. "Turks." In *Communities and Identities in Bulgaria*, edited by Anna Krasteva, 287–306. Ravenna: Longo.

Zonis, Ella. 1973. *Classical Persian Music: An Introduction*. Cambridge, MA: Harvard University Press.

CONTRIBUTORS

Samer Akkach is a professor of architecture history and theory and the founding director of the Centre for Asian and Middle Eastern Architecture at the University of Adelaide, Australia. He has published widely on the theory of architecture and landscape, Islamic art and architecture, and Islamic intellectual history in the early modern period with special attention to Syria. He is the author of *Cosmology and Architecture in Premodern Islam: An Architectural Reading of Mystical Ideas* (2005); *ʿAbd al-Ghanī al-Nābulusī: Islam and the Enlightenment* (2007); *Letters of a Sufi Scholar: The Correspondence of ʿAbd al-Ghanī al-Nābulusī* (2010); *Intimate Invocations: Al-Ghazzī's Biography of ʿAbd al-Ghanī al-Nābulusī* (2012); *Damascene Diaries: A Reading of the Cultural History of Damascus in the Eighteenth Century* (2015); and *Istanbul Observatory* (2017).

Glaire D. Anderson is an associate professor of art history at the University of North Carolina at Chapel Hill. Her research and publications center on Islamic art, architecture, and civilization during the age of the caliphs, with a research focus on Umayyad Córdoba and the western Mediterranean. Anderson is the author of *The Islamic Villa in Early Medieval Iberia: Aristocratic Estates and Court Culture in Umayyad Córdoba* (2013) and a coeditor of *Revisiting al-Andalus: Perspectives on the Material Culture of Islamic Iberia and Beyond* (2007).

Ali S. Asani is a professor of Indo-Muslim and Islamic Religion and Cultures at Harvard University and former director of the university's Prince Alwaleed Bin Talal Islamic Studies Program. A scholar of Islam in South Asia, his research focuses on Ismaili and Sufi devotional traditions in the region. He is particularly interested in the role of the arts in fostering religious and cultural literacy about Islam. His books include *Celebrating Muhammad: Images of the Prophet in Muslim Devotional Poetry* (coauthor; 1995); and *Ecstasy and Enlightenment: The Ismaili Devotional Literature of South Asia* (2002).

Saida Daukeyeva is a Georg Forster Research Fellow at Humboldt University, Berlin. A music historian and ethnographer with expertise in the Middle East and Central Asia, she published the book *Philosophy of Music by Abu Nasr Muhammad al-Farabi* (2002) and coedited the textbook *The Music of Central Asia* (2016). Her current research explores issues of identity, gender, social memory, mobility, spirituality, and politics in relation to Kazakh instrumental performance and ritual practice in western Mongolia and Kazakhstan.

Nina Ergin is a visiting associate professor in the Department of Archeology and History of Art at Koç University, Istanbul. Her research activities and publications have focused on Ottoman architectural history and the art history and visual culture of the Islamic world. Her article "The Soundscape of Sixteenth-Century Istanbul Mosques: Architecture and Qur'an Recital" (*Journal of the Society of Architectural Historians* 67, no. 2 [2008]: 204–221) pioneered the theme of the present edited volume.

Michael Frishkopf is a professor of music, the director of the Canadian Centre for Ethnomusicology, and an adjunct professor of religious studies at the University of Alberta, Canada. His research centers on music and sound in Islam, the Arab world, and West Africa, including an edited collection, *Music and Media in the Arab World* (2010). Frishkopf has served as member of advisory or editorial boards for the journals *Ethnomusicology*, *Asian Music*, and *Review of Middle East Studies*; he founded the Society for Arab Music Research and served on the board for the Society for Ethnomusicology.

Irene Markoff teaches music in the Department of Music at York University, Toronto, and also contributes to the graduate programs in music and anthropology. Since 1981, her research and many publications have focused primarily on Alevi-Bektaşi religiosity, performance practice, rituals, and identity politics in Turkey and, more recently, Bulgaria and Canada. Markoff is known for her performances of Alevi vocal repertoire and the accompaniment she provides on the sacred plucked lute, the *bağlama*.

Kamil Khan Mumtaz was a professor in and the head of the Department of Architecture at the National College of Arts in Lahore from 1966 to 1980. He has led a distinguished career both as a practicing architect in Pakistan and abroad and as an architectural thinker. His extensive, pioneering publication activity on architectural heritage and conservation and urban planning in Pakistan includes the two volumes *Architecture in Pakistan* (1989) and *Modernity and Tradition: Contemporary Architecture in Pakistan* (1999).

John Morgan O'Connell is a reader in and director of the program in ethnomusicology at the School of Music, Cardiff University. His many publications concern the musical traditions of the Islamic world, including Turkey and the Middle East. He has recently completed a monograph on music and memory during World War I (under review). He has also published a monograph on Münir Nurettin Selçuk (2013) and edited a collection entitled *Music and Conflict* (2010).

Cynthia Robinson is a professor of medieval and Islamic art in the Department of History of Art and Visual Studies at Cornell University. Her prolific publication activity on the visual, literary, courtly, and religious manifestations of cultural and confessional interchange in the medieval Mediterranean world includes the book *In Praise of Song: The Making of Courtly Culture in al-Andalus and Provence, 1005–1134 A.D.* (2002).

D. Fairchild Ruggles is a professor of Islamic architecture, art, and landscape at the University of Illinois, Urbana-Champaign. Her research areas include the built environment of the Islamic Mediterranean and South Asia, cultural heritage, and women as patrons of art and architecture in Islamic societies. Among her publications are the award-winning *Islamic Gardens and Landscapes* (2008) and *Gardens, Landscape, and Vision in the Palaces of Islamic Spain* (2000).

Jonathan H. Shannon is a professor of anthropology at Hunter College, City University of New York. He is the author of *Among the Jasmine Trees: Music and Modernity in Contemporary Syria* (2006), *A Wintry Day in Damascus: Syrian Stories* (2012), and *Performing al-Andalus: Music and Nostalgia across the Mediterranean* (2015), as well as of numerous articles in journals devoted to culture and anthropology. He has conducted extensive research into musical aesthetics and cultural politics in the Arab world and the Mediterranean and is an accomplished performer of the *'ūd* (fretless lute).

Paul A. Silverstein is a professor of anthropology at Reed College, Portland, Oregon. He is the author of *Algeria in France: Transpolitics, Race, and Nation*

(2004) and of numerous contributions on ethnicity, expressive culture, and urban spaces among North African communities in France.

Federico Spinetti is a professor of ethnomusicology at the University of Cologne, Germany. His research has primarily focused on the political economy of music in Soviet and post-Soviet Central Asia, particularly Tajikistan; on musical relations across the Mediterranean Sea (including his edited collection *Giuseppe Donizetti Pasha: Musical and Historical Trajectories between Italy and Turkey*, 2010); and on contemporary Italian popular music. Since 2006 he has been researching the music-architecture nexus in the context of the Iranian traditional martial arts gymnasium (*zūrkhāneh*), directing a documentary film on this topic (*Zurkhaneh: The House of Strength—Music and Martial Arts of Iran, 2010*).

Anthony Welch is a professor of Islamic art and architecture, Iranian painting, and architecture of Muslim India at the University of Victoria, Canada. He is the author of numerous articles in scholarly journals and a number of books on Islamic art, including, among others, *Shah ʿAbbas and the Arts of Isfahan* (1973) and *Calligraphy in the Arts of the Muslim World* (1979).

INDEX

Page numbers in italics refer to figures.